Gertrud M. Backes · \

Gender, Health and A

Alter(n) und Gesellschaft
Band 13

Herausgegeben von

Gertrud M. Backes
Wolfgang Clemens

Gertrud M. Backes
Vera Lasch
Katja Reimann (Eds.)

Gender, Health and Ageing

European Perspectives on Life Course, Health Issues and Social Challenges

VS VERLAG FÜR SOZIALWISSENSCHAFTEN

Bibliografische Information Der Deutschen Nationalbibliothek
Die Deutsche Nationalbibliothek verzeichnet diese Publikation in der Deutschen Nationalbibliografie; detaillierte bibliografische Daten sind im Internet über <http://dnb.d-nb.de> abrufbar.

1. Auflage Dezember 2006

Lektorat: Monika Mülhausen

Der VS Verlag für Sozialwissenschaften ist ein Unternehmen von Springer Science+Business Media.
www.vs-verlag.de

Umschlaggestaltung: KünkelLopka Medienentwicklung, Heidelberg
Satz: Anke Vogel
Druck und buchbinderische Verarbeitung: Krips b.v., Meppel

Printed in the Netherlands

ISBN 978-3-531-14980-6

Acknowledgements

This volume emerges as result of two European research workshops: "Ageing, Health, and Gender" 29.-30.04.2005 and "Networking for Women's Health across Regional Diversity in Europe: Experiences, Concepts and Strategies" 8./10.10.2004, both have taken place in Kassel, Germany.

The focus of the workshops has been on gender-specific conditions and possible strategies for managing resources and strains, and their effects on health and life-situations in old age. Thus the emphasis has been on strategies promoting "successful" coping with the changes brought on by old age, but also the roles of gender, gender-relations and social environments in old age. The objectives of the workshops have been the cross-border exchange of information on models, best practice and conducive conditions, and the question of how to possibly implement such models and strategies. Two volumes[1] now emerge as a result of the workshops, which examine in several articles different aspects of the topic from various national contexts. A main point of interest has particularly been to strengthen the East-West dialogue as well as the co-operation with researcher from the new EU member states.

We thank the Hessen's Ministry of Higher Education, Research and the Arts (Hessischen Ministerium für Wissenschaft und Kunst), and the Group on Gender Research (Interdisziplinäre Arbeitsgruppe Frauen- und Geschlechterforschung) at the University of Kassel, Germany for funding. Without their support neither the workshop nor the books would have been realised. We want to thank also Bärbel Sauer, Verena Koslowsky, Simone Happel and Bettina Hegemann for their exceptional assistance in organisation and Stefani Ross for her excellent and patiently translation work.

Kassel, Juli 2006
Katja Reimann, Vera Lasch & Gertrud M. Backes

1 The 2nd one is: Lasch, Vera; Freitag, Walburga;, Sonntag, Ute (Ed.): Gender, Health, and Cultures. Networking for a better Future for Women within an enlarged Europe. Kassel university press, 2006.

Table of Content

Foreword

Pasqualina Perrig-Chiello

Certain books are eagerly anticipated and long overdue. „Gender, health, and ageing“ is such a book. Its topic is relevant in many different ways. The demographic and societal changes of the past decades, such as longevity and improvement of public health, have definitely created new and often very distinct realities for men and women. However, these diversities have only marginally and fragmentally been the topic of research endeavours. There is, for example, a general growing awareness for the societal phenomenon of „feminization of old age“, yet the topic and its psychosocial and health-related consequences haven't attracted the scientific interest they would have deserved. It is noteworthy, that still until a few decades ago, the majority of geriatric and gerontological studies were oriented towards male standards without considering gender effects. Even though subsequent studies increasingly began to focus on differences between women and men, they referred mainly to the biological sex of a person and not to their gender belonging. Due to these scientific neglects and limitations, the state of the art in the field of gender, health and ageing is sketchy and often enough contradictory (Perrig-Chiello & Höpflinger, 2004). Do older women really have more physical and mental health problems than older men, or are these findings influenced by a gender bias, due to a different awareness and understanding of health and illness? Is there truly a higher incidence for Alzheimer's dementia for women than for men, or is the apparently higher incidence simply the consequence of women's higher life expectancy? What are the physical and mental health costs of being the main caregiver of spouses, in-laws and partners, considering that this is a role many women have to fill from middle-age on? It's impossible to find satisfactory answers to all these questions without considering the cultural and social living context of the subjects studied, and without adopting a life course perspective (Perrig-Chiello & Höpflinger, 2003). The inclusion of gender as a social reality in the broadest sense is therefore an absolute prerequisite for gaining valid information.

Gender is not only a neglected, but also a highly complex construct, which cannot be allotted to one single discipline and thus demands a multi- or even an interdisciplinary approach. In view of the complexity of the issue it is furthermore frustrating to see that a large majority of scientific work done so far was not only mono-disciplinary but also to a large extent purely descriptive and theory poor. As a consequence, we are faced with the impossibility to grasp the underlying complex causes and mechanisms of gender, health, and ageing. However, in order to enable optimal age- and gender-appropriate assessment, prevention, and intervention in-depth, multi-causal, and innovative approaches are needed.

Based on what has been stated so far, the book „Gender, health, and ageing" is of particular significance. Its editors, Gertrud Backes, Vera Lasch, and Katja Reimann, did not balk at tackling such a complex and demanding issue. They have compiled a reader that identifies the research gaps already mentioned and proposes a multidisciplinary view of the topic. In addition, the international lineup of authors permits a comparative, European perspective of the issue. The authors manage to reveal in an impressive manner the necessity of a gender perspective in aging and health research, as well as the necessity of an age and health-related perspective in gender research. Various contributions adopt a life course approach and include further aspects of body, physicalness and identity, which have previously been neglected by the social sciences. In a society in which „anti-ageing" has become a buzzword, scientific analyses of ageism – which is not infrequently paired with sexism – form a crucial basis for a differentiated understanding of the constituents of illness and health in old age (Perrig-Chiello, 2005).

All things considered, this book contains a wealth of data integrated in a coherent theoretical framework, thus yielding vital elements for a gender and age-appropriate health practice.

References

Perrig-Chiello, Pasqualina, 2005: Frauen im Alter: Vorurteile und Fakten. In: Freiburger Frauen Studien, Zeitschrift für Interdisziplinäre Frauenforschung, 16: 199-219.

Perrig-Chiello, Pasqualina & Höpflinger, François (Eds), 2003: *Gesundheitsbiographien – Variationen und Hintergründe*. Bern: Huber.

Perrig-Chiello, Pasqualina & Höpflinger, François (Eds), 2004, 2nd edition: Jenseits des Zenits. Frauen und Männer in der zweiten Lebenshälfte. Bern: Haupt.

Gender, Health, and Ageing: An Introduction

Vera Lasch, Katja Reimann & Gertrud M. Backes

1 Introduction

The worldwide increase of life expectancy, coupled with a decreasing birth rate, has led to populations with increased numbers of more-than-60 year-olds, in terms of percentage as well as in absolute numbers. The longer lifespan necessarily also lengthens the phase of life termed 'old age', so that today we differentiate between a third and a fourth age (Laslett 1995). The consequences of this development are manifold. More and more people may expect a late active phase of life, after employment. The positive aspects for those affected notwithstanding, this development also creates a whole set of challenges. The European societies need to adapt to these changes, particularly in reference to topics such as the political and the societal integration of the elderly; to changing needs, particularly in the field of institutional care, but also for the development of concepts for the reconciliation of care-giving and employment. The topic of health – the health-issues of the elderly, preventive strategies in the life course as well as in old age, and their effects on the quality of life –, plays a vital role within this framework, particularly in the later stages of old age. According to the WHO, health of older women is an increasingly important field, as due to the higher life expectancy of women the majority of the old, and particularly the oldest old, will be women. Ageing, knowledge of resources and coping strategies, and experience in the implementation of this knowledge will turn into decisive factors, societally, politically and economically.

In this context, the societal base of knowledge (in research and theory) on the phenomenon of ageing is increasingly important. The question of what we actually know, and which questions still need to be answered, is also relevant to the policies of research. The European research programmes, most markedly the 5. Research Framework, have created knowledge on the central issues of demographic change, and have built up networks (see Lasch, Reimann in this volume). However, Malcolm Johnson's statement in the "Cambridge Handbook of Age and Ageing " is still true:

> "Theoretical work remains a remarkably neglected area of gerontological work. So the oft-repeated observation that gerontology is 'data rich and theory poor' is demonstrably still the case" (Johnson 2005: XXIII).

In this volume we dedicated our attention to the important intersections of three topics – „Gender, Health, and Ageing". Gender and health are both factors decisively shaping ageing, thereby impacting quality of life in old age, and which are relevant in recognizing societal developments as well as in formulating adequate strategies for facing the challenges of ageing.

2 Gender, Health, and Ageing – Research Strategies, Missing Links and Integrated Views

There are at least three missing links and some promising ideas for a discussion in future research. The first one is the discussion about gender impact on ageing, as well as on health in old age; the second is the formulation of research approaches, which develop insights out of developmental, biographical and life-course perspectives (cf. Backes et al. in this volume). The third link encompasses the development of perspectives focussing on the cultural images of ageing bodies and identities, their effect on health and their gender impact. On a global perspective, it is a matter of improving research strategies, which describe ageing in a more differentiated way, and which integrate the vital impact of societal developments. Also still missing is a broader concept for an interdisciplinary compilation of the socio-political developments, connecting them with the issue of ageing. The following comments are just a few examples of the complexity of this field of research. The topic of care for the elderly may no longer be discussed without including the context of reconciliation of gainful employment and care-giving. While health is an essential component of successful care, it is the economic situation in old age (poverty and financial resources), which is expressive of historical and biographical life courses and „Lebenslagen" (see Backes et al. in this volume), and is equally relevant to a satisfactory situation in old age. The discourse on societal participation in old age, be it politically or in volunteer settings, requires a re-orientation on social and societal co-responsibility; that is, it requires attention to the cultural connotations of age and of gender; positive strategies for the integration of the elderly and those in need of support may only be formulated as a cross-generational effort.

The following three chapters emphasize the relevance of integrating three different research perspectives: gender, life course perspective and new approaches towards health, ageing, body and identity. Particular attention is given to the complex interconnectedness of many issues, pointing out the lack of cross-disciplinary references, and identifying those intersections, where a change of perspective, – from gender-research to age-research, focussing sociology, or health research, may serve to connect research approaches.

2.1 The Need for Gender Perspectives

Since the 70ties in feminist research *Gender* has been understood as the social classification into male and female, as a social construct of a dual gender system and as a matter of culture (Gildemeister 2004; Hirschauer 1989, 1994; Meuser 2005; Pasero, Braun 1995; Schaufler 2002; Villa 2001). Gender and age(ing) are social constructions interwoven with each other as well as with identity and social structure. Both are structural principles impacting social conditions, personal strategies of life, identities and concepts of creating and adapting. It is therefore not only a question of „doing gender“ and „doing age“, but also of „a gender lens on aging“ und „an aging lens on gender“ (Calasanti, Slevin 2001; also cp. Arber, Davidson, Ginn 2003; Arber, Ginn 1991, 1995; Backes 2002, 2004, 2005b, 2006; Bury 1995; Cruikshank 2003; Hatch 2000; McMullin 1995). The interaction of both of these factors with a multitude of societal sub-areas is currently one of the most important research paradigms. What is needed is an integrated analytical perspective, opening the view for the central relevance of „gender“ in gerontological research.

Particularly in the German-language gerontology, the word „Geschlecht“ is used primarily as an empirical factor for differentiating between two groups in society, between “men” and “women”. The discussion focuses on gender-specific differences and inequalities of “Lebenslagen” within the life courses and in old age, as well as on the differences in life expectancy and the affectedness by health problems. The considerations primarily remain on a descriptive level; basic theoretical perspectives opening a view on gender as a societal principle of order and in its generation processes are largely missing. A term used in this context is the feminization of old age (Tews 1993; Kohli 1990), addressing the purely quantitative predominance of women in the 60+ population (Tews 1993) as well as the approximation of the gender roles in old age (Kohli 1990), which is mainly effected by men’s post-retirement entrance to the “female” sphere of the household. In the English-language sphere, this approximation of gender roles in old age is also discussed under the key term „androgyny“; however, this discussion is based on relatively static and universal statements on male and female gender roles (cp. Hatch 2000: 71ff). Contrary to the thesis of a structural „feminization“ of old men is the thesis of a continuation of gender-specific sociations over the entire life course, all the way into old age; a process which under certain social constellations could also be associated with a superficial approximation of gender roles (cp. Backes 1997, 1999, 2002).

A gender-perspective in gerontology would entail a research approach taking both the differences as well as the shared traits of men and of women into account. It would also include the specific social problems, different „Lebenslagen" and resources of men and of women (for the German-language area, cp. Backes 1999, 2002, 2004, 2005b; Fooken 1986, 1999; Höpflinger 1997, 2002; Perrig-Chiello, Höpflinger 2000), interpreting gender as a dynamic and relational category. The research process needs to clear of unreflected, inapplicable stereotypes, as well as creating gender-specific blind spots in the generation of data, and the analysis of differentiated facts (for the research field of health, see Fuchs, Babitsch 2006: 85-96).

Above all, what is missing in gerontology is a reception of the concepts and the theories of gender research, with a view on the societal construction processes and *Doing Gender* in social interactions (cp. Calasanti 2004). This conceptualization of gender as a social construction would scrutinize a variety of aspects, such as educational and employment opportunities, life courses, value orientations, problematic health situations, life-expectancy and ageing, leaving behind the level of simply describing differences.

In the same way that gerontology rarely integrates the theories and approaches of gender research, gender research in turn neglects the topic of age(ing) and gerontological approaches. The examination of gender constructions within the process of ageing, respectively within the life course (particularly at a later age) is still largely missing. What is most frequently thematized is developments in adolescents and in middle-age adults. Nevertheless, the theories of gender-research contain important approaches, the application of which to developments in old age, respectively with a perspective on the life course, could be extremely useful.

The theoretical discourse on the category of gender requires perspectives on the connections between gender and other factors of social inequality, which cumulate during the life course, and which are connected to the differentiation of "Lebenslagen" and social inequality in old-age (Clemens, Naegele 2004; Moen 1996, 2001; O'Rand 1995, 1996; Sørensen 1990).

> Class, Race, and Ethnicity or being part of a minority are together with gender, factors that we know shape social situation and influence ageing, and even health in old age (Markides 1989: 14f).

Only the synopsis of diverse structural categories such as gender, age, but also class and ethnicity can result in more differentiated analyses and theoretically sound perspectives on life-situations, resources and strains, and their consequences for health in old age. The hitherto existing results show that women, by their greater reported levels of disability than older men therefore may experience more difficulties in social life, everyday mobility and social integration (Arber, Cooper 1999). It is also women who struggle more with economic problems and poverty in old age (Arber, Ginn 1991; Backes 2002; Sørensen 1990). Old age, multiple disabilities have been identified as predispositions for entry into institutional care (Oldman, Quilgars 1999 according to Arber 2003: 3).

Questions and controversies of gender research, gerontology, life course research and social policy therefore need to be connected and broadened by a focus on life-quality and health. Debates are necessary on the consequences of the societal construction of gender, on the theses of the feminization of age, and the acumination of gender differences in old age; actually the old issues of levelling, continuity, cumulation and diversity of genders (specifically in old old age), of hierarchization, complementarity and power distribution among the genders in old age, and on the effects of ageism, sexism and racism. What is needed, in addition to analyses of equal opportunities in the various societal segments and in the life course, is a more accurate description of the effects of gender assignations, of stereotyping or of gender ignorance, e.g. in research on ageing and health.

2.2 Ageing within a Life Course Perspective

It is important to understand ageing phenomena as a result of structural developments within the life course, as resources (such as finances) and potentials (such as education) are accumulated over a lifetime. In old age, these resources serve as a basis for coping with the process of ageing. This does not imply that ageing and personal development are mutually exclusive, it does however mean that (socio-political as well as individual) strategies for coping with ageing need to be established at a much earlier point in life. This also has consequences for gendered differences in the area of health, and for strategies for coping with ageing: in addition to gender-related differences in morbidity and mortality, old-age-health is influenced by resources and strains of the previous stages of life, which are difficult to influence ex post. Gender-related inequalities in lifetime work experience, social network and health status developed over the life course, cumulate in old age and determine differences of „Lebenslagen", socio-economical status, health status, health behaviour and well-being. Gender norms and roles determine ways of handling the ensuing strains and resources in the life course, therefore also influencing the development of strategies for coping with day-to-day challenges. For example, as women are the main bearers of care burdens in case a family-member is afflicted, they are also the ones affected by the necessity of reconciling employment and family. The cultural and social gender norms are generated in complex connections with other social structural categories; in addition to the already-mentioned categories such as strata and class, cultural and ethnic group, categories such as education play an important role. Particularly education has turned out to be an important resource for successful reorientation in old age; it is closely tied to old age health and is a resource for coping strategies in old age. Due to the interplay of these different categories, different and socially unequal „Lebenslagen" cumulate over the life course, and together determine life conditions and health in old age (Clemens, Naegele 2004; Moen 1996, 2001; O'Rand 1995, 1996).

Furthermore it is necessary to take into consideration the political and structural changes and upheavals, such as changes in family structures, labor-market developments, political reforms, European as well as global migratory movements, the growing influence of transnational players on national policy makers, the resulting effects on the development dynamics in the individual countries and therefore also the respective „Lebenslagen" of the elderly.

Particularly the establishment of a life-course-oriented approach, including biological as well as social factors, offers interesting possibilities for the integration of biological-medical with social-scientific perspectives within one theoretical approach. Health situations, social lifestyles as well as societal health cultures could thereby be integrated and evaluated to improve health prevention, health services, and rehabilitation.

Certain research approaches have already been established, such as the WHO Life Course Approach, providing indications of life course risks and attempting to quantify the resulting risk burdens. This raises several questions, such as to the type of coping strategies (political and private) appropriate for offering support from high risks in a life-course. An investigation into the differences generated by gender and by socio-political frameworks could serve to foster understanding of cultural barriers. Correspondingly it would be possible to identify stages for the creation of resources, coping-competence and social capital.

2.3 Health, Ageing, Body and Identity

The topic of ageing and health shows a vital gender-specific component, just as it is inextricably linked with body and identity. There are certain, gender-specific differences in old age health, such as the generally longer life-expectancy of women, as well as the differing rates of leading chronic conditions. Men and women develop different patterns of chronic conditions, with women exhibiting higher rates of nonfatal chronic diseases, and higher rates of fatal diseases for men (Verbrugge 1989). To these differences may be added numerous disease-specific differences in morbidity and mortality in old age, all of which are known from health research. In the field of Public Health gender factors are well known: poverty, unequal access to resources, discrimination and violence lead to gender disparities in communicable disease, occupational health, mental health and reproductive health (Sen, George, Östlin 2002). Gender analysis of health sector reform programs stress the importance of understanding women's roles as both providers and consumers of health care, of identifying inequalities in health resources and health needs between women and men, and of ways in which institutional reforms can have gender implications (Standing 2002).

The body is particularly relevant within the context of ageing and the connected increase of complaints and decrease of capabilities. On the one hand the body is affixed with societal constructions such as gender, age, ethnicity, and their naturalization (Bourdieu 2005, Foucault 1977), while at the same time being shaped and designed by societal and individual physical practice such as sports (Sobiech 1994), beauty activities (Degele 2004), nutrition (Setzwein 2003), and sleep (Hislop, Arber 2003). Similar to institutional body-work, such as in care, these individual body-practices are closely tied to societal norms and cultural images. However, particularly within the contexts of caring for the ageing body, complex concepts of physicalness are largely neglected. (Backes 2005a, Twigg 2004). Just as is medical care, care for the elderly is oriented by a bio-medical body-model, ignoring any social dimensions of physicalness. (Uschok 2005).

The relevance of body-images is illustrated by the increasing willingness to use surgical means for designing the body, accompanied by efforts to medically/surgically restrain the ageing body; by the proliferation of anti-ageing medicine and the modern trend to wellness and fitness activities. All of these may be seen as indicators of an ideological transition from a „given" body to an „influenceable" body, which is therefore totally within individual responsibility. The body is turned into an instrument of self-expression and design, and as a social basis of life and – similar to gender – a social construct is increasingly relevant.

The long-standing absence of social sciences from the realm of the body is rooted in the Western philosophical traditions with their dualistic pair of opposites „body and soul", analogue to nature and culture. For the past couple of years however, the body has become a much-discussed topic in sociology. In gender studies, body and body practices are seen within a social constructive perspective. They are highly influenced by gender and other social categories, and the body is a crucial location, where gender is identified, constructed and validated and naturalized (see Duden 1987, Laqueur 1992, Butler 1997, Lindeman 1993, 1999, Villa 2001, Bourdieu 2005). In other disciplines such as identity research (e.g. Gugutzer 2002) and sports sciences (e.g. Sobiech 1994) the theme of 'body' is also present. In medicine and care sciences the bio-medical notion of the body have so far dominated; social dimensions of the physical body are thematized within the context of daily activities, if at all. In German gerontology, the discussion on body and ageing has been very limited, while in the English-language sphere much more has been published. (Among others Twigg 2004, Kontos 1999, Öberg et al. 1999, Biggs 1997). Here, the topic "Body and ageing" is discussed in the context of changing identities and the impact of physical ageing on self-images in old age (cp. the discussion on the „mask of ageing", the „masquerade of ageing" and on the „ageless self" by Biggs 1997).

A much stronger interdisciplinary gain in knowledge could be generated by perceptions aiming at researching the body and questioning the relevance of body, body practices, health practices on or with the body, in connection with an understanding of the body in the ageing process, and the way both genders handle physical ageing. It would be particularly valuable to connect medical, geronto-psychological, socio-scientific, care-scientific and feminist insights and questions, most notably in view of the development of application-oriented concepts in ageing and care sciences (see Reimann, Backes in this volume).

The analyses of the phenomenon of ageism, which may be interpreted as a negative connotation of age and ageing woven into the socio-cultural pattern, need critical examination, particularly in respect to the fields dealing with body-related ageing-phenomena. To which degree are existing connotations of ageing responsible for the precarious medical care in old age? The existence of such phenomena is well-known, but to which degree do they influence old-age quality of life? Which changes are necessary in the medical image of humanity? The links between gender-specific strategies of ageing, the health opportunities in age and the role of identity-development and presentation in old age have not yet been explored and compiled to a sufficient degree.

3 Outlook

For research in the field of ageing it is important to compile the already-existing results in the various disciplines, and to expand the body of knowledge on the complex interconnections between ageing, gender and health. This includes knowledge on the interplay of individual behaviour, social economy, cultural conditions and social environment, and their effects on old-age health and „Lebenslagen“. Attention needs to be given to gender as a social construct in the already-mentioned realms, with a focus on its effects on the identities and needs of elderly women and men.

Also requiring exploration are the impacts of concepts of health and of ageing developed over a life course, the individual strategies for coping with changes and losses, lifestyles, and gender-allocated resources and strains. Particularly cultural i.e. country-specific differences could serve to demonstrate the influence of societal frameworks, and could open up new venues for the discussion of causes and consequences. Another very interesting question is how the various societies react to the challenges created by demographic change (e.g. the raised need for care) and the changing societal structures; which developments are relevant in individual countries and which strategies are implemented politically. One example here could be the gendered organization of care-giving and country-specific strategies for the improvement of the support for private caregivers. Here, too, it would be possible to learn more about the country-, i.e. culture-specific differences via the reception of sociopolitical differences, making it easier to formulate the right questions on strategies for change. International research and cross-border cooperation account for the fact that in spite of very different health, pension and social systems, employment-market characteristics and family traditions, all of these countries face similar challenges. They need to address the problems and demands brought on by demographic changes, an ageing population and rising costs for their health and pension systems. At the same time, globalization and the increasing coalescence of the European economic area necessitate cross-border descriptions of problems and strategies for their solution. However, it is necessary that the research focus should remain on the change pressure on the day-to-day lives of older and of younger cohorts. Not only financial feasibility of social systems, but also life quality and equal opportunity as relevant socio-political factors.

Research should focus on the question as to which knowledge is actually needed in order to meet the upcoming challenges, and which promising strategies or models are already existent in individual countries or as cross-national models. In doing so, it is particularly important to elicit the framework conditions of the respective strategies and models of good practice, in order to examine their transferability onto other contexts.

In Brief: Combining research knowledge, needed questions and debates

Multidisciplinary views on:
▪ Intersections between ageing, health and gender with a focus on gender ▪ Integration of Gender Theories in Ageing and Health Studies ▪ Research on health in old age based on the life course approach ▪ Gender focus on older men's health ▪ Intersections between gender, body, identity, health and ageing in the life course
Questions for Research on Healthy Ageing
▪ Which resources and strains are responsible for health inequality and diversity over the life course? ▪ Which specific strategies do different groups have to balance resources and strains? ▪ Which strategies exist in different countries to support health in old age? ▪ Are there gender differences in these issues? ▪ Which life-long strategies for balancing strains and resources are developed over the life course? Are there models of good practice in order to societally promote these strategies, and to implement successful ones? How does this impact health and quality of life in old age?
Questions for Research on Gender Issues in Healthy Ageing
▪ Which cultural gender constructions affect health and ageing issues? ▪ How are they currently changing? ▪ Which challenges will be brought on by future developments such as the increasing number of ageing men?

4 About the Articles in this Volume

In the present volume, different aspects of the topic „Gender, Health and Ageing" will be presented.

In the first chapter *„Gender Impacts on the Life Course and Old-age Health"*, gender is the central perspective for developing insights into the topics of "life course" and "health". Gertrud M. Backes, Ludwig Amrhein, Vera Lasch and Katja Reimann provide a detailed account of the dynamics and changes in the living conditions of ageing men and women over the life course, their resources and strains, and their impact on the living conditions in old age in Germany. They thereby introduce the German „Lebenslagen"-concept and link it with a life course approach in order to show the future challenges of gender equity in ageing. The contribution on men in later life, by Katja Reimann and Gertrud M. Backes, introduces a gender perspective on ageing men and health. It offers insights into different research concepts, results and theoretical approaches towards masculinities, men's health as well as on embodiment, broadening the perspective on old age health of men. Brigitta Lindencrona and Barbro Westerholm report on the results of the MERI research project in their contribution: "Mapping Existing Research and Identifying Knowledge Gaps Concerning the Situation of Older Women in Europe (MERI)". The overview of accessible data in twelve European countries allows identification of general and country-specific research gaps and necessary emphases of future research.

In the second chapter "Issues of Health Research in the Context of Gender and Old Age" are at the focus. There are also contributions showing the complex meanings of health, gender and ageing in different European cultural contexts. Friederike Kendel and Monika Sieverding point out how important it is to differentiate patients according to gender and age in cardiovascular medicine. As risk factors work gender-specifically (like smoking) and gender specific factors influence manifestation, course and prognosis of diseases (for example of cardiovascular diseases) health care and health research need to integrate both factors more carefully. Csilla T. Csoboth provides insight into the health status of Hungarian women and the process of ageing in Hungary. Beata Tobias-Adamczyk writes on the complexity of social resources and their influence on health status and gender differences in Poland. Majda Pahor, Barbara Domajnko and Valentina Hlebec offer an overview of quality of life of older women in Slovenia and discuss the importance of social networks for health issues. Mónika Erika Kovács discusses quality-of-life factors and their impact on health, gender and ageing, supplying a wealth of data on the intersections of these factors in Hungary. Bridget Penhale focuses on the dynamics of mental health and elder abuse and describes causation and management of elder abuse.

The last chapter on *Challenges of Care – Gender and Health Perspectives* focuses on discussions on demographic change and challenges for European societies. Vera Lasch and Katja Reimann discuss an overview of European comparative research, explaining the need for reviewing different results from the 5th European Research Framework Program into national and future research strategies, as well as the need for a debate on theoretical models and an overall interpretation on heterogeneous single project results. Hildegard Theobald presents results from a European research project "Care for the aged at risk of marginali-

Hislop, Jenny, Arber, Sara (2003): Sleep as socials act: a window on Gender Roles and Relationships. In Sara Arber, Kate Davidson, Jay Ginn (Eds.): Gender and Ageing. Changing Roles and Relationships. Maidenhead, Philadelphia: Open University Press: 186-205.

Höpflinger, François (1997): Frauen im Alter – Alter der Frauen. Ein Forschungsdossier. 2. Aufl. Zurich: Seismo.

Höpflinger, Francois (2002): Männer im Alter. Eine Grundlagenstudie. Zurich: Pro Senectute.

Johnson, Malcolm L. (Ed.) 2005: The Cambridge Handbook of Age and Ageing. Cambridge University Press

Kohli, M. 1990: Das Alter als Herausforderung für die Theorie sozialer Ungleichheit. In: Berger, P. A.; Hradil, S. (Eds.): Lebenslagen, Lebensläufe, Lebensstile. Soziale Welt, Göttingen: 387-406.

Kontos, Pia C. 1999: Local biology: bodies of difference in ageing studies. In: Ageing and Society 19: 677–689.

Laqueur, Thomas 1992: Auf den Leib geschrieben. Die Inszenierung der Geschlechter von der Antike bis Freud. Frankfurt a.M., New York: Campus.

Laslett, Peter (1995): Das Dritte Alter. Historische Soziologie des Alterns. Weinheim, Munich: Juventa.

Lindemann, Gesa 1993: Das paradoxe Geschlecht: Transsexualität im Spannungsfeld von Körper, Leib und Gefühl. Frankfurt a.M.: Fischer.

Lindemann, Gesa 1999: Bewußtsein, Leib und Biographie. Biographische Kommunikation und die Verkörperung doppelter Kontingenz. In: Alheit, Peter; Dausien, Bettina; Fischer-Rosenthal, Wolfram; Hanses, Andreas; Keil, Annelie (Eds.): Biographie und Leib. Gießen: Psychosozial-Verlag: 44–72.

Markides, Kyriakos S. (Ed) 1989: Aging and Health. Perspectives on Gender, Race, Ethnicity, and Class. SAGE Publications, Newbury Park, London, New Delhi

McMullin, Julie (1995): Theorizing age and gender relations. In: Arber, Sara; Ginn, Jay (Eds.): Connecting gender and ageing: A sociological approach. Buckingham, Ph.: Open University Press: 30–41.

Meuser, Michael (2005): Frauenkörper – Männerkörper. Somatische Kulturen der Geschlechterdifferenz. In: Schroer, Markus (Ed.) (2005): Soziologie des Körpers. Frankfurt a. M.: Suhrkamp: 271–295.

Meuser, Michael 2002: Körper und Sozialität. Zur handlungstheoretischen Fundierung einer Soziologie des Körpers. In: Hahn, Kornelia; Meuser, Michael, (Eds.): Körperrepräsentationen: die Ordnung des Sozialen und der Körper. Konstanz: UVK: 19–44.

Moen, Phyllis (1996): Gender, Age, and the Life Course. In: Binstock, Robert H.; George, Linda K. (Eds.): Handbook of Aging and the Social Sciences. 4th Edition. San Diego, Calif.: Academic Press: 171–187.

Moen, Phyllis (2001): The gendered life course. In: Binstock, Robert H.; George, Linda K. (Eds.): Hand-book of Aging and the Social Sciences. 5th Edition. San Diego, Calif.: Academic Press: 197–196.

O'Rand, Angela M. (1995): The Cumulative Stratification of the Life Course. In: Binstock, Robert H.; George, Linda K. (Eds.): Handbook of Aging and the Social Sciences. 4. Edition. San Diego, Calif.: Academic Press: 188–207.

O'Rand, Angela M. (1996): The Precious and the Precocious: Understanding Cumulative Disadvantage and Cumulative Advantage Over the Life Course. The Gerontologist 36: 230–238.
Öberg, Peter; Tornstam, Lars 1999: Body images among men and women of different ages. In: Ageing and Society 19/5: 629–644.
Oldmen, C.; Quilgars, D. 1999: The last resort? Revisiting ideas about older people's living arrangements. In: Ageing and Society, vol 19/ 3: 363-384.
Pasero, Ursula; Braun, Friederike (Eds.) (1995): Konstruktion von Geschlecht. Pfaffenweiler: Centaurus.
Perrig-Chiello, Pasqualina; Höpflinger, Francois (Eds.) (2000): Jenseits des Zenits. Frauen und Männer in der zweiten Lebenshälfte. Bern, Stuttgart, Vienna: Paul Haupt,
Schaufler, Birgit (2002): „Schöne Frauen – starke Männer". Zur Konstruktion von Leib, Körper und Geschlecht. Opladen: Leske + Budrich.
Sen, Gita; George, Asha; Östlin, Piroska (Ed.) 2002. Engendering International Health. The Challenge of Equity. MIT Press, Cambridge, Massachusetts, London
Setzwein, Monika (2003): Ernährung – Körper/Leib – Geschlecht. Zur sozialen Konstruktion von Geschlecht im kulinarischen Kontext. Diss. Phil. Fac. Univ. Kiel.
Sobiech, Gabriele 1994: Grenzüberschreitungen: Körperstrategien von Frauen in modernen Gesellschaften; Opladen.
Sørensen, Annemette (1990): Unterschiede im Lebenslauf von Frauen und Männern. In: Mayer, Karl Ulrich (Ed.): Lebensverläufe und sozialer Wandel. Special issue 31 of the KZfSS. Opladen: Westdeutscher Verlag, p. 304–321.
Standing, Hilary 2002: Frameworks for Understanding Health Sector Reform. In: Sen, Gita; George, Asha; Östlin, Piroska (Ed.) 2002. Engendering International Health. The Challenge of Equity. MIT Press, Cambridge, Massachusetts, London: 347-371
Tews, H. P. 1993: Neue und alte Aspekte des Strukturwandels des Alters. In: Naegele, G.; Tews, H. P. (Ed.): Lebenslagen im Strukturwandel des Alters. Alternde Gesellschaft – Folgen für die Politik. Opladen: 15-42.
Twigg, Julia 2004: The body, gender, and age: Feminist insights in social gerontology. In: Journal of Aging Studies 18/1: 59–73.
Uschok, Andreas 2005: Körper und Pflege. In: Schroeter, K. R.; Rosenthal, T. (Eds.): Soziologie der Pflege. Grundlagen, Wissensbestände und Perspektiven, Weinheim, München: Juventa Verlag.
Verbrugge, Lois M. 1989: Gender, Aging, and Health. In: Markides, Kyriakos S. (Ed): Aging and Health. Perspectives on Gender, Race, Ethnicity, and Class. SAGE Publications, Newbury Park, London, New Delhi: 23-77
Villa, Paula-Irene 2001: Sexy Bodies. Eine soziologische Reise durch den Geschlechtskörper. 2. Auflage. Opladen: Leske + Budrich.
Winkler, Ines; Buyantugs, Lamjav; Petscheleit, Andreas; Kilian, Reinhold; Angermeyer, Matthias C. 2003: Die interkulturelle Erfassung der Lebensqualität im Alter: Das WHOQOL-OLD-Projekt. In: Zeitschrift für Gerontopsychologie & -psychiatrie, 16/4: 77-192.
World Health Organization WHO 2000: A Life Course Approach to Health

World Health Organization WHO 2002: Active Ageing. A Policy Framework.. Noncommunicable Disease and Mental Health Cluster, Noncommunicable Disease Prevention and Health Promotion Department, Aging and Life Course.

I. Gender Impacts on the Life Course and Old-age Health

Gendered Life Course and Ageing – Implications on „Lebenslagen“ of Ageing Women and Men

Gertrud M. Backes, Ludwig Amrhein, Vera Lasch & Katja Reimann

For Ingrid and Heinz between Tradition and Modernity of Gender Relations.

1 Introduction: Gender and Ageing – a Well Known Field of Social Inequalities and its Research Perspectives

For the longest time, the societal and individual relevance of the interaction of gender and ageing had been missing from the list of topics appropriately represented and treated in German-language sociology of ageing, or in research on women and on gender. Only slowly and sporadically have these topics been accepted into the realms of gerontology and sociology of ageing (cp. Fooken 1987, 1994; Backes 1993a, 1993b, 1999a, 1999b, 2002, 2005, 2006; Höpflinger 1994; Perrig-Chiello, Höpflinger 2000, 2001), and in part also into the feminist critique of the social systems (cp. Kickbusch, Riedmüller 1984). First continuative approaches may for instance be found in the discussion of the "Effects of Female Longevity on Ways of Life and Generational Relations“ (Höpflinger 2000, 2002a) and the transition of women from a working life to retirement. (Cp. Clemens 1993, 1997), as well as most recently in the considerations on the "different" ageing of men (cp. Fooken 1986, 1999, Höpflinger 2002b). Meanwhile, gender has been accepted as an essential differentiating criterion also in terms of age. The necessity of this differentiation as much as the subsequent analysis has repeatedly been proven by pertinent data and facts (cp. Backes 2001, 2003). Studies on life-course, ageing and life-circumstances now commonly differentiate according to gender, or at least emphasize the particularities of the female process of ageing as opposed to male ageing; in doing so, they serve to expose substantial differences and inequalities between the genders (Sørensen 1990).

But still there is a gap between the outstanding societal and individual relevance of a gendered life course and its implications on „Lebenslagen“[1] up into a very high age on the one hand and the somewhat scant attention this has so far received in scientific research, at least as far as the German-speaking cultural sphere is concerned (for the Anglo-American area cp. Arber, Davidson, Ginn

2003; Arber, Ginn 1995; Moen 1996, 2001; O'Rand 1995, 1996). Therefore gender-specific differentiation happens primarily on a descriptive level, such as in the description of disparate lifespans (what draws most interest here, again and again, is the question as to why women generally live longer than men) and the unequal effects these social problems have on women in old age, particularly very old age. Other studies concentrate on "feminine" age(ing) in the sense of the ageing of women and the social problems they encounter. The term used is the "feminization of age" (Tews 1993, Kohli 1990), which is justified not only quantitatively, by the much higher proportion of women, but also qualitatively, as female forms of sociation (in the meaning of the German term "Vergesellschaftung") seem to dominate life at a high age. Old men are even ascribed an approximation to female forms of sociation, as their gender-typical social integration via employment comes to an end after retirement. A more in-depth analysis of gender-relations onto the life course and their effects on "Lebenslagen" of both genders still needs to be done.

Furthermore, the public and political discussions on the social problems faced by old and oldest old women are dominated by the societal and financial burdens (such as caused by care-services) accompanying old age. The high proportion of women in the group of the oldest old characterized by increasing polymorbidity, dementia and need for care, has caused them to be compared to the shorter lifespan of men, and has caused them to be perceived as a greater burden to their social environment and society in general. Usually this equation includes only publicly noticeable burdens and resources, while neglecting privately performed services (such as caring) by women, which often complement or even replace public services. In contrast, post-professional activities of men are frequently emphasized (compare Kohli/Künemund 2000). This biased assignation, which is also supported by corresponding scientific studies, presents women as a burden to society, while at the same time featuring men as resources.

For research on the topic(s) of women, gender and age(ing) the field of gender-relationships and relations, and the correlation of gender and age(ing) raises a number of questions, particularly relevant for the future. The theoretical foundation certainly needs to draw on considerations already formulated regarding social structure, social inequality and "Lebenslagen", on the division of labor between genders, and on constructions on gender and on age(ing).

Correspondingly, the key to an appropriate analysis of the complex individual and societal relevance and the consequences of gender and ageing, - this at least is our thesis- is an analysis of the forms of sociation of both genders and their collusion over the course of one's life, as well as their connection to „Lebenslagen". In modern societies, these generally consist of hierarchically complementary structured gender relations, correlating with social inequality up until high age. In reference to a well-founded empirical analysis it would be useful to implement a survey on the "Lebenslagen" of the genders in the life-course, in addition to conducting the appropriate theoretically based studies. What deserves particular attention in the light of the prognosis and prevention of individual, social and societal problems caused by age(ing), are the changing living and working conditions of men and of women.

In the following, a few important aspects of gendered life course and ageing and its implications on „Lebenslagen"[1] will be exemplarily highlighted. The rather descriptive chapters 2 and 3 will set forth the empirical basis for the analysis of the changing gender-relationships and relations over the life course, with the consequences for "Lebenslagen" up into an advanced age. The empirical dimensions of „Lebenslagen" (material situation, employment, social network and health) serve as the conceptual framework. Chapter 2 will deal with social inequality in a gendered life course and „Lebenslagen", and the potentially cumulative social risks for elderly women. Chapter 3 will treat the social processes of change and their effects on female and male conditions of life and work in a gendered life course. The issues at question are the new risks, opportunities and contradictions in the gendered life courses as well as their implications on future ageing. Finally, in chapter 4, the thesis of the (hierarchical) complementariness of the gender relations up into a high age will be analytically founded. The concept of a „gendered life course" i.e. of „ageing as a gendered process" on the one hand and „Lebenslagen" on the other hand will serve as the conceptual cornerstones. As a conclusion, chapter 5 will provide a summary and a short preview on research questions and developments to be expected.

2 Empirical Perspectives on Social Inequality in Gendered Life Course and "Lebenslagen" – Cumulation of Risks for Women?

„Lebenslagen" here (chapter 2 and 3) primarily serves as the empirical-descriptive concept of social inequality, in order to systematically present the individual situation in a social context, exemplarily illustrated by central dimensions such as material situation (income, residence), social integration by employment (work) and social network, health situation and provision of related services (including care). For further use of this concept of "Lebenslagen" it is necessary to integrate objective as well as subjective dimensions (such as diagnosed disorders and subjective state of health). It is also necessary to include

1 The German concept of "Lebenslagen" contains several dimensions to describe socially unequal life situations. The characteristic of the concept is the integration of objective conditions of action and subjective scope of action.

historical time (cohorts) and individual lifetime (personal data and biography) in order to appropriately recognize the variations of "Lebenslagen" in the societal as well as the individual developmental process (social change, individual changes). Socially unequal „Lebenslagen" in a gendered life course are therefore directly related to other dimensions of social differentiation, such as class, stratum, region, ethnicity or religion. (see chapter 4; on the concept of „Lebenslage" cp. Hradil 1987, Clemens 1994, Backes 1997b).

Geared to this concept of interwoven dimensions of social inequality, ageing and to be old as a woman under the current historical and biographical conditions means to bear a double risk for the „Lebenslage": the threats of facing social problems structurally tied to age(ing) (concerning financial security and residence, employment and social integration, social network, health/care and dependency on others) are felt to a much higher degree by old women today, than by men. Accompanied by other characteristics of social differentiation, ageing women experience a much greater degree of socially problematic „Lebenslagen" (such as poverty, unemployment, dependency on non family members for support in old age).

Gendered division of labor to the majority of the currently old women meant that, at least for large periods of their lives, they took on the roles of housewives and homemakers (in spite of different experiences made during and directly after the war), and that employment had not been normative, or at least, served only temporary purposes. The 'old', respectively 'traditional' risks consisted of a primarily familial orientation and the resulting dependency for material survival and purpose in life. Studies on elderly women univocally show that women are not only more satisfied, but also healthier, more secure, and socially more integrated, if they enjoyed and enjoy a variety of contacts and activities outside their homes. It seems as if a concentration onto family creates not only a higher risk of poverty in old age, but also interferes with social and psychological health, and that, to put it bluntly, qualified and continuous employment is the best „geroprophylaxis" (promotion of health in old age) (cp. Lehr 1977, 1982; Szinovacz 1982; Clemens 1992, 1993, 1997).

All in all it seems as if currently female age(ing) in our society is more contradictory, ambivalent and socially more problematic than male age(ing). This includes other and principally more impairments, but also different and frequently greatly varied subjective forms of coping. A short review on the "Lebenslage" of today's old women in comparison to today's old men will exemplify this view (cp. Lehr 1978; Fooken 1994, 1999; Backes 1983, 1999b; 2001; Krüger 1983; Gather et al. 1991; Höpflinger 1994; Stuckelberger, Höpflinger 1996):

Due to their gender-specific, prevalently discontinuous working lives, their generally lower professional status and their primary orientation towards marriage and family women are more often, and more often severely, affected by material and partly also immaterial poverty. Their conditions of life and of work have mainly been relegated to familial and activities. Very often these conditions were involuntarily accepted, and simply continued to enforce the strains and contradiction of a "woman's life". Additionally, they are more often dependent on help by third parties, – also family-external – and are more frequently subjected to violence and abuse, or neglect. Even though women generally live longer than men, they more frequently suffer from chronic diseases, psychosocial emergencies and experience need for care. Longevity and quality of "Lebenslagen" here have an inversely proportional relationship. Within the gender-specific female ageing-problem there are highly individual situations: living and working conditions, age, stratum, biographical features, individual lifestyle and subjective attitudes, region, residential environment and neighborhood, familial conditions and personal interests may all contribute to the actual "Lebenslage" of a women in old age. These old-age risks are particularly potent if disadvantages are cumulated: on the one hand for women who come from the lower strata of society, and have not managed to rise socially, who live in infrastructurally disadvantaged regions, and have limited resources in terms of health, social contact and adequate material provision; and on the other hand for women who are disadvantaged materially and immaterially, or for whom poverty, isolation, unemployment, excessive strain and disease have altogether created difficult situations, and who do not have any opportunity to make up for losses in one area by resources to be found in another.

The quantitatively and qualitatively different female and male opportunities and risks in age(ing) are for example visible in the fact that women today typically need to arrange themselves at least twice, but normally four times within their lives, with the loss of life course and "Lebenslagen"-determined functions and relationships. In modern society, it is possible to differentiate among four gender-typical risky transition phases in the lives of the presently old and elderly women (Backes 1993a, 1993b, 1999a, 2001; also cp. Fooken 1994, 1999; Perrig-Chiello, Höpflinger 2000, 2001). These periods of transition are sketched here, and are exemplarily contrasted with the respective transitions experienced by ageing men. All in all this is a field of research with many open questions, to most of which the answers available are justified assumptions or fragmentary.

First period: In middle age, after children have left the house and women search for a new orientation regarding their prospects of life and of work. Even if the ideal of the 'normal female biography' (employment, interrupted or reduced for several years of child-rearing, employment) and the concentration onto the family has long become fragile, or is at least no longer the most desirable model, the traditional societal images of women persist. They result in penalties against those who behave differently, or who try to do so. Even single women without children and with an undivided orientation towards their professional lives experience different stigmatizations and segregations than men. For these women, too, their femininity and desirability are measured by their age and possibly also by whether they 'need' to work for a living at all. The accordant self-images are well-known. The best conditions for coping with this stage of life are strong interests and relationships also outside of the family sphere. In addition to work-related contacts these could also include other forms of sociation, such as volunteer activities. To men, however, middle age does not (yet) as a rule represent comparable challenges to their reorientation-capacities. On the other hand, they are frequently confronted with the demands created by a "senior"-position, often facing the need for relearning, loss of status, relocation, and early retirement (cp. Clemens 2001; Barkholdt 2001; Herfurth, Kohli, Zimmermann 2002). The fact that these conditions do not bypass women is largely ignored by the public as well as by science. (cp. Clemens 1997, 2001)

Second period: At so-called 'Old Age' (beginning at 60/65 years), the age at which retirement begins, – either because a woman herself retires or because her husband's employment comes to an end. What is initially important is coming to terms with the loss of a function, an assignment, for which the role of a housewife – contrary to popular assumption – does not offer adequate compensation (cp. Clemens 1993; 1997). This is often accompanied by the coping-support women provide for their husbands after these have left gainful employment (Backes 1987b). The new life-prospects and perspectives come along with complex losses and requirements, for men as well as for women. Depending on their previous conditions of life and of work, resources for coping may differ considerably. Again, those manage best who have extensive out-of-home contacts and activities as well as working conditions, which leave or have left them with opportunities for developing further contacts and interests. So far this has mainly been the case for men. The fact that women are and were responsible for housekeeping may offer them support and grounding, but may also lead to risks, restrictions and additional strains. On the other hand, due to their primarily out-of-home orientation, men tend to experience more freedom in exploring new activities for their retirement, while sometimes lacking orientation in the familial sphere (cp. Clemens 1997; Gather 1991, 1996).

Third period: After the loss of their spouse or partner, which for the majority of women happens towards the end of their 8th or 9th decade. At this time, women are again forced to substantially reorient themselves, while often having to accept material losses. At the same time new, unexpected leeway and freedom arises, revealing challenges and excessive demands, opportunities and limitations. Freedom from and freedom to exist side by side. Both may be contradictory and may be felt as ambivalent: to be freed of the burden of caring for an ailing husband, but also to be free in the sense of having lost intimate companionship, security and closeness. But also to be free for new contacts, which may be felt as an opportunity, but which may also cause fear and present an unwelcome effort. Men much less frequently find themselves in this situation, at least today: they are often (re)married to or living together with a much younger partner, and are therefore rarely confronted with the necessity of having to care for their spouses.

Fourth period: After losing the capacity to live independently, particularly when the need for care arises, and is accompanied by material dependency on others. Being dependent on support by relatives or strangers seems to be more difficult to bear for women than for men (cp. Lehr 1986). This caesura is feared most of all problems associated with ageing, and great efforts are made to avoid it. This attitude is probably one reason for the comparatively large number of unreported cases of female age-related poverty. Need of care to them turns into a decisive point-of-no-return on the way to unwanted material and immaterial dependency. Their problems as oldest old in nursing homes as well as in private situations are manifold. Objective situation and the subjective difficulties of having to rely on others concur. A taboo is only slowly being lifted from abuse of elderly women (such as in situations of in-patient or at-home care).

These four typical periods of transition, their timing and their importance, are also subjected to change as male and female conditions of life and work transform. And, new ones are added: divorce, unemployment (Backes 1993b, 1999a) or (enforced) mobility. Some of these developments have already emerged in the lives of today's old, and they are on the increase: more and more women are already affected by a pluralization of female ways of life (cp. Herlyn, Vogel 1989, 1991; Ostner 1990; Beck-Gernsheim 1983; Beck, Beck-Gernsheim 1990), which will also have consequences for their ways of ageing.

3 Empirical Perspectives on Gendered Life Courses, Social Change and Prospective on Future Ageing of Women and Men

3.1 Social Change in Work and Life Conditions – Consequences on "Lebenslagen"

Together with the continuous integration into the workforce, emancipation from 'typically female family orientation', individualization and pluralization, there are several changes affecting both men and women, and which, in view of their age(ing) and their "Lebenslagen" contain contradictions, risks and opportunities.

To those men and women who are elderly or old today the colourful mosaic of conditions and ways of life has already widened substantially, to include entirely new hues, has become much more complex and heterogeneous. It now contains many more obligations and demands, which may be met only with great personal efforts, and by creating a strong supportive social network (cp. Beck-Gernsheim 1986). The differences between various 'types' of male, but particularly female lives at old age are growing. The transition between the two female 'risk-types', – the 'traditional, old' one and the 'modern, new' one – is blurred. There have always been women who were forced to work in order to survive financially, at the same being responsible for household-chores, while today, there are (still) women who orient themselves along the traditional model of marriage without them working outside their homes. But women's work is (still) a relatively precarious and insufficient basis for securing an independent existence; this is not only true for the underprivileged class.

All in all, the dissolution of the exclusive orientation along the traditional role of women is discernible (cp. Feldmann-Neubert 1991). However, this liberation from the biographical obligation to be a wife and mother has been accompanied by an only seemingly free choice between contrary ways of life (orientation either towards family or career). This normally presents women with an insolvable dilemma and a life accompanied by discrepancies. Women are forced to give up one or the other, but still without enjoying the chosen option. To have both at the same time is at best to live only parts of both, and is possible only if she is willing to bear multiple strains and to balance a series of contradictory demands. Up until today, men have rarely been forced to face the same dilemma. Professional career and family are parallely possible, without ever forcing them to accept comparable career disadvantages or familial work.

As a downside, the gain of personal freedom is accompanied by a loss of social security, which possibly needs to be compensated by social security systems (Buhr et. al. 1988: 655). But these systems are so far not able to counterbalance existing discrepancies, but in turn continue gender-specific discrimination (cp. Weg 1988; Riedmüller 2000). For example, the state pension funds still send out „contradictory signals“ regarding women's participation in the work force (Bäcker 2001: 185f.; also cp. Michaelis 2000; Schmähl 2000).

In the face of increasing pluralization and individualization of life, and the dissolution of the primary orientation along traditional gender roles, the in many ways anachronistic (at least in Germany) social, family and labor market-policy orientation along the hitherto existing male and female 'normal biographies' and the traditional role model represents additional social risks for women. (cp. Ostner 1983, 2000; Hohmann-Dennhardt 1988; Gerhard 1990; Deutsches Institut für Altersvorsorge 2000). Economization and positive sanctioning of the model of the temporarily unemployed wife and mother relates to the socio-political trend of propagating unpaid (female) work within the family and in the social sphere. 'Motherliness' is again discovered as a social resource and an ideological value, and attempts are made to promote it further (cp. Riedmüller 2000). Women, particularly those of middle age, are seen as searching for 'meaningful' work, less than in need of employment and material independence. Accordingly, they are primarily assigned social volunteer activities, and the private care for old and ailing people (Wand 1986; Backes 1987a, 1991, 2001). Ideologically, this revives an antiquated traditional family-model, which in its idealized form was never valid. Economizing measures and postponed plans of reform have always hit women, – and particularly elderly and old women – to a much greater degree. This is true for the exploitation of 'female work' in families, 'self-help-organizations', and social professions, but also for their access to appropriate forms of support (cp. Peace 1986).

For men, too, new patterns of life and of work emerge, which will remain valid up into old age: changing conditions on the labor market (more frequent interruptions of gainful employment, the necessity to be mobile regionally) and – if only rudimentarily relevant to them – changed familial demands (the reconciliation of family and career necessary to women also confronts their partners with new challenges) cause the male 'normal biography' to become frayed, opens up new choices and necessities, altogether creating an increase of hitherto unknown multiple responsibilities. Compensatory efforts by wives/partners can no longer be taken for granted. Instead, men are now also expected to balance career and familial needs, or a private life, if they do not want to or cannot fall back onto old partnership models. And these are increasingly difficult to realize in times of at least temporarily insecure employment prospects and changing female role models. The growing numbers of single households is probably to be seen within the context of these developments. But all in all, the field of these changing male life courses, up into a high age, is still a largely unexplored field, the research of which – in combination with changes in the lives of women, – will, in our opinion, be indispensable for the future of sociology of age(ing).

3.2 Risks, Chances, Contradictions and Changes

The trends described above are all indicators of the individualization and pluralization of (male and female) life and work. The question as to the relevance of these social changes to women in regard to their age(ing) needs to reflect on the inherent risks, opportunities and contradictions (cp. Beck 1986; Herlyn, Vogel 1989, 1991). Particularly for women, these changes represent extremely contradictory developments, while under current conditions the risks seem to prevail. While they, too, are increasingly forced to sell their labor during their entire lifetime, they often do not enjoy the necessary freedom from other obligations. On the labor-market, women and men are expected to perform at equal levels; this, however, does in no way take into consideration the inequality of their prerequisites concerning the freedom to negotiate their value on the labor market. Specifically women are often subjected to multiplex strains, obligations and orientations. They are forced to use a multiple approach. This results in a perpetuation of the well-known gender-specific discrimination on the labor-market (cp. Mayer et al. 1991; Krüger, Born 1991; Allmendinger 2000; Maier 2000). Old certainties have dissolved, while at the same time new ones, particularly in reference to their own employment and the state-subsidiarity in case of emergency, are not as secure to them as they are to men. Due to the still existing gender-hierarchical attribution-criteria, safeguarding their independent existence is still structurally more precarious, discontinuous, and quantitatively and qualitatively on a lower level than is men's (cp. Bäcker 2001). This is accompanied by dwindling traditional protective measures, without the emergence of sufficient material and psychosocial equivalents. Furthermore, women are still more frequently excluded from important societal spheres, such as the public sphere and leisure time activities, at least temporarily (during periods of child-rearing and while caring for older family members). But particularly these spheres are important for quality of life and satisfaction in old age.

The new freedom is much more risky for less qualified women with discontinuous working lives and socially problematic living conditions, than for well-educated and socially privileged women. An important question is which women have which options during the course of their ageing, and whether the new freedom is not actually an illusionary improvement, offering benefits to few, while deteriorating the "Lebenslagen" of the majority. The paradox characterizing the structural changes in female life and work is that even though women have become more qualified and greatly participate in the labor market, the still-effective gender-hierarchical mechanisms of attribution and exclusion continue to render autonomy and life, with and without family, more risky for them than it is for men: In reference to the life-situation of women the buzzword of 'individualization' may be interpreted as a dissolution of solidary communalization within the family, liberation from social family ties and relations, or – in the handy wording by Beck-Gernsheim – as the enforcement of the aspiration for one's own 'share of life'. The gain in freedom is offset by a more of insecurity, which needs to be compensated (by official security systems)" (Buhr et al. 1988: 655; cp. Ostner 2000)

A female 'normal biography' is something to be expected less in future (cp. Herlyn, Vogel 1989, 1991; cp. Allmendinger 2000), even if it is still a desirable model to many. Disruptions of the work-biography – and therefore increased risks at old age – no longer adhere to the previously common, classical 'three-phase-pattern', but are based on unforeseeable risks such as unemployment, divorce or single parenthood (cp. Maier 2000). On the one hand this creates more insecurity and decreasing reliability of traditional patterns. But it may also result in more self-reliance, in the sense of self-determination in the arrangement of life and of work. However, these positive developments are often thwarted by adverse parameters (how much freedom of choice is available when several children need to be raised under financially narrow circumstances?) In reference to the formerly (and currently) relevant 'intersections of female ageing', (see chapter 2) – depending on the decisions made on family, career or both, – it is assumable that the process of pluralization and differentiation will go on:

First: The so-called empty-nest-phase and women's subsequent return to employment, i.e. the revived concentration on professional activities and perhaps an increase of working hours may no longer be concentrated onto middle age, but will be spread onto a longer period of life-time. There will be a greater variety of patterns of how women attempt to reconcile career and family. The question of generativity and its limitation will remain a central issue in female ageing.

Second: Efforts for a continuous, qualified integration into the labor market will increase. In how far this will be realizable or whether this will be accompanied by even more fragility (such as unemployment) will differ for each woman, depending on the economy, qualification, social status, and familial strains. According to the existing knowledge about women's integration into the labor-market (see above) it can be assumed that there will be a 'hard core' of unplanned discontinuity.

Third: The period of transition into retirement will probably increase in importance for women themselves, while their role as 'crisis manager' of their husbands' retirement will be somewhat reduced. Depending on the individual's life course, we may expect a variety of different courses.

Fourth: The last-mentioned intersection, survival without a partner, to be left behind alone in old age, will increase in importance as compared to today, but will probably be spread over a longer period and will more often be due to other reasons than death of a partner (e.g. divorce). Also showing a tendency to increase is the danger for women to become dependent on institutions or on relatives. Their life expectancy is still rising. And there is no indication for the assumption that as oldest old they will be less bothered by chronic degenerative diseases, dementia, multimorbidity or limited capacity of independently handling their everyday lives, than today.

The flexibilization and individualization of female work- and lifestyles will not per se result in a reduction of risks, but rather in an increase of potential social threats. Ostensibly, increased female integration into the labor force gives rise to hopes for a reduced risk of poverty in old age. However, in combination with the tendency for disintegration of the familial social security, and when taking a closer look at the type, duration and quality of female employment this positive prognosis cannot be upheld. On the one hand, there will be more and higher pension entitlements for women, on the other hand derived pensions will be less, and will be available to fewer women. And in addition to workplace and wage discrimination, discontinuous employment considerably lowers pension entitlement. This does not only include planned 'breaks' for familial reasons, but particularly the recurring (registered or concealed) phases of unemployment and/or part-time employment, or even illicit employment. Financially, this often means a downward spiral in terms of sufficient or even independent livelihood. For many women, old age poverty is the logical consequence of taking into account only one particular type of work as entitling to a pension at the end of a life filled with work (cp. Gerhard 1990; Gather et al. 1991; Allmendinger et al. 1991; Schmähl, Michaelis 2000).

However, the qualitative deficits and negative developments of female employment do not only result in material losses, but will also create health-related and social disadvantages (Allmendinger et al. 1991; Allmendinger 2000). The described female (multiple-)strains in addition to material risks are accompanied by health-related, psychological and social hazards. Whether these can be appropriately counterbalanced by a gain in social contacts and self-affirmation is still questionable. The rates of morbidity and mortality of multiply strained women in highly-stressful jobs seem to validate these assumptions. (cp. Falck 1990). All of these factors together may, – even though there have been developments towards female autonomy, – lead to age(ing)-relevant losses in women's material and immaterial quality of life.

What is principally true for both genders is even truer for women: while (at least potential) old safety systems are lost, the new ones have not yet been adequately developed and may not be relied on. Instead, new risks and insecurities have been added, but also new opportunities. What has remained for women is a good proportion of the old, gender-specific risks of ageing: poor conditions for material security and independent existence in old age, little self-determination in discontinuous life courses and working lives, and restricted development of leisure-time interests, particularly for women with high or multiple strains (mainly women from underprivileged groups). What has been added – through the structural changes in female education and occupation, – is a batch of new risks, which may however be seen as new forms of the old gender relations: materially risky employment histories accompanied by a reduction of (the already before precarious) social security offered by marriage/family; immaterially risky life-orientation, which becomes evident in the difficulty or impossibility to structurally reconcile certain areas.

In the 'new' federal states, in East Germany, 'emancipation' and the accompanying improvement of social chances for women could not be equated with neutralization of women-specific discrimination in old age. Here too, observation of everyday-lives and facts seems to suggest a specific multiple strain, which will rather lead to a modified pathology of problems in age(ing) than to an equalization of social opportunities in old age. The critical changes accompanying the 'Wende' are already reflected in the „Lebenslagen" of today's elderly women. In the future, material and immaterial "Lebenslage" of old women (and a rising proportion of future old men) in the new federal states will increasingly show the effects of discontinuity of employment, unprotected employment, risky but unavoidable balancing acts between job and family, and the chances and risks of job mobility (On the development during the first ten years after the 'Wende' and a first cautious forecast based on these observations, cp. Backes 2001).

All in all, the question as to the effects of changed risks of age(ing) for women and their opportunities in old age seem to indicate that the gender-specific discrimination concerning material, social and individual risks has changed on a formal level, i.e. has changed symptoms, but has not been abrogated. If risks of age(ing) should be kept at a minimum or be counterbalanced, women need to flexibly alternate between options in their life course, need to be mobile and use multiple approaches. Also in reference to the age(ing) risks of men, the combination of individualization and pluralization with other developments relating to employment will contribute to less secure prognoses for a sustainably secure quality of "Lebenslagen" in old age.

4 Analytic Perspectives on Ageing in the Context of "Lebenslagen" and of the Gendered Life Course

As already mentioned, the concept of „Lebenslagen" on the one hand offers empirical-descriptive competence, which was particularly referred to in chapters 2 and 3. On the other hand, it includes explanatory-analytical competence, linking up theories of social structure and social change, as well as to theories of action. It therefore, via the life course, links up with concepts of gender relations and gender structures. These will exemplarily be dealt with below. Corresponding with the initial thesis (cp. chapter 1) the key to an appropriate analysis of the multi-layered relevance of gender and ageing is to be found in an analysis of the forms of sociation of both genders, and their mutual interwovenness up into old age. In previous parts of this article, hierarchical-complementarily structured sociation (being tied into conditions of life and of work) and the respective "Lebenslagen" for present and future old women and men were presented empirically. In the following, this structure and its effects shall be explained in more detail, by embedding them into a sociological analysis of age(ing) in the context of „Lebenslagen" and a gendered life course. In doing so, we shall initially explore the so-called "Feminization of Age" (Tews 1990, 1993, Kohli 1990), a topic frequently treated in gerontology, and shall contrast it with our thesis of the complementarity of gender relations up into old age (Backes 1999b, 2002). Subsequently, the concepts of ageing as a gendered process (s. gendered life course) on the one hand, and gender and ageing as social structures undergoing change on the other, will be sketched in terms of their contribution to an analysis of gender and ageing and their implications on „Lebenslagen".

4.1 „Feminization of Old Age" vs. Complementarity of Gender Relations up into Old Age

The thesis of the "Feminization of Old Age" is the first, at least in the German-language area, to respond to gender relations and the respective changes in "Lebenslagen" in old age (Tews 1990, 1993, Kohli 1990). It therefore acknowledges at least qualitative changes with the transition to so-called old age. It does however suggest associations to the effect that men – or at least male ways of life – had (nearly) disappeared from old age, as if their gender-specific sociation (primarily via employment) had totally lost its relevance. This condensed quantitative description of the quality of age(ing), the structure of "Lebenslagen" and their societal relevance somewhat falsifies the picture. Because qualitatively – and this is our thesis – old age is still characterized by a (hierarchical) gender-structure assigning lower quality of life to "female" old age as compared to "male" old age, and this in spite of the quantitatively higher proportion of women and of female forms of sociation.

Not only due to war-induced losses on the side of men, but mainly due to the higher life-expectancy of women, far more elderly and old women than men live in today's society. Two thirds of the over-60-year-olds and three quarters of the over-75-year-olds are women. While the proportion is still nearly balanced among the 60-65-year-olds, there is a striking imbalance among those 85 and older, with women making up more than three quarters (cp. Statistisches Bundesamt 1995, 1996, no year given; for an explanation of gendered differences in life expectancy cp. Höpflinger 2000).

But in spite of the superficial plausibility of the thesis of an approximation of the ways of life in old age (Kohli 1990) men and women live differently, also in old age (cp. Backes 1994b; 1999b): Their „Lebenslagen" and lifestyles differ in socially unequal (hierarchical) ways, depending on gender (in addition to other socio-structural differentiations, such as class/stratum, cohort, region or nationality). The „female" and „male" life courses and forms of sociation obviously find their extension in old age, if maybe on another level. Concretely, the following social gender-differences in old age may be described:

On the one hand, the likelihood of women being affected by a socially problematic „Lebenslage" is much higher than for men. As has already become apparent, women are much more frequently financially restricted, often living alone and with precarious material and immaterial facilities; they are more often forced to "earn something on top" or to oblige familial demands, which are often no longer appropriate in consideration of their state of health. They more often suffer from chronic illnesses, but live longer, so that they are more frequently dependent on institutional care, all the way to institutional nursing-home arrangements (cp. Backes 1994a, 2001). While they themselves have taken care of and cared for their husbands until the event of their spouses' death, this type of support is rarely available to them. They often end their lives as widows, or solitarily. Until then, they have undergone more and more frequent phases of reorientation, such as when children leave home, the end of their own employment, the end of their husbands' employment, their husbands' diseases and possible need of care, his death, and finally, their own decreasing autonomy and increasing neediness (cp. Backes 1983; 1993a, 2001; Fooken 1987; Lehr 1987; Naegele et al. 1992; Niederfranke 1994; Clemens 1997). Old-age-men, however, are comparatively less affected by social problems (such as poverty, disease and neediness without adequate daily support available in the immediate environment).

On the other hand, due to a gendered life course, old age offers several advantages to women, while offering disadvantages to men. This is effective all the way to the age-specific reorientation processes. Probably due to the higher frequency of reorientation and the necessity to reconcile contradicting demands, women are often much better prepared to cope with changes and losses, or at least to come to terms with them (cp. Clemens 1997). Men on the other hand, at least initially seem to experience more difficulties when making the transit to the so-far totally unaccustomed old-age-specific way of life, unstructured by the demands of employment. At the same time they have adequate employment-derived resources (money, qualification), which may serve to alleviate this transition. And they are, at least generally, less burdened by (familial) obligations limiting them in the development of new pursuits.

But even if old age principally represents a socially doubly precarious situation for women (see chapter 2) this is not true for all old women, and vice versa, not for all old men. A cumulation of disadvantages is often to be found for widconstructions, among others by age, which in turn is also a social construction, influenced, among other factors, by gender. In other words: „Ageing is a gendered process“ (Arber, Ginn 1991: 2).

What both means is that gender-typical ways of sociation are subjected to different processes of change in old age. While that of men moves into the background, a vital proportion of the female ways gains importance; for both genders, with women playing a more active role, and men taking on a receptive one. But that does not mean that the "Lebenslagen" of both genders are not still dominated by male and by female sociation and their mutual hierarchical attributions. The hierarchy of the gender-relations is basically maintained; it finds its expression in the increased unburdening of men, and in their better access to "Lebenslage"-relevant resources and discrimination in reference to "Lebenslage"-relevant resources on the side of women.

This complementarity of the gender-relations i.e. the relation of both genders with each other is hierarchical in so far as, while female sociation is quantitatively dominant at old age, this does not lead to it being perceived as more valuable or even as equally valuable. Instead, its social esteem remains lower: What is noticeable as 'negative', such as the burden to be borne by society, is described as 'feminine'; whatever is positively noticeable, such as post-professional activities as a resource, is described as 'male'. In old age too, female resources remain largely privatized, thereby marginalized, while male resources show a tendency 'to go public', thereby receiving much more acknowledgement. It is still common practice to draw on the reservoir of elderly and old women as a care-resource, without in turn providing them with an entitlement to the same services (such as receiving mainly private care). The currently rising number of men involved in care-giving, and the support and relief-systems available to private care-givers since the introduction of the care-insurance are first indicators of change.

5 Gender and Age(ing) as Social Structures Undergoing Change

The above explorations allow the following conclusions: The division of labor and the ways of sociation of the genders up into old age are to be seen as a fundamental element of the changing social structure in modern societies. They affect the individual and the societal meaning of age(ing), as well as the solutions for coping with related problems. Within the context of comprehensive demographic and age-structural changes the above-described fact that age(ing) is determined by gender-specific sociation processes is extremely consequential to both genders as well as to society as a whole (cp. Backes 1997a, 2001). It leads to developments, which will quantitatively increase forms of female sociation in old age, and will foster their increased importance:

1. Within the changes of the age structure, quantitative feminization is closely tied to oldest old age and singularization; both of these dimensions indicate typical social endangerment areas of old age. The larger proportion of social problems in old age are de facto problems of old and oldest old women. The socially endangering consequences of the specific sociation of women outside or on the fringes of a 'normal working life' finds its expression here. Social security, 'late freedom' and equality, balanced to include the entire life course are rather an exception for women. What is 'normal' is the deviation from this societally defined 'normality' and concomitant objectives for age(ing). In terms of social security and freedom in old age, women are structurally affected by a twofold inequality. In view of the societal and socio-political objectives this represents a double legitimatory and practical challenge. The more deviations from 'normal life' in the sense of a normal working life develop into social problems in old age, the greater the demands on social control and processing, and the greater the probability that the available societal resources turn out to be insufficient for creating solutions. The "Lebenslage" of women in old age therefore appears to be a societally generated situation, much more so than an individually created burden (as is often insinuated).
2. At the same time, women, – up into a very high age, - represent a vital societal support potential for the care of the old and oldest old, as well as of younger people (particularly families and those suffering from illness). They also represent a substantial reservoir of self-help potential for coping with their own age(ing)-problems. If women are addressed as "the secret resource of social policy" (Beck-Gernsheim 1991), this actually includes the entirety of their life courses and working lives. However, the resources available and actually made available for everyday informal support, all the way to care-giving in a familial, extended-family and neighborly context, are mostly those of elderly and old women. In addition to their employment (at least as long as they are still employed) these women provide help to the younger as well as to the older generation. From middle age on they find themselves in a sandwich-position, and are much less prepared, or forced, than younger women to consider the safeguarding of their own existence and autonomy as equally relevant or even more important than the provision of familial help (cp. Borcher, Miera 1993; Clemens 1997). In so far, women represent another, – equally sociation-induced, – substantial relief system for meeting societal demands and costs of age(ing).

3. This may now begin to change: intergenerational support, the greatest part of which was previously performed by women, was and is a basic point of reference in social policy. In view of the short, middle and long term future the question raised since the beginning of the 1990s is: "Who will take care of us when we are old?" (Kytir, Münz 1991; cp. also Bengtson, Schütze 1992). In addition to the demographically-caused and, as is to be foreseen, progressively dwindling numbers of the younger potential care-givers, today many more women are employed as a parallel activity to child-rearing and care-giving. They are forced to do so by their life-conditions (such as single parents, divorcees and women with unemployed partners). And accordingly, these women more frequently orient themselves, at least principally, by the norm of maintaining at least part of their independence and selfrealization.

   This begins to undermine the matter-of-fact nature of primarily or exclusively female care of old and diseased parents or parents-in-law, or even of spouses. A decisive resource for curtailing social costs induced by longevity is threatening to run dry. So far, this is not counterbalanced by rising concern for old and diseased relatives by men, or by qualified and increased social services. It is currently a wide open question in which way and to which extent care-insurances and (planned) qualification measures may provide sustainable long- and mid-term relief.
4. Temporally parallel with this development the expansion of the old-age phase-of-life, care and support of the old and particularly the oldest old is turning into a significant quantitative, but also qualitative challenge to society. As has become apparent above, the traditional familial, relational and in part neighborly patterns of support have become brittle, and are, in any case, quantitatively insufficient. Still, even if in modified form, the largest proportion of care services is provided in the private realm, and there is performed by daughters and by daughters-in-law. However, even if numbers are still relatively insignificant, an increasing amount of this care is performed by old men (cp. Wand 1986; Backes 1992a; 1992b; Naegele, Reichert 1998). New forms of compatibility of employment and home-care-provision are tested individually, but are structurally inadequate as long-term-solutions for larger numbers of people (Beck et al. 1995; Backes 1996, 1998). With the introduction of the care insurance, certain moments of relief were created for care-giving relatives (see support by ambulant care; remuneration); their effects in the "Lebenslagen" of care-givers, however seems contradictory (e.g. if money is accepted instead of care services, but pressure on care-giving women to provide full-time care is increased; cp. various contributions in Naegele, Reichert 1998).

5. Seen against backdrop of the above-described developments, it is imaginable that on the one hand the hitherto-available precarious social security and freedom will be adequate for less and less women, and that on the other hand, as a parallel development, there will be substantially less opportunities for independent social security. Female sociation (in its old and in its new forms) is a risky factor in terms of age(ing). However, it also leads to the development of immaterial compensation and coping capabilities, which will probably also be the case in the future.

Conclusion: In accordance with the similarly hierarchically structured societal valuation of phases of life, 'female' sociation seems to gain importance in old age (the societally less valued phase of life). 'Male' sociation moves to the background. However, it still directly or indirectly – such as mediated by the pension-entitlement 'earned' during employment, – determines the available resources and therefore quality of life. Basically, the complementarity of both types of sociation remain valid in their socially unequal, hierarchical structure, even if contents and meaning, and their forms of relating to each other are somewhat modified according to age. Particularly in women's lives, the ideology of equality of the genders and the reality of a still hierarchically structured inequality built over a lifetime drift apart in old age. Due to their different ways of sociation they have not managed to adapt, or have only partially adapted, to the (male) 'normal course of life', which leads to social security in old age, and a period of 'late freedom'. Up into their own old age they are involved in caring for others, or performing other, family-related work, so that the advantage of 'late freedom' is not available to them. At the same time, their own provision with these same services and financial security is inadequate. Choicelessness, insecurity and inequality respectively injustice are much too often the consequences of a life deviating from 'normal' sociation. The more this increases quantitatively (with increasing feminization of old age), while at the same time qualitatively violating the prevailing societal ideals (the notion of a free, secure old age and a just reward for a lifetime spent working), the more this development should lead to legitimatory problems and to raising questions on the sociation of age(ing).

References

Allmendinger, Jutta (2000): Wandel von Erwerbs- und Lebensverläufen und die Ungleichheit zwischen den Geschlechtern im Alterseinkommen. In: Schmähl, Michaelis (Ed.): 61-80.

Allmendinger, Jutta; Brückner, H.; Brückner, Erika (1991): Arbeitsbedingungen und Lebensarbeitsentlohnung: Zur Entstehung von finanzieller Ungleichheit im Alter. In: Mayer, Allmendinger, Huinink (Eds.): 423-459.

Arber, Sara; Davidson, Kate; Ginn, Jay (Eds.) (2003): Gender and Ageing. Changing Roles and Relationships. Open University Press, Maidenhead Philadelphia.

Arber, Sara; Ginn, Jay (1991): Gender and later life. A sociological analysis of resources and constraints. London/Newbury Park/New Delhi: Sage Publications.

Arber, Sara; Ginn, Jay (Eds.) (1995): Connecting gender and ageing: A sociological approach. Buckingham, Philadelphia: Open University Press.

Bäcker, Gerhard (2001): Zur Alterssicherung von Frauen nach der Rentenreform. In: Barkholdt (Ed.): 177-208.

Backes, Gertrud M. (1983): Frauen im Alter. Bielefeld: AJZ (1. edition 1981).

Backes, Gertrud M. (1987a): Frauen und soziales Ehrenamt. Zur Vergesellschaftung weiblicher Selbsthilfe. Augsburg: Maro.

Backes, Gertrud M. (1987b): Krisenbewältigung als Frauenarbeit - Zur Privatisierung der Folgen beruflicher Frühausgliederung, In: Backes, Gertrud M.; Clemens, Wolfgang (1987) (Eds.): Ausrangiert!? - Lebens- und Arbeitsperspektiven bei beruflicher Frühausgliederung. Bielefeld: AJZ: 184-203.

Backes, Gertrud M. (1991): Ehrenamtliche Arbeit älterer und alter Frauen - ein Beitrag zu ihrer sozialen Integration? In: Frauenforschung, 3: 389-100.

Backes, Gertrud M. (1992a): „Krise“ der Familie oder der Vergesellschaftung von Hilfe und Pflege? In: Forum Demographie und Politik, Heft 1 Mai 1992: Moderner Sozialstaat und alternde Gesellschaft. Bonn: 33-48.

Backes, Gertrud M. (1992b): Soziales Ehrenamt. Handlungsperspektiven für Frauen im Alter. In: Karl, Fred; Tokarski, Walter (Eds.): Bildung und Freizeit im Alter. Bern/Göttingen/Toronto: Hans Huber: 93-110.

Backes, Gertrud M. (1993a): Frauen zwischen ‚alten' und ‚neuen' Alter(n)srisiken. In: Naegele, Tews (Eds.) (1993): 170-187.

Backes, Gertrud M. (1993b): Frauenerwerbslosigkeit und Alter(n). In: Mohr, Gisela (Ed.) (1993): Ausgezählt. Theoretische und empirische Beiträge zur Psychologie der Frauenerwerbslosigkeit. Deutscher Studien Verlag: Bremen: 66-86.

Backes, Gertrud M. (1994a): Alter(n)smedizin gleich Frauenmedizin? - Oder: Alte Frauen als Herausforderung an die Kompetenz geriatrischer Versorgung. In: Zeitschrift für Gerontopsychologie & -psychiatrie 7: 117-126.

Backes, Gertrud M. (1994b): Männer und Frauen: Unterschiedliche Lebensbedingungen und Orientierungen im Alter. In: Evers, Adalbert; Leichsenring, Kai; Marin, Bernd (Eds.) (1994): Die Zukunft des Alterns. Sozialpolitik für das Dritte Lebensalter. Graz: Styria: 177-196.

Backes, Gertrud M. (1996): Familienbeziehungen und informelle soziale Netzwerke im sozialstrukturellen und demographischen Wandel. In: ZfGG 29: 29-33.

Backes, Gertrud M. (1997a): Alter(n) als ‚gesellschaftliches Problem'? - Zur Vergesellschaftung des Alter(n)s im Kontext der Modernisierung. Opladen: Westdeutscher Verlag.

Backes, Gertrud M. (1997b): Lebenslage als soziologisches Konzept zur Sozialstrukturanalyse. Zeitschrift für Sozialreform 43/9: 704-727.

Backes, Gertrud M. (1998): Zwischen Erwerbsarbeit und häuslicher Pflege – Perspektiven der Vereinbarkeit für Frauen und Männer in Deutschland. In: Naegele, Reichert (eds.): 107-124.

Backes, Gertrud M. (1999a): Erwerbslosigkeit im Lebensverlauf als soziales Alter(n)srisiko für Frauen. In: Naegele, Gerhard; Schütz, Rainer-Maria (Eds.): Soziale Gerontologie und Sozialpolitik für ältere Menschen: Gedenkschrift für Margret Dieck. Opladen: Westdeutscher Verlag: 101-119.

Backes, Gertrud M. (1999b): Geschlechterverhältnisse im Alter. In: Jansen, Birgit; Karl, Fred; Radebold, Hartmut; Schmitz-Scherzer, Reinhard (Eds.) (1999): Soziale Gerontologie. Ein Handbuch für Lehre und Praxis. Weinheim/Basel: Beltz: 453-469.

Backes, Gertrud M. (2001): Lebenslagen und Alter(n)sformen von Frauen und Männern in den neuen und alten Bundesländern. In: DZA (Ed.): Expertisen zum Dritten Altenbericht der Bundesregierung, Band 3, Lebenslagen, soziale Ressourcen und gesellschaftliche Integration im Alter. Opladen: Leske + Budrich: 11-116.

Backes, Gertrud M. (2002): „Geschlecht und Alter(n)" als künftiges Thema der Alter(n)ssoziologie. In: Backes, Gertrud M./Wolfgang Clemens (Eds.): Zukunft der Soziologie des Alter(n)s. Opladen: Leske + Budrich: 111-148

Backes, Gertrud M. (2003): Frauen – Lebenslagen – Alter(n) in den neuen und alten Bundesländern. In: Reichert, Monika/Nicole Maly-Lukas/Christiane Schönknecht (Eds.): Älter werdende und ältere Frauen heute. Zur Vielfalt ihrer Lebenssituationen. Wiesbaden: Westdeutscher Verlag: 13-34

Backes, Gertrud M. (2005): Alter(n) und Geschlecht: Ein Thema mit Zukunft. Aus Politik und Zeitgeschichte 49-50: 31-38

Backes, Gertrud M. (2006): Editorial: Geschlecht und Alter(n). Zeitschrift für Gerontologie und Geriatrie 39 (1): 1-4

Barkholdt, Corinna (Ed.) (2001): Prekärer Übergang in den Ruhestand. Handlungsbedarf aus arbeitsmarktpolitischer, rentenrechtlicher und betrieblicher Perspektive. Opladen: Westdeutscher Verlag.

Beck, Brigitte; Dallinger, Ursula; Naegele, Gerhard; Reichert, Monika (1995): Vereinbarkeit von Berufstätigkeit und Pflege - eine neue sozialpolitische Herausforderung. In: Theorie und Praxis der Sozialen Arbeit, 46: 384-388.

Beck, Ulrich (1986): Risikogesellschaft. Auf dem Weg in eine andere Moderne. Frankfurt a.M.: Suhrkamp.

Beck, Ulrich; Beck-Gernsheim, Elisabeth (Eds.) (1990): Das ganz normale Chaos der Liebe. Frankfurt a.M.: Suhrkamp.

Becker-Schmidt, Regina (1995): Transformation und soziale Ungleichheit, soziale Ungleichheit und Geschlecht. Vortrag auf dem 26. Kongreß der Deutschen Gesellschaft für Soziologie. Halle: Manuskript.

Beck-Gernsheim, Elisabeth (1983): Vom „Dasein für andere" zum Anspruch auf ein Stück „eigenes Leben": Individualisierungsprozesse im weiblichen Lebenszusammenhang. In: Soziale Welt 34: 306-340.

Beck-Gernsheim, Elisabeth (1986): Von der Liebe zur Beziehung? Veränderungen im Verhältnis von Mann und Frau in der individualisierten Gesellschaft. In: Soziale Welt 44: 209-233.

Beck-Gernsheim, Elisabeth (1991): Frauen - die heimliche Ressource der Sozialpolitik? - Plädoyer für andere Formen der Solidarität. In: WSI Mitteilungen 44: 58-66.

Bengtson, Vern; Schütze, Yvonne (1992): Altern und Generationsbeziehungen: Aussichten für das kommende Jahrhundert. In: Baltes, Paul B.; Mittelstraß, Jürgen (Ed.): Zukunft des Alterns und gesellschaftliche Entwicklung. Berlin, New York: de Gruyter: 492-517.

Borchers, Andreas; Miera, Stephanie (1993): Zwischen Enkel-Betreuung und Altenpflege. Die mittlere Generation im Spiegel der Netzwerkforschung. Frankfurt a.M./New York: Campus.

Buhr, Petra; Leibfried, Stephan; Meyer, Thomas; Riedmüller, Barbara (1988): Individualisierung und soziale Sicherung der Frau (Preface by the editors). In: Zeitschrift für Sozialreform 11/12: 655-658.

Clemens, Wolfgang (1992): Arbeit – Leben – Rente. Biographische Erfahrungen von Frauen bei der Deutschen Bundespost. Bielefeld: Kleine Verlag.

Clemens, Wolfgang (1993): Verrentung und Ruhestandsanpassung erwerbstätiger Frauen. In: Zeitschrift für Gerontologie 25: 344-348.

Clemens, Wolfgang (1994): „Lebenslage" als Konzept sozialer Ungleichheit – Zur Thematisierung sozialer Differenzierung in Soziologie, Sozialpolitik und Sozialarbeit. In: Zeitschrift für Sozialreform, 40. Jg., Heft 3: 141-165.

Clemens, Wolfgang (1997): Frauen zwischen Arbeit und Rente. Lebenslagen in später Erwerbstätigkeit und frühem Ruhestand. Opladen: Westdeutscher Verlag.

Clemens, Wolfgang (2001): Ältere Arbeitnehmer im sozialen Wandel. Von der verschmähten zur gefragten Humanressource? Volume 3 of the Series Alter(n) und Gesellschaft. Opladen: Leske + Budrich.

Deutsches Institut für Altersvorsorge (Ed.) (2000): Repräsentative Befragung Frauen und ihre Altersvorsorge. Fakten und Meinungen. Eigenverlag: Köln.

Falck, Ingeborg (1990): Alte und kranke Frauen. In: Schmitz-Scherzer, Reinhard; Kruse, Andreas; Olbrich, Erhard (Eds.): Altern - Ein lebenslanger Prozeß der sozialen Interaktion. Darmstadt: Steinkopff: 163-176.

Feldmann-Neubert, Christine (1991): Frauenleitbild im Wandel 1948-1988 (Von der Familienorientierung zur Doppelrolle). Weinheim: Deutscher Studien Verlag.

Fooken, Insa (1986): Gerontologie eine Männerwissenschaft oder: Der Mann im Alter das unbekannte Wesen? In: Zeitschrift für Gerontologie 19: 221-222

Fooken, Insa (1987): Älterwerden als Frau. In: Kruse, Andreas; Lehr, Ursula (Eds.): Gerontologie, eine interdisziplinäre Wissenschaft. München: Bayerischer Monatsspiegel Verlag: 164-237.

Fooken, Insa (1994): Alter(n) – Umbruch und Kontinuität. Akzentsetzungen von Wissenschaftlerinnen, Essen: Die Blaue Eule.

Fooken, Insa (1999): Geschlechterverhältnisse im Lebensverlauf. In: Jansen, Birgit; Karl, Fred; Radebold, Hartmut; Schmitz-Scherzer, Reinhard (Eds.) (1999): Soziale Gerontologie. Ein Handbuch für Lehre und Praxis. Weinheim/Basel: Beltz: 441-452.

Gather, Claudia (1991): Der Übergang in den Ruhestand bei erwerbstätigen Paaren. Theoretische Überlegungen zur Chance einer Veränderung der geschlechtsspezifischen Arbeitsteilung. In: Gather et al. (Eds.): 207-222.

Gather, Claudia (1996). Konstruktionen von Geschlechterverhältnissen. Machtstrukturen und Arbeitsteilung bei Paaren im Übergang in den Ruhestand. Berlin: Edition Suhrkamp.

Gather, Claudia; Gerhard, Ute; Prinz, Karin; Veil, Mechthild (Eds.) (1991): Frauen-Alterssicherung. Lebensläufe von Frauen und ihre Benachteiligung im Alter. Berlin: edition sigma.

Gerhard, Ute (1990): Geschlechtsspezifische Sozialpolitik und die soziale Unsicherheit weiblicher Lebenslagen. In: Döring, Dieter; Hanesch, Walter; Huster Ernst-Ulrich (Eds.): Armut im Wohlstand. Frankfurt a. M.: Suhrkamp: 311-331.

Herfurth, Matthias; Kohli, Martin; Zimmermann, Klaus F. (Eds.) (2002): Erwerbsarbeit in einer alternden Gesellschaft. Forschungsstand, Problembereiche, Entwicklungstendenzen. Opladen: Leske + Budrich.

Herlyn, Ingrid; Vogel, Ulrike (1989): Individualisierung: Eine neue Perspektive auf die Lebenssituation von Frauen. In: Zeitschrift für Sozialisationsforschung und Erziehungssoziologie 9: 62-178.

Herlyn, Ingrid; Vogel, Ulrike (1991): Individualisierungskonzept und Analyse weiblicher Lebensformen. In: Frauenforschung 9: 59-67.

Hohmann-Dennhardt, Christine (1988): Soziale Sicherung der Frau im Widerspruch von Familien- und Sozialrecht. In: Zeitschrift für Sozialreform 11/12: 673-676.

Höpflinger, Francois (1994): Frauen im Alter – Alter der Frauen. Ein Forschungsdossier, Zürich: Seismo.

Höpflinger, Francois (2000): Auswirkungen weiblicher Langlebigkeit auf Lebensformen und Generationenbeziehungen. In: Perrig-Chiello, Pasqualina, Höpflinger, Francois (Eds.): Jenseits des Zenits. Frauen und Männer in der zweiten Lebenshälfte. Bern/Stuttgart/Wien: Paul Haupt: 61-74.

Höpflinger, Francois (2002a): Frauen im Alter – die heimliche Mehrheit. http://www.my-page.bluewin.ch/hoepf/fhtop/fhalter1K.html

Höpflinger, Francois (2002b): Männer im Alter. Eine Grundlagenstudie von Francois Höpflinger. Zurich: Pro Senectute Fachverlag

Hradil, Stefan (1987): Sozialstrukturanalyse in einer fortgeschrittenen Gesellschaft. Von Klassen und Schichten zu Lagen und Milieus. Opladen: Westdeutscher Verlag.

Hradil, Stefan (1995): Die Modernisierung des Denkens. Zukunftspotentiale und ‚Altlasten' in Deutschland. In: Aus Politik und Zeitgeschichte, Beilage zu Das Parlament, B 20/95: 3-15.

Kickbusch, Ilona; Riedmüller, Barbara (Eds.) (1984): Die armen Frauen. Frauen und Sozialpolitik. Frankfurt a. M.: Suhrkamp.

Kohli, Martin (1990): Das Alter als Herausforderung für die Theorie sozialer Ungleichheit. In: Berger, Peter A.; Hradil, Stefan (Eds.) (1990): Lebenslagen, Lebensläufe, Lebensstile. Göttingen: Schwartz & Co.: 387-406.

Kohli, Martin/Harald Künemund (Eds.) (2000): Die zweite Lebenshälfte. Gesellschaftliche Lage und Partizipation im Spiegel des Alters-Survey. Opladen: Leske + Budrich.

Kreckel, Reinhard (1992): Politische Soziologie der sozialen Ungleichheit. Frankfurt a.M./New York: Campus.

Krüger, Dorothea (1983): Lebensrealität und Lebensorientierung von Frauen in der Nachkinderphase,. In: Backes, Gertrud; Krüger, Dorothea (Eds.): „Ausgedient!?" - Lebensperspektiven älterer Frauen. Bielefeld, AJZ: 37-70.

Krüger, Helga; Born, Claudia (1991): Unterbrochene Erwerbskarrieren und Berufsspezifik: Zum Arbeitsmarkt und Familienpuzzle im weiblichen Lebenslauf. In: Mayer, Allmendinger, Huinink (Eds.): 142-162.

Kytir, Josef; Münz, Rainer (1991): Wer pflegt uns im Alter? In: Zeitschrift für Sozialisationsforschung und Erziehungssoziologie 11: 332-354.

Lehr, Ursula (1977): Psychologie des Alterns. Heidelberg: Quelle & Meyer (3. edition, 1. edition 1972).

Lehr, Ursula (1982): Zur Lebenssituation von älteren Frauen in unserer Zeit. In: Mohr, Gisela; Rummel, Martina; Rückert, Dorothea (Eds.): Frauen. Psychologische Beiträge zur Arbeits- und Lebenssituation. München/Wien/Baltimore: Urban & Schwarzenberg: 103-122.

Lehr, Ursula (1986): Was bedeutet Familie für ältere Menschen und was bedeuten ältere Menschen für die Familie? In: Gesamtbericht über den 71. Deutschen Fürsorgetag 1986 in München, Familie und soziale Arbeit. Familienideal, Familienalltag - Neue Aufgaben für die soziale Arbeit Schriften des Deutschen Vereins für Öffentliche und Private Fürsorge. 266, Frankfurt a.M./Stuttgart: Kohlhammer: 474-493.

Lehr, Ursula (1987): Zur Situation der älter werdenden Frau. München: Beck.

Lehr, Ursula (Ed.) (1978): Seniorinnen. Zur Situation der älteren Frau, Darmstadt: Steinkopff

Maier, Friederike (2000): Empirische Befunde zur Arbeitsmarktsituation von Frauen. In: Schmähl, Michaelis (Eds.): 81-96.

Mayer, Karl Ulrich; Allmendinger, Jutta; Huinink, Johannes (Eds.) (1991): Vom Regen in die Traufe. Frauen zwischen Beruf und Familie. Frankfurt a.M./New York: Campus.

Michaelis, Klaus (2000): Alterssicherung von Frauen – Bestandsaufnahme und Reformüberlegungen für die gesetzliche Rentenversicherung. In: Schmähl, Michaelis (Eds.): 147-163.

Moen, Phyllis (1996): Gender, Age, and the Life Course. In: Binstock, Robert H.; George, Linda K. (Eds.): Handbook of Aging and the Social Sciences. 4. edition. San Diego, Calif.: Academic Press: 171–187.

Moen, Phyllis (2001): The gendered life course. In: Binstock, Robert H.; George, Linda K. (Eds.): Handbook of Aging and the Social Sciences. 5. edition. San Diego, Calif.: Academic Press: 197–196.

Naegele, Gerhard, Tews, Hans Peter (Eds.) (1993): Lebenslagen im Strukturwandel des Alters. Alternde Gesellschaft - Folgen für die Politik. Opladen: Westdeutscher Verlag.

Naegele, Gerhard; Heinemann-Knoch, Marianne, Hollstein, Betina; Korte, Elke; Niederfranke, Annette; Reichert, Monika (1992): Landessozialbericht Band 1: Armut im Alter. Untersuchung zur Lebenslage ökonomisch unterversorgter älterer Frauen in Nordrhein-Westfalen durch die Forschungsgesellschaft für Gerontologie e.V. Institut für Gerontologie im Auftrag des Ministeriums für Arbeit, Gesundheit und Soziales des Landes Nordrhein-Westfalen. Duisburg: WAZ-Druck.

Naegele, Gerhard; Reichert, Monika (Eds.) (1998): Vereinbarkeit von Erwerbstätigkeit und Pflege. Nationale und internationale Perspektiven I. Dortmunder Beiträge zur angewandten Gerontologie. Hannover: Vincentz

Niederfranke, Annette (1994): Pluralisierung und Individualisierung als Bestandteil weiblichen Älterwerdens. In: Fooken, Insa (Ed.): Alter(n) - Umbruch und Kontinuität. Akzentsetzungen von Wissenschaftlerinnen. Essen: Verlag Die Blaue Eule, Siegener Studien Band 55: 69-80.

O'Rand, Angela M. (1995): The Cumulative Stratification of the Life Course. In: Binstock, Robert H.; George, Linda K. (Eds.): Handbook of Aging and the Social Sciences. 4. edition. San Diego, Calif.: Academic Press: 188–207.

O'Rand, Angela M. (1996): The Precious and the Precocious: Understanding Cumulative Disadvantage and Cumulative Advantage Over the Life Course. The Gerontologist 36: 230–238.

Ostner, Ilona (1983): Kapitalismus, Patriarchat und die Konstruktion der Besonderheit „Frau". In: Kreckel, Reinhard (Ed.): Soziale Ungleichheiten. Göttingen: Schwartz & Co.: 277-297.

Ostner, Ilona (1990): Der partikularistische Sozialstaat - Das Beispiel der Frauen. In: Dressel, Werner; Heinz Walter R.; Peters, Gerd; Schober, Karin (Eds.): Lebenslauf, Arbeitsmarkt und Sozialpolitik. Beiträge zur Arbeitsmarkt- und Berufsforschung 133. Nürnberg.

Ostner, Ilona (2000): Wandel von Haushaltsformen, Ehe und Familie. In: Schmähl, Michaelis (Eds.): 46-60.

Peace, Sheila (1986): The forgotten female: Social policy and older women. In: Phillipson, Chris; Walker, Alan (eds.): Ageing and social policy. A critical assessment. Hants/Vermont: Gower: 61-86.

Perrig-Chiello, Pasqualina; Höpflinger, Francois (2001): Zwischen den Generationen. Frauen und Männer im mittleren Lebensalter. Zürich: Seismo.

Perrig-Chiello, Pasqualina; Höpflinger, Francois (Eds.) (2000): Jenseits des Zenits. Frauen und Männer in der zweiten Lebenshälfte. Bern/Stuttgart/Wien: Paul Haupt.

Riedmüller, Barbara (2000): Frauen- und familienpolitische Leitbilder im deutschen Alterssicherungssystem. In: Schmähl, Michaelis (Eds.): 36-45.

Schmähl, Winfried (2000): Alterssicherung von Frauen im Prozess ökonomischen, gesellschaftlichen und politischen Wandels – zugleich zur Einführung in das Thema des Kolloquiums. In: Schmähl, Michaelis (Eds.): 9-35.

Schmähl, Winfried; Michaelis, Klaus (Eds.) (2000): Altersicherung von Frauen. Leitbilder, gesellschaftlicher Wandel und Reformen, Opladen: Westdeutscher Verlag.

Sørensen, Annemette (1990): Unterschiede im Lebenslauf von Frauen und Männern. In: Mayer, Karl Ulrich (Eds.): Lebensverläufe und sozialer Wandel. Sonderheft 31 der KZfSS. Opladen: Westdeutscher Verlag: 304–321.

Statistisches Bundesamt (Eds.) (1995): Statistisches Jahrbuch 1995 für die Bundesrepublik Deutschland. Stuttgart: Metzler-Poeschel.

Statistisches Bundesamt (Eds.) (1996): Statistisches Jahrbuch 1996 für die Bundesrepublik Deutschland. Stuttgart: Metzler-Poeschel.

Statistisches Bundesamt (Eds.) (without year): Statistisches Jahrbuch für die Bundesrepublik Deutschland. Stuttgart/Berlin/Köln/Mainz: Kohlhammer.

Stuckelberger, Astrid; Höpflinger, Francois (1996): Vieillissement différentiel: hommes et femmes. Dossier de recherche. Zürich : Seismo.

Szinovacz, Maximiliane (1982): Women's Retirement. Policy Implications of Recent Research. Beverly Hills, London, New Delhi: Sage

Tews, Hans Peter (1990): Neue und alte Aspekte des Strukturwandels des Alters. In: WSI Mitteilungen 43: 478-491.

Tews, Hans Peter (1993): Neue und alte Aspekte des Strukturwandels des Alters. In: Naegele, Gerhard/Hans Peter Tews (Eds.): Lebenslagen im Strukturwandel des Alters. Alternde Gesellschaft - Folgen für die Politik. Opladen: Westdeutscher Verlag: 15-42

Wand, E. (1986): Ältere Töchter alter Eltern. Zur Situation von Töchtern im 6. und 7. Lebensjahrzehnt. Schriftenreihe des BMJFFG, Band 13, Stuttgart et al.: Kohlhammer.

Weg, M. 1988: Frauenarbeit und ihre Folgen für die soziale Sicherung, in: Zeitschrift für Sozialreform, 11/12: 677-686.

Men in Later Life: Perspectives on Gender, Health, and Embodiment

Katja Reimann & Gertrud M. Backes

1 Introduction

With the demographic change in European societies, we will face an increase not only of the elderly as a whole and with a majority of women, but also an increase of the proportion of men in the older population. With this increase we need to integrate certain needs of older men in concepts of health and social care and health promotion in old age, and in other topics such as participation, living arrangements and, voluntarily activities. Ageing men are, even if they are the underlying norm of most research on ageing and old age, mostly neglected under a gender focus. In gerontology, a gender focus is often misunderstood as a perspective on the differences and inequalities of women's life in regard to an abstract (male) norm (Calasanti 2004, Backes 2002, 2005, 2006). But gender is not only a single factor shaping individual life situation, it is furthermore a complex relational and dynamic category that organizes social institutions, and identities as well as power relations between men and women, but also among men. We therefore need to take power relations and differences between men, their different life situations, access to resources, as well as different images and norms of masculinity into account, when if we investigate ageing and old men (see Reimann, Lasch 2006).

The crucial point where a damaging impact of traditional masculinity occur is in health issues, and health is an important factor determining life quality in old age. In regard to old age health, there are gender differences in mortality and morbidity, respective the higher proportion of women with chronic ill health or disabilities, and the significant shorter life expectation of men compared to women (difference between 5 – 8 years in European countries), which are not yet fully understood. Therefore especially health should be investigated under a 'gender lens'. In 1999, the WHO suggested:

> „While gender-specific approach is often used to identify persistent inequalities in the status of women, the specific situation of men, particularly older men, also requires investigation and further studies, especially with regard to the determinants of health. For example, why is it that men continue to be at higher risk of most of the

important causes of mortality? Why is it that life expectancy for men at all ages is still shorter than for women in almost every country?" (WHO 1999: 9)

To enter this very complex field of ageing men's health under a gender lens, we want to give insight into several research results and theoretical concepts. These may provide an idea of, how we may explore the impact of masculinity on health in old age on the one hand, and the relevancy of the ageing body in regard to health issues on other, from a gender and social scientific perspective. Doing so is a difficult undertaking, dealing with very different research concepts and questions, with quantitative as well as qualitative research results, and with approaches from different contexts and disciplines. In this article it is our my aim to sketch out a research perspective that allows to integrate these approaches into a social sciences framework, with which we can gain more detailed and complex insights within the intersections and conditions of old men's health.

2 Men's Health and Ageing

In the mainstream of medicine and health research a huge range of differences in mortality and morbidity of (ageing) men and women have been shown statistically. Men are at higher risk to suffer from fatal severe illness, such as cardiovascular diseases and cancer, and to die several years earlier than women. They also exhibit higher rates of dying from suicide, accidents and due to violent acts (Bründel, Hurrelmann 1999: 103ff). Even though in Germany the mortality rates for cardiovascular diseases and cancer have been on the increase for women over 65, men are still at higher risk to die earlier (Merbach, Brawlers 2004: 70; Hahn, Maschewsky-Schneider 2002: 100). In the morbidity rates, based on diagnosis rates, there are differences as well. Women show a higher prevalence to suffer from chronic diseases, such as allergies, diabetes and mental health problems, but also to suffer from cerebro-vascular diseases (Merbach, Brähler 2004: 71ff), while men suffer more from hypertension and heart attack, lung and bronchial diseases as lung cancer, and liver diseases like liver cirrhosis. Furthermore, men's rates for death by suicide increase with age, whereas suicide rates for women decrease with ageing. These differences in causes of death as well as in prevalence of diseases in men and women are due to biological-genetic as well as to social and behavioural factors. As the biomedical model does not sufficiently explain these differences due to its mono-causal explications, there is a need to search for explanations of the gender gaps within a socio-cultural model of health (Sabo, Gordon 1995: 2ff).

> "Within the socio-cultural model, in contrast, health and illness are understood primarily in light of cultural values and practices, social conditions, and human emotion and perception." (Sabo, Gordon 1995: 3)

Within such a socio-cultural model of health, several differences between men's and women's behaviour are discussed as health-related: men have higher rates of risk behaviour, such as consumption of alcohol and other drugs; men are more involved in dangerous sports activities and in physical arguments and fights and their diets are more often unhealthy; they work in more burdening and dangerous working conditions. On the other hand, men have a better self-reported health status, report less health disorders and symptoms, and they use less professional health care services (see Babitsch 2002: 191; Bründel, Hurrelmann 1999: 103 ff, Sieverding 2000; Courtenay 2003). Or as the clinical social worker and psychologist, Courtenay puts it for the U.S.:

> "Men and boys, in general, have less healthy lifestyles than women and girls, and they engage in far fewer health-promoting behaviours." (Courtenay 2003: 3)

In psychological health research, these differences in risk-taking and (ill-)health-related behaviour are explained by the male gender role. As Sabo & Gordon pointed out, four different components shape the male gender role in western European and North American countries:

> "1. No Sissy Stuff: the need to be different from women
> 2. The Big Wheel: the need to be superior to others
> 3. The Sturdy Oak: the need to be independent and self-reliant
> 4. Give'Em Hell: the need to be more powerful than others, through violence if necessary." (Sabo, Gordon 1995 : 6)

These different components of the male gender role, beside other factors, influence the behaviour and perceptions of men during the life course and therefore have an effect on health in old age as well. For example, men have, as Waldron pointed out for the United States, "higher scores on measures of hostility and mistrust of other, which are psychological characteristics, that are associated with increased risk of ischemic heart disease" (Waldron 1995: 25).

It is also recognized that especially traditional or stereotypical beliefs of masculinity are linked with unhealthy behaviour (Courtenay 2003: 7). For example the German psychologist Sieverding (2000, 2004) investigated the coherence of the orientation on a traditional male image, with the perception and representation of symptoms, and with the utilization of prevention courses. She thereby ascertained that the higher the agreement of the self-concept with traditional masculinity ideals are, the fewer symptoms and disorders are reported, and the more negative attitudes towards prevention courses are reported. This can be seen in the context of "The Sturdy Oak" and "No Sissy Stuff" components of the male gender role. Men need to represent independency and in order to not appear feminine by showing others their own vulnerability.

In the ageing process, some of the factors representing masculinity, such as physical strength, sexual function, and capability may decline. Therefore Thiele (2000) investigates the impact of ageing on the well-being of older men in the concept of the "Gender Role Strain" (Thiele 2000: 126), and shows a high level of stress for ageing men due to a higher orientation towards the traditional male role.

But the gender role explanation is limited, as it is a static model that does not consider the dynamics and the differences between men in different social contexts. With Connell (2000) we can assume that masculinity is not singular, but that societal and cultural norms promote a specific hegemonic masculinity, which differs historically and culturally. Men do not need to deal with one universal gender role, but with an underlying hegemonic gender norm that also organizes the power relation between different groups of men. This male gender norm privileges some men who represent the ideal hegemonic masculinity and marginalizes or dominates others' masculinities, such as working class men, gay men, migrant or black men.

3 Doing Gender

If we shift our perspective, from a given, static and external male gender role to a more dynamic and relational concept of gender, we can take differences between men into account, as their resources, their power relations as well as their representations, perceptions and images of masculinity. From a sociological perspectives, gender and masculinity can be theorized as a cultural and social category that is constructed and reproduced within social interactions and practices. In their approach West and Zimmerman (1991) set the notion of *Doing* Gender against the scientific and everyday belief that we do always already *have* a gender (West, Zimmerman 1991, Gildemeister 2004). In this perspective, social behaviour is used to construct and represent masculinity in social interactions.

Therefore social behaviour, including health-related behaviour, is embedded in the hierarchical gender system, shaped by gender norms, habits and roles and at the same time reproduces this system through seemingly individual actions and interactions. Saltonstall (1993) pointed out that even explicit health practices are used to 'do' and represent gender. Saltonstall (1993) argues, that

> "[...] doing of health is a form of doing gender. This is not because there is a essential difference between male and female healthiness, but because of social and cultural interpretations of masculine and female selves – selves which are attached to biological male and female bodies. Health activities can be seen as a form of practice which constructs the subject (the person) in the same way that other social and cultural activities do." (Saltonstall (1993: 12)

In the context of masculinity, Courtenay (2000) clarifies some normative ideals of hegemonic masculinity that influence health-related believes and behaviours:

> "[...] health related beliefs and behaviours that can be used in the demonstration of hegemonic masculinity include denial of weakness or vulnerability, emotional and physical control, the appearance of being strong and robust, dismissal of any need for help, a ceaseless interest in sex, the display of aggressive behaviour and physical dominance." (Courtenay 2000: 1389)

Thus, we have to keep in mind that even the hegemonic masculinity with its standards is dominant, it is a cultural and societal norm, and not a trait shared by all men. The norms and ideals of masculinity, and therefore the meaning and utilization of specific behaviour and practices to demonstrate masculinity, differ for men of other social categories, like age, ethnicity, social class and sexuality.

> "Although men may endorse similar masculine ideals, different men may enact these ideals in different ways. For example, although most young men in the United States may agree that a man should be 'tough', how each man demonstrates being 'tough' will be influenced by his age, ethnicity, social class and sexuality. Depending upon these factors, a man may use a gun, his fists, his sexuality, a mountain bike, physical labor, a car or the relentless pursuit of financial strength to construct this particular aspect of masculinity." (Courtenay 2000: 1390)

With a 'Doing Gender' approach towards men's health beliefs and behaviours we can integrate perspectives on gender roles and on different positions and resources available to men. It also allows us to see that men are not victims of their role instructions, but are also active agents (Courtenay 2000: 1388). Even if the ideals of masculinity lead men to hold on to types of behaviour that harm their health, they do have advantages from this behaviour within social power relations. Furthermore this reproduces norms of masculinity. On the other hand, there are always also men who cultivate other behaviours and social practices. Within the perspective of doing gender, a huge range of behaviours, practices, interaction patterns and resources could be used to research constructions of masculinity and it allows us to integrate resistant practices into the concept as well. And, these possible new ways of doing gender i.e. due to social change in the field of men, masculinity, and health, especially in old age, could let us gain knowledge and insights into strategies of how to improve health behaviour, if applicable.

Looking at socially disadvantaged groups of men, who do not have financial, social or ability resources to demonstrate dominant or hegemonic masculinity such as for example young lower class urban men, or who are subordinated within the power gender relations, such as gay men, Courtenay (2000) suggests that they may use risky behaviour, e.g. smoking, drug and alcohol use, street fighting, crime or sexual excesses to compensate the lack of other resources to validate their masculinity in other ways. This thesis should be tested, because it supposes first of all negative effects of being outside of hegemonic masculinity. But there could also be positive ways to respond to unattainable masculinity norms within these groups of men. Maybe these groups could give insights into different images and norms of masculinity represented and whether these representations have a different impact on health beliefs and behaviour, and on body practices, for example by investigating gay men or drag queens.

Furthermore, doing gender is a life-long and dynamic process, altering due to the specific social context and within the life course. But how the ideals and norms of masculinity are performed in the process of ageing, how this might influence health in old age, is also an unstudied subject. We suggest that the lower self-care and low use of prevention and health promotion services are also part of doing masculinity in old age, which are determining and affecting old men's health. To investigate how the different groups of ageing men adapt to the ageing process in regard to the hegemonic masculine ideals, how they perform masculinity, is a promising research field to improve our knowledge and understanding of the determinants of old men's health and lives. Particularly if we take into account that critical life events in the process of ageing may change central aspects of male identity, such as physical strength and capabilities, labour and activities, and social relationships, and that they affect health-related beliefs and behaviours of ageing men. This knowledge could be used to develop better social and health policy strategies to reach different kind of men and to promote male images and behaviour designed to improve the health situation of ageing men.

4 Male Habitus

To deepen our perspective on the intersection between gender (or class, race etc.), health and ageing, we can learn from the sociological discussion about the *habitus* concept of Bourdieu. In sociology of the body, his work is used to conceptualize the intertwining of social structure and social practices located within the body.

Originally, Bourdieu in his work investigates the stability of domination within society and the reproduction of class relations and structures. He also studies male domination and gender power relations (Bourdieu 2005).

He argues that gender as well as class are bound to distinct learned and incorporated behaviour, attitudes, gusto, preferences and value judgements. He named this incorporated and embodied distinction *habitus*. This incorporation of social structure shapes unconscious and subjective pattern of perceptions, thoughts and behaviour (cp. Schwingel 2000:57ff). These patterns are fundamentally embedded in the embodiment, in body movement, in attitudes and everyday practices (see Schwingel 2000: 62). The *habitus* is shaped by very early learning within a certain position of social structure. Therefore it is modified by class, race, age and gender. The crucial point of the gendered *habitus* is the construction of two antagonistic and distinct gender identities, the female and the male. The gendered *habitus* shapes perception, expression and habits of one's body, and has an effect on the gendered identities as well as on behaviours and social practices (see Krais, Gebauer 2002: 48ff.)

For studying our subject, we can learn from the *habitus* concept that gender is not "only" something to do, but also embedded and incorporated in our bodies. Or as Brandes (2002) supposes that one can differentiate between three dimensions of masculinity to deal with the complexity of the term masculinity. Brandes identifies 1. the embodied dimension of the male habitus, 2. the dimension of male gender identity, and 3. the dimension of cognitive attitudes and judgements towards the gender relations (Brandes 2002: 86). The incorporated *habitus* can be seen as a specific part of masculinity shaping male behaviour, attitudes, values and thoughts. As we have seen before, a range of behaviour and social practices influence health and well-being, and are also used to represent and validate masculinity. With the *habitus* concept we can see that the social structure even shapes i.e. what kind of exercise or what kind of diet one will prefer; we can also suggest just how deep one's attitude towards seeking help from health professional could be embedded and shaped by social norms. In this context, we can suggest, that behaviour is very probably difficult to change by cognitive decisions alone.

What this means for men in later life, how the *habitus* is modified by ageing, and whether this affects health beliefs and behaviours of ageing men is still unknown. Here we can suppose that the concept of the *habitus* might give us an instrument to theorize attitudes, beliefs and behaviours concerning health and illness of ageing and old men, including their unconscious attitudes and images.

5 Male Embodiment

The sociological concept of the body or of embodiment gives us additional insights into underlying perceptions and attitudes, which presumedly affect determinants of old men's life and health. In medical or even gerontological terms, body is often only used within a biomedical perspective. But, especially in English gerontology, approaches towards a social understanding of the body, the meaning of the ageing body, i.e. in the context of identity in old age, as the thesis of the ageless self (Kaufman 1986) or the mask of ageing (Biggs 1997, 2004; Featherstone, Hepworth 1991, Hepworth 1991), are discussed. A social understanding of the body tries to enhance the biomedical view of body and to counter the naturalization of power relation, which refers to a natural basis of gender relations in one's sex. Especially gender researcher did a huge body of work on theorizing the meaning/role of the body in gender relations.

To discuss the body or embodiment in regard of ageing and health, first of all, we have to identify the meaning of the term body. We therefore need to have a look into the phenomenology dealing with the body. Plessner (1941) notices that the human relationship to the body is shaped from two different sides: firstly, we *are* our body, we are bound to space and time, we can experience internal feelings and emotions; but secondly, we also *have* a body, we can consider and treat our body as an external object. Both of these aspects of the body are inseparably bound to each other. In German language, we are able to differentiate the body in two terms; one is "Leib" as the *being a body* or the lived body, the internal view and experience, the other is "Körper" as *having a body*, describing the external, instrumental, usable body. To demarcate these different aspects of the body in English language, Watson (2000: 43) for example uses among others, the term *embodiment* to describe the *"embodied basis of being"*. For a better understanding, we will use the English terms 'body' and 'embodiment' here.

In the sociology of the body one finds on the one hand approaches focussing on the structural or macro level, on how the body is produced, regulated through norms, discourses or – to speak with Foucault – through power-knowledge complexes (Foucault 1976, Butler 1997). The body also is seen as representing and symbolizing social values, norms and structures (Douglas 1974). The other way around, the body is also seen as producing social interaction, due to the bodily basis of social actors. In the case of ageing, we cannot ignore the bodily changes and their impact on identities of ageing people. Therefore the sociology of the body studies the body as link between social structure and social action (Gugutzer 2005: 140ff). For this the *habitus* concept of Bourdieu is a useful theoretical background, as we have seen before.

But, to explore masculinity and health empirically, there is also research based on a concept of embodiment. Watson (2000, et al. 1996) supposes the concept of embodiment to theorize male health beliefs and behaviours and the impact of the social structure and discourse on everyday life and practices, and to develop empirical research strategies in the field of men's health. From such a health research perspective, he criticizes the lack of subject centred research and searches for useful qualitative research concepts. In his exploration of male bodies and health practices in North East Scotland Watson (2000) interviewed men between 30 – 40 years of age and living in a lasting relationship. As a result, he outlines 'being in shape' as a heuristic concept to investigate male embodiment. He differentiates four main dimensions of male embodiment in a 'male body schema' (Watson 2000: 114 ff): The *normative embodiment* as ideals and images of shape, health and masculinity; the *pragmatic embodiment* as functional body use in everyday context to fulfil specific roles and demands; the *experiential embodiment* as experienced site of the physical body and emotions like 'well–being', 'feeling good'. This is actually the space where the social and physical boundaries touch, and the *visceral embodiment* as underlying, biological and physiological processes that support bodily function. With this male body schema, he tries to describe the different levels in which his "informants perceive, compose and experience embodiment in the context of everyday life" (Watson 2000: 121).

Another health researcher, Robertson, adapts Watson's 'male body schema' for his own research and argues that it provides an analytical concept of embodiment to investigate male health and body without reducing the body to be either a physical entity or a discursive construction (Robertson 2006: 451). He is specifically interested in the intersections and linkages between the different dimensions of the body within the schema and argues that Watson's results have too strongly emphasized the pragmatic body. He also affirms the necessity to look in "[...] more detail at how, when and where these elements interact with each other, and with the men's conceptualisations of health, to influence health practices and health outcomes." (Robertson 2006: 450). He also suggests taking other aspects of male lives and identity into account, particularly class and ethnicity, but also the "changing nature of male embodiment in respect to health through the lifecourse" (Robertson 2006: 452).

Herewith Robertson strengthens a social constructivist perspective (for social construction perspectives see Helduser, Marx, Paulitz, Pühl 2004) on embodiment and health, but even so takes the material basis and changes of the body into account. To investigate the impact of masculinity norms and construction on men's health and ageing, this integrated view provides a useful new perspective on gerontological and health research.

In the context of ageing and health, the lay-perspective on health and embodiment of older men, the impact of identity and embodiment on health beliefs and behaviour is rarely studied. A concept of embodiment contains the possibility to analyze the intersections of masculinity norms, the effects of health perceptions and of the realization of subjective strategies in empirical research by emphasizing body practices. Due to the embodied basis of being, and the relevance of bodily changes in ageing, a perspective of these intersections could give us more detailed and complex perspectives on the process of ageing, and provide ideas to develop strategies to acquire, promote, and maintain old men's health.

6 Outlook

Looking at this complex field and the intersections between doing masculinities, power relations, resources and practices, as well as health beliefs and behaviour, opens up new perspectives in gender studies and gerontology as well as in health research. The theoretical approaches outlined help us to ask new questions and to get more detailed knowledge about the impact of doing masculinity and male gender norms on life situations and health in old age, but also on images of and attitudes towards i.e. being a carer, for different kind of men. This perspective also stimulates theoretical debates about research concepts and questions. In the outlined perspectives, we have to face and integrate a variety of dynamics and changes: on one hand the perceptions, practices and behaviours of men differ within the life course, i.e. the impact of critical life events on `doing´ masculinity, on health beliefs and behaviour are rarely studied, on the other hand, the impact of societal changes, such as changing male images and ideals, changing biographies through the crisis of the 'male-breadwinner-working-his- whole-life' model, changing access to resources by i.e. increasing levels of unemployment as risk factors of living conditions in old age or less social resources for men due to the higher level of divorces and women in employment, on ageing men have to take into account. What do these changes mean for men and their representation of masculinities, how does it impact old age, and how does it impact health beliefs and behaviours, should be considered also in future research.

Within gender studies first of all a dynamic perspective on the life course and the cumulation of resources and strains during the gendered life course (see Backes, Amrhein, Lasch and Reimann in this volume) should be included. In gerontology, the concepts and debates of gender, i.e. gender as social construct, or the approach of Doing Gender should be integrated, as this perspective could serve to broaden understanding and knowledge about the specific conditions of male and female life course and ageing processes. Within the health research debates, men's health is an increasingly important subject. Furthermore, life course approaches towards health are an accepted perspective. But how the dynamics and changes of gendered life course and of the gender system and norms influence health and especially health in old age is an additionally promising issue. With more detailed knowledge about men's experiences and practices within the life course, we may create a wider basis to improve health education and promotion, as well as health care services to reach different types of (ageing) men. For future research, the following question should be faced:

How do men address their bodies to produce health? Where are there connections between the subjective addressing of the body, health information and a change of attitude towards health during the life course? How can health services appropriately address older men, what do they need to know about differences in older men? How can concepts in health promotion and health education be developed by including knowledge about men's gender, embodiment and *habitus* within the ageing process? Which strategies are most effective? How can we integrate certain male coping strategies, such as ignoring health symptoms and disorders, i.e. by addressing men not within terms of health risks but with positive images, e.g. 'Being in Shape' as a concept of male embodiment as Watson has shown?

A promising focus could also be on deviating masculinities, life styles, and life courses of men. It can offer us insights into different ways of constructing gender, into risks, potentialities and conditions of resistant behaviour, but also in other and new possibilities and chances by new combinations of resources, risks and coping strategies. Examples are the different ways to deal with masculinity ideals of older gay men. What kind of practices dealing with the body, embodiment or health practices have different groups of men developed during their life course? What is changing in the process of ageing in regard to health and body issues? What impact do the orientation towards masculinity norms and the necessity to do gender have? In which context do men see health risks and health related behaviour? Are there different types of ageing men when it comes to dealing with embodiment and health risks?

The concept of embodiment should be a basis to explore these phenomena and to open the discussion for new questions. It can broaden our understanding of the intersections of masculinities, embodiment, health and ageing.

References

Babitsch, Birgit 2002: Gesundheitskonzepte und Gesundheitshandeln. In. BMFSFJ: Bericht zur gesundheitlichen Situation von Frauen in Deutschland. Eine Bestandsaufnahme unter Berücksichtigung der unterschiedlichen Entwicklung in West- und Ostdeutschland. Stuttgart: Kohlhammer: 188-198.

Backes, Gertrud M. 2002: „Geschlecht und Alter(n)“ als künftiges Thema der Alter(n)ssoziologie. In: Backes, Gertrud M./Wolfgang Clemens (eds.): Zukunft der Soziologie des Alter(n)s. Opladen: Leske + Budrich: 111-148

Backes, Gertrud M. 2004: Alter(n): Ein kaum entdecktes Arbeitsfeld der Frauen- und Geschlechterforschung. In: Becker, Ruth; Kortendiek, Beate (eds.): Handbuch Frauen- und Geschlechterforschung. Theorie, Methoden, Empirie. Wiesbaden: Verlag Sozialwissenschaften: 395–401.

Backes, Gertrud M. 2005: Alter(n) und Geschlecht: Ein Thema mit Zukunft. Aus Politik und Zeitgeschichte 49-50: 31-38

Biggs, Simon 1997: Choosing not to be old? Masks, bodies and identity management in later life. Ageing and Society 17 (5): 553–570.

Biggs, Simon 2004: Age, gender, narratives, and masquerades. Journal of Aging Studies 18 (1): 45–58.

Bourdieu, Pierre 2005: Die männliche Herrschaft. Frankfurt/M.: Suhrkamp.

Brandes, Holger 2003: Männlicher Habitus und Gesundheit. In: Blickpunkt Der Mann 2/2003: 10-13.

Bründel, Heidrun; Hurrelmann Klaus 1999: Konkurrenz, Karriere, Kollaps. Männerforschung und der Abschied vom Mythos Mann. Stuttgart, Berlin, Köln: Kohlhammer.

Butler, Judith 1995: Körper von Gewicht. Die diskursiven Grenzen des Geschlechts. Frankfurt/M.: Suhrkamp.

Calasanti, Toni 2004: Feminist Gerontology and Old Men. In: Journal of Gerontology: Social Sciences Vol. 59B, No 6: S305-S314.

Courtney, Will H. 2000: Constructions of masculinities and their influence on men's well-being: a theory of gender and health. In: Social Science & Medicine Vol. 50: 1385-1401.

Courtney, Will H. 2003: Key Determinants of the Health and the Well-Being of Men and Boys. In: Journal of Men's Health, Vol. 2, No. 1:1–27.

Courtney, Will H.; Keeling, Richard P. 2000: Men, Gender, and Health. Toward an Interdisciplinary Approach. In: Journal of American College Health Vol. 48: 243-246.

Douglas, Mary 1974: Ritual, Tabu, Körpersymbolik. Sozialanthropologische Studien in Industriegesellschaft und Stammeskultur. Frankfurt/M.: S. Fischer.

Featherstone, Mike; Hepworth, Mike 1991: The mask of ageing and the postmodern life course. In: Featherstone, Mike; Hepworth, Mike; Turner, Bryan (eds.): The body: social process and cultural theory. London: Sage: 371–389.

Foucault, Michel 1976: Überwachen und strafen. Die Geburt des Gefängnisses, Frankfurt/M.: Suhrkamp.

Gildemeister, Regine 2004: Doing Gender: Soziale Praktiken der Geschlechtsunterscheidung. In: Becker, Ruth; Kortendiek, Beate (eds.): Handbuch Frauen- und Geschlechterforschung. Theorie, Methode, Empirie. Wiesbaden: 132-140.

Gugutzer 2004: Soziologie des Körpers. Bielefeld: transcript Verlag.

Hahn, Daphne; Maschewsky-Schneider, Ulrike 2002: Lebenserwartung und Mortalität im Geschlechtervergleich. In: BMFSFJ: Bericht zur gesundheitlichen Situation von Frauen in Deutschland. Eine Bestandsaufnahme unter Berücksichtigung der unterschiedlichen Entwicklung in West- und Ostdeutschland. Stuttgart, Berlin, Köln: Kohlhammer: 95-101.

Helduser, Urte; Marx, Daniela; Paulitz, Tanja; Pühl, Katharina 2004: under construction? Konstruktivistische Perspektiven in feministischer Theorie und Forschungspraxis. Frankfurt/M.: Campus Verlag.

Hepworth, Mike 1991: Positive ageing and the mask of age. In: Journal of Educational Gerontology 6: 93–101.

Kaufman, Sharon R. 1986: The ageless self: Sources of meaning in late life. Madison: University of Wisconsin Press.

Krais, Beate; Gebauer; Gunter 2002: Habitus. Bielefeld: transcript Verlag.

Merbach, Martin; Brähler, Elmar 2004: Daten zu Krankheiten und Sterblichkeit von Jungen und Männern. In: Altgeld, Thomas (Ed.): Männergesundheit. Neue Herausforderungen für Gesundheitsförderung und Prävention. Weinheim, München: Juventa: 67-84.

Plessner, Helmut 1941: Das Verhältnis des Menschen zu seinem Körper. In: Plessner, Helmut: Phiolosophische Anthropologie. Frankfurt/M.: S. Fischer Verlag: 31-55.

Reimann, Lasch 2006: Differenzierte Lebenslagen im Alter. Der Einfluss sexueller Orientierung am Beispiel homosexueller Männer. In: Zeitschrift für Gerontologie und Geriatrie 39: 13–21.

Robertson, Steve 2006: 'I've been like a coiled spring this last week': embodied masculinity and health. In: Sociology of Health & Illness, Vol. 28, No. 4: 433-456.

Saltonstall, Robin 1993: Healthy Bodies, Social Bodies. Men's and Women's Concepts and Practices of Health in Everyday Life. In: Social Science & Medicine: An International Journal Vol. 36, No. 1: 7–14.

Schwingel, Markus 2000: Pierre Bourdieu zur Einführung. Hamburg: Junius Verlag.

Sieverding, Monika 2000: Risikoverhalten und präventives Verhalten im Geschlechtervergleich: Ein Überblick. In Zeitschrift für Medizinische Psychologie 1/2000: 7-16.

Sieverding, Monika 2004: Die männliche Rolle gefährdet ihre Gesundheit! In: psychomed Vol. 16 No. 1: 25-30.

Watson, Jonathan 2000: Male Bodies. Health, Culture and Identity. Buckingham, Philadelphia: Open University Press.

Watson, Jonathan; Cunningham-Burley, S.; Watson, N.; Milburn, K. 1996: Lay theorizing about 'the body' and implications for health promotion. In: Health Education Research Vol.11 No.2: 161-172.

West, Candace; Zimmerman, Don H. (1991): Doing gender. In: Lorber, Judith; Farell, Susan A. (eds.): The social construction of gender. Newbury Park: Sage: 13–37.

WHO 1999: Men Ageing And Health. Achieving health across the life span. Available under http://whqlibdoc.who.int/hq/2001/WHO_NMH_NPH_01.2.pdf, access date 10/05/06.

Williams, Clare 2000: Doing health as doing gender: teenagers, diabetes and asthma in: Social Science & medicine: an international journal 50/3: 387–396.

Mapping Existing Research and Identifying Knowledge Gaps Concerning the Situation of Older Women in Europe (MERI). From the Swedish National Report

Birgitta Lindencrona & Barbro Westerholm

During the 20th century the average expected lifetime increased by some 25 years in Europe. This means that almost every fifth person in Europe is a woman aged 50 or more years. Despite this fact, efforts by researchers and statisticians to compile information on the living conditions of older women have shown a tendency to neglect this group in scientific studies and official statistics (Stiehr, Huth, 2001).

Within a European seminar, which took place in 2001, a catalogue of measures for future research was drawn up and agreed with representatives of the European Commission, national governments within the European Union (EU), EFTA and accession countries, as well as relevant European and national umbrella associations, among them the Swedish Association of Senior Citizens. This formed the basis for an application to the Commission from representatives of twelve of the, at that time, fifteen EU countries, for a project with the following main objectives

- to increase knowledge about the specific living conditions and problems faced by older women
- to improve the empirical basis for
  - work by national and European associations aimed at older women and/or intergenerational relations,
  - government tasks at the level of social policy, and
  - current and future research work on the living conditions of older women
- to raise the awareness of the general public of the situation of older women.

The present paper summarizes studies on living conditions and statistics on older women available in Sweden for the study period 1993 – 2003, particularly emphasizing the health aspects, as shown in scientific studies and official statistics.

The MERI-project deals with many other matters that in various degrees may have an impact on the lives of older women, such as education, work and the material situation, social integration, participation and other social issues, interest representation, crime/violence/abuse/neglect. We will not deal with all these matters here. The full report is included in the comparative *European overview of available statistics and the research situation on living conditions of older women (MERI)* in the twelve European countries participating in the project (www.own-europe.com).

Methodological Proceedings

Definition of the Target Group of Research

In the MERI-project it was agreed to comprise and take the definition of an "older women" as being those aged 50+. This definition does not agree with the definition used in Swedish research and statistics, where 65+ is regarded as the borderline between older middle-aged and older women. Since the words "old", "older" or "elderly" were used in the search process for this report, most of the research on older women in Sweden refers to the age group 65+.

Similarly, official statistics use the age 65 as an indicator for old age since 65 was for a long time the official pension age. It has recently been changed to 67 years by a Parliamentary decree which, though, has been questioned by some labour unions. Since most statistics contain all age groups from 0 up to 85+ years, finding the age groups below 65 years presents no problem. However in some official statistics there is no differentiation within the age group 45 – 64, thus not allowing for an analysis of the 50 – 64 year olds.

Sources Used to Find Research on Older Women

Research on women and men is conducted at universities and other academic research centres, but also by governmental agencies, county and municipality councils, regional social insurance offices etc. This survey includes studies published in scientific journals using referees, doctors' dissertations and monographs published by universities. It also includes the results of parliamentary investigations and surveys that focus on women. Research results taken from these are presented, in combination with data gleaned from studies performed in Swedish municipalities and counties, which, even though they were carried out by scientifically trained people, are not necessarily linked to universities.

In order to find publications on research it was decided to write to universities and other academic research centres, including those performing gender-focussed research and to request papers published during the study period 1993 – 2003. The main research funds were also contacted for information about research projects funded by them. In total some 60 persons were contacted; the answers received from one third of these were either affirmative, i.e. with papers and publications, or negative ("our research is not gender oriented"). Some senior researchers kindly passed on our request to other members of their research groups or partners. Additionally the homepages and local databases of Swedish universities were searched. Searches were also made in free access databases such as MEDLINE[1] and LIBRIS, the union catalogue of Swedish research libraries[2].

In Sweden there are a number of research centres conducting epidemiological studies on ageing. As all Swedes have an identity number, denoting year, month and date of birth and a four digit check number, there are ample opportunities for epidemiological and longitudinal research in Sweden. Many of such studies commenced long before 1993, the starting year of this survey. These studies comprise cohorts that include both women and men, who are contacted and followed up at regular intervals, and who have now reached an advanced age.[3]

Gender Results in Statistical Data

The history of the statistical databases in Sweden goes back to the seventeenth century, when the registration of citizens was initiated in order to form a basis for taxation. From 1686 on it was the responsibility of the church to keep a register of the inhabitants. Population statistics have been available in Sweden since 1749. In 1756 a governmental agency, now the Statistics Sweden (SCB), was established. Since then statistics have been collected from an increasing number of fields. At first many of the tables and figures were unisex but gradually data on women and men were presented separately. In 1994 the Swedish Parliament decided that all official statistics related to individuals should be disaggregated by sex, unless there are special reasons for not doing so.

According to the project plan the MERI project only comprises statistics that are easily available and free of charge. In Sweden, as in many other countries, there is a distinction between official statistics and other public statistics.

1 http://www.ncbi.nlm.nih.gov/entrez/queri.fcgi

2 http://websok.libris.kb.se/websearch/form?lang=eng

3 Because of the vast number of studies it is not possible to list them all among the references added to this paper. A complete set of references can instead be obtained from one of the authors: barbro.westerholm@spfpension.se.

Official statistics are produced according to the statistical act and ordinance and published as required by official regulations.

The Official Statistics Act states that official statistics are to be used for public information, planning and research purposes in specified areas produced by appointed public authorities in accordance with the provisions issued by the Government. According to the Act official statistics shall be objective and made available, free of charge, to the public. An appendix to the Official Statistics Ordinance (SFS 2001:100) defines the areas covered by official statistics and states the authorities responsible for the statistics in these areas (statistical authorities). This means that the responsibility for the official statistics in Sweden remains not only with Statistics Sweden, but also with 24 additional Government authorities. They may, however, order and buy their statistics from Statistics Sweden (which is also often the case).

Among the Government authorities and agencies responsible for the official statistics of Sweden and which may be of interest in this connection are, besides Statistics Sweden, the National Agency for Education, the National Agency for Higher Education, the National Council for Crime Prevention, the National Board of Health and Welfare, the National Mediation Office, the National Social Insurance Board, the Swedish National Council for Cultural Affairs, the Swedish Institute for Growth Policy Studies and the Swedish Work Environment Authority.

All of these authorities are expected to annually provide an updated description of every subject they are responsible for. Most of these authorities publish statistics on the Internet. Since January 1997, Statistics Sweden has databases available on the Internet, allowing users to easily download information to their own computers. The English version of the website is not complete but will eventually have the same general content as the Swedish website (www.scb.se).

Public statistics are found in governmental publications on selected subjects, e.g. care of older people. These publications are also used to answer questions raised by MERI.

The above-mentioned authorities, as well as the Swedish counties and municipalities, and a number of research centres, also produce statistics which they find necessary to answer specific questions. These statistics are publicly available, mostly in publications that can also be found on the Internet. Examples of such publications are *Jämställd vård* (National Board of Health and Welfare, 2004a) and *Jämställd socialtjänst* (National Board of Health and Welfare, 2004b) both published in 2004 by the Swedish National Board of Health and Welfare.

The statistics used for the analyses made in this project are listed under *Statistics-websites*. Since finalising this paper *Women and Men in Sweden. Facts and figures 2004* has been published. It contains data for the year 2003 and some information on care of the elderly, gainful employment, and violence and crime, which have not been included in previous issues. The new data do, however, not change the conclusions and recommendations presented in the Swedish national overview.

As a framework for the analysis of the living conditions of older women in Sweden, the MERI research group set up a number of themes and sub themes with hypotheses to be tested. The Swedish National review uses these themes and layout.

Overview of Findings Concerning the Living Conditions of Older Women in Sweden

Health, Functional Ability and Services

There is a vast amount of research conducted on the health situation of older people. Relevant statistics are extensive.

Of great interest are the longitudinal studies, such as the gerontological and geriatric population studies in Gothenburg, called the H 70 study. A summary of all of their findings has recently been published in the publication *To become old. H 70* (Steen, 2004). It is comprised of people born 1901-02, 1906-07, 1922 and 1930. In addition, women born 1908 – 1922 were studied separately from 1968-69 and onwards.[4] Other cohorts, who have been followed over a long period of time, are to be found in the cities of Stockholm, Malmö, Lund and Jönköping. Hundreds of papers have been published over the time-period studied, presenting results from these studies. [5]

Of the 110 papers and monographs analysed here, some present data from the longitudinal studies, some from other studies designed to answer special questions as well as available official statistics. A gendered approach in general health aspects is becoming more acknowledged. There are a couple of on-going longitudinal studies analysing the living conditions of the oldest old and gender differences in health and survival – a life course perspective. The *Study of Living*

4 Populationsstudien av kvinnor i Göteborg/ The Population Study of Women in Gothenburg. The Department of Primary Health Care, http://www.sahlgrenska. gu.se/allmed/forskning/index_kv_pop.jsp.

5 For the Stockholm and national longitudinal studies, see http://www.aldrecentrum.se/ eng.html, http://www.neurotec.ki.se/doge/arc/. For the longitudinal studies in Jönköping, see http://mars. hhj.hj.se/hhj%5Fsql/default.asp?V_DOC_ID=831, which (in Swedish) gives the links to the various projects, among those The OCTO-TWIN Project, http://www.cdhg.psu.edu/octotwin/ index.html.

Conditions of the Oldest Old, SWEDOLD[6] has revealed that health problems in the oldest old have increased during their later years, especially among women (Hemström, 2001). For a study using the *Swedish Twin Registry* (Gold et al., 2002)[7], all living pairs of unlike sex-twins born between 1906 and 1925, in total 605 twin pairs, were sent surveys asking them to assess health and other facts. The results showed that women had more health problems, with most of these problems showing a lesser degree of severity than the diseases found in men. Men had more seriously life-threatening health conditions and cardiovascular conditions. There is overwhelming support for the thesis, both in available research and official statistics, that it is more common for older women than for older men to present symptoms in general, and that incapacitating illnesses increase with age. One consequence of the higher life expectancy of older Swedish women is that they more often live alone than older men.

Many symptoms, disorders and disabilities are found to be more common in older women than men. In some of the longitudinal studies attempts are made to relate gender to risk factors. Dementia can serve as an example.

A higher risk for Alzheimer's disease has been found in subjects with low levels of vitamin B12 and in subjects living alone or without any close social ties. Low diastolic blood pressure is predictive of dementia. Light-to-moderate alcohol consumption in late life may decrease the risk of dementia in very old people.[8] Women who developed dementia between ages 79 and 88 years were found to be overweight compared with non-demented women. These associations were not found in men (Lernfelt et al. (2003). Dementing disorders shortens life especially among women (Aguero-Torres et al., 1999). An association between dementia, hypertension and stroke (Liebetrau et al., 2003) as well as hip fracture has been found in women (Johansson et al., 1996).

Another area worth mentioning is grief, bereavement and loneliness, which have been studied among others by Grimby (1993, 1997) and Holmén (1994). Loneliness is common especially among people with impaired cognition. This has been found despite the fact that they were visited by relatives more frequently than subjects with intact cognition. Almost all psychological conditions tended to be more frequent among the women, but the gender differences were significant only for anxiety and concentration. Pessimism and financial worries were more common among women than men. Despite these findings older

---

6 Homepage of the project: http://www.neurotec.ki.se/doge/arc/index.htm. See also Lundberg Olle et al.: Swedold II. A follow-up of the living conditions of the oldest old. CHESS, Stockholm University, http://www.chess.su.se/projects.php?PId=5.

7 See also http://www.mep.ki.se/twinreg/about/index_en.html.

8 The Aging Research Centre in Stockholm (ARC) http://www.neurotec.ki.se/doge/arc/.

women seem, according to the statistics and some research data, less likely to commit suicide than older men.

From available statistics it can be concluded that overall, the self-reported health of older people aged 65 – 84 improved from 1980 onwards, more so in men than in women. There is no corresponding reduction in the prevalence of long-term illness. Older women are less mobile than men and it is more common for women to use aids to move about, such as sticks, walking frames or wheelchairs. Women report pain to a greater extent than men and this goes for older women, too.

Official statistics reveal differences between older men and women with regard to causes of death and mortality rates, incidence, prevalence and trends in infectious diseases, neoplasms, blood diseases and immunity disorders etc. It can be noted that a number of diseases decreases in both women and men aged 45+ e.g. of the circulatory, respiratory and, genitourinary systems. Arthritis and arthrosis are more common among older women than older men. Furthermore hip joint replacement is more common among women, with the reason for this operation being arthrosis. Statistics are in accordance with the findings in the longitudinal studies, that older women are more likely to suffer from depression and dementia than older men.

Cardiovascular diseases deserve mentioning with regard to gender inequalities. There are gender and age differences in prevalence, prognosis and manifestation of cardiovascular diseases. Because of the gender difference in prognosis, investigation and treatment, special measures need to be applied in the care of female cardiovascular patients. This has been summarized in a number of reviews, e.g. by Swan (1999) and by Schenk and Gustafsson (2003).

Worth noticing are a number of cohort studies in Sweden, the aim of which was to study mammography service screening and mortality in breast cancer. In the study of organised service mammographic screening in seven Swedish counties, covering approximately 33% of the population of Sweden, it was found that there was a 40 – 45% reduction in breast carcinoma mortality among women actually screened (Duffy et al., (2002).

Statistics support the research findings that older women make use of medical consultations more often than men, but these statistics do not present the full picture as at the same time, there are data showing that women refrain from medical treatment more often, citing the ensuing costs as their reason. There are also indications that women more often abstain from dental care and medicines because of cost, but evidence has not been found as to whether older women as a result of their worse financial situation, have less access to technical support than older men. There is no support for the hypothesis that older women from ethnic groups and other especially vulnerable older women are at risk of inferior medical treatment, but this question should be investigated further since there is a gap in knowledge on the subject.

Since the 1980-ies the number of hospital beds has decreased considerably in Sweden. The aim has been to treat health problems as much as possible in outpatient care. The number of geriatric wards has diminished and many patients who used to be cared for there 25 years ago are now either living at home or in special residential homes which are not defined as hospitals. It is therefore difficult to make comparisons with other countries where developments may have been different, particularly evident with respect to home care.

There is no indication of discrimination against Swedish women with regard to hospitalisation. More women than men suffering from dementia are treated in hospital, but in most cases this is due to the fact that they are older and also have other diseases. In the age group 75 – 79 years, more men are treated in hospital because of stroke than women. In the age group 80+ the situation is reverse, as in this age group more women than men are taken ill with stroke.

In the age group 65 – 89 years, more men than women are hospitalized because of cancer. In the age group 90+ there is no difference between the two sexes.

More women than men are hospitalized because of hip fracture, which reflects the higher prevalence of osteoporosis in women

Older women are prescribed more medicines than older men, but the patterns of the two sexes differ. While for example antacids, laxatives, vitamin B12 and folic acid and thiazides are prescribed more often for women 45+, insulin and oral drugs used in diabetes, anticoagulants, cardiac glycosides and vasodilators are prescribed more often to men. This reflects the differences in disease pattern between women and men.

Women are prescribed hypnotics, sedatives and antidepressants to a much higher extent than men, and there has been a dramatic increase from 1998 to 2002. While these differences between the two sexes were already observed in Sweden in the 1970-ies, there is still no explanation as to why this is so.

The use of oestrogen by women increased according to sales and prescription figures up to 1998/99. Thereafter there has been a drop probably because of the altered recommendations for use, based on new findings on adverse effects following long-term treatment with oestrogen.

A surprising finding is that the average cost per prescribed drug is lower for women than for men. The explanation seems to be that men are prescribed newer and more expensive cardiovascular drugs.

Swedish statistics on the use of medicines should be further developed in order to aid correct interpretation. We need to know why medicines are prescribed and how they are taken. We know from many studies that there is a difference between what people are prescribed and what they actually use. It would therefore be an advantage if Sweden introduced a system for individual registration of drugs prescribed and used, and the indications for treatment.

Obesity is more common among older men than older women. Women 50+ smoke less and use less alcohol than men of the same age. These findings, though, cannot be taken as support for the statement that Swedish older women are more aware of healthy lifestyles than older men. Both sexes appear to be aware of the importance of physical exercise and healthy nutrition.

The Department of Domestic Sciences, Uppsala University, paid special attention to the issue of nutrition in *Meals, Eating habits and Nutritient intake among Elderly Women (the MENEW project).* The results indicate that elderly women still living in their homes seem to manage a sufficient dietary intake despite disability and high age. The reported energy intakes in all groups of women were low, which might be explained by an actual low intake and/or underreporting. In the highest age group small portion sizes could lead to lower intakes of some nutrients, indicating that nutrient density should be given greater consideration. Meal patterns were found to be regular and the distribution of main meals and snacks satisfactory. It has also been shown that many elderly women are influenced by the prevailing health messages and try/make an effort to eat a healthy diet. It is also important to them to enjoy their preferred foods (Andersson, 2002; Gustafsson, 2002).

Care at Home and in Institutions

In a recent dissertation Ylva Hellström (2003) provides evidence that people receiving help with ADL were mostly women, widowed, and living alone, were older, had had more children, a higher number of self-reported diseases and complaints, and were less able to be alone at home by themselves than those without help.

The parliamentary investigation SENIOR 2005 summarizes available data supporting the hypothesis that more elderly women than men are in need of care. Swedish policy is, as mentioned above, that individuals should have the possibility to stay at their home as long as they wish. This is true for both sexes. There are homes for patients with dementia and for the very old, but they are not sufficient to meet needs. Statistics show that more women than men live in these homes. One reason is that the women have survived their husbands, for whom they cared when they were alive. The majority of elderly men receive care from spouses, whereas elderly women more often rely on relatives or public elder care

Family members are an important source of support for both older women and older men. SENIOR 2005 estimates that family members are responsible for at least 60 per cent of the care of older people. Large gender differences have been found when both home help services and the help of relatives were factored in. A greater proportion of men received practical household help than did women.

According to national statistics the trend is that family members and other relatives have increased their care of elderly family members since 1994. An interesting finding is that in couples, where both partners are alive and live together, husbands (65+) twice as often take care of their wives, as the other way around. This finding, though, needs to be confirmed by further studies as up until now men have been found to receive more care from spouses, whereas elderly women often rely on relatives or on public elder care. Daughters and female relatives live up to the expected picture, as they provide help more often than sons and male relatives.

Statistics support the statement that the population in residential care is essentially female, very old, single or widowed.

Education

Education, perhaps especially the lack of education, can certainly be a health factor. There are, however, few scientific studies on the education of older women in Sweden. Thus our main source for information is the extensive *statistics* that Statistics Sweden presents regularly.

From these the following conclusions can be drawn: in the overall statistics, the levels of education are found to be fairly evenly distributed between the sexes. Older women in Sweden are not disadvantaged concerning basic reading and writing skills, and age cohorts are increasingly better educated. Older women are at least equal to older men in participating in "Third Age Universities" and similar institutions.

Work

We found surprisingly few scientific papers on older women, but the ones we found, however, pointed at the influence of working conditions during a life span on health in old age. There is also a correspondence between health and the ability to participate in working life and to be gainfully employed till the official age of retirement.

Lena Lannerheim (1993; 1998) has studied women 45+ in a number of working careers. She found that there are differences when it comes to physical strain and psycho-social stress between the trades and professions, but also within each category. The well-being of both women and men was related to the degree to which the work was perceived as stimulating and engaging. Social class and occupation are factors, which contribute to how we age. Aging is more of an individual and personal process than a biological one. In this investigation, women as a group, reported more stress but also greater engagement in their jobs than men did. The similarities in the answers between women and men in gender-neutral occupations were greater than in the gender-dominated occupations.

Similar results were obtained by Forssén and Carlstedt (1999), who analyzed the life stories of twenty women born in the 1919s and 1920s. Women who responded to the demands and needs of others felt confirmation, strength and a sense of meaning, but simultaneously it could keep (hinder does not go with from) them from developing their own interests. Loss of previously held responsibility could lead to poor health, in their gainful employment as well as in their unpaid work. To most women in the study, constant negotiations over responsibility and power, and a continual balancing and reconciliation between the two largely determined health and ill health. The conclusion drawn from this study was that when meeting an older woman in the health care system one should ask: How much have you worked in your life, in which occupation and in what kind of work environment.

Gunnarsson (2000, 2002) has studied the economic and social situation of retired women, who had low incomes during their active years. She summarizes her results as follows: In Europe, older women are more likely than older men to be living in poverty, and this disparity is directly related to their domestic roles and labour market position during earlier phases of their life course. Despite the well-developed social security system in Sweden, this generalization applies to its older women. The women studied in this research had been main carers of their children, and had worked part-time or in low-wage jobs. Their formal employment histories are the foundation of their subsequent vulnerable economic situation in older age, for which the Swedish social security system gave insufficient support. Unless the bases and assumptions of the social security model are changed, the number of older women living a life of poverty or near poverty will remain substantial.

At the National Institute of Working Life, several studies have been performed on the working conditions of women and men, older and younger, and some studies have aimed at looking specifically at women (Lagerlöf, 1993). The results show that older women in the labour force are a vulnerable group. They have a higher number of sick days, many cases of early retirement and they are found in occupations where little formal education is needed. They take part in a labour market that sometimes places too high a demand on their physical capacities, and with little flexibility in their work schedules. Older women are also often regarded as secondary workers and reserve labour force.

The authors conclude that the attraction of early retirement must be counterbalanced by a work design that suits older people better. Such redesign could range from improved work organization, such as flexible working hours, to improved opportunities for training in new skills and improved ergonomics at work. Such actions must however be taken at an early stage because rehabilitation after 55 – 59 will not achieve the expected goal.

The motivation to stay active in the labour market until retirement age varies from individual to individual, but health and working conditions remain crucial elements in this decision.

A project based on an inquiry in 2000 of 6637 men and women age 25 – 75, launched by researchers at the National Institute of Working Life, deals with the working conditions and attitudes to retirement from the labour market by older people. This has resulted in a first report (Torgén et al., 2001). This confirms that more older women experienced the strains of physically heavy work than older men. Older women also more often found that recent changes at their place of work had been negative. Very few young men or women (11% and 18%) — reported that older people lack flexibility and adequate competence or that they did not want to learn new things. Most negative in this respect were older men (27%) whereas older women were equal to younger workers in terms of positive thinking. About one third of the respondents thought that employers discriminated against older people. This was most keenly felt by the oldest women, 42% of the 65 –75 year olds and 35% by the 45 – 65 year olds. Only 32% of the men in the same age groups believed this was true. Both men and women wanted more part time jobs for older people or jobs allowing for de-escalation at an advanced age. More older women (62%) than older men (56%) reported missing possibilities to work at a more easygoing tempo. In this research no general opinion emerged that early retirement of older people was due to their deficiencies, but rather to the attitudes of co-workers, employers and bosses, ill-health and the lack of adaptations of the work to the conditions and needs of older people, that were similar for both women and men.

Very few studies validate the impression that mental abilities regress or deteriorate over the adult period. Application of youth-related criteria may falsely induce the impression of regressive trends, while a more reasonable interpretation is progression.

A general conclusion is that work control may be a fruitful concept in studies of older women's situation in working life and that more research is needed.

What Statistics Tell and Don't Tell About Older Women and the Labour Market

There is a number of statistical series, entrances and tables produced by Statistics Sweden. Most of the statistics are in Swedish and not always easy to translate. The age groups relating to older manpower are usually 45-54 and 55-64 and 65+ without further age group breakdown.

From the statistics it can be concluded that the overall labour market participation rate of older women is lower than of older men. Thus in 2002, 90.2% of all men and 87.0% of women aged 45-54 were active in the labour force. For the age group 55 – 64 the corresponding figures are 72.2 and 65.5%

For the category married/cohabitating 93.2% of the men and 88.3% of the women aged 45 – 54 years were in the labour force. For the age group 55 – 64 the corresponding figures are 74.9 and 66.3%.

The figures for the categories single men and single women show a different picture. Here 79.9% of the men and 80.3% of the single women aged 45-54 are active in the labour force. For the age group 55 – 64 years the figures are 61.9% and 63.3% respectively. Further studies are needed to explain why the picture is different. One hypothesis is that single men more often have retired because of disease or disability, another that single women are in greater need of an income of their own.

More women than men receive unemployment benefits, and when it comes to studies during unemployment, more than three times as many women are engaged.

The employment sectors in which older women are concentrated are typically "female" professions. To be found in the 20 most common occupational groups for women are personal care and related workers (89% women), office clerks (82%), numerical clerks (89%), nursing and midwifery professionals (93%) etc. Typically "male" professions are building and related trade workers (99% men), mechanics and fitters (98% men), and metal moulders (98% men) etc. It should be mentioned that statistics give figures for a varied sample of 114 professions/occupations as well as the educational background for women and men working in the age groups 16 – 64.

The statistics on occupations and salaries are also presented in detail on the Internet. It is clear that in the older age groups men generally do have higher incomes than women. Vast gaps between the salaries of male business professionals and females are evident. Even in professions involving personal care and related work, men have higher salaries than women. The ten most common occupational groups include 43% of all employed women and 34% of all employed men. In nine of these ten occupational groups, women are paid lower average salaries than men.

The statistics support the hypothesis that older women are more likely than older men to work, or have been working, in part time positions and that they are at higher risk of health problems and disability.

Available official statistics do not support the statement that the career development of older women is often restricted by care obligations within their families. On the other hand support for this statement can be found in the background papers for the present Swedish pension system introduced in 2003. This has led to the parliamentary decision that childcare creates an entitlement to a pension. Furthermore, women and men receive the same level of basic state pension and pension based on total life income despite the fact that women live longer.

At work, older women are three times as often exposed to sexual harassment than are older men. Discrimination is more difficult to assess through available statistics. A more thorough analysis is required to find an answer to this hypothesis.

Statistics support the statement that women's permanent retirement from the labour market takes place at an earlier time than that of men, even though the differences seem to be minute. Women more frequently than men report age-related difficulties in coping with assignments. Women more often than men state that the following changes are needed to enable them to stay in employment until regular retirement age: shorter work hours, a change of time in working hours, changes in physical working conditions, changes in the psychosocial working conditions and a change in the speed work is performed at.

Women are more affected by long-term unemployment than men at the end of their working life, and this is a growing tendency.

No statistics have been found to support the hypothesis that older women feel less negative about their exit from the labour market than older men, but there are some smaller studies supporting this statement.

There have been two national surveys on how women and men spend their time, one in 1990/91 and one in 2000/01, both ordered by the Government and conducted by Statistics Sweden. The former was comprised of individuals 20 – 64 years, the latter 20 – 84 years old. The age group 65 – 84 years was included following pressure from associations representing older people.

Among the findings it can be noted that women spend more time than men on household chores; men heat the house, chop wood and do the bulk of repair and maintenance of vehicles as well as other kinds of repair and maintenance. Both men and women take part in the care of grandchildren and care of others, but women spend more time on this.

In the public statistics there are data on care given by spouses and family members. However, by using "spouse" as the statistical relevant criterion, no difference is made between husband and wife. There are figures related to daughters.

As mentioned earlier, the Swedish National Board of Health and Welfare published a survey on gender perspectives on health care. No significant differences were found between men and women concerning the quality of care, measured as survival, life quality and functional ability.

Women more often reported adverse drug reactions, which might be due to the fact that they are prescribed more drugs than men and that therefore there is a higher risk of interactions between different drugs. Older women complain more often to the governmental agencies about malpractice than men (60% versus 40%).

The National Board of Health and Welfare concludes that more research is needed on gender aspects of care, treatment, medical and social interventions and the consequences of structural changes of the organization of the care of health and welfare. Clinical trials should always include women representing the age groups for which the medicines are intended. Research and statistics should include follow – up of treatment results and resource allocation.

The Material Situation of Older Women

One of the main themes of the MERI project has been to study the material situation of older women. We found little research published on this issue. Most of the information here is therefore based on official statistics. Gunnarsson (2000, 2002), as mentioned above, reported that older women are at risk of poverty leading to means-tested benefits. How this risk is distributed amongst the many immigrant groups living in Sweden seems not to have been investigated.

The material situation of the population and its effects on living conditions is one of the themes of ULF, the Swedish *Survey on living conditions,* which has been conducted since 1975 and covers the age groups 16-84 years. The survey, which is published online[9] as well as in printed reports, presents statistics in which gender, age group and marital status are considered. There are a number of socioeconomic subgroups, within which gender usually is taken into account, but not sufficiently correlated to age groups.

It is thus possible to obtain information on total income from employment and business, basic pension and supplementary pension, disability pension and temporary disability pension, savings for retirement etc.

9 http://www.scb.se/templates/Amnesomrade_12184.asp.

According to ULF, older women are poorer than older men and worry more about their personal economic situation than men do. The age group presented, however, is 65 – 84 years of age which is too large too be a good variable.

There are detailed statistics on immigrants (not born in Sweden or with at least one parent not born in Sweden) with the same indicators as for statistics on native Swedes. The statistics are, however, presented in a way that makes it impossible to determine the situation of older immigrant women as a group, despite the fact that their numbers, ages and marital status are known.

The hypothesis that at least parts of social protection systems (including welfare schemes or invalidity pensions) have negative effects on the material situation of older women cannot be tested without extensive statistical analyses. Statistics capable of shedding light on the statement that widows are an especially vulnerable group within the present framework of the social protection system are not readily available.

We have no figures on whether older women assess their housing conditions more negatively than older men, nor do we know anything about financial support given to family members.

Social Integration, Participation and Other Social Issues

A person's health may be affected by her or his social life and status. The hypotheses put forward in this section are to a limited extent answered by *research*. On the other hand there is an abundance of official *statistics* shedding light on the situation of women and men with regard to social integration, participation and other social issues.

The statement that widowhood is more common among older women than among older men can be commented as follows: the percentage of those married at older ages has risen. In 1950 46% of the 65+ were married. In the years 2000 and 2002, the corresponding figure was 51%. In the age group 80+ 20% were married in 1950, in the year 2000 the corresponding figure was 31% and in 2002 32%. In absolute numbers the number of marriages, which had lasted for 50 years or more, was 14% in 1960, 18% in 1980, 20% in 1990 and 24% in 2000. The explanations are increased life expectancy, decreased age differences between wives and husbands and the fact that people married earlier 60 years ago. Never before have people in Sweden been married for so long to the same person as today!

It should also be noted that many older people today live as "sambos", cohabiters, without being married. Of course, divorces also occur among older couples. In 1950 the figure was 2%, in the year 2000 it was 10%.

The view that older women are more likely to live alone than older men, is supported by statistics. Among men 45 – 64 years of age, the figures for the period 1992/93 to 2000/ 2001 varied between 17.2% and 19.0%. For the age group 65 – 84, the corresponding figures are 23.8% – 26.8%. For women 45 – 64 years of age, the figures vary between 17.3% and 18.8%, and for the group 65 – 84 years, between 51.5% and 53.2%.

Statistics cannot tell whether it is more difficult for older women to find a new partner since "new" older couples usually do not marry. Therefore we cannot answer the question whether older men have a higher probability of having "free-love" relationships than older women. In Sweden there has been little interest in the distinction between "married" and "cohabitating" relationships. "Free-love" or not is not much of an issue, especially not if you have reached a certain maturity. "Joint taxation" (when it comes to taxed property assets) is probably a hotter issue, something which older persons who are not married and have no children together have certain possibilities to avoid. Additionally if you are not married you may keep your widow's/widower's pension.

The question has been raised whether older single men have a higher probability of remarrying than older single women. The statistics here are not transparent. There are figures on the average age at marriage and we have tables giving the age of the bride and groom but we do not know the numbers of married men and married women at any given age; the same goes for divorced, unmarried and widowed.

The hypothesis "Older women have fewer living relatives than men" might be true, if the term 'relatives' is limited to relatives of the same age. If children and grandchildren are included the picture is quite different. The longer you live, the greater the chance to have more relatives, if you have children of your own.

Statistics show that among the 75+, 10% live in the same house as or in a neighbouring house with their children. 64% have one child within 15 km distance from their home, and most live within 1.5 km from a child.

There are detailed statistics on the percentages of women and men aged 45–64, 65–74 and 75–84 having their own families (men > women), having social intercourse with a close relative every week (men < women), having no social intercourse with close relative (men > women), having no social intercourse except with close relatives (men>women), having social intercourse with friends every week (men<women), having social intercourse with neighbours every week (men<women), possessing no close friend (men>women)and having little social intercourse (men>women)[10].

10 < stands for less than, > more than.

The question has been asked whether the ease of access of older women to daily life infrastructure (e.g. shops) has declined as a result of external changes. The health statistics show that the percentage of disabled women is higher than that of disabled men, but the figures decreased during the period 1980 – 2000. In 2001 the figures increased again for reasons we do not know. When you are very old, mobility in daily life becomes more difficult. The statistics show that the percentage of older women and men with no car and a 500 m + distance to the closest bus stop decreased during the period 1980 – 2001. That older women more often depend on public means of transportation than older men is probably true since they more seldom own a car or have a drivers licence. However, there is a trend towards increased motorization among older women. And there are no statistics available as to which extent older women use the cars formally owned by their husbands.

That grandmothers and grandfathers play an important part in intergenerational relations is indirectly shown by the time utilization study performed by Statistics Sweden mentioned earlier. It can be seen from the figures that they spend considerable time looking after their grandchildren. The available statistics on leisure and cultural activities show that older women were more likely to have gone to the cinema at least once during the previous 12 months than older men. More older men, on the other hand, visited sport events at least once during the last 12 months. More older women visited the library at least once during the last 12 months, while older men played musical instruments more often. Older women more often than older men write poems, letters etc. or keep a diary. They also read books more often, visit the theatre and attend divine services.

Engagement in all kinds of associational life is very thoroughly investigated and reported in discussions and detailed statistics with many variables, including age and sex. Some of the engagement in voluntary work can be spotted this way. Women and men are both active, but not always in the same kinds of organization. In some, women are more active; in others men show a higher rate of activity.

Ageism has been one of the most important questions discussed in SENIOR 2005. Ageism in its different forms has been described by Prof. Lars Andersson who has presented the work performed on this issue (SENIOR 2005). However, no systematic research on the occurrence of various types of ageism was found.

Trossholm (2000) has presented a thesis about female pensioners' lives in a class and life course perspective. She showed that despite the fact that old people of today live longer and are much healthier than in the beginning of the 20th century, there is a prevalent misconception of them as being invalid and needing much more care in their old age than is the case. The picture is often polarized and represents the pensioners as decrepit versus active, a burden versus a resource, or old and wise versus conservative and rigid. In addition, Trossholm illuminates the spectra between those dichotomies.

Although there are no scientific papers or official statistics on this, there are indications that a number of recently retired men and women miss contacts to their professional life. The organization Pensionsforum has conducted a number of surveys (interviews with representative samples of Swedes) that show that some miss contacts related to their work place while others do not. A small study conducted by Ohlin and Rinman published by the Swedish Association of Senior Citizens supports this (Ohlin, Rinman, 2002).

The statistics do not include data on older women from ethnic minorities. Research is presently being carried out on this subject at various universities, i.e. in the Department of Social Work, Stockholm University, where Emilia Forssell (2004) is currently completing her doctoral thesis on informal care of elderly immigrants. She has based her work on interviews with relatives of elderly immigrants from a variety of different countries.

Sexuality

Two books have been published about sex and older people based on non-representative interviews with a limited number of women. The authors conclude that older women do have an interest in sexual life but the investigations do not live up to scientific standards. There is also an investigation initiated by the Swedish Board of Public Health (National Institute of Public Health, 1996) based on interviews with a sample of 5,400 persons aged 18 – 74 years about their sex habits. It includes tables on age at first masturbation, orgasm and intercourse, with a focus on the age-groups of 50 – 65 and 66 – 74. The survey also describes to what extent couples have had abortions, sexually transmitted diseases, and subfertility, and asked for help because of fertility problems. It also describes time for menarche, spermarche, frequency of sexual problems and value of sexual life.

Violence, Abuse and Neglect

There is very little research on violence, abuse and neglect suffered by older women and men within families, but two studies are worth mentioning. Lundgren et al. (2001) asked 10,000 women about their experience of violence. 70% replied. Among women aged 45 – 54 years and 55 – 64 years 9% had been exposed to violence during the previous year. 44% of the younger of the two groups had been exposed to violence once or several times since they were 15 years old. Of the group 55 – 64 years the corresponding figure was 36%. The study describes variables such as education, profession, income, country of birth, civil status, family situation, abuser etc.

In the area of the city of Umeå in Northern Sweden a study comprised of older people 65 – 80 years old – was carried out in order to find out to what extent violence or injustice occurred within close relationships (Eriksson, 2001). 1,502 questionnaires were sent out and 1,091 replies were obtained. The results showed that 16% of the women and 13% of the men had been exposed to violence or injustice of some kind after 65 years of age. Neglect was most common – 190 women and 130 men/1000. Harassment and threats came next, 64 women and 82 men/1000 inhabitants. The offender was a partner, child or sometimes persons outside the family. Types of violence can be categorized as physical, psychological, sexual, financial or neglect.

Recently a study from two municipalities in Western Sweden (Kristensen, Risbebeck, 2004) showed that older men slightly more often had been the victims of neglect, while older women more often encountered threats, physical and financial abuse as well as harassment, also sexual harassment.

According to official statistics older women are generally less exposed to violence in their middle years. There is no difference between women and men aged 45 – 64 and 65 – 84. If one looks at the more detailed yearly statistics over the period 1981 – 2001 there are variations between years but the general picture is that there are not significant differences between older women and men with regard to any threat or violence, any kind of violence causing physical injury, any kind of street violence or threat, any kind of violence or threat within the homes. The figures are also low in comparison with the youngest age group 16 – 24 years.

Men are more often exposed to threats or harassment from their partners, while women are more often exposed to extreme abuse. Every second man has sought help while only one woman out of four has done so.

What stands out is that older women (45 – 64, 65 – 74 and 75 – 84) are much more frightened than other groups – both women and men - of going outside in the evening for fear of being exposed to violence although they are not the prime targets of violence.

Studies on violence in homes for older people seem to be lacking but we know from case reports that violence can occur between caretakers and carers, with both parties involved as either perpetrators or as victims.

Conclusions and Recommendations

How we age is an individual process/experience, and t it may therefore be misleading to describe groups of people primarily according to their chronological age. In the MERI project older women were defined as 50+. But there is a great difference between being 50 years of age or 100 years old. If chronological age groups are to be used to describe the situation of women and men, five-year intervals should be used.

Statistics sometimes stop at 64, sometimes 74 or 84 years. With regard to the fact that during the 20th century some 25 years have been added to our lifetime suggest that no upper age limit should be used.

Statistics for both women and men have been included in our reports to the MERI project since a gendered perspective must be included when studying the situation of either sex.

As relevant data become available, it is important that categories are combined in such a way as to make it possible to see sex + age + the subject criterion under study. Currently, for example, the numbers of immigrants in Sweden and their origins, their age groups and educational backgrounds, are available by gender. But in the readily available statistics it is difficult to determine the educational backgrounds of older immigrant women.

Sweden has a remarkable tradition of longitudinal research. It is most important – perhaps the most important of all research issues – that the continuity of these on-going studies is not broken or threatened.

Research on various aspects of growing old, on the living conditions, health and well-being of older people is going on at many universities and other institutions in Sweden. Usually these studies take both sexes into account and separate women and men as categories. Gender research in the strict sense is less common. It is very important that the knowledge that has been obtained and the results of all the on-going studies are distributed and diffused in ways that will make them useful to the widest possible audience, even if extra resources are required.

Health

Within this area there are both longitudinal studies and abundant statistics, which give a good picture of the health situation of women and men. Despite this gender analyses are rarely made. There are some gaps which are summarized here and for which measures should be taken:

- There is a lack of research and statistics on health and the health care of older immigrant women and men
- Despite the fact that there is much data on prescribed medicines, there is a lack of follow-up of as what extent the medicines are actually used and the outcome of the medication.
- There is therefore a need to introduce a national registration of medication on an individual basis. This register should include the identity No. of the patient, drugs used, amounts, dosages and indications and be protected by secrecy legislation.
- Since Sweden offers very good facilities for epidemiological research and its patient registers are not used to their full extent for research it would be an advantage to make them accessible also for foreign scientists. One way to make that possible would be to establish an International/European Institute for Register-based Research (IIRR/EIRR). By means of this it would be possible to evaluate the therapeutic effects, risks and cost /effectiveness of various treatments used in care, in this case care of older people.
- That such data are missing is obvious from the systematic compilation of existing scientific literature in *Geriatric Care and Treatment* published by the Swedish Council on Technology Assessment in Health Care in 2003 (Akner, 2003). Here it is stated that there is a need for evaluation of the care of older people regarding the following aspects: cognitive disorders, drug treatment, stroke, infections, skin ulcers, geriatric rehabilitation, chronic obstructive pulmonary disease and depression. Furthermore there is a need for clinical treatment research in the care of older people for: palliative care, confusion/delirium, chronic pain, malnutrition, emergency geriatric care, Parkinson's disease, high blood pressure, urinary incontinence, heart failure and osteoporosis.

The Swedish National Board of Health and Welfare (2004) would like to see initiatives taken regarding the following:

a. Knowledge and research on the situation of women and men within the social welfare sector
b. Gender-differentiated statistics on work and resources so that the distribution of resources between men and women can be traced/determined. Statistics based on the individual would increase these possibilities considerably.

Education

There are extensive statistics on the educational level of older women and men. There is some lack of data for the 65+ and statistics should be presented in five-year age groups.

One important gap is our scarce knowledge of how older women use computers and have access to the Internet. According to statistics, older women have less access to computers and the Internet. It should be investigated which obstacles are preventing women from using these facilities.

Work

More research is needed on how the work environment and family situation influence women and their ability to continue to work up to regular retirement age.

Research is also needed to show what value older women's and men's work represent in terms of life experience, knowledge and monetary value. Conditions relating to the exit from the labour market is another topic where further investigations are needed. i.e. to what extent does the loss of work constitute a loss of life quality?

The voluntary work undertaken by older women and men should be analyzed in further detail and be valued also in monetary terms. Gender aspects should be taken into account. Of special importance is to initiate research on old people's relation to children and young people, not least grandparents' relation to grandchildren and the support given to their parents.

Statistics should include also those aged 65+.

Material Situation

Statistics should be split into five-year subgroups. Both research and statistics on the situation of immigrants is needed.

Housing conditions and how they are assessed is another area on which information is needed. This is true also for the financial support given to family members.

What criteria should be used to give a valid picture of the material situation of older women should be a matter for discussion. The objects used in measuring the living conditions in Sweden might reflect ideas of what should constitute material wealth/standards held by a younger generations of men. A woman of a certain age, who lives in a small household of one/two persons and is used to washing up after each meal, may not find owning a dishwasher very important. A study of what older people/women value and find important when it comes to their material situation would be useful.

Ageism is an area in which very little research has been conducted. We base much of our opinion on case reports. Therefore research in this area should be promoted.

Far too little is known about the situation of immigrants. Research is going on and more studies are certainly needed.

Very little is known about sexuality in old age. We actually do not know whether women's sexual ability and desire vanishes after menopause and whether older women have more difficulties in finding a new partner and how they feel about that. Studies should be initiated in order to obtain a basis for help that older women and men may need.

Violence and Abuse

Statistics are available on violence and abuse met by older women and men outside their homes are available. Far too little is known about abuse occurring in close relations and in homes for the elderly. Here research is needed.

Final Remark

Research on old age and older persons, whether related to health and care or in the various social sciences, appears to be a dynamic field engaging individual researchers as well as research groups. New results and new projects are constantly being presented. As has been pointed out, sex and gender are nowadays usually (but not always) taken into account and included in analyses. Some university departments and research groups have very informative, sometimes professionally managed and updated web-sites with good English versions. In other cases it takes experience, great determination and a good command of the Swedish language to find the information one wants, if one gets it at all. Since websites in Swedish with little or no information in English are of little value to people who do not speak Swedish, these are not listed in the source section below. In addition there are no references to personal web-pages of individual researchers. Thus the listed resources do not give the full picture of research on older women in Sweden. What is published as books or articles in official and scientific series and journals is fairly easy to find, at least for other researchers.

Descriptions of on-going research may (sometimes) be found by penetrating the websites of the various Swedish universities and university colleges.

References

Aguero-Torres H, Fratiglioni Laura, Guo Z, Viitanben M, Winblad Bengt, (1999): Mortality from dementia in advanced age: a 5-year follow-up study of incident dementia cases. Journal of clinical epidemiology. Aug; 52 (8):737-43. PMID:10465318 [PubMed-indexed for MEDLINE.

Akner, Gunnar (ed) (2003): Geriatric Care and Treatment. A systematic compilation of existing scientific literature. (Evidensbaserad äldrevård. En inventering av det vetenskapliga underlaget.) Stockholm. The Swedish Council on Technology Assessment in Health Care. Pdf fulltext: http://www.sbu.se/www/index.asp.

Statens räddningsverk (2003): Äldres skador i Sverige : äldreskadeatlas med data och trender på nationell, läns-, kommungrupps- och kommunnivå 1987-2001 (Accidents among elderly in Sweden) Karlstad. Räddningsverket.

Andersson, Jenny (2002): Older Women and Food. Dietary Intake and Meals in Self-Managing and Disabled Females Living at Home. Uppsala. Diss. Acta Universitatis Upsaliensis. Faculty of Social Sciences. For summary, see http://publications.uu.se/theses/abstract.xsql?dbid=2558 .

Berleen, Göran (2004): A healthier elderly population in Sweden. Stockholm: National Institute of Public Health, Sweden [Statens folkhälsoinstitut], 2004 (Sandviken : Sandvikens tr.).

Carlstedt, Gunilla, Forssén, Annika, (1999): Mellan ansvar och makt: en diskussion om arbete, hälsa och ohälsa utifrån tjugo kvinnors livsberättelse. Diss. Medical Sc. Luleå . Luleå tekniska universitet.

Carlstedt, Gunilla, Forssén, Annika, (1999): Between responsibility and power. A discussion of work, health and ill health from the life-histories of twenty women. English summary of a dissertation: Mellan ansvar & makt . Luleå. See also: http://www.luth.se/depts/arb/genus_tekn/GAsummary.htm.

Duffy S.W., Tabar L., Chen H.H., Holmqvist M., Yen M.F., Abdsala S., Epstein B., Frodis E., Ljungberg E., Hedborg-Melander C., Sundbom A., Tholin M., Wiege M., Akerlund A., Wu H.M., Tung T.S., Chiu Y.H., Chiu C.P., Huang C.C., Smith R.A., Rosén M., Stenbeck M., Holmberg L (2002): The impact of organised mammography service screening on breast cancer mortality in seven Swedish counties. Cancer. 2002 Aug 1; 95 (3):458-69. PMID: 12209737 [PubMed - indexed for MEDLINE].

Eriksson, Hjelde (2001): Ofrid?: Våld mot äldre kvinnor och män – en omfångsundersökning i Umeå kommun. (Be at strife. Violence against women and men) Brottsoffermyndigheten (The Crime Victim Compensation and Support Authority). Umeå : Brottsoffermyndigheten ; Stockholm : Fritzes offentliga publikationer [distribution].

Fjellström Christina, Sidenvall, Birgitta, Nydahl, Margareta (2001): Food Intake and the Elderly – Social Aspects. In Frewer, L, Risvik, E, Schifferstein, H. (eds) (2001): Food, People and Society. A European Perspective of Consumers' Food Choices. Berlin ; New York : Springer.

Forssell, Emilia (2004): Skyddandets förnuft : en studie om anhöriga till hjälpbehövande äldre som invandrat sent i livet. Summary in English: The logic of protection: a study of informal caregiving to elderly family members in immigrant families. Stockholm. Diss. Stockholms universitet. Department of Social Work. Rapport i socialt arbete.

Forssén, Annika, Carlstedt, Gunilla (2003): Varsågod och var stark : om kvinnors liv, arbete och hälsa under 1900-talet. Lund : Studentlitteratur, Lund.

Fratiglioni Laura, Viitanen M, von Strauss Eva, Tontodonati V, Herlitz Agneta, Winblad Bengt (1997): Very old women at highest risk of dementia and Alzheimer's disease: incidence data from the Kungsholmen Project, Stockholm. Neurology.; 48:132-8 PMID:9008508 [PubMed - indexed for MEDLINE].

Gold, Carol H., Malmberg Bo, McClearn Gerald E., Pedersen Nancy L., Berg, Stig (2002): Gender and health: a study of older unlike-sex twins. The Journals of gerontology. Series B: Psychological sciences and social sciences. May; 57 (3): 168-76. [PubMed – indexed for MEDLINE].

Granqvist, Lena, Ståhlberg, Anne-Charlotte (2003): Occupational Pensions in Sweden from a Gender Perspective. In Hughes, Gerard and Stewart, Jim (eds.)(2004): Reforming Pensions in Europe: Evolution of Pension Financing and Sources of Retirement Income. Cheltenham Glos & Northampton MA. Edward Elgar.

Grimby, Agneta (1993): Bereavement among elderly people: grief reactions, post-bereavement hallucinations and quality of life. Acta psychiatrica Scandinavica; 87:72 – 80. [PubMed - indexed for MEDLINE].

Grimby, Agneta, Svanborg, Alvar (1997): Morbidity and Health-related Quality of Life in Old Age. Aging (Milano). Oct;9(5):356-64. [PubMed - indexed for MEDLINE].

Gunnarsson Evy (2000): Kvinnors fattigdom - om könsperspektivet i forskningen om socialbidrag och fattigdom. (The Poverty of Women – on the gender perspective in research on social assistance and poverty). Socialvetenskaplig tidskrift årg. 7:1-2: 57-71; Reprint series No. 113. Department of Social Work, Stockholm Univ.

Gunnarsson Evy (2002): Det utsatta livsloppet i skuggan av de gynnade generationerna. Om medelålders och äldre kvinnors försörjning. (The vulnerable life course in the shadow of the favoured generations. On the maintenance of middle-aged and older women). Socialvetenskaplig tidskrift årg 9:4: 357-374; Reprint series 132. Department of Social Work, Stockholm Univ.

Gunnarsson Evy (2002):The vulnerable life course: poverty and social assistance among middle aged and older women. Ageing and Society vol. 22:709-728. Cambridge. Cambridge University Press; Reprint series no 135, Department of Social Work, Stockholm University.

Gustafsson Kerstin (2002): Meals and Food in Older Women. Health Perceptions, Eating Habits and Food Management. Dissertation. Uppsala Acta Universitatis Upsaliensis. http://publications.uu.se/theses/abstract.xsql?dbid= 2638.

Hälften vore nog – om kvinnor och män på 90-talets arbetsmarknad : slutbetänkande av Utredningen om kvinnors arbetsmarknad /Half would be enough – about women and men in the labour market of the 90ies/ (1996), Swedish Government official reports.SOU 1996:56. Stockholm. Fritze.

Hellström Ylva (2003): Quality of life among older people receiving ADL help. Help, help providers, and complaints. Lund. Diss. Department of Nursing, Lund University, Sweden. Bulletin No.13.

Hemström, Örjan(2001): Biological and social conditions: hypotheses regarding mortality differences between men and women. In Östlin, Piroska, Danielsson, F. Diderichsen F., Härenstam A.,& Lindberg G. (eds.) (2001): Gender inequalities in health: a Swedish perspective. Boston. Cambridge: Harvard University Press.

Holmén Karin (1994): Loneliness among elderly people: implications for those with cognitive impairment. Stockholm, Norstedt. Karolinska Institutet Diss.

Jansson, Wallis (2001): Family-based dementia care: Experiences from the perspective of spouses and adult children Stockholm. Norstedt. Karolinska institutet Diss.

Johansson C, Skoog, Ingmar (1996): A population-based study on the association between dementia and hip fractures in 85-year olds. Aging (Milano) Jun;8 (3):189-96.

Kristensen, Kerstin, Risbäck. M.arie (2004): De sista ljuva åren – om utsatthet och erfarenheter av våld hos personal och vårdtagare inom hemtjänsten. /The last nice years – on exposure to and experiences from violence of the staff and the care-takers in home-based care/. Göteborg. Rondo Grafisk Kommunikation AB.

Lagerlöf, Elisabeth (1993): Panel of experts on women work and health: national report Sweden; OECD Working Party on the Role of Women in the Economy. Stockholm. Ministry of Social Affairs. Ds 1993:98. Fritzes. Chapter 5 pp 93 – 98. Special risk factors for women. Working women after 45.

Lannerheim, Lena (1993): Vinnare och förlorare. En studie av medelålders och äldre kvinnors arbetsmiljö. Slutrapportering. (Winners and losers. A study of the working conditions of middle-aged and older women). Final report, Lund. Gerontologiskt Centrum. Wallin & Dalholm.

Lannerheim, Lena (1998): Arbete, genus och hälsa. En studie av medelålders och äldre personers arbetsmiljö. (Work, gender and health. A study of middle-aged and older persons´ working conditions), Lund. Gerontologiskt Centrum.

Larsson, Kristina (2004): According to need?: Predicting use of formal and informal care in a Swedish urban elderly population. Diss. Stockholm Univ. Stockholm Studies in Social Work, Stockholm: Dept. of Social Work. http://publications.uu.se/su/theses/abstract.xsql?dbid=109.

Lernfelt Bodil, Samuelsson O, Skoog, Ingmar, Landahl Sten (2003): An 18-year follow-up of overweight and risk of Alzheimer disease. Archives of gerontology and geriatrics Mar- Apr 36 (2):127 – 40.

Lewin, Bo (ed.) (1998): Sex i Sverige. Om sexuallivet i Sverige 1996 (Sex in Sweden. About Sex Habits in Sweden in 1996), Stockholm. Statens Folkhälsoinstitut (National Institute of Public Health). 1998: 11. Summary in Swedish pdf: http://www.fhi.se/templates/Page_930.aspx.

Liebetrau Martin, Steen Bertil, Skoog Ingmar (2003): Stroke in 85-Year-Olds. Prevalence, Incidence, Risk Factors and Relation to Mortality and Dementia. Stroke. Nov;34 (11):2617-22. Epub 2003 Oct 16. [PubMed - indexed for MEDLINE].

Lundberg Olle et al.(2002-2004): Swedold II. A follow-up of the living conditions of the oldest old. CHESS, Stockholm University, www.chess.su.se/chosen_projects.php?projectid=5&action=get.

Lundgren, Eva, Heimer, Gun, Westerstrand, Jenny, Kalliokoski, Anne-Marie (2001): Slagen Dam. Mäns våld mot kvinnor i jämställda Sverige – en mfångsundersökning. Brottsoffermyndigheten och Uppsala Universitet. Umeå.

Lundgren, Eva, Heimer, Gun, Westerstrand, Jenny, Kalliokoski, Anne-Marie (2002): Captured queen: men's violence against women in "equal" Sweden: a prevalence study ; Umeå : Brottsoffermyndigheten ; Uppsala: Univ. ; Stockholm: Fritze [distribution] Full text pdf: http://www.brottsoffermyndigheten.se/informationsmaterial/Captured%20queen.pdf/Captured%20Queen%20.pdf.

Mattsson Sydner, Ylva (2002): Den maktlösa måltiden: Om mat inom äldreomsorgen. (The Unempowered Meal – About food and meals in the elderly-care). Uppsala. Uppsala University. Department of Domestic Sciences. Written in Swedish with an English summary: http://publications.uu.se/ theses/abstract.xsql?dbid=2534.

National Board of Health and Welfare (2004): Framtidens anhörigomsorg - Kommer de anhöriga vilja, kunna, orka ställa upp för de äldre i framtiden? (Families/relatives and care of the elderly in the future) Stockholm : Socialstyrelsen.

National Board of Health and Welfare (2004a): Jämställd vård? Könsperspektiv på hälso- och sjukvården. (A gender perspective on Swedish health care). Stockholm : Socialstyrelsen. Pdf-fulltext: http://www.socialstyrelsen.se/Publicerat/2004/5153/2004 -103-3.htm Summary in English: http://www.socialstyrelsen.se/Publicerat/2004/5153/Summary.htm.

National Board of Health and Welfare (2004b): Jämställd socialtjänst? Könsperspektiv på socialtjänsten (Gender perspectives on social welfare). In Swedish only. Stockholm: Socialstyr.elsen.

Nilsson, Lotta (2002): Våld mot kvinnor i nära relationer (Abuse of women in close relations). Brottsförebyggande rådet, BRÅ (The National Council for Crime Prevention) Report 2002:14. http://www.bra.se/web/english/ (English).

Ohlin, Hellen, Rinman, Ingrid (2002), Upplevelsen av pensioneringen : rapport från en intervjustudie våren 2001. (The Experience of Retirement). Stockholm : SPF förl.

Oskarson, Maria, Wängnerud, Lena (1990): Kvinnor som väljare och valda : om betydelsen av kön i svensk politik (Women as electors and elected. The significance of sex in Swedish politics). Lund : Studentlitteratur, 1996.

Östlin, Piroska, Danielsson, F. Diderichsen F., Härenstam A., Lindberg G. (eds.) (2001): Gender inequalities in health: a Swedish perspective. Boston. Cambridge: Harvard University Press

Rennemark, Mikael (1999): Wellbeing in old age. Life history, sense of coherence and social networks in relation to health. Lund. Diss. Univ. Lund: KFS

Rydenstam, Klas, Engberg, Tobias, Berlin, Marie (2003): Tid för vardagsliv : kvinnors och mäns tidsanvändning 1990/91 och 2000/01 (Time for everyday life : women's and men's time use 1990/91 and 2000/01). Levnadsförhållanden. Rapport nr 99 /Living Conditions. Report no 99. Stockholm : Statistiska centralbyrån (SCB).

Schenk-Gustafsson, Karin. (ed.,) (2003): Kvinnohjärtan – hjärt och kärlsjukdomar hos kvinnor (Women's hearts – cardiovascular diseases in women) In Swedish. Lund. Studentlitteratur.

SENIOR 2005. Parliamentary investigation. Äldrepolitik för framtiden (2003) (Policies for elderly people in the future). Swedish Government official reports, SOU 2003:91. Stockholm. Fakta info direct

Statistisk årsbok för Sverige (Statistcal Yearbook of Sweden) 2002. Årgång / Volume 88. Stockholm: SCB ; Örebro: Publikationstjänsten, SCB.

Steen, Bertil, (ed.) (2004): To Become Old. The Gerontological and Geriatric Population Studies in Göteborg, Sweden, 1971-2002. Göteborg. Department of Geriatric Medicine, Sahlgrenska Academy at Göteborg University.

Stiehr Karin, Huth Susanne (2001): Web witches and other older women: www.sophia-net.org: Exchanging information and discussing experience on the Internet; a publication of Bundesarbeitsgemeinschaft der Senioren-Organisationen (BAGSO), Bonn; [findings of a project in Austria, France and Germany], in: Karin Stiehr ; Susanne Huth (ed.). In co-operation with Europäisches Zentrum für Wohlfahrtspolitik und Sozialforschung, Wien, [Transl.: Pauline Cumbers ; Stephen Richards] Verlag Peter Wiehl, Stuttgart-Marburg-Erfurt.

Sundin, Elisabeth (ed.) (1997): Om makt och kön : i spåren av offentliga organisationers omvandling: rapport till Utredningen om fördelningen av ekonomisk makt och ekonomiska resurser mellan kvinnor och män (About power and sex during reorganisation of public institutions). Statens offentliga utredningar (SOU) / Swedish Government official reports 1997:83. Stockholm. Fritzes offentliga publikationer

Swahn W. (1999) The care of patients with ischaemic heart disease from a gender persective. European Heart Journal. Nov; 20 (21):1600.

Torgén, Margareta, Stenlund Carin, Ahlberg Gunilla, Marklund, Staffan (2001): Et,t hållbart arbetsliv för alla åldrar. (A sustainable working life for all ages) Stockholm. Arbetslivsinstitutet. http://arbetslivsinstitutet.se/isbn/2001/isbn9170456119.pdf

Trossholm, Nina (2000): Tid till eftertanke: kvinnligt pensionärsliv ur ett klass- och livsloppsperspektived (Time for reflection. Female pensioners-life in a class- and life-course perspective). In Swedish with an English summery. Skrifter från Etnologiska föreningen I Västsverige no. 32. Göteborg. Diss. Department of Ethnology, Göteborg University.

Ty makten är din: myten om det rationella arbetslivet och det jämställda Sverige : betänkande / av Utredningen om fördelningen av ekonomisk makt och ekonomiska resurser mellan kvinnor och män – (Kvinnomaktutredningen)(1998) (The power is yours. Swedish Government official reports) SOU 1998:6. Stockholm. Fritzes offentliga publikationer.

Välfärd och ofärd på 90-talet. En temabok om: Ekonomi - Åldrande - Inkomst - Hälsa och omsorg - Jämlikhet - Sociala nätverk - Demokrati - Fritid - Sverige i världen. Levnadsförhållanden Rapport nr 100. Del 5 Åldrande och äldres välfärd. / Good Times and Hard Times in Sweden during the 1990s. Livning Conditions no. 100. Vol. 5. Aging and the welfare of the elderly.(2003). Örebro Statistiska centralbyrån / Statistics Sweden.

Women and Men in Sweden (2004). Statistics Sweden. http://www.scb.se/templates/publdb/publikation_2725.asp&plopnr=1738.

Official and Other Public Statistics

Swedish Work Environment Authority (SWEA) Arbetsmiljöverket , responsible for the information system on accidents at work (ISA): http://www.av.se/statistik/eng/default.asp (Engl.).

The Swedish Institute for Transport and Communications Analysis, SIKA, statistics on traffic accidents: http://www.sika-institute.se/english_fr.html.

Adverse drug reaction register: http://www.mpa.se/eng/index.shtml.

Swedish statistics on medicines: http://www.apoteket.se/rd/d/2215/a/3336.

CAN (Swedish Council for Information on Alcohol and Other Drugs): http://www.can.se/sida.asp?navId=19.

Statistics Sweden/ Statistiska Centralbyrån, SCB: http://www.scb.se/.

Surveys of Living Conditions/Undersökningarna av levnadsförhållanden, ULF: http://www.scb.se/ templates/Product____12187.asp (Engl.).

Gender statistis .Women and Men in Sweden: http://www.scb.se/templates/Product____12237.asp (Engl.).

Work Environment Surveys: http://www.scb.se/templates/Product____21021.asp (Engl.).

Labour Force Survey (LFS): http://www.scb.se/templates/Product____23276.asp (Engl.).

National Board of Health and Welfare http://www.sos.se/sosmenye.htm (Engl.).

National Board of Health and Welfare is responsible for several official registers, including the cause-of-death register, the cancer register, the cancer-environment register, the Hospital discharge register, the Myocardial infarction register, which can all be found by way of the statistics department: http://www.sos.se/sose/sos/omsos/statist.htm (Engl.).

European Home and Leisure Injury Surveillance System, EHLASSS.: http://www.sos.se/epc/english/ehlasseng.htm (Engl).

Some Additional Addresses for Research and Research Groups in Sweden

The Aging Research Center in Stockholm (ARC), the Division of Geriatric Epidemiology, Karolinska Institutet, and the Sophiahemmet – DOGE research group: http://www.neurotec.ki.se/doge/index.html.

The Stockholm Gerontological Research Center: www.aldrecentrum.se/english.html.

The Swedish National Study on Ageing and Care (SNAC): http://www.aldrecentrum.se/snack/ ; http://www.snac.org/engelsk.html.

The Kungsholmen Project: http://www.neurotec.ki.se/doge/kungsholmen/.

CHESS, Centre for Health Equity Studies of the Stockholm University and Karolinska Institutet: http://www.chess.su.se/index.php.

SWEOLD .The Swedish Panel Study of Living Conditions of the Oldest Old study: http://www.sweold.se/.

Swedold II. A follow-up of the living conditions of the oldest old. CHESS, Stockholm University: http://www.chess.su.se/projects.php?PId=5.
Gender differences in health and survival – a life-course perspective: http://www.chess.su.se/projects.php?PId=38.
The Swedish Institute for Social Research (SOFI), Stockholm University: http://www.sofi.su.se/indexe.htm.
The Department of Social Work, Stockholm: http://www.socarb.su.se/forskning savdelningen/forskpublikat.htm.
Swedish Twin Register: http://www.mep.ki.se/twinreg/index_en.html.
The Department of Primary Health Care, Göteborg, with Populationsstudien av kvinnor i Göteborg (The Population Study of Women in Gothenburg): http://www.sahlgrenska.gu.se/allmed/forskning/index_kv_pop.jsp.
H 70. The gerontological and geriatric population studies in Göteborg, Sweden, are performed at Department of Geriatric Medicine, Göteborg University: http://wwhost.gu.se/geriatrik/.
The Social Gerontology Group, Uppsala University: http://www.soc.uu.se/research /gerontology/.
SENIOR FOOD-QOL – Quality of Life and Management of Living Resources. Choosing foods, eating meals: sustaining independency of life in old age Vårdvetenskap, Uppsala University: http://www.pubcare.uu.se/care/care/forskningsprojekt/ mat1.htm.
Division of Geriatric Medicine, Lund University http://www.med.lu.se/english/hvs/geriatric_medicine/research
The Lundby Study – 50 years of psychiatric epidemiology: http://search.lu.se/search/medfak-lu/?q=Lundby&submit=S%F6k
The Lund Longitudinal Dementia Study. A neuropsychiatric, http://www.research.med.lu.se/en_projektdetaljer.php?Proj=429
The Aged and the Economy, Departments of Economics and Economic History and School of Social Work, Lund University: http://www.ekh.lu.se/ed/English/research/elderly_economy.htm
School of Health Sciences, Jönköping, Inst. of Gerontology: http://mars.hhj.hj.se/hhj%5Fsql/default.asp?V_DOC_ID=831
The Octo Twin Project: http://www.cdhg.psu.edu/octotwin/index.html
The Gender Study. Aging in Women and Men. A Second Follow-up in a Longitudinal Twin Study of Gender Differences in Health Behavior and Health Among Elderly:
http://mars.ws.hj.se/hhj%5Fsql/default.asp?V_DOC_ID=1027
The NONA Study, Publications and Presentations: http://mars.hhj.hj.se/hhj%5Fsql/default.asp?V_DOC_ID=835
The Betula Project – Aging, Memory, Dementia: http://www.psy.umu.se/memory/Betula.html (Engl.).
The National Institute of Working Life (Arbetslivsinstuitute is the national centre of knowledge for issues concerning working life and carries out research and studies): http://www.arbetslivsinstitutet.se/en (English)

II. Issues of Health Research in the Context of Gender and Old-age

The Impact of Gender and Age on Cardiovascular Health in Germany

Friederike Kendel & Monika Sieverding

1 Introduction

When women in Germany are asked what they regard to be their greatest personal health risk, over two-thirds report that breast cancer is the disease they fear the most. According to a survey conducted by a German health insurance fund, only 25% of women cite cardiovascular disease in this context (Deutsche Angestellten Krankenkasse DAK, 2002). However, according to information from the German Federal Statistical Office, a total of 17,173 women died in Germany from mammary carcinoma in the year 2003, compared to 29,550 women who died from acute myocardial infarction (Figure 1). Why is the risk of cardiovascular events so drastically underestimated by women themselves, as well as by those around them?

Figure 1: Mortality rates among women (per 100,000 population) for breast cancer and myocardial infarction according to age 2003 (StBa, 2005)

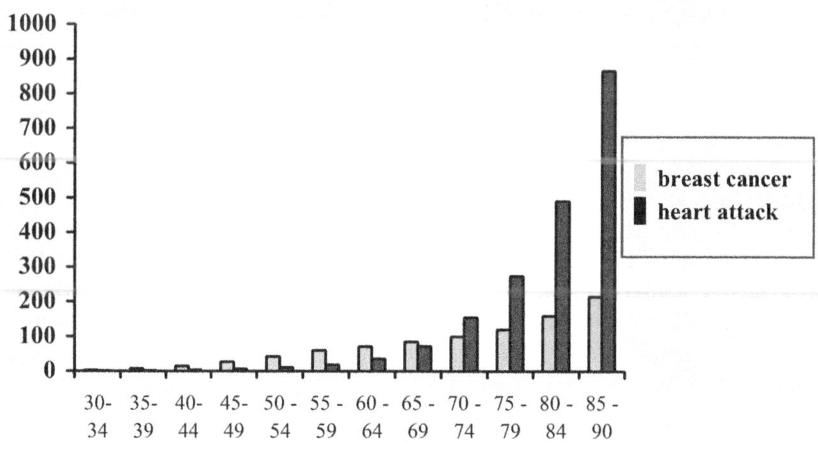

Myocardial infarction has long been viewed as a disease primarily of men; and, indeed, it is true that more men than women in Germany die from heart attacks each year. However, despite the higher prevalence in men, in absolute numbers women actually account for 46% of all lethal heart attacks in Germany (StBA, 2005), and the trend is rising. The relative proportion – calculated per 100,000 population – is somewhat lower due to the longer life expectancy of women (Figure 2).

Figure 2: Acute myocardial infarction according to age and gender per 100,000 population in 2003 (based on information from the StBa, 2005)

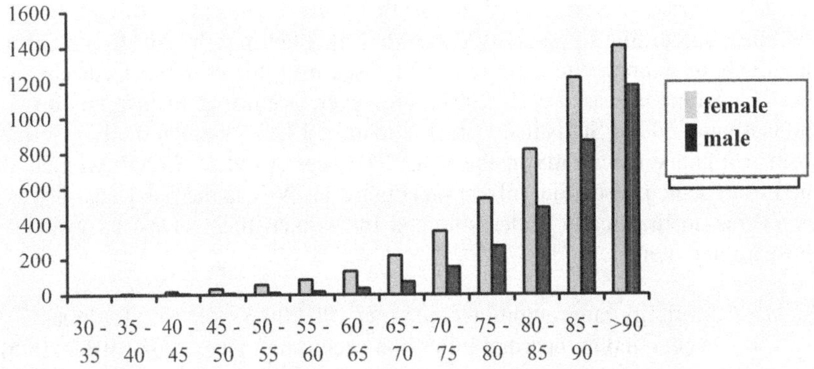

The fact that the relative rate of myocardial infarction among women is lower than among men is only one of the reasons why women and those around them are less aware of the danger of heart attacks. Another reason is the age of those affected. On the average, men are at least ten years younger than women when they suffer their first heart attack. Between the ages of 50 and 65, men are four times more likely than women to suffer a myocardial infarction (Figure 2). Consequently, men are more likely to be gainfully employed at the time and are, thus, more strongly a part of public consciousness. In addition, men and women differ with regard to initial symptoms, as well as to the extent and the effect of risk factors. Only in recent years has attention been drawn to these differences. Indeed, well into the 1990s, coronary heart disease was studied primarily in men. The extent to which the findings of such studies can be applied to women has increasingly been called into question.

2 Developments in Research

For several decades now, cardiovascular disease has been the leading cause of death in Western industrialised nations. Germany is no exception: cardiovascular diseases – and coronary heart disease (CHD) in particular – are the number one cause of death among both men and women in this country (StBa, 2005). Although it is clear that CHD does not overwhelmingly affect men, the vast majority of research on CHD in Germany to date has been conducted almost exclusively in male populations (see Mittag, 2002:13). The findings of epidemiological studies have frequently been extrapolated to women, despite the fact that there is a great variety of biological differences between men and women that make such a generalisation highly questionable. It has been known for some time that there are gender-specific differences in risk factor profiles, as well as in symptom manifestation and issues related to starting and managing therapies. Nonetheless, gender differences in cardiovascular risks did not become an important focus of research on an international scale until the early 1990s. This was triggered by an editorial written in 1991 by the then director of the US National Institutes of Health (NIH), Bernadine Healy, in which she criticised the lack of attention paid to women in medical research (Healy, 1991). As part of a larger NIH initiative, study findings on the aetiology and course of cardiovascular diseases were compiled in 1992, leading to the discovery of a large deficit in research on the situation of female patients (Blumenthal & Matthews, 1993).

Increasingly, cardiology research in Germany is also taking gender-related factors into account. Several important German studies investigating gender differences in CHD have recently now been published. An important basis for examining coronary risk factors in this country is the MONICA Study (Monitoring Trends and Determinants in Cardiovascular Disease), conducted in the Augsburg region. This project was initiated in the early 1980s by the World Health Organisation. Its goal was to describe the risk factors for cardiovascular disease in different world regions. The risk factors were determined by means of 3 independent cross-sectional surveys conducted between 1984 and 1995 at 5-year intervals on random population samples (see Löwel et al, 2005). This survey is of enormous significance for trend analyses and gender-specific examinations of risk factors. In addition, Schannwell et al (2000) conducted an elaborate gender-comparison study on symptomology and diagnostics in coronary heart disease. Yet another important basis for further research can be found in studies on cardiological rehabilitation. Whereas Grande, Leppin, Mannebach, Romppel & Altenhöner (2002) and Mittag (2002) focus primarily on the question of whether women are disadvantaged in cardiological rehabilitation programmes, Härtel, Gehring, Klein and Symannek (2003b) examine gender-specific differences in the success of rehabilitation measures following patients' first myocardial infarction.

3 Risk Factors

A number of risk factors for the development of cardiac diseases have been identified. Data on their prevalence represent an important basis for estimating the relative risk of developing coronary disease. However, there are striking gender- and age-related differences in risk factor profiles among individuals. The classical risk factors for cardiac infarction affecting both men and women include cigarette smoking, diabetes, obesity, low high-density lipoprotein (HDL) cholesterol levels, and hypertension. The impact of any particular risk factor can, however, vary according to gender. In addition, there are a variety of risk factors, such as oral contraceptive use, that only affect women. The relative changes in risk factor burden seen in the MONICA study survey clearly show that the risks have increased, especially among women (Löwel et al, 2005). Recently there has been increased discussion about the role played by depression and lack of social support with regard to age and gender in the development of CHD. In contrast, the notion of Type A personality appears to have declined in importance, as can been seen in the comprehensive meta-analysis conducted by Myrtek on the associations between CHD, Type A behaviour, and hostility (Knoll, Scholz, & Rieckmann, 2005; Myrtek, 2001).

3.1 Somatic Risk Factors

Cigarette smoking is the most important single risk factor for the development of coronary heart disease in women and men. In the early 1980s it was already becoming clear that smoking and oral contraceptive use were the two risk factors in younger female patients (<50) that were tied to issues of social status as well as to those related to family and career planning (Weidemann, Meyer, Fischer, & Wetzel, 2003). Importantly, whereas the older female patients had begun smoking between the ages of 20 and 30, the younger women had already started between 15 and 18 years of age. Between 1983 and 2003 the number of women smokers steadily increased from 27% to 30% among women aged 25 to 69. In contrast, smoking among men over the same period showed a decline from 42% to 38%. In the year 2003, a total of 34% of women in the 18-29 years age group were classified as daily smokers (men: 39%) (Lampert & Burger, 2004). The increase in smoking prevalence among women has been attributed in particular to changes in gender roles; today, for example, smoking is no longer viewed as "unfeminine" (see Waldron, 2002). Studies conducted in the 1980s also show that smoking among women is often associated with emotional stress, whether this be related to work or other psychosocial burdens (Weidemann et al, 2003). As a risk factor for CHD, smoking appears to be particularly harmful to women. In one study, current female smokers had a relative risk for myocardial infarction of 2.24 compared with non-smokers; for male smokers, however, the relative risk was 1.43 (Prescott, Hippe, & Schnohr, 1998:1043). Furthermore, the younger women are when they begin smoking, the greater their risk. Female smokers who use oral contraceptives and started smoking before the age of 15 are 13 times more likely to develop CHD (Hennekens, Evans, & Peto, 1989). In addition, active smoking is associated with a drastic reduction in the age of onset for first myocardial infarction: in one study, the average age reduction was 19 years for women (from 79 to 60 years of age) and 7 years for men (from 71 to 64). This means that women who are heavy smokers have their first myocardial infarction an average even of 4 years earlier than male smokers (Hansen, Andersen, & von Eyben, 1993).

Smoking plays a less important role in the cardiovascular risk profile of older women, which is characterised instead by a combination of hypertension, overweight, and diabetes (Weidemann et al, 2003:56). The prevalence of hypertension in both men and women increases steadily with advancing age. Until the age of 60, the prevalence of hypertension is higher in men than in women, but the gender gap closes in older age groups. For example, in the 70-79 years age group, approximately 70% of men *and* women are affected. From an epidemiological standpoint, a rise in blood pressure is a consequence of aging; this is in contrast to the increase in LDL cholesterol and decrease in HDL cholesterol levels seen in older women, for which the association with menopause has been confirmed (Härtel, 2003a:29).

In her analysis of data from the German Federal Health Survey [*Bundesgesundheitssurvey*] from 1998, Härtel (2003a:31) shows that women in the youngest age group and women aged 50 years or older demonstrated a higher prevalence of hypercholesterolemia than did men. The greatest differences could be seen in the 60-69 year age group: 65% of the women and 44% of the men in this population suffered from hypercholesterolemia. Only in women 70 years of age or older did the prevalence decrease, thus narrowing the gender gap to some extent. A comparison of these objective figures with self-assessments by survey participants shows that individuals of both genders greatly underestimated their cholesterol levels. However, the false self-assessment among women over the age of 50 is particularly striking.

Diabetes is another risk factor that has more serious implications for women than for men in the context of CHD. It appears that younger women lose the protection normally afforded by estrogen if they develop diabetes (Härtel, 2003a:26). Indeed, diabetes increases the risk of myocardial infarction by 6-fold in women, and 4-fold in men (Löwel et al, 1999). Diabetes also increases premature mortality after a heart attack by 18% for women, but only 9.9% for men (Löwel, Koenig, Engel, Hormann, & Keil, 2000).

In summary, it is clear that known risk factors for cardiovascular disease in men also apply to women. However, comparing the prevalence of risk factors in women and men is of limited value only. With regard to several risk factors – especially smoking and diabetes – the relative risk of suffering a myocardial infarction differs markedly between men and women, as well as between different age groups. Both smoking and diabetes represent a considerably higher coronary risk for women than for men. Because of the increase in smoking among young women in particular, the prevalence of CHD in intermediate age groups is likely to rise as well. The MONICA Index in Augsburg, Germany appears to confirm this supposition: whereas in men the number of myocardial infarctions decreased by 2.3% per year between 1985 and 1995, it only decreased by 0.7% per year in women. Furthermore, this decrease was not distributed evenly across the different age groups: whereas women between the ages of 55 and 74 showed a reduction of 2% per year, younger women (aged 25-54) actually showed an annual increase of 3.8% (Verbundprojekt zur gesundheitlichen Situation von Frauen in Deutschland, 2001:120). This trend in younger women runs contrary to the general tendency towards a decrease in myocardial infarctions and thus deserves special attention.

3.2 Psychosocial Risk Factors

Over the past several years, a growing body of evidence has made clear that not only somatic, but also psychosocial risk factors play a role in the development and clinical manifestation of coronary heart disease. Of course, it should not be forgotten that psychosocial and biological factors often influence each other in a reciprocal manner, and that somatic risk factors such as smoking, overweight, or hypercholesterolemia are often the result of lifestyle behaviours developed in response to stressful life events.

Traditionally, gender research in medicine has focused on the health consequences of the double burden faced by women as they strive to find a balance between career and household work (Mittag, 2002:18). However, the notion that this double burden increases the risk of coronary heart disease has not always been confirmed by the available data. Paid work and career building have a number of positive effects that can protect against other harmful factors – including, most notably, economic and social independence, greater social support, and more emotional and intellectual stimulation (Sieverding, 1995). The converse is true, however, when the stress caused by women's double burden comes to outweigh the positive aspects of paid work. Above all, it is women with a low socioeconomic status who experience the greatest burden in this regard: compared to female college graduates, women in unskilled positions are at a far greater risk of developing CHD (Wamala, Mittleman, Horsten, Schenck-Gustafsson, & Orth-Gomer, 2000). For both men and women, low socioeconomic status is associated with lifestyle behaviours that increase one's susceptibility to cardiac disease: heavy smoking, increased stress, unhealthy eating habits, and physical inactivity (Brezinka & Kittel, 1996). However, socioeconomic status appears to have a stronger effect on women than it does on men.

A lack of social support has also been frequently cited as a risk factor for CHD. However, in order to clarify this term, it is important in gender research to draw a distinction between the qualitative and quantitative aspects of social networks. For example, men and women differ with regard to the size of their networks: women tend to have large social networks, whereas men often depend on fewer social contacts. At the same time, men profit more from the support provided by women than vice versa. This is particularly true of middle-aged men. Older individuals can often compensate for the lack of a partner by means of a well-functioning social network. Cardiac events occur more frequently in individuals who are socially isolated and have little social support. This effect is stronger in men than in women (Schwarzer & Rieckmann, 2002:195). On the other hand, a spouse is frequently the person who is able to call for help when his or her partner is experiencing an acute heart attack. Because women in older age groups have a higher risk of myocardial infarction than their younger counterparts (see Figure 2), it is more likely that they no longer have a partner and are living alone. The lack of a close companion who can call for medical assistance in the event of an emergency may thus have a particularly unfavourable effect on the recognition and treatment of myocardial infarction in older women.

Chronic stress has been cited frequently as a behavioural, and thus modifiable, risk factor in men and women alike. However, in contrast to the most frequently investigated somatic risk factors, elucidating the exact role played by stress in myocardial infarction has been difficult. This may be due to the fact that insufficient attention has been paid to the affective manifestations of chronic emotional distress, such as feelings of "burn out", exhaustion, or pessimism about the future – all of which can contribute to depression or depressive moods (Ladwig, Erazo, & Rugulies, 2004). Individuals with coronary heart disease often have concomitant depression. Frequently, depressive moods are prodromal to an infarction, although it is not always possible to diagnose these in an objective manner. Such "premanifest" illness behaviour, characterised by energy loss and exhaustion, may be relatively non-specific. The question as to whether these factors independently influence the course of disease is still largely unexplored (Ladwig et al, 2004:11). Depression is associated with a number of behavioural risk factors, such as smoking, alcohol abuse, and physical inactivity. On a physiological level, these behaviours correspond, for example, with overweight, diabetes, and hypertension.

4 Diagnosis and Prognosis After Cardiac Events

In the sections above we described how individual risk factors affect cardiovascular health. But how do men and women differ with regard to disease manifestation and outcome after myocardial infarction and bypass surgery?

4.1 Manifestation and Acute Care of Myocardial Infarction

An elaborate study by Schannwell and colleagues (2000) recorded and analysed clinical symptoms and history in more than 5000 patients (50% women) who had been admitted to hospital due to suspected CHD. The findings of this study clearly underline the problems involved in diagnosing CHD in women versus men: almost 60% of the women in the study indicated experiencing atypical anginal symptoms compared to 19% of the men. This may very well be one of the main reasons why CHD is underestimated among women in clinical practice. This finding is in accordance with the fact that women were much more likely to visit a general or non-medical practitioner prior to hospital admission (Table 1). In fact, 68% of women vs. 4% of men in whom CHD was eventually diagnosed indicated that they had visited at least two medical specialists before being admitted to hospital for an invasive investigation. Interestingly, there were also differences in the type of specialists that had been consulted: only half as many women as men consulted a cardiologist (see Table 1). These factors undoubtedly contributed to the delay in the diagnosis of CHD in women. The average length of time between the onset of clinical symptoms and the actual diagnosis was a startling 77 months for women vs. 9 months for men. One can only speculate on the extent to which the cardiac function of these patients may have deteriorated during this period of time and what consequences this might have for their prognosis. The delay in diagnosis also translates into considerably higher health care costs.

Table 1: Epidemiological data on prehospital diagnosis of CHD (Schannwell et al, 2000)

	Women with CHD	Men with CHD
Age at time of diagnosis	67±4.1	57±2.3
Number of months with prior angina pectoris	77±8	9±2
Prehospital diagnosis		
General practitioner („Praktischer Arzt“)	65 %	43 %
Internist	22 %	57 %
Non-medical practitioner	13 %	0 %
Number of specialists		
1	11 %	73 %
>2	68 %	4 %
Type of specialists		
Cardiologist	41 %	82 %
Orthopaedist	83 %	47 %
Neurologist	42 %	19 %
Psychotherapist	31 %	15 %

Because the manifestations of infarction in women are more complex, and because many women are unaware that they are at risk, there is also a long delay between symptom onset and eventual diagnosis in cases of *acute* myocardial infarction. Men who experience severe chest pain are probably more likely to suspect a heart attack and seek medical help, either of their own accord or at the prompting of someone else. Women, in contrast, may possibly wait longer before seeking assistance (Mittag, 2002:65). Myocardial infarction is still regarded as a "man's disease", especially by younger women and those around them. The prodromal symptoms of acute myocardial infarction are often non-specific in women. Women are more likely than men to have symptoms that differ from those of typical angina pectoris, experiencing, for example, only shortness of breath, nausea, sweating, or neck pain. This difference in the premonitory manifestation of infarction may be one of the reasons for the higher mortality rate in women following a heart attack. Not only women themselves, but also their attending physicians, often appear to be interpreting their symptoms incorrectly, leading to delayed hospital admission. In women, the symptoms of an impending infarction are more likely to be attributed at first to spinal disorders or gastric complaints (Härtel, 2003a:47). This is one of the reasons why women reach the emergency room an average of 60 minutes later than men after noticing initial symptoms (Grande et al, 2002:150). Analyses of data from the MONICA Study in Augsburg, Germany, also point to a clear association between marital status and mortality. A total of 39% of the women vs. 4% of men in this population who experienced sudden death after acute myocardial infarction were widowed. When women suffer a heart attack, they are more likely to be alone and lacking a partner who would be able to call an ambulance (Mittag, 2002:65). Because the decision to call for medical assistance usually depends on the presence of a friend or relative, it may well be that a number of female heart attack patients die due to delays in treatment (Härtel & Löwel, 1991). Thus, the fact that women are admitted to hospital later than men should not be interpreted solely as the result of poor quality health care.

4.2 Prognosis After Myocardial Infarction and Bypass Surgery

Since the early 1990s a large number of epidemiological and clinical studies have focused on the question of whether women have an increased risk of premature death after myocardial infarction compared to men. Data from the MONICA Project of the World Health Organisation have shown that this is the case in the majority of the 21 countries that participated in the study (see Härtel, 2003a:14). Men may be more likely than women to suffer heart attacks – but women are more likely to die from them. Data from the Augsburg Index from 1985/95 for individuals between the ages of 25 and 74 show that, of the heart attack victims who died prematurely from the event, 34% did so before reaching the emergency room. Another 20% died on their first day in hospital, and another 5% between the second and twenty-eighth day in hospital. This means that only 41% of those affected were still alive after 4 weeks (Verbundprojekt zur gesundheitlichen Situation von Frauen in Deutschland, 2001).

The fact that rates of premature death among women changed only minimally from 1985/87 to 1995/97 is surprising considering the frequent claims that the quality of acute treatment in myocardial infarction no longer differs between men and women, as it once did (Härtel, 2003a:15). At first glance, a logical explanation for higher mortality in women would be that they are, on the average, older than men when they experience their first infarction. Whereas in men CHD mortality increases in a linear fashion starting at the age of 35, in women the curve is shifted up by approximately 10 years and shows a strong increase in mortality starting at approximately the age of 65 (see Figure 2). More than 95% of CHD-related deaths in women occur in this age group. In contrast, only 37% of CHD-related deaths in men occur in individuals above the age of 65 (Mittag, 2002:11). In addition, women in this age group often suffer from other age-related diseases and are treated in a less "aggressive" manner. However, a closer look at the available epidemiological data reveals that the older average age of women who present themselves with CHD is not a sufficient explanation for their higher mortality rate. As was demonstrated by Vaccarino, Parsons, Every, Barron and Krumholz (1999) in a prospective cohort study in the United States, younger women showed higher mortality following a heart attack than did older women. Younger women (<50 years of age) in the study were also more than twice as likely to die after a heart attack than age-matched men – a gender gap which did not close until approximately the age of 70.

Coronary heart disease is often treated with bypass surgery, a method by which a blood vessel taken from the tissues of the chest, arms, or legs is used to route blood around blockages in the coronary arteries. The number of women who undergo this procedure has risen continually in recent years; today women comprise almost 30% of all bypass patients. However, it should be noted that the increased use of such invasive methods is not always associated with better chances of survival. Women are generally older than men at the time of diagnosis, and their treatment is made more difficult by the fact that their coronary system differs from that of men in a variety of respects. As a result, less "aggressive" treatment in women is not necessarily a sign of disadvantage, but rather is based on the fact that women who are diagnosed as suffering from coronary disease are older and have a different clinical picture than men. The role played by the expectations and gender-specific stereotypes of physicians has yet to be determined.

There is a general consensus that women have a poorer prognosis than men following bypass surgery (Regitz-Zagrosek et al, 2004; Vaccarino et al, 2003). The only German study on this topic to date examined in-hospital mortality of 17,528 consecutive inpatients who underwent coronary artery bypass grafting between 1992-2001 at the German Heart Institute in Berlin (Regitz-Zagrosek et al, 2004). Compared to men, women in the study had a 1.5-fold higher risk of death following the bypass operation. This increased risk was not evenly distributed among the different age groups, however. Whereas women who were under 50 had a 2.4-fold higher risk, the gender gap closed with advancing age; at approximately the age of 70, men and women showed a comparable risk of mortality (Figure 5).

Figure 3: Mortality risk ratio according to age group in women vs. men after bypass surgery (Regitz-Zagrosek et al, 2004)

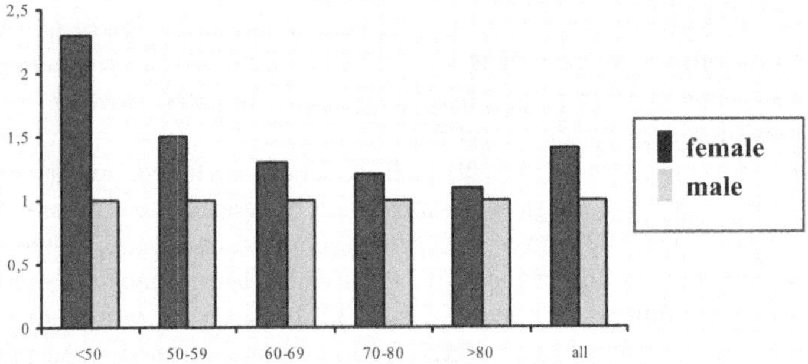

This does not appear consistent with the observation that premenopausal woman are protected from coronary heart disease. It is conceivable that women who undergo bypass surgery at a relatively young age comprise a special risk group.

Women have a poorer prognosis than men, both following myocardial infarction and after bypass surgery. In both of these contexts, it is especially younger women who have a markedly higher risk of mortality compared to men (Regitz-Zagrosek et al, 2004; Vaccarino et al, 1999). Currently known risk factors cannot fully explain this gender difference, however. As a result, one can only speculate on the age and gender interactions observed in the abovementioned studies. Clinical parameters that have been suggested in this context include genetic risk profiles and hormone status (Regitz-Zagrosek et al, 2004). Depression has also been identified in a number of studies as a predictor of mortality following coronary artery bypass surgery (Blumenthal et al, 2003) and after myocardial infarction (Frasure-Smith, Lesperance, Juneau, Talajic, & Bourassa, 1999). Because women in Germany are almost twice as likely to suffer from depression as men (Brüggemann & Haltenhof, 2002), this may prove to be an explanatory approach to higher mortality rates in women.

Another reason for the poorer prognosis for women with CHD may be due to an inability to reduce the number of household activities they perform, giving them less opportunity to recover after myocardial infarction or bypass surgery. Several studies in the United States have examined the association between household activities and health status after cardiac events. In a prospective longitudinal study (15 men, 15 women), Rose, Suls and Green (1996) showed that the spouses of female patients assumed greater responsibility for domestic tasks in the first weeks after the heart attack. As early as 10 weeks after the heart attack, however, the female patients were already performing substantially more domestic work than their spouses. The support provided by male spouses was thus limited primarily to the time directly following discharge from hospital. In contrast, men were able to markedly reduce the number of household activities they performed following myocardial infarction, allowing for a longer recovery period. In general, it appeared to be difficult for patients to forgo traditional sex-typed activities. In a later American longitudinal study with 63 patients, the correlations between the symptoms reported and activities performed were quite variable with respect to gender. In men, there was a reverse correlation: the more symptoms they reported, the more they limited their household activities. In contrast, female patients appeared to pay little or no heed to their symptoms (Lemos, Suls, Jenson, Lounsbury, & Gordon, 2003:13). Despite their functional limitations and more severe symptoms, women continued to perform their usual activities and appeared to pay less attention to their own needs. This pattern of behaviour may place female patients at particular risk, especially considering the fact that household activities are often not distributed evenly throughout the day, but rather are concentrated within a certain period of time (Jenson, Suls, & Lemos, 2003). In the early postoperative phase, when patients are instructed to avoid physical strain – in particular of their upper body – such behaviour undoubtedly represents an increased risk. As far as we know, to date, no studies have been conducted in Germany on the burden of household work in women following myocardial infarction or bypass surgery.

5 Gender- and Age-Related Aspects of Rehabilitation

In Germany, approximately 280,000 persons experience a myocardial infarction each year, and hundreds of thousands of patients require bypass surgery or undergo procedures to widen narrowed coronary arteries (StBA, 2003). Acute cardiac events interrupt the everyday working lives of affected individuals and deprive them of their normal social environment. Current cardiac rehabilitation programmes were developed in the 1960s and 1970s with younger men in mind and had the primary goal of helping these individuals return to work. However, with health care resources becoming increasingly scarce, it is today more important than ever to determine precisely which measures are needed most, and to evaluate the effectiveness of these measures, in an evidence-based fashion.

5.1 Are Women Disadvantaged With Regard to Health Care?

In 1991 the Rehabilitation Commission of the German Association of Pension Funds [*Verband Deutscher Rentenversicherungsträger*, VDR] presented a series of recommendations on the further development of medical rehabilitation in Germany. In its report, the Commission noted that rehabilitation services for several diagnoses were still utilised much less frequently by women than men in this country (VDR/Reha-Kommission, 1992:187). A little over a decade later, however, the situation has changed. None of the three recent rehabilitation studies (Grande et al, 2002, Mittag, 2002, Härtel et al, 2003b) focusing on gender discrepancies was able to find any evidence that women were disadvantaged in a quantitative manner with regard to access to services or service utilisation. However, this does not answer the question as to the appropriateness of particular services. When they begin rehabilitation programmes, women are considerably more impaired physically and psychologically than comparably aged men. This applies to disease severity, exercise tolerance, comorbidity, risk factors, and health-related quality of life. In women, anxiety and depressive symptoms appear to be especially pronounced at the start of rehabilitative therapy compared to men – a difference that could also be clearly seen at the end of rehabilitation in at least one German study on the topic (Härtel, 2005:11). In the rehabilitation study by Mittag (2002:68), younger women, in particular, experienced depression as a result of their illness. They more frequently reported feeling that their personal health was dependent on chance or fate, seeing as a result fewer opportunities to influence the state of their health through treatment or, for example, a change in lifestyle. At the same time, younger women suffered considerably more disease-related worries compared with men or, in particular, older women. Younger women also reported experiencing pronounced vital exhaustion (Mittag, 2002:68). This can be explained by the personal circumstances of many younger women, for whom family- and work-related stress often represent an especially large burden. Moreover, the disease often appears in a completely unexpected manner at this time of life and requires a great deal of adjustment. And in the study by Mittag (2002:68) it is precisely the younger women who described their situation as unclear, difficult to manage, or unsatisfying. According to traditional concepts of the family, women are assigned the expressive role – that is, they are responsible for providing their husbands and children with socioemotional support. The lack of control over one's own life can set in motion a vicious circle that eventually leads to severe depression (e.g. Nolen-Hoeksema, Larson & Grayson, 1999:1061).

Differences in personal circumstances also appear to influence the reasons reported by men and women for not participating in outpatient rehabilitation programmes, such as in supervised exercise groups. Women most often give practical reasons for non-participation, citing for example that the programme is too far from their home or that they have no means of transportation. The main reasons for non-participation cited by men include lack of interest or the opinion that the programme is "not fun" (Härtel, 2003a:51). Because of this, Härtel et al (2003b:45) recommends therapy programmes that take the special circumstances of women into account. Programmes like these are based on separate, women-only groups that deal specifically with the multiple comorbidities common to women, that teach self-confidence, and that provide instructions on how to make use of what they have learned in everyday life. The emphasis lies on the psycho-social and familial burdens, fears, and depressions typically experienced by women. To date, such programmes have met with strong approval by female patients (Härtel, 2005:12). It may be that new social structures are able to develop in women's groups like these, leading to greater mutual support.

5.2 *The Role of Age in the Allocation of Health Care Services*

According to the findings of the three rehabilitation studies described above, gender does not have an effect on the allocation of health care services among patients with CHD. A patient's age, however, does appear to play an important role in this regard (Grande et al, 2002:151). Grande et al assert that younger patients receive a larger number of diagnostic interventions, such as exercise ECG testing and coronary angiography. In addition, there were clear age-related differences with regard to discharge medication and patients' use of rehabilitation services. Participants in rehabilitation programmes and supervised exercise groups were an average of 3 to 4 years younger than non-participants. The older the patients were, the less they made use of services such as bicycle ergometer training, psychological counselling, and/or anti-smoking classes (Grande et al, 2002:151). These differences are not a sign that care was being tailored to the needs of certain groups of individuals, however, because older patients simply received fewer, rather than different, services (Grande et al, 2002:157). These findings show that some of the differences, which at first glance appear to be based on gender, are in reality due to age. Indeed, age appears to be a more important factor than gender with regard to the allocation of health care services (Grande et al, 2002:151). Focusing too narrowly on gender can easily obscure this fact by confounding the pre-existing sociodemographic and medical characteristics that lead a patient to make use of, or receive, particular health care services. In the acute care phase of treatment, the greater prevalence of multimorbidity, the less favourable risk factor profile, and the poorer state of health in older patients undoubtedly play an important role. Furthermore, during the rehabilitation phase – if not much earlier – patients themselves also influence the type of care they receive insofar as they consent to, or decline, certain services. Differences in patients' subjective perception of disease, which have been found in a number of studies, may exert a substantial influence in this context (Grande et al, 2002:154). Because the number of older patients in rehabilitation care is expected to rise considerably in the future, it is essential that new rehabilitation services be developed that are tailored specifically to the needs of this particular age group (Grande et al, 2002:154).

6 Conclusions

The differences in CHD rates between men and women begin to level out as patients grow older. Due to the aging of society and changes in the risk factor profiles of younger women, it is very likely that the number of female heart patients will increase dramatically in the future. The findings of recent risk factor analyses underscore the importance of differentiating patients according to gender and age in medical research and treatment. Indeed, there are clearly risk factors, such as smoking, that exert a greater influence on the incidence of coronary heart disease in women than in men, and that interact with other risk factors in different ways or to a different extent depending on gender. Gender-specific factors also influence the manifestation, course, and prognosis of cardiovascular diseases. In contrast, age appears to be the major determinant in the allocation of health care services. Whereas men and women, in general, receive comparable health care services, older patients receive fewer services than younger patients, regardless of their gender. The reasons for these differences and the roles played by patients and physicians cannot be fully explained based on the available data. However, the overarching goal of achieving "fairness" or "equality" in health care cannot be reached by completely standardising the services provided. Standardisation carries with it the danger of neglecting the unique characteristics and needs of certain groups. Studies have repeatedly shown that the positive effects of rehabilitation programmes are difficult to sustain (Willich et al, 2001). In order to account for changes in lifestyles and health-related behaviour, it will be necessary to develop new concepts that differentiate patients according to gender and age.

Younger female patients appear to comprise a special risk group. To date, few studies in Germany have focused explicitly on the role played by gender in coronary heart disease. Almost no research has been conducted in this country on the extent to which family- and work-related stress influences CHD, patient recovery following myocardial infarction, or bypass surgery. It is difficult to generalise the findings of studies from America or Scandinavia, for example, because of sociocultural differences. As a result, new studies in Germany that focus on these issues are urgently needed. In Europe, the first "Institute of Gender Related Medicine" was founded in Sweden in 2001 at the Karolinska Institute. The first such institution in Germany, the Centre for Gender in Medicine [Zentrum für Geschlechterforschung in der Medizin, GiM], was established in 2004 at the Charité University Medical Centre in Berlin. The task of the GiM is to investigate why the prevalence, course, and manifestation of many diseases differ between women and men. The example of gender- and age-related effects in cardiovascular disease makes clear that gender research in medicine is, by definition, an interdisciplinary field. In which cases do the effects of age contribute more than the effects of gender to our understanding of variance? To what extent can different examples of variance in medicine be traced back to biological factors, or to social ones? In the English-speaking countries, "gender" has become an established concept and is used to distinguish between the social and cultural characteristics of men and women and their biological sex (see Legato, 2004). Societies assign different roles and allocate different resources to men and women, and they judge their contributions to the community according to different standards, as well. How much of what we describe as "masculine" or "feminine" can be attributed to biological sex and thus cannot be influenced? And how much is acquired and thus subject to change? The process of investigation and discovery in this field of inquiry has been set in motion, but there are many important questions that still need to be answered.

References

Blumenthal, J. A., Lett, H. S., Babyak, M. A., White, W., Smith, P. K., Mark, D. B., Jones, R., Matthew, J. P., & Newman, M. F. (2003). Depression as a risk factor for mortality after coronary artery bypass surgery. *The Lancet, 362*, 604-609.

Blumenthal, S. J., & Matthews, K. A. (1993). Psychosocial aspects of cardiovascular disease in women: Introduction and overview. *Annals of Behavioral Medicine, 15 (2-3)*, 109-111.

Brezinka, V., & Kittel, F. (1996). Psychosocial factors of coronary heart disease in women: a review. *Social Science & Medicine, 42*, 1351-1365.

Brüggemann, B., & Haltenhof, H. (2002). Der Beitrag soziokultureller Faktoren zum Verständnis der Geschlechterverteilung depressiver Störungen. *Zeitschrift für Klinische Psychologie, Psychotherapie und Psychiatrie, 101-132.*

Deutsche Angestellten Krankenkasse, DAK (2002). *"Was wissen Frauen über den Herzinfarkt?"*Emnid/DAK.

Frasure-Smith, N., Lesperance, F., Juneau, M., Talajic, M., & Bourassa, M. G. (1999). Gender, depression, and one-year prognosis after myocardial infarction. *Psychosomatic Medicine, 61*, 26-37.

Grande, G., Leppin, A., Mannebach, H., Romppel, M., & Altenhöner, T. H. (2002). *Geschlechtsspezifische Unterschiede in der kardiologischen Rehabilitation*: Abschlussbericht Universität Bielefeld.

Hansen, E. F., Andersen, L. T., & von Eyben, F. E. (1993). Cigarette smoking and age at first acute myocardial infarction and influence of gender and extent of smoking. *American Journal of Cardiology, 71*, 1439-1442.

Härtel, U. (2003a). Ist-Analyse Prävalenz der Herz-Kreislauferkrankungen bei Frauen in NRW. Gutachten im Auftrag der Enquete-Kommission "Zukunft einer frauengerechten Gesundheitsversorgung in NRW. Düsseldorf. URL: http://www.landtag.nrw.de/portal/WWW/GB_I/I.1/EK/EKALT/13_EK2/aktuelles.jsp.

Härtel, U., Gehring, J., Klein, G., & Symannek, C. (2003b). Untersuchung geschlechtsspezifischer, biomedizinischer und psychosozialer Einflüsse auf den langfristigen Erfolg von Reha-Maßnahmen bei Patienten mit koronarer Herzkrankheit: Abschlussbericht (1. Förderphase) BMBF Bericht.

Härtel, U. (2005). Geschlechtsspezifische Unterschiede in der kardiologischen Rehabilitation. *informiert! Nr.9.*

Härtel, U., & Löwel, H. (1991). Familienstand und Überleben nach Herzinfarkt. Ergebnisse des Augsburger Herzinfarktregisters. *Münchner Medizinische Wochenschrift, 133*, 464-468.

Healy, B. (1991). The Yentl syndrome. *The New England Journal of Medicine*(325).

Hennekens, C., Evans, D., & Peto, R. (1989). Oral contraceptive use, cigarette smoking and myocardial infarction. *British Journal of Family Planning, 5*, 66-67.

Jenson, M., Suls, J., & Lemos, K. (2003). A comparison of physical activity in men and women with cardiac disease: do gender roles complicate recovery? *Women and Health, 37*(1), 31-47.

Knoll, N., Scholz, U., & Rieckmann, N. (2005). *Einführung in die Gesundheitspsychologie.* München: Ernst Reinhardt Verlag/UTB.

Ladwig, K.-H., Erazo, N., & Rugulies, R. (2004). Depression, Angst und Vitale Erschöpfung vor Ausbruch der koronaren Herzkrankheit. Frankfurt a.M.:VAS

Lampert, T., & Burger, M. (2004). Rauchgewohnheiten in Deutschland - Ergebnisse des telefonischen Bundes-Gesundheitssurveys 2003. *Das Gesundheitswesen, 66*, 511-517.

Legato, M. (Ed.). (2004). *Principles of Gender-Specific Medicine.* Amsterdam: Academic Press

Lemos, K., Suls, J., Jenson, M., Lounsbury, P., & Gordon, E. E. I. (2003). How do female and male cardiac patients and their spouses share responsibilities after discharge from the hospital? *Annals of Behavioral Medicine, 25*, 8-15.

Löwel, H., Döring, A., Schneider, A., Heier, M., Thorand, B., & Meisinger, C. (2005). The MONICA Augsburg Surveys - Basis for Prospective Cohort Studies. *Gesundheitswesen, 67 Sonderheft 1*, S13-S18.

Löwel, H., Koenig, W., Engel, S., Hormann, A., & Keil, U. (2000). The impact of diabetes mellitus on survival after myocardial infarction: can it be modified by drug treatment? Result of a population-based myocardial infarction register follow-up study. *Diabetologia, 43*, 218-226.

Löwel, H., Stieber, J., Koenig, W., Thorand, B., Hörmann, A., Gostomzyk, J., & Keil, U. (1999). Das Diabetes-bedingte Herzinfarktrisiko in einer süddeutschen Bevölkerung. Ergebnisse der MONICA-Augsburg Studien 1985-1995. *Diabetes und Stoffwechsel, 8*, 11-21.

Mittag, O. (2002). *Vergleich der Verläufe nach erstem Herzinfarkt bzw. ACVB-Opration oder PTCA bei Frauen und Männern*:B-1 Projekt im Norddeutschen Forschungsverbund. Abschlussbericht 1. Förderphase.

Myrtek, M. (2001). Meta-analyses of prospective studies on coronary heart disease, type A personality, and hostility. *International Journal of Cardiology, 79*, 245-251.

Nolen-Hoeksema, S., Larson., J., & Grayson, C. (1999). Explaining the gender difference in depressive symptoms. *Journal of Personality and Social Psychology*, 77, 5,1061-1072.

Prescott, E., Hippe, M., & Schnohr, P. (1998). Smoking and risk of myocardial infarction in women and men: Longitudinal population study. *British Medical Journal, 316*, 1043-1047.

Regitz-Zagrosek, V., Lehmkuhl, E., Hocher, B., Goesmann, D., Lehmkuhl, H. B., Hausmann, H., & Hetzer, R. (2004). Gender as a risk factor in young, not in old, women undergoing coronary artery bypass grafting. *Journal American College of Cardiology, 44* (11), 2413-2414.

Rose, G. L., Suls, J., & Green, P. J. (1996). Comparison of adjustment, activity, and tangible social support in men and women patients and their spouses during the six months post-myocardial infarction. *Annals Of Behavioral Medicine, 18*, 264-272.

Schannwell, C. M., Schoebel, F. C., Lazica, D., Marx, R., Plehn, G., Leschke, M., & Strauer, B. E. (2000). Besonderheiten der koronaren Herzkrankheit in der klinischen Symptomatik und Erstdiagnostik bei Frauen. *Deutsche Medizinische Wochenschrift, 125*, 1417-1423.

Schwarzer, R., & Rieckmann, N. (2002). Social Support, Cardiovascular Disease, and Mortality. In G. Weidner & M. S. Kopp & M. Kristenson (Eds.), *Heart Disease: Environment, Stress and Gender* (pp. 185-194). Amsterdam: IOS Press.

Sieverding, M. (1995). Die Gesundheit von Müttern - Ein Forschungsüberblick. *Zeitschrift für Medizinische Psychologie, 4*, 6-16.

StBA. (2005). Gesundheitswesen. Todesursachen in Deutschland 2003.Wiesbaden: Statistisches Bundesamt.

Vaccarino, V., Lin, Z. Q., Kasl, S. V., Mattera, J. A., Roumanis, S. A., Abramson, J. L. & Krumholz, H. M. (2003). Gender differences in recovery after coronary artery bypass surgery. *Journal of the American College of Cardiology, 41*, 307-314.

Vaccarino, V., Parsons, L., Every, N. R., Barron, H. V., & Krumholz, H. M. (1999). Sex-based differences in early mortality after myocardial infarction. *New England Journal of Medicine, 341*, 217-225.

VDR/Reha-Kommision (Ed.). (1992). Bericht der Reha-Kommission des Verbandes Deutscher Rentenversicherungsträger. Empfehlungen zur Weiterentwicklung der medizinischen Rehabilitation in der gesetzlichen Rentenversicherung. Frankfurt am Main:VDR.

Verbundprojekt zur gesundheitlichen Situation von Frauen in Deutschland (2001). Bericht zur gesundheitlichen Situation von Frauen in Deutschland *(Schriftenreihe des Bundesministeriums für Familie, Senioren, Frauen und Jugend, Band 209)*. Stuttgart: Kohlhammer.

Waldron, I. (2002). Trends in gender differences in coronary heart disease mortality-relationships to trends in health-related behavior and changing gender roles. In G. Weidner, M. S. Kopp & M. Kristenson (Eds), Heart Disease: Environment, Stress and Gender. *Amsterdam: IOS Press*, 80-98.

Wamala, S. P., Mittleman, M. A., Horsten, M., Schenck-Gustafsson, K., & Orth-Gomer, K. (2000). Job stress and the occupational gradient in coronary heart disease risk in women. The Stockholm Female Coronary Risk Study. *Social Science & Medicine, 51*, 481-489.

Weidemann, H., Meyer, K., Fischer, T., & Wetzel, A. (2003). Frauen und koronare Herzkrankheit. Altersverteilung, Rauchen und orale Kontrazeption, klassische Risikofaktoren, psychosoziale Konstellationen, körperliches Training. Frankfurt a.M.:VAS

Willich, S.N., Müller-Nordhorn, J., Kulig, M., Binting, S., Gohlke, H., Hahmann, H., Bestehorn, K., Krobot, K. & Völler, H. (2001). Cardiac risk factors, medication and recurrent clinical events after acute coronary disease - a prospective cohort study. *European Heart Journal, 22*, 307-313.

Health of Ageing Women in Hungary

Csilla T. Csoboth

1 Introduction

Although the concept of women's health in Hungary has only emerged in the past decade, the study of women's health and how it develops from youth to old age is important for many reasons. The political, social, and economic changes, which have occurred in the past fifteen years, have affected the lives of women, especially those of middle and old age, bringing changes in income, social roles, etc. (Kleiverda, Csoboth, Ceapchi, 1999). Joining the European Union, within which the life expectancy of women is on average five years more than of Hungarian women, it is of the greatest importance to increase both the physical and the mental state of health of women in Hungary. Hungarian women should not be at a disadvantage in terms of health, economic productivity, or social disposition, just because interventions did not specifically target their health needs and didn't address the most important issues influencing their health.

Hungarian older middle-aged and elderly women and men comprise a generation, which has experienced hardships ranging from wars and revolution, dictatorship, socialism, to capitalism. They are the ones whose lives were influenced by change in political, economic, and the social system. These changes affected their private as well as their work lives and had a tremendous impact on both their physical and mental health. For most, the political change from communism to democracy did not result in an increase in the quality of life. In fact many suffered and still suffer from the disadvantages of the free market, which has resulted in a widening of the social and economic gap. During the communist era, this gap was much more narrow, almost invisible. Unemployment was non-existent and most people had a secure minimum income, and were therefore able to afford basic goods and services.

Thus the health of Hungarian elderly women has suffered from both physical and mental hardships, a situation which has continued into the present. These hardships, partially due to the higher average life expectancy compared to men and high rate of widowhood, include low pensions, high prices of daily living, lack of infrastructure equipped for the elderly, low quality health care facilities, low social acceptance and tolerance for the elderly, and difficulties in the execution of daily tasks. All factors result in a low quality of life, impaired well-being, and an objectively and subjectively worse health-state.

2 Social and Demographic Trends

2.1 Demography

The percentage of elderly people in general above the age of 65 years has increased from 13.4% to 14,6% between 1980 and 2000, which is a slightly lower increase compared to the European Union (from 13,97% to 15,97%, respectively) (Johann Béla Hungarian National Health Promotion Program, 2003). Elderly women comprise a large proportion of the population, 17,6% of the Hungarian female population is over 65 years old. This proportion is 11.4% among men. In 2005, there were 1,364 and 1,863 elderly women per thousand males in the age-groups of 60- 69 years and 70 + years, respectively (Central Statistical Agency, 2005). The old-age dependency ratio, measured as the number of people 65 years of age or older for every 100 people of working age (15 to 64 years of age) in Hungary was 22,7 in 2005. The ageing index has increased to 99,9 in 2005 (Central Statistical Agency, 2005). In comparison in 1960 the ageing index, which is the ratio of older people to children, was 35,2, in 1990 it was 64,5 and in 2000 it was 88,5.

Due to the decrease in the number of elderly men and the rise in divorces, living alone is the predominant trend among Hungarian women. The older a woman, the higher the odds are for her to live in a one-head household. The following table (Table 1.) shows the magnitude of elderly women living alone, 48.6% of 60-69-year-olds and 76.5% of those above 70 were not married. 62% of 60-69 years and 91% of the 80 years or older population lived in single households (Central Statistical Agency, 2002).

Table 1: Marital status among elderly Hungarian women (Central Statistical Agency, 2002)

Age group (years)	Never Married (%)	Widowed (%)	Divorced (%)	Total number of the female population in the given age-group
60-69	3,3	35.8	9.37	594,042
70+	4.4	66.2	8.1	682,080

2.2 *Employment, Retirement, Social Benefits*

Although some studies (Buss et al., 1994) found that the level of poverty and low income does not explain health status differences between countries, the unfavourable economic situation of elderly Hungarian women increases their risk for ill health. Pensions are extremely low, especially among elderly women, and the quality of life of retired women is substantially lower compared to those who are economically active. According to a survey conducted by the Central Statistical Agency, elderly women living in one-head households are at the greatest risk for living in poverty (Central Statistical Agency, 2002). The poverty risk for elderly women living alone is 2,5 times higher than for the average of households. In general 21.2% of one-headed households over the age of 75 years live in poverty.

Until recently the retirement age for women was 55 years, compared to 60 years for men. In 2005, the retirement age for women was raised to 60, and 62 years for men. This age-difference will be equalized to 62 years for both genders by 2009 (National Strategic Report, 2005). The average age for retirement was 58.6 years among women and 59,7 years among men in 2003. The average working years for both genders was 37,7 years. The value of pensions in regard to the net income received in the last year of employment is significantly higher among men (Kempelen Farkas Digitális Tankönyvtár, 1999). While pensions are the main source of income of elderly women, they are 23% less than pensions received by men (National Strategic Report, 2005). This difference is mainly due to the fact that the average income received for the same number of working years is lower among women, as for a variety of reasons women are unable to participate in the economically more dynamic sectors. There is a strong employment segregation, and women usually have family obligations to fulfil, such as childcare and elderly care, which all add up to lower income. Other reasons for this economic disadvantage is that women retire earlier than men and also live longer, thus increasing the total number of years spent living in retirement (the average years spent in retirement is 22-23 years for women and 16- 17 years for men).

The guaranteed minimal pension is granted to those who have paid social security contributions for at least twenty years. On January 1st, 2005, the minimum pension was 24.700 HUF (less than 100 Euro) (National Strategic Report, 2005). In 2003, the average pension was 52.360 HUF (circa 200 Euro), which is 59% of the national average net income. Widows' pensions consist of 50% of the pensions of the deceased, for widows in the retirement age without individual income, and 30% of the deceased's pension if the widow has individual income. In January 2005, 62% of the retired received below-average pensions. Pensions only slightly higher than the minimum pensions were paid to 10-13% of retirees.

To this day, care facilities and services for the elderly are substantially insufficient. The majority of social care consists of financed meals, home-care, and day care facilities for the elderly. The number and quality of long-term care facilities for the elderly is low (the numbers being unknown). Public meals are assured by 71% of the Hungarian municipalities (National Strategic Report, 2005). 61% of the municipalities offer organized home-care for the elderly, services that are mainly missing in small rural villages and towns (National Action Plan, 2005).

Due to their low income, elderly women have diminished opportunities to enjoy their retirement. "Luxuries", such as travelling, going to the movies or theatre, even owning a telephone, are far from being a matter of course. The availability of cars for the elderly is very limited in Hungary and the accessibility of and satisfaction with public transport is low, therefore decreasing the mobility of Hungarian elderly (Mollenkopf et al., 2004). In addition, rural areas offer very few opportunities to pursue leisure activities to their elderly population. These socio-economic limitations often lead to depression and suicide, which will be discussed later on in this chapter.

3 Health Indicators

If we look at the average life expectancies at birth (Central Statistical Agency, 2004) of Hungarian women (76,91 years) and men (68,59 years) they are considerably lower than the EU average of 80 years for women and 74 years for men (EC, 1997). This disadvantage compared to the EU is somewhat lower at the age of 60 and 65 years (for women 2,9 and 2,6 years and for men 3,5 and 3 years respectively) (National Strategic Report, 2005). Life expectancy did not increase significantly from 1970 to 1995 in Hungary, (4,83 years) compared to other countries in the EU, where it increased at an average of 5,5 years (EC, 1997).

Another interesting phenomenon is the difference in life expectancy between genders (8,3 years), which is much higher in Hungary (Central Statistical Agency, 2002) than in other Western countries. In Sweden, for example, the difference is 5.2 years, in Austria it is 6,5 years (Kopp, Réthelyi, 2004). Therefore it can be postulated that even though Hungarian women live longer than Hungarian men, their health and illness state is much worse than in other countries.

In a comparative study between elderly Hungarians and Americans, Hungarians were in much poorer health as measured by functional status, symptomatology, medical condition, and subjective health status (Buss et al., 1994). According to ratings of self-perceived health status, elderly women in Hungary regard themselves as less healthy than other women living in the EU. Compared to the average of women living in the EU, of whom 39% of 65 to 74 of age and 32,3% of 75 years and older women rated their own health as good or very good (EC, 1997), 40% of women over the age of 65 in Hungary rated their health bad or very bad, 50% rated it satisfactory, and only 10% rated it good or very good (Johan Béla National Center for Epidemiology, 2003). This means an increase in low subjective rating of health, since 35% of the same age-group rated their health bad or very bad in the year 2000.

3.1 Trends in Mortality

Mortality rates have increased significantly among women since 1960 (9,6/1000 inhabitants). After a peak rate in 1999 (12,8/1000 inhabitants) there was a decline to 12.08/1000 inhabitants in 2004, but this rate is still higher than rates (11.6/1000) up to 1975 (Central Statistical Agency, 2005). Mortality rates for women increase significantly at the age of 50 and over, but are significantly lower than rates among men. Table 2 shows the mortality rates of women and men according to age-groups.

Table 2: Mortality rates in Hungary per thousand according to gender and age-groups (Central Statistical Agency, 2005)

Age-groups (years)	Women	Men
40 – 49	3,28	8,24
50 – 59	6,85	17,38
60 – 69	14,4	33,43
70+	65,5	87,82

The major causes of death among elderly women (65 years or older) are other ischaemic heart disease, cerebrovascular disease, and acute myocardial infarction, the first two resulting in a higher number of deaths among women compared to men. Table 3 shows mortality rates among women according to diseases by selected age-groups.

Table 3: Mortality rates (mortality per hundred thousand inhabitants belonging to the corresponding age-group of the deceased) among Hungarian women by selected age-groups (Central Statistical Agency, 2005)

Disease	60 – 64 years	65 – 69 years	70+ years
Other ischaemic heart disease	102,37	230,21	1.554,01
Cerebrovascular disease	111,48	220,3	1.138,11
Acute myocardial infarction	83,22	154,42	425,56
Malignant neoplasm of trachea, bronchus and lung	94,21	112,63	143,77
Bronchitis, emphysema, asthma	30,15	43,92	151,47
Diseases of the liver	83,85	76,86	53,2
Motor vehicle accidents	5,97	6,73	11,34
Intentional self-harm	16,96	17,00	26,74

It is especially important to compare these mortality rates to figures in the other EU countries and unfortunately, alarming differences can be found. For example the mortality rate for respiratory system cancer for women of all ages in the EU was an average of 6,63 and was the highest in Denmark (34,88) in 1992, whereas the same rate is 81,72 for all Hungarian women in 2004. A significant difference can also be seen regarding cerebrovascular disease, where the EU average for women of all ages was 75,93 in 1992, while the mortality rate in Hungary was 172,82 in 2004 (EC, 1997; Central Statistical Agency, 2004).

Breast cancer is one of the most common types of cancer among women in Hungary and the European Union. The mortality rate for breast cancer was 22,91 in Hungary (Central Statistical Agency, 2005) compared to the EU average of 31,25 in 1992 (EC, 1997). Most deaths occurred among women over the age of 65 years (1.376 cases). Mortality due to malignant neoplasm of the ovary - with a mortality rate of 6,59 per hundred thousand inhabitants - is the second highest among gynaecological cancers, the number of deaths being highest among those over the age of 65 (392 cases). Mortality caused by malignant neoplasm of the cervix uteri was 4,88 in 2004, but the number of deaths was higher among women in the age-group of 35-64 years (293 cases). The EU average mortality due to cancer of the cervix was 2,28 per 100.000 inhabitants in 1992. These Hungarian data show the same trend as data in the EU, namely a substantial decline in cancer mortality for women under the age of 65.

3.2 Morbidity

More than 45% of elderly women over the age of 65 years suffer from participation restriction, which hinders them in executing daily tasks and fulfilling social roles (Gallup Institute, 2000). Back pain is one of the most common complaints causing disability; more than 70% of women over the age of 65 years reported feeling pain around their spine. Household injury and traffic accidents were the most common causes of injuries among elderly women.

As mentioned before, the main cause of mortality, as well as of morbidity and disability among Hungarian elderly women are the disorders of the heart and blood vessels. These diseases are related mostly to life style and to social class. More than 70% of Hungarian women over the age of 65 years suffer from cardiovascular disease. Risk factors, such as obesity, high cholesterol diet, and sedentary life style, are also highly prevalent among older Hungarian women. In one study concerning urban women and men over the age of 50 years, 50% of women were found to be obese, but the prevalence declined with age. The authors hypothesized that the decrease was due to the changing eating habits of the elderly population, as the elderly cannot afford food with high cholesterol contents (Kiss et al., 2003) and also due to more exercise (in the form of daily walking, etc.). A survey conducted in the capital of Hungary found that the quantities of milk, dairy products, fish, meat, fruits, and fresh vegetables consumed by the elderly were far below the amounts recommended (Rurik & Antal, 2003) and the average time spent with outdoor activity was only 12 hours per week. Another aspect of mobility and of physical exercise is the possibility of taking trips, representing an important contribution to the well-being of older persons (Mollenkopf, 2004). The MOBILATE study, a comparative study of European countries, found that Hungarian elderly have the highest incidence of walkers (58%) and that they also more likely to use the bicycle, therefore ensuring daily physical exercise for some of the elderly. Nevertheless Hungarian elderly were the least satisfied with mobility, and compared to other European countries, achieved less mobility in their daily lives.

Regarding other risk factors for premature death, diabetes was present in almost 20% of the female population (Johann Béla National Center for Epidemiology, 2003). In 2003, seven percent of elderly women reported drinking alcoholic beverages moderately, and three percent reported heavy drinking. The prevalence of tobacco use increased among women over the age of 65 years; in 2000, 4% of those questioned reported being a daily smoker, while in 2003, this rate increased to 7%. Interestingly, in the National Health Survey 50% of elderly women reported having an induced abortion in their medical history (Gallup Institute, 2000).

3.3 Health Care Utilization

The use of health care services for the treatment of disease is widespread among elderly women. On the other hand preventive services are underutilized by this population. Fifteen percent of women over the age of 65 years have not been to see their General Practioner in the past 12 months (Gallup Institute, 2000). Prevention of circulatory disease would require regular blood pressure monitoring. In the National Health Interview Survey, 10% of elderly women have not had their blood pressure measured in more than 12 months (Johann Béla National Center for Epidemiology, 2003). According to general medical recommendations, women aged 45-65 years should be screened for breast cancer at least once every two years, but despite these guidelines approximately one-third of the high-risk population has not had a mammography in two years (Johann Béla National Center for Epidemiology, 2003). Regular gynaecologist visits are also infrequent among elderly women, 65% of elderly women have not been to see their gynaecologist in more than 5 years. Dental hygiene is also very underdeveloped among the elderly: more than 85% of elderly women have not been to see the dentist in the past year (Gallup Institute, 2000).

3.4 Mental Health

Mental disorders and symptoms are a major public health concern in Hungary, but preventive interventions are scarce and treatment facilities are lacking. The report of the World Health Organization on Mental Health (2001) identified the three groups within society to be most at risk of mental health disorders to be women, the elderly, and persons living in lower socio-economic status. This signifies the fact that elderly women, who usually live in the lower socio-economic levels, are at an even greater risk for mental health problems, due to their concurrent membership in all three of these risk groups. In the National Health Interview Survey dated 2000, 18% of elderly women over the age of 65 years were found to show a reduction in mental functionality compared to men, whose rate was only 13% (Gallup Institute, 2000).

Many factors contribute to poor mental health among the elderly, such as isolation, feeling of lack of security, and reduced mobility. Hungarian elderly living in the countryside were found to have the greatest levels of insecurity in the MOBILATE study (Mollenkopf, 2004). As mentioned before, loneliness is common among Hungarian elderly; in a European comparative study the proportion of elderly living alone was higher than 30% (the lowest proportion being in Italy, 18%) and single-headed households were more frequent in the countryside than in the cities.

Depression. According to world health statistics, depression is the second most common disease world wide, with a lifetime prevalence of 15%, perhaps as high as 25% among women (Kaplan, Sadock, 1998), with women suffering from unipolar major depression approximately twice as often as men (Regier, Burke, Burke, 1990).

Data collected by the HUNGAROSTUDY in 1988, 1995, and 2002 showed that the prevalence of depressive symptomatology has increased in the past fifteen years. Kopp et al. (1996) found that 33% of Hungarian women reported depressive symptoms in 1995, representing an increase of 29% since 1988.In 1995, older women showed a four times higher risk for depressive symptoms (measured by the shortened Hungarian version of the Beck Depression Inventory[1]) than those who were under 40 years of age (Kovács, Jakab, Kopp, 2001). The average Beck Depression score was 15,4 points[2] among the 60 years and older women, meaning that elderly women on average experience mild depressive symptoms.

According to the data of the HUNGAROSTUDY 2002[3] (Kovács, Kopp, Rózsa, 2003), the occurrence of all categories of depressive symptoms increased with age (Figure 1). Elderly women proved to have the highest prevalence of depressive symptoms (48,3%), almost half had a score of 10 points or higher on

1 Depressive symptomatology was measured by the Hungarian version of the Shortened Beck Depression Inventory (BDI), which according to several studies is a reliable measure of screening depressive symptom severity in community surveys. This adaptation contained the 9 items from the 21-item version of the BDI and showed a strong correlation with the total BDI (Kopp, Skrabski, Szedmák, 1995).

2 Scores of the shortened Beck Depression Inventory were transformed into the original score by multiplying the total score with 2.3 (Réthelyi, Berghammer, Kopp, 2001). The scores were grouped in the following categories: normal: 0-9 points; mild: 10-18 points; moderate: 19-25 points; severe: 26 points or higher.

3 HUNGAROSTUDY 2002, a national representative survey of the Hungarian population over the age of 18 years, conducted by the Semmelweis University Institute of Behavioral Sciences in 2002. The sample included 6987 women, and was representative according to age and region. Age groups were formed: 18 to 25 years; › 25 to 35 years; › 35 to 45 years; › 45 to 55 years; › 55 to 65 years; and > 65 years. Mid-age was defined from 45 to 65 years and old-age from > 65 years.

the Beck Depression Inventory (BDI) with severe depressive symptoms being in almost one-fifth of the oldest age-group. These again are higher figures than those found in other international studies of elderly women, for example Heikkinen (2004) found 36% prevalence of depression in elderly women (using the CES-D scale (Center for Epidemiologic Studies Depression Scale). Stage et al. (2001) found reports of a 10-15% prevalence of depressive symptoms over the age of 65 years. The difference according to age-groups in frequency of severe depressive symptomatology measured by the BDI was especially significant. While only 2,1% of the youngest age group (18 – 25 years) reported severe depressive symptoms, 19,0% of the oldest age group (>65 years) reported severe depressive symptomatology.

When analysing according to employment status, depressive symptoms showed a high prevalence among the retired (42,6%). The occurrence of anxiety also increased with age. While 26,0% of the youngest age group (18 – 25 years) reported anxiety symptoms, 32,6% of the middle-aged group (46 – 55 years) reported frequent anxiety symptoms and a slight decrease could be seen in the oldest age-group (28%; $p<0,001$). Frequent alcohol consumption was more common in the older age-groups, 1,1% of 18 – 25 year olds reported drinking four or more times a week compared to women older than 65, who represented 38,2% of frequent drinkers ($p<0.001$).

Figure 1: Prevalence of depressive categories according to age-groups

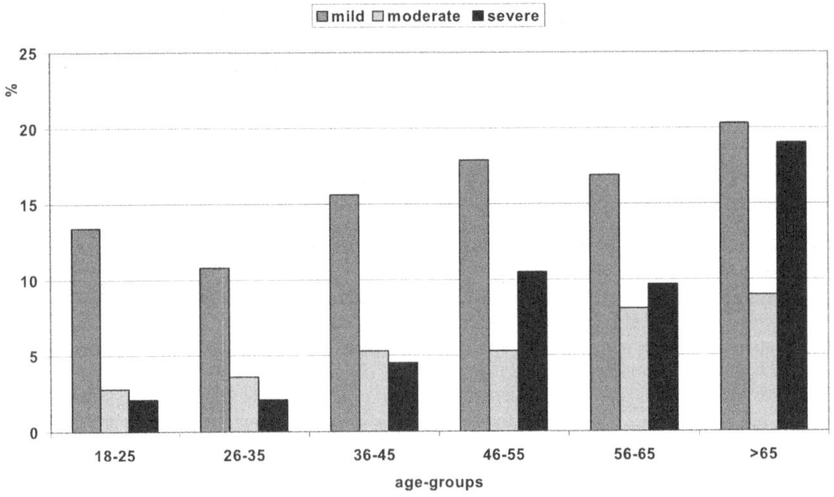

Suicide. In 2004, 293 women over the age of 60 years committed suicide. The number of suicides increases with age (See Figure 2). Suicide rates have decreased significantly among elderly women. During the past decades, rates among women over the age of 60 – 74 years, rates decreased from 61/100,000 in 1982 to 15/100,000 in 2002 (WHO, 2002). Studying suicide rates in a different age-group, namely women above 65 years, the mortality rate peeked in 1977 by 74/100,000 and decreased to 22/100.000 by the year 2002. Elderly women over the age of 75 years are most at risk of committing suicide. The suicide rate was 95/100,000 in 1980, which decreased to 36/100.000 by 2002, but is considerably higher than the average suicide rate of 27.13/100.000 of the whole population. In comparison, the EU average suicide rate was 6,24 among women in 1992.

Figure 2: Increase in suicide rates among women according to age-groups, 2001 (Central Statistical Agency, 2002)

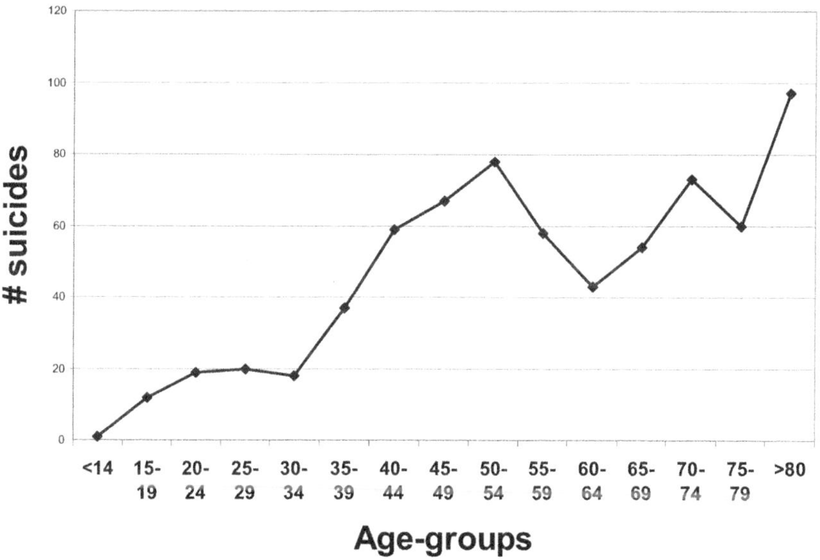

4 Violence against Elderly Women

Data regarding violence against Hungarian elderly women is scant. The data of the HUNGAROSTUDY 2002 showed that physical abuse was reported by 12,7% of the oldest age-group, but was still lower compared to middle- aged women, who had the highest frequency of reporting abuse (21,4%), and the youngest (19%) of the sample.

5 Conclusions

The health status of Hungarian elderly women is much poorer than of their peers in other European or North American countries. Interestingly, the level of poverty alone does not explain health status differences; this finding warrants further research on this health disadvantage. The Hungarian health and social system should pay more attention to health promotion, prevention, and primary care in order to increase the level of health and quality of life of elderly women. Also importantly young and middle-aged women need to be targeted through health promotion and disease prevention interventions in order to prevent the further decline in the state of health of the elderly female population.

References

Buss TF, Beres Cs, Hofstetter CR, Pomidor A (1994). Health status among elderly Hungarians and Americans. Journal of Cross-Cultural Gerontology 9(3): 301- 322.

Central Statistics Agency (2002). Statistical Year Book of Hungary 2002, Budapest: KSH.

Central Statistical Agency (2005). Statistical Yearbook of Hungary 2004, Budapest.

Elekes Z (1999). Devianciák, mentális betegségek. In: T Pongrácz, IG Tóth (Eds.), Szerepváltozások. Budapest: TÁRKI, Szociális és Családügyi Minisztérium Nőképviseleti Titkársága, pp. 125- 141.

European Commission (1997). The state of women's health in the European Community. Luxembourg: Office for Official Publications of the European Communities.

Gallup Institute Budapest (2000). Executive summary of the national health interview survey. http://gallup.hu/olef .

Heikkinen RL, Kauppinen M (2004). Depressive symptoms in late life: a 10-year follow-up. Archives of Gerontology and Geriatrics 38(3): 239-50.

Johann Béla Hungarian National Health Promotion Program, 2003, p. 15-16.

Johann Béla National Center for Epidemiology (2003). National Health Interview Survey 2003 Hungary. Http://www.antsz.hu/olef .

Kaplan HI, Sadock BJ (1998). Kaplan and Sadock's synopsis of psychiatry: Behavioral sciences/clinical psychiatry (8th ed.). Baltimore, MD: US Williams & Wilkins Co.

Kempelen Farkas Felsőoktatási Digitális Tankönyvtár (1999). A nyugdíjak jövedelempótló képessége. www.hik.hu .

Kiss C, Poór G, Donáth J, Gergely P, Paksy A, Zajkás G, Antal M (2003). Prevalence of obesity in an elderly Hungarian population. European Journal of Epidemiology 18: 653-57.

Kleiverda G, Csoboth C, Ceapchi N (1999). Women's health in Central and Eastern Europe, Advances in Women and Health Research,. In: A Kolk, M Bekker, K van Vliet, (Eds.), Tilburg University Press, pp.: 199-217.

Kopp MS, Skrabski Á, Szedmák S (1995). Socioeconomic factors, severity of depressive symptomatology, and sickness absence rate in the Hungarian population. Psychosomatic Research 39(8): 1019- 29.
Kopp MS, Skrabski Á (1996). Behavioural sciences applied to a changing society. Budapest: Biblioteca Septem Artium Liberalium.
Kopp MS, Réthelyi J (2004). Where psychology meets physiology: chronic stress and premature mortality- the Central-Eastern European health paradox. Brain Research Bulletin 62: 351-67.
Kovács M, Jakab E, Kopp M (2001). Középkorú és idős nők lelki egészsége. In: Nagy I, Pongrácz T, Tóth IG (Eds.), Szerepváltozások 2001. Budapest: TÁRKI- Egészségügyi és Szociális Minisztérium, pp. 222-237.
Kovács M, Kopp M, Rózsa S (2003). Hazai adatok. In: M Kovács (Ed.) Időskori depresszió és szorongás. Budapest: Springer Tudományos Kiadó. pp. 44-54.
Mollenkopf H, Marcellini F, Ruoppila I, Széman Zs, Tacken M, Wahl HW (2004). Social and behavioural science perspectives on out-of-home mobility in later life: findings from the European project MOBILATE. European Journal of Ageing 1: 45-53.
National Action Plan (2005). Beszámoló a Kormány részére a Társadalmi össyetartozásról szóló nemzeti cselekvési terv 2004. évi megvalósulásáról és a 2005. évre tervezett intézkedésekről. www.3sz.hu.
National Strategic Report (2005). Nemzeti Stratégiai Jelentés a megfelelő és fenntartó nyugdíjakról Magyarország, 2005 július. http://europa.eu.int/
Regier DA, Burke JD, Burke KC (1990). Comorbidity of affective and anxiety disorders in the NIMH Epidemiologic Catchment Area program. In JD Maser, CR Cloninger (Eds.), Comorbidity of mood and anxiety disorders. Washington, D.C.: American Psychiatric Press, pp. 113-122.
Réthelyi JM, Berghammer R, Kopp MS (2001). Comorbidity of pain-associated disability and depressive symptoms in connection with sociodemographic variables: results from a cross-sectional epidemiological survey in Hungary. Pain 93: 115-121.
Rurik I, Antal M (2003). Nutritional and lifestyle practice of elderly people in Hungary. Acta Alimentaria 32(1): 77- 88.
Stage KB, Bech P, Kragh-Sorensen P, Nair NPV, Katona C, Danish University Antidepressant Group (2001). Differences in symptomatology and diagnostic profile in younger and elderly depressed inpatients. J of Affective Disorders 64: 239-48.
Szádóczky E (2000). Kedélybetegségek és szorongásos zavarok prevalenciája Magyarországon. Budapest: Print-Tech Kiadó.
World Health Organization (2001). The World Health Report: 2001: Mental Health: New understanding, new hope. Geneva: World Health Organization, pp. 27-33.
World Health Organization (2003). Health statistics. www.who.int .
Zonda T, Bartos É, Nagy G (2000). Affektív zavarok szűrése egy budapesti kerület lakosai körében. Orvosi Hetilap 141: 601- 607.

Social Resources and Health Status in Older Polish Women

Beata Tobiasz-Adamczyk

1 Introduction

There is a large body of evidence derived from epidemiological as well as from medical sociological studies, demonstrating differences in the health status of women and men, and the effect of these differences on the quality of life in older age (Arber 1993, Bonita 1996, Macintyre 1996, Arber 1997, Verbrugge 1985, Grundy 2003, Jefferys 1996, Krause 1995).

Among the different gender-related factors that play an important role in differentiating the health status in older age groups are psychological (work force participation, multiple roles, role quality) and cultural determinants of the quality of life (Rodin 1990). Also, the role of earlier life experiences in the quality of life in older age has been confirmed in the studies conducted (Grundy 2000, Macintyre 1996, Hibbard 1991).

The generation of Polish women who are now at the beginning of old age, in the earlier stages of their lives shared both the models of traditional family roles together with occupational activity. The difficulties experienced in their everyday lives determined that their life-circles concentrated almost entirely on familial social environment and work place environment.

Numerous studies have been trying to explain women's attitudes to work activity as a result of economic difficulties and their lack of real expectations on life, associated with professional achievements, professional carrier and self-esteem, and job satisfaction (Titkow 1993, 1999; Tobiasz-Adamczyk 1999).

Different questions, referring to the role of family and work environment as a significant resource of social network and social support, and meaningful determinants of health-related quality of life at the beginning of older age, have emerged. The protective role of marriage has been given much attention and the observations made have confirmed the relationship between marital status and mortality, morbidity and different dimensions of subjective health (Wyke, 1992, Waldrom 1996).

2 Aim of the Study

The aim of the study was to identify gender-related differences in social resources and to analyse how social characteristics from the previous stages of life (family life, occupational history- past and present occupational activity, daily living activity, leisure time activity, social network, life-style, stressful life events, satisfaction with the past and the present life) influence life at the beginning of older age. The study was conducted on the cohort of 65-years-old women and men.

The influence of gender-related inequalities in social characteristics on different dimensions of subjective health as well as on health-related quality of life was also evaluated (Baron-Epel 2001, Benyamini 2003, Fylkesnes 1992, Verbrugge1997, Gibson 1986-7, Manderbacka 1996, Tobiasz-Adamczyk 2005).

In formulating the aims of the study we referred to the WHO Quality of Life Groups definition (1993), and specified our focus as being on

> "an individual perception of their position in life in the context of the culture and value systems in which they live and in relation to their goals, expectations and standards and concerns." (WHOQOL 1995, Farquhar 1995).

The influence of life-experiences and social resources on health status in different stages of life has been defined in terms of "life course approach", which explains many determinants of women's health in older age (Ben Shlamo 2002, Wadsworth, 2003).

The contribution to health outcomes in later life of the various social factors acting independently, interactively, and cumulatively during the life-span, i.e. self-rated health, general well-being, psychological well-being, functional status, was analysed.

3 Material and Methods

In the study, face-to-face interviews were used in the randomly chosen sample of the cohort of 65 years old women and men (control group), all of them citizens of Cracow. The database consists of 412 interviews with women and 321 with men, aged 65.

The structured questionnaire used in the study consisted of several parts addressing socio–demographic characteristics of the respondents' living arrangement: material and financial conditions, marital status and family history; occupational history, size and quality of social network, activity of daily living, leisure time activity, life style (diet, smoking habit, alcohol consumption, physical activity), characteristics of 24 chronic conditions, as well as different dimensions of subjective health.

The description of the family system covers information about marital status, number and type of family members living in one household, family ties and relationships, accordance between expected and real model of family life; emotional support coming from partner, children, grandchildren, expectations and satisfaction with family emotional support, feelings of being loved, emotional ties, stressful life events in the family: alcohol or drug problems, financial problems, retirement, unemployment, life-threatening diseases, disability, death, bereavement, increasing conflicts, separation, divorce.

Occupational history covers past and present activity, kind of duties performed, workplace, position of supervisor, cooperation with co-workers, attitudes toward work, relation with co-workers, job satisfaction, keeping relation with previous work environment in spite of retirement.

Activities of daily living concentrated on participation in household chores, church activities, meetings with family and friends, different kinds of support (instrumental, social) to family member, care of grandchildren, etc.

The quality of life has been assessed from general health perception perspective as well as with a focus on social activity and satisfaction with life. The general health perception dimension has been evaluated on the scales included in the Medical Outcome Study General Health Questionnaire SF-36 test (Steward and Ware 1988), consisting of 8 subscales and concentrating on: general health perception, health potential perception, psychological well-being, physical functioning scale, role functioning limitations due to health status or emotional problems, social life limitation scale and body pain scale. Other quality-of-life dimensions measured included: depression symptoms (Geriatric Depression Symptoms – Geriatric Depression Scale), functional status scale (Groningen Activity Restriction Scale, Kempen 1996), and satisfaction with life (Life Satisfaction Index A, Neugarten 1961).

Statistical analyses were conducted using SPSS 11 Pl for Windows. Differences regarding nominal variables were evaluated by Chi^2 independence test, and differences in distribution of interval variables in groups defined by values of nominal variables using the Mann-Whitney test. The influence of social resources on self-rated health and on particular dimensions of the quality of life was explored in uni- and multivariate logistic regression models.

4 Results

4.1 Demographic Characteristics

Table 1 presents demographic and social characteristics of 65 year-old women in comparison to same-age men involved in the study and shows significant statistical differences in their marital status: 61.8% of the women and 89.1% of the men were married, over one fourth of women were widows (26.5%) in comparison to 6.2% of men, and twice as many women (6.6%) than men (2.8%) were never married. Living alone was reported by 22.5% of the women versus 8.5% of the men (statistically significant differences).

4.2 Social Determinants of Chosen Dimensions of Health-related Quality of Life.

Significant differences in education between women and men have been observed: more women than men had primary and secondary school education, and twice as many men than women had a vocational education. Only 2.2% of the women were never involved in occupational activity, however most women (87.3%) and men (76.3%) had worked in the past; 10.5% of women and twice as many men (23.7%) continued their work activity in spite of retirement.

A supervisory position during work activity was held by 35.3% of women and 49.8% of men (significant differences). Differences in the levels of income were found. Three times more women (25.2%) than men (7.2%) reported low income; high level of income confirmed 15.5% women and 26.2% men (tab. 1).

Significant differences between the mean values of some predictors of health-related quality of life were observed. The number of chronic conditions was higher in women (4,2) than in men (3,5), depression symptoms were higher in women (5,0) than in men (4,4), psychological well-being was better in men (37,0) than in women (35,2), life satisfaction with the present stage of life was higher in men (6,1) than in women (5,6), as was general life satisfaction: 9,5 in men and 8,7 in women (tab. 2).

Contrary to expectations, statistical differences in self-rated health between women (poor health 16.5% – average 2,25, SD 0,79) and men (poor health 13.1%; average 2,35, SD 0,78) have not been confirmed

Table 1: Demographic and social characteristics of respondents

Variables		Women N = 412 n	Women %	Men N = 321 n	Men %	Chi^2 test
Marital status	Married/with partner	254	61,8	286	89,1	Chi^2 = 70,64 *
	Widowed	109	26,5	20	6,2	
	Divorced	21	5,1	6	1,9	
	Single	27	6,6	9	2,8	
Children		360	87,6	303	94,4	Chi^2 = 10,28*
Living alone		92	22,5	27	8,5	Chi^2 = 25,70*
Education	Primary school	109	26,5	49	15,3	Chi^2 =36,08 *
	Occupational school	71	17,2	109	34,1	
	Secondary school	145	35,2	85	26,6	
	Graduated from university	87	21,1	77	24,1	
Occupational History	Never paid worker	9	2,2			Chi^2 = 33,08 *
	Ex paid worker	359	87,3	245	76,3	
	Present paid worker	43	10,5	76	23,7	
Income	Low	104	25,2	23	7,2	Chi^2 = 45,74 *
	Medium	244	59,3	214	66,6	
	High	64	15,5	84	26,2	
Supervisory position		142	35,3	159	49,8	Chi^2 = 15,42 *

* statistically significant differences

Table 2: Mean values of several indicators of quality of life

	Women	Men	SS
Number of chronic conditions	4,2	3,5	*
Independence in everyday activity (GARS)	16,4	16	
Depression symptoms (GDS)	5,0	4,4	*
Psychological well-being	35,2	37	*
Self-rated health	2,25	2,35	
Life satisfaction with previous stages of life	3,2	3,4	
Life satisfaction with present stage of life	5,6	6,1	*
Life satisfaction	8,7	9,5	*

* statistically significant differences

The determinants of poor self-rated health in relation to resources coming from work environment were analysed by the multivariate logistic regression model. The findings showed that in women, perceived need of self-development in professional skills, social interaction with co-workers after stopping work activity and high level of income lowered the risk of poor self-rated health scores, while in men, the corresponding risk was lowered if their occupation required intellectual effort, they were satisfied with salaries, and had social interaction with co-workers after stopping work activity (tab. 3).

With regard to the role of occupational environment, the risk of low self-rated health increased in women who reported being involved in a job requiring intellectual effort, being exposed to unhealthy agents and job stress, while in men no negative associations were found between the work-place-related factors and a heightened risk of low self-rated health (tab. 3).

The role of family environment influenced risk of low self-rated health in a different way: in women, a large social network consisting largely of family members as well as partners available for attending cultural events decreased the number of low self-rated health scores; while correspondingly in men, such factors as support from partner (wife), large size of social network (family members), partners available for attending cultural performances significantly lowered the number of low self-rated health scores. A multivariate logistic regression model showed that being a victim of physical abuse and low life satisfaction increased the risk of higher numbers of low self-rated health scores in women, and in men low life satisfaction played the same role (tab. 4).

Table 3: Determinants of poor self-rated health in relation to characteristics of work environment (multivariate logistic regression model)

	Women			Men		
Factor	RR	95% CI		RR	95% CI	
Perceived need of self-development in professional skills	0,40	0,18	0,89	1,47	0,64	3,38
Occupation requiring intellectual effort	2,72	1,21	6,09	0,41	0,17	0,96
Exposure to unhealthy agents	2,65	1,46	4,81	1,09	0,58	2,05
Job stress	1,85	1,05	3,26	0,94	0,49	1,79
Assessment of salaries as satisfied	0,99	0,56	1,76	0,49	0,26	0,90
Social interactions with co-workers after stopping professional activity	0,32	0,17	0,60	0,26	0,13	0,53
Income level: high vs. low and medium	0,13	0,04	0,45	0,19	0,04	0,85

In model included: psychological effort, too many duties, job control, job autonomy, personal conflicts at work, job satisfaction, positive self-evaluation of social interactions at workplace, high self-esteem due to occupational status, visiting workplace, number of friends recruited from coo workers, education, supervisor position. Adjusted for: number of chronic conditions, psychological well-being, functional independency.

The analysis of all predictors of self-rated health coming from different resources using multivariate models of regression analysis confirmed that friendly atmosphere at work, size of social network in women and high salaries, as well independence in daily living activities in men significantly influenced higher general self-rating of health. The number of chronic conditions, depression symptoms and worsening of health during the last year in both genders as well as the intention to spend more money on medicines and treatment in women and occupation requiring physical effort and poor assessment of one's health potential remained significant predictors of poor self-rated health.

Table 4: Determinants of poor self-rated health in relation to characteristics of family environment (multivariate logistic regression model)

	Women			Men		
Factor	RR	95% CI		RR	95% CI	
Support from partner	0,80	0,49	1,31	0,48	0,23	0,99
Large social network	0,82	0,73	0,93	0,84	0,74	0,95
Attending cultural events	0,83	0,69	1,00	0,81	0,67	0,96
Victim of physical abuse	2,54	1,14	5,57	0,83	0,33	2,12
Low life satisfaction	2,80	1,69	4,64	2,77	1,60	4,80

In model included: agreement between real and ideal model of family, giving support to children, receiving support from: children, parents, brothers and sisters, size of social network, attending cultural events, stressful relations with: partner, family and social environment (neighbours). Adjusted for: psychological well-being, functional independency.

Table 5: Determinants of number of reported chronic conditions in relation to work environment (multivariate logistic regression model)

	Women			Men		
Factor	RR	95% CI		RR	95% CI	
Education: university vs. primary and secondary schools	1,52	0,66	3,51	0,21	0,06	0,74
Supervisory position	2,10	1,21	3,63	2,85	1,43	5,65
Harmful conditions at work	1,83	1,11	3,02	1,90	1,05	3,43
Conflicts at workplace	1,49	0,77	2,88	3,33	1,62	6,86
Social interactions with co-workers after retirement	0,52	0,30	0,90	0,49	0,25	0,95

Included in model: need of self-development in occupational skills, physical and psychological effort, too many duties, job control, job autonomy, job stress, job satisfaction, positive self-evaluation of social interactions at workplace, satisfactory level of salaries, high self-esteem due to occupational status, visiting workplace, number of friends recruited from co–workers, income level. Adjusted for: psychological well-being, functional independency.

The number of reported chronic condition scores increased with holding a supervisory position and harmful work conditions in both genders, and additionally with personal conflicts in work-place in men. For both genders, social interactions with co-workers after retirement and university education in men significantly lowered the number of reported chronic conditions (tab. 5).

Determinants such as stressful relationships with partner, being a victim of physical abuse and low life satisfaction (also in men) significantly increased the reported number of chronic conditions. Support from children lowered the risk of chronic conditions in men (tab. 6).

Table 6: Determinants of number of chronic conditions in relation to family environment (multivariate logistic regression model)

	Women			**Men**		
Factor	RR	95% CI		RR	95% CI	
Support from children	0,63	0,35	1,14	0,45	0,25	0,81
Stressful relations with partner	1,40	1,14	1,75	0,86	0,65	1,14
Victim of physical abuse	2,05	1,03	4,07	2,07	0,80	5,38
Low life satisfaction	1,85	1,45	3,00	2,42	1,37	4,26

Included in model: agreement between real and ideal model of family, giving support to children, receiving support from: partner, parents, brothers and sisters, size of social network, attending cultural events, stressful relations with: family and social environment (neighbours), being a victim of physical abuse, life satisfaction. Adjusted for: number of chronic conditions, psychological well-being, functional independency.

Social interaction with co-workers and an extended social network significantly lowered the risk of depression symptoms in women; in men medium or high level of income and attendance at cultural events decreased risk of depression symptoms. Being a victim of physical abuse and low life satisfaction in women and such factors as stressful relations with wife (partner), being a victim of physical abuse and low life satisfaction in men significantly increased depression symptoms (tab. 7, 8).

Table 7: Determinants of depression symptoms in relation to characteristics of work environment (multivariate logistic regression model)

	Women			**Men**		
Factor	RR	95% CI		RR	95% CI	
Social interactions with co-workers after stopping professional activity	0,50	0,29	0,87	0,83	0,43	1,57
Income level: medium and high income vs. low income	0,64	0,38	1,07	0,34	0,12	0,97

Included in model: need of self-development in occupational skills, physical and psychological effort, too many duties, exposure to unhealthy agents, job control, job autonomy, job stress, personal conflicts at work, job satisfaction, positive self-evaluation of social interactions at workplace, satisfied level of salaries, high self-esteem due to occupational status, visiting workplace, number of friends recruited from coo workers, education level, supervisor position. Adjusted for: number of chronic conditions, functional independency, life satisfaction.

Table 8: Determinants of depression symptoms in relation to characteristics of family environment (multivariate logistic regression model)

	Women			**Men**		
Factor	RR	95% CI		RR	95% CI	
Large social network	0,86	0,76	0,95	0,90	0,77	1,05
Attending cultural events	1,05	0,85	1,30	0,76	0,60	0,95
Stressful relations with partner	1,19	0,94	1,52	1,61	1,16	2,23
Victim of physical abuse	2,99	1,35	6,63	3,14	1,06	9,35
Low life satisfaction	7,56	4,29	13,3	6,48	3,33	12,6

Included in model: agreement between real and ideal model of family, giving support to children, receiving support from: partner, children, parents, brothers and sisters, stressful relations with: family and social environment (neighbours). Adjusted for: number of chronic conditions, functional independency, life satisfaction

Unhealthy work environment, stressful relations with husband (partner) and low life-satisfaction increased risk of low psychological well-being in women; while in men conflicts with co-workers, stressful relations with social environment and low life-satisfaction remained predictors of low psychological well-being (tab. 9, 10).

In women, support coming from children, large size of social network as well as attending cultural events, social interactions with co-workers after stopping work activity, high or medium income in men decreased the risk of low psychological well-being (tab. 9, 10).

Table 9: Determinants of low psychological well-being in relation to work environment (multivariate logistic regression model)

	Women			**Men**		
Factor	RR	95% CI		RR	95% CI	
Unhealthy work environment	1,89	1,14	3,16	1,16	0,65	2,08
Conflicts with?of co-workers	0,88	0,43	1,83	4,64	1,96	9,63
Social interactions with co-workers after stopping professional activity	0,64	0,37	1,11	0,45	0,24	0,84
Income level: high and medium income vs. low income	0,85	0,51	1,42	0,22	0,07	0,70

In model included: need of self-development in occupational skills, physical and psychological effort, too many duties, job control, job autonomy, job stress, job satisfaction, positive self-evaluation of social interactions at workplace, satisfied level of salaries, high self-esteem due to occupational status, visiting workplace, number of friends recruited from co-workers, education level, supervisor position. Adjusted for: number of chronic conditions, symptoms of depression, functional independency.

Our data confirmed that such determinants as the number of friends among previous co-workers, income high or medium, support from husband (partner), large size of social network in women and high self-esteem due to occupational status, support coming from wife (partner), attending cultural events significantly decreased the risk of low satisfaction with the past stages of life (tab. 11, 12).

Table 10: Determinants of low psychological well-being in relation to family environment (multivariate logistic regression model)

	Women			Men		
Factor	RR	95% CI		RR	95% CI	
Support from children	0,47	0,24	0,92	0,83	0,49	1,54
Large social network	0,85	0,75	0,95	0,86	0,75	0,99
Attending cultural events	1,00	0,82	1,23	0,81	0,66	0,91
Stressful relations with social environment	0,96	0,59	1,56	2,10	1,11	4,00
Stressful relations with partner	1,30	1,01	1,68	1,23	0,91	1,67
Low life satisfaction	5,16	3,10	8,59	3,81	2,16	6,71

Included in model: agreement between real and ideal model of family, giving support to children, receiving support from: partner, parents, brothers and sisters, stressful relations with partner and family, being a victim of physical abuse. Adjusted for: number of chronic conditions, symptoms of depression, functional independency.

The risk of low satisfaction with the past stages of life increased in women with stressful relation with partner and being a victim of physical abuse; in men such factors as conflicts in workplace, necessity of giving support to children, stressful relation with wife (partner) and being victim of physical abuse remained predictors of low satisfaction with the past stages of life (tab. 11, 12).

The risk of low satisfaction with the present stage of life decreased in women, who assessed their salaries as satisfactory, had social interaction with co-workers after stopping occupational activity, received support from husband (partner), had an extended social network, and correspondingly increased in women who reported stressful relation with husband (partner) (tab. 13, 14).

Table 11: Determinants of low satisfaction with past stages of life in relation to work environment (multivariate logistic regression model)

	Women			Men		
Factor	RR	95% CI		RR	95% CI	
Conflicts at workplace	0,71	0,34	1,51	2,64	1,21	5,74
High self-esteem due to occupational position	1,14	0,65	2,02	0,36	0,20	0,65
Number of friends among co-workers	0,56	0,32	0,99	0,88	0,43	1,81
Income level: medium and high income vs. low income	0,52	0,31	0,87	0,61	0,21	1,80

Included in model: need of self-development in occupational skills, physical and psychological effort, too many duties, exposure to unhealthy agents, job control, job autonomy, job stress, personal job satisfaction, positive self-evaluation of social interactions at workplace, satisfied level of salaries, social (informal) interactions with co-workers after stopping occupational activity, visiting workplace, education level, supervisor position. Adjusted for: self-rated health, number of chronic conditions, psychological well-being, functional independency.

Table 12: Determinants of low satisfaction with past stages of life in relation to family environment (multivariate logistic regression model)

	Women			Men		
Factor	RR	95% CI		RR	95% CI	
Giving support to children	1,23	0,74	2,06	1,96	1,08	3,53
Support from partner	0,24	0,14	0,41	0,31	0,15	0,66
Large social network	0,79	0,70	0,90	0,89	0,78	1,01
Attending cultural events	1,09	0,91	1,31	0,80	0,67	0,97
Stressful relations with partner	1,57	1,22	2,03	1,42	1,06	1,91
Victim of physical abuse	5,43	2,21	13,3	2,83	1,01	7,92

Included in model: agreement between real and ideal model of family, receiving support from: children, parents, brothers and sisters, stressful relations with family and social environment (neighbours), life satisfaction. Adjusted for: self-rated health, number of chronic conditions, psychological well-being, functional independency.

Table 13: Determinants of low satisfaction with present life in relation to work environment (multivariate logistic regression model)

	Women			Men		
Factor	RR	95% CI		RR	95% CI	
Assessing own salaries as satisfactory	0,55	0,32	0,93	0,83	0,47	1,47
Social interactions with co-workers after stopping professional activity	0,49	0,27	0,86	0,58	0,31	1,08
Income level: medium and high income vs. low income	0,49	0,28	0,85	0,47	0,16	1,37

Included in model: need of self-development in occupational skills, physical and psychological effort, too many duties, exposure to unhealthy agents, job control, job autonomy, job stress, personal conflicts at work, job satisfaction, positive self-evaluation of social interactions at workplace, high self-esteem due to occupational status, visiting workplace, number of friends recruited from co-workers, education level, supervisor position. Adjusted for: self-rated health, number of chronic conditions, psychological well-being, functional independency.

Table 14: Determinants of low satisfaction with present life in relation to family environment (multivariate logistic regression model)

	Women			Men		
Factor	RR	95% CI		RR	95% CI	
Giving support to children	0,90	0,56	1,46	2,47	1,32	4,63
Support from the partner	0,44	0,27	0,72	0,14	0,06	0,32
Support from brothers and sisters	0,82	0,43	1,58	0,35	0,15	0,82
Large social network	0,88	0,79	0,99	0,81	0,70	0,92
Attending cultural events	0,88	0,73	1,05	0,78	0,65	0,95
Stressful relations with partner	1,42	1,13	1,80	1,23	0,90	1,68

Included in model: agreement between real and ideal model of family, receiving support from: children, parents, stressful relations with family and social environment (neighbours), being a victim of physical abuse. Adjusted for: self-rated health, number of chronic conditions, psychological well-being, functional independency.

The risk of low satisfaction with the present stage of life decreased in men who received support from wife (partner), support from brothers and sisters, had large size of social network, attended cultural events. The corresponding risk increased in men giving every kind of support to children (tab. 14).

5 Summary

Demographic and social characteristics of the cohort of 65-year-old Polish women and men (control group) confirmed gender-related significant differences in social resources at the beginning of older age.

The early stage of the older age has been characterized by gender-related differences in the areas of health status and quality of life influenced by determinants coming from previous stages of life; in the stage of advanced age observed differences in health status decreased.

From a historical perspective, and in comparison to others from West-European countries last twenty years, Polish women have been started their work activity on labour market earlier but these cohorts of women presented poorer educational level and mostly have been vocationally active because of economic reasons. In comparison to older cohorts presented, the cohort of 65-year-old Polish women belongs to a generation characterized by a higher level of education (56.3% of the respondents presented a higher level of education, among them 15.8% university level; 18.9% held high occupational position, 35.3% had position of supervisor) and for this generation occupational activity remained a very important dimension of their life (84% confirmed satisfaction with vocational activity) although most of them have been strongly influenced by having to fill both the occupational role and the traditional home role and domestic duties.

Presented data showed that gender-related differences in social determinants stemming from family and work environment significantly influence specific dimensions of health-related quality of life. The same determinants affected the quality of life in women and men in different ways.

Comparison between older Polish women and women at the same age from other West European countries is more complicated. Differences in quality of life vary according to cultural variations in family patterns and intergenerational relations between older mother and adult children and grandchildren. Due to the traditional role in family, older women in Poland have been still strongly involved in an instrumental way, giving social and financial support to their adult children and grandchildren. For many women, retirement means systematical unpaid work focused on help in housekeeping , household chores, caring for grandchildren as well as sharing their retirement pension with children and grandchildren. Excess of older women to care for younger generations of their families remains a significant factor of their tiredness and health outcomes.

In Poland health outcomes in relation to exposure to different environmental and life-style risk factors have concentrated mostly on males due to their high morbidity and mortality especially in middle age groups, less attention has been paid to the role of life-span social determinants on health-related quality of life in women.

Contrary to the generally accepted conclusions our findings confirmed that meaningful relationships with co-workers are important throughout the period of work activity, and continuation of these relationships after stopping occupational activity is perceived as an important social resource especially for women.

Arber (1997) showed that professional qualifications based on the level of education remained a significant predictor of self-rated health in women. Ren (1997) found that women with marital status dissatisfaction or dissatisfaction with informal partner relationships have been perceived as a group with a higher risk of poor self-rated health. Satisfaction with family roles significantly influenced self-rated health in women (Arber 1997).

Marmot (1997) suggested that the relation between social status and self-rated health can be clearly explained in men but in women mentioned relation remained more complicated. Other data (Borg 2000) showed that the relation between previous social status and self-rated health could be explained by social and economical resources stemming from the life experiences

Our data corresponding with other studies mentioned (Arber 1997, Ren 1997, Marmot 1997, Borg 2000) confirmed the significant role of socio-economic position in earlier stages of life on the quality of life in older women as well as showing that for the cohort of 65-year-old women the „ladder" of vocational achievements was associated with many barriers.

Presented data showed that health-related quality of life in Polish women at the beginning of older age will be a strong predictor of their situation in later stages of old age, because of their financial independence, social network consisting of non-relative individuals, experiences based on occupational activity, experiences associated with activity out of family circle, and having learned coping strategies with difficulties of everyday life.

References

Arber S.: Comparing inequalities in women's and men's health: Britain in the 1990. Soc. Science and Medicine, 1997, 44/6: 773- 787.

Arber S., Ginn J.: Gender and inequalities in health in later life. 1993. Soc. Sci. Med. 36/1: 33-46.

Baron-Epel O., Kaplan G.: General subjective health status or age-related subjective health status: does it make a difference? 2001, Soc. Sci. Med., 53/10: 1373.

Ben-Shlomo Y., Kuh D.: A life course approach to chronic disease epidemiology: conceptual models, empirical challenges and interdisciplinary perspectives. 2002, International Journal of Epidemiology, 31: 285-293.

Benyamini Y., Leventhal E. A., Leventhal H.: Elderly people's rating of the importance of health -related factors to their self-assessments of health. 2003.

Bonita R., Howe A.: Older women in an aging world: Achieving health across the life course. 1996, w: Health security for women. World Health Statistics, 49/2: 134-141.

Borg V., Kristensen T.S.: Social class and self-rated health: can the gradient be explained by differences in life style or work environment? 2000, Soc. Sci. Med., 51/7: 1019.

Farquhar M.: Elderly people' s definitions of quality of life. Soc. Sci. Med. 1995, 41/10: 1439-1446.

Fylkesnes K., Forde O.H.: Determinants and dimensions involved in self-evaluation of health. Soc. Sci. Med. 1992, 35/3: 271-279.

Gibson D.M., Interaction and Well-being in Old Age. Is it Quantity or Quality that Counts. Int L J. Aging and Human Development. 1986-87, 24, 1, 29-40.

Grundy E., Holt G.: Adult life experiences and health in early old age in Great Britain. 2000, Soc. Sci. Med., 51/7: 1061.

Grundy E., Sloggett A. Health inequalities in the older population: the role of personal capital, social resources and socio-economic circumstances. 2003, Soc. Sci. Med., 56/5: 935-947.

Hibbard H.J., Pope R.C.: Effect of domestic and occupational roles on morbidity and mortality. 1991, Soc. Sci. Med. 32/7: 805-811.

Jefferys M.: Cultural aspects of ageing: gender and intergenerational issues. 1996, Soc. Sci. Med., 43, 5, 681.

Kempen G.I.J.M., Miedema I., Ormel J., Molenaar W., The assessment of disability with the Groningen Activity Restriction Scale. Conceptual framework and psychometric properties. Social Science and Medicine, 40/11: 1601-1610, 1996.

Krause N.: Sex, marital status, and psychological distress in later life: a comparative analysis. Archivers of Gerontology and Geriatrics, 1995, 21: 127-146.

Macintyre S., Hunt K., Sweeting H.: Gender differences in health: are things really as simple as they seem ? 1996, Soc. Sci.Med., 42,4,617-624.

Manderbacka K., Lundberg O.: Examining points of reference of self-rated health" among Swedish oldest old. Archives of Gerontology and Geriatrics, 1996, 23: 47-60.

Marmot M., Ryff C.D., BumpassL.L., Shipley M., Marks N.F.: Social inequalities in health: next questions and converging evidence. 1997, Soc. Sci. Med., 44/6: 901-910.

Neugarten BL, Havighurst RJ, Tobin SS. The measurement of life satisfaction. J of Gerontology 1961; 16: 134-143.

Rodin J., Ickovics J.R.: Women's Health. Review and Research Agenda as We Approach the 21st Century. American Psychologist, 1990, 45/9: 1018-1034.

Stewart AL., Hays RD, Ware JE jr, The MOS Short-Form General Health Survey: reliability and validity in a patient population. Med. Care 1988; 26: 724-735.

Titkow A.: Historical and social determinants of identity of Polish women. Historyczno-społeczne uwarunkowania tożsamości kobiet w Polsce. 1999, Promocja Zdrowia Nauki Społeczne i Medycyna. 16/VI: 11-10.

Titkow A.: Stress and social life, Polish experiences. Stres i życie społeczne Polskie doświadczenia, PIW, W-wa, 1993.

Tobiasz-Adamczyk B.: Wybrane elementy jakości życia kobiet starszych wiekiem. (Chosen elements of quality of life in older women) 1999, Promocja Zdrowia Nauki Społeczne i Medycyna. 16/VI: 68-83.

Tobiasz-Adamczyk B., Przyski P.: Psychosocial work conditions as predictors of quality of life at the beginning of older age. International Journal of Occupational Medicine and Environmental Health, 2005, 18/1: 43-52.

Verbrugge L., M.: Disability in Later Life Aeging and Quality of Life red. Abeles R.P., Gift H.C, Ory M.G., 1997, Springer Publishing Company, New York.

Verbrugge L., M.: Gender and Health: An Update on Hypotheses and Evidence, 1985. J. of Health and Social behavior 26: 156-182.

Wadsworth M.: Health inequalities in the life course perspective. 1997, Soc. Sc. Med. 44/6: 859-869.

Waldron I., Hughes E., Brooks T.: Marriage protection and marriage selection – prospective evidence for reciprocal effects of marital status and health. 1996, Soc. Sci. Med.,43/1: 113-123.

Wyke S., Ford G.: Competing explanations for associations between marital status and health, 1992. Soc. Sci. Med. 34/5: 523-532.

Double Vulnerability: Older Women and Health in Slovenia

Majda Pahor, Barbara Domajnko & Valentina Hlebec

1 Introduction

Demographic trends in Slovenia follow the same pattern as in other developed countries: for the last twenty years they have showed birth rates decreased by almost 50 per cent, and a constantly increasing number of older citizens (Jakoš, 2002). At the moment, there are 14.6 % of people above 65 (Šelb-Šemerl et al, 2004) and according to a demographic projection, it is expected that older people will represent approximately 16.5 % of the total population in 2020 (Jakoš, 1999). This trend is reported to be on the rapid increase – in the year 2040 the calculations for Slovenia predict 30% of the population to be older people than 65 years of age (Hvalič Touzery, 2005). With respect to gender there is a noticeable misbalance especially in the oldest old stage of life, the majority of the old people being women.

This age distribution is a historically new situation – never before have societies had such a large proportion of older people, therefore new forms of social and political organization are needed. Taking into account a broader socio-political frame, new kinds of risks are brought about by modernization, globalization and, in case of Slovenia, also transition. In this context, the aging of the Slovenian population is for the most part perceived as a new set of problems, not as a great individual and social challenge and achievement. There is little doubt that old strategies regarding employment and retirement, health and social care, social inclusion, housing etc. are no longer adequate. The challenge for decision-makers and politicians in all countries is how to enhance the advantages of this situation and how to support the previously unknown social and economic vulnerabilities. In this chapter vulnerability is interpreted as being exposed to life situations or conditions that make people susceptible to being disadvantaged in physical, emotional and/or economic manners. Vulnerable people can further be interpreted as lacking the knowledge, abilities and/or resources to deal with these disadvantages or risks (Schroder-Butterfill, Marianti, 2006; Grundy, 2006).

In this chapter, the authors address the health-related situation of older women in Slovenia. Our hypothesis is that older women are a progressively vulnerable social group. We take into account the role and importance of social networks and examine the ways they could help to explain gender differences in health and health related support in older women. Our starting point is the gender-related experience of older women in Slovenia. Several studies of the condition of women in Slovenia consistently confirmed their greater workload, nearly complete responsibility for childrearing, underprivileged position in public life and economic deprivation (Kanjuo Mrčela, 2000, Černigoj Sadar, 2000, Jogan, 2000, Švab, 2003). There is no doubt that women are not a homogenous group, and there are significant differences in their status, wealth and autonomy, but still, as Doyal pointed out (1995), they are all more or less underprivileged. Older women were born in the first half of the 20th century and went through its dramatic changes, including the slow (and incomplete) decline of patriarchal patterns in the society. Of course both men and women were involved in these changes and needed to adapt, but our focus here is on women and their condition.

In order to get a broader picture, we will first look at some demographic characteristics of older people and especially women in Slovenia, and summarize results of related studies, which will give us an idea of how older women live in Slovenia, seen through statistics and numbers. We will then look into the scientific and expert literature on the health of older people, published in the last ten years in Slovenia. How do health and social care experts see older women? Do they notice them at all? Thirdly, we will introduce the concept of social networks as a co-determinant of human health and, on the basis of a research study, present sources of support in case of illness of older women. We use data from two representative studies conducted in 1987 (The Stratification and Level of Living Survey in Yugoslavia, 1987; see Boh et al. 2000) and 2002 (Social support networks of residents of Slovenia; see Ferligoj et al. 2002) to compare the provision of social support in case of illness with respect to the transition period in Slovenia.

2 Older Women in Statistic Figures

According to SORS (Statistical Office of the Republic of Slovenia, 2006) although more boys are born than girls, women outnumber men by 2% in Slovenia. Women who died in the year 2004 lived on the average 76.9 years and outlived men of their generation by 8.5 years, while girls who were born that year can expect to live up to 81 years. They will outlive boys born in the same year by 7.6 years. Up to the 58th year of age, there are more men than women in Slovenia. After that age, the relative number of women increases each year. Among people older than 100 years, 84% are women, and people older than 103 years are women only. Among EU 25, the Slovenian girls' life expectancy ranks 15th, and first among the new member states, together with Malta and Cyprus.

Figure 1: Population by age and gender in Slovenia

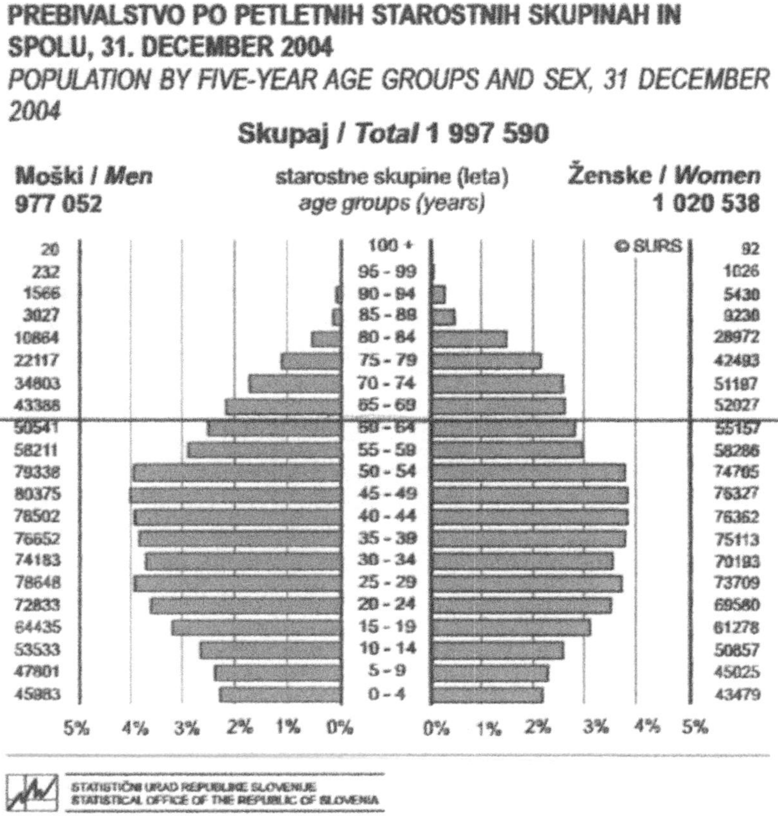

(Source: Slovenia in figures [in Slovene]. Ljubljana: Statistical Office of the Republic of Slovenia, 1994-(2005): 15)

Aging index, which shows relation between old population (over 65) and young population (0 to 14 years), shows gender differences. In 2005, it was 77.0 for men and 134.4 for women, meaning that there are more young than old men in the population and more old women than young ones. Death rate per 1000 population has been stable for the last 15 years – 9.3. Life expectancy has increased in the last 15 years by 5 years for men (from 69 to 74) and by 4 years for women (from 77 to 81) (Statistical Office of the Republic of Slovenia, 2006).

In order to contextualize the process of aging of women in Slovenia, it will be useful to review some data about Slovenian women in general.

Slovenian women work a lot. They represent 44% of the active population, 85% of those between 25 and 49 years of age are employed. Those who are employed mostly work full time (40 hours a week). Paid work and housework take them on the average, employed as well as unemployed, nearly 8 hours a day – only Lithuanian women work more. Meals and personal care take them only 2 hours a day, similar to Finnish and Estonian women, while Italian and French women use much more time for these activities. With four and a half hours of leisure time per day, Slovenian women are on the 10th place out of 15 countries studied. Norwegian women have the longest time available for themselves, nearly six hours per day, plus one more, because they do not need as much time as for household chores as do Slovenian women. In general, Slovenian women have 65 minutes less leisure time a day than men, and this is the largest discrepancy in all of the EU countries (SORS, 2006).

According to the Slovenian health behaviour survey 2001 (Zaletel-Kragelj, Pahor, 2005) the overall prevalence of frequent perception of stress in adults (age 25-64), is 24.3%[1]. It is significantly higher in women (27.0%) than in men (21.0%) (Zaletel-Kragelj, Pahor, 2005). Stress is recognized as one of the basic risk factors influencing a variety of disorders and diseases. It is often related to mental disorders, but lately a lot of research in different countries has been conducted on the connection between stress and cardiovascular diseases (Bosma et al, 1997, Lindbohm, 1999).

If we look at how perception of stress is distributed among women, we see that it is connected with the educational level. It shows a marked "U distribution", meaning that those women with the lowest and the highest educational levels report the highest stress level. This is in accordance with the results of another recent study, which showed that in Slovenia the lowest and the highest educated population groups receive the lowest level of support at their workplace

1 Stress and related feelings were assessed on the basis of two questions: (a) "How often do you feel tense, stressed, or under a lot of pressure?" (1–never; 2–rarely; 3–sometimes; 4–frequently, 5–every day), and (b) "Do you feel that you are able to cope with these feelings?" (1–I can cope with them easily; 2–I can cope with them with moderate effort; 3–I can cope with them with major effort; 4–I can barely cope with them, 5–I cannot cope with them at all). The observed outcome was defined on the basis of cross-classification of both questions: frequent (frequently or every day) perception of tension, stress, or heavy pressure with at least minor difficulties in coping with these feelings. In short we called it "stress".

(Černigoj Sadar, 2002), least of it from superiors. Why is this so? Women with low education level and no professional qualification, who perform subordinate jobs, experience stress due to low income, repetitive work and non-autonomous positions at work. On the other hand, women who have reached high education and compete for better-paid positions on the job market are often seen as "deviant" as they do not comply with the traditional picture of women (Kanjuo Mrčela, 2000, Černigoj Sadar 2000). One of the reasons for stress is a permanent threat of loosing employment, which is extremely important in Slovenia, as women's contribution to the family budget is substantial (for nurses, for example 53%) (Klemenc, Pahor, 2001). In Slovenia women are generally slightly more educated than men (in 1996: women 10.8, men 10.6 years of education) (Hanžek, 1998). Also, their level of education is increasing more rapidly than that of men (Hanžek, 1998). About 57% of higher education students and about 60% of graduates are women (Hanžek, 1999). Also the education of women is more adapted to job requirements (Mohorčič-Šolar et al, 1995). But they work mostly in sectors requiring fewer skills and frequently find themselves at much lower levels of the employment hierarchy. Their professional engagement is limited to specific tasks, which generally do not involve managerial positions associated with higher levels on the hierarchical scale and consequently also with higher prestige (Hanžek, 1998, Javornik, Korošec, 2003). The results of a recent study on the distribution and the amount of housework in Slovenia showed that women spend on the average 28.5 hours per week doing housework (men 7 hours), and 27.3 hours looking after and bringing up children (men 17.9 hours) (Hanžek, 1998). Given the above-mentioned 85% employment rate among women aged 25-49, this workload means a double burden for them. All these separate views on women's position in Slovenia are also reflected in more synthetic indicators, such as the gender empowerment measure (GEM). It measures women's active participation in the public sphere, and is rather low. In the year 2000, Slovenia was on the 25th place out of 66 countries (Javornik, Korošec, 2003).

2.1 The Context of Transitional Changes

Transitional changes in the contemporary Slovenian society and in particular the changes of the social and health care systems can provide some further context to understand the circumstances of the life of older women in Slovenia. Slovenia introduced market economy with strong liberal elements instead of planned economy in the early 1990s. It also started reorganizing the welfare system, including its partial privatization. Previously people had been accustomed to the fact that the costs for health care were covered by the obligatory insurance. Along with the transitional process, the state budget and/or obligatory health insurance cover pay increasingly less for health care. A new system of additional, individual health insurance has been introduced, gently forcing people to invest in advance in a system they do not yet trust.

Due to these changes in the economy as well as in health and social care, it may be argued that old age is becoming an important health risk factor. It affects the health-related quality of life for older people: it influences their decisions regarding the provision of healthy food, sufficient amount of exercise, appropriate housing, life in a healthy environment etc. by turning these factors (or the lack of them) into health risks. This process can be traced on at least two levels.

On the one hand, old age is becoming a risk factor at the material level. Older people's pensions have remained practically unchanged, whereas the health care system (as explained above) is changing in the direction of placing greater financial burdens on individuals. As a result older people's living standard is decreasing. As some of the studies show (Novak, 1998), this was not the case in the former political system. The new financial challenges, brought about by the change of the political and economical systems, are not adequately addressed by relevant adaptations of the social and health care systems to provide equal quality-of-life opportunities for all generations.

On the other hand, the transitional process also bears influence on older people at the psycho-social level. Within the context of health promotion, there is a growing tendency to interpret care for one's health as one's individual responsibility. This concept of self-care is efficient if people have the ability to identify their specific needs, if they are able and know how to make responsible choices regarding a healthy life-style. Taking responsibility for these choices is the other side of taking part in decision-making. But health professionals and policy makers tend to conceptualize older people in Slovenia as passive in relation to health care (see literature review below, section 2.). The voice of older people is largely ignored and their autonomous and critical stance is not supported. The relations of power within health care institutions and health professional–patient communication still do not follow the democratic model (Toš, Malnar 2002, Ule 2003). It seems as if democratization in Slovenia had not yet gone deep enough to include everyday encounters between professionals and service-users in institutional settings.

How does this affect older women? Taking into account the feminization of old age, it actually means that the issues (explained in the previous paragraphs) have predominantly turned into older women's problems.

Gender (together with education, occupation, class and corresponding benefits) is a powerful risk factor. Matcha (1996) talks about the feminization of poverty; some of its elements are also relevant for Slovenian context. It has already been said that in Slovenia 85% of women (aged 24-49) are employed. In spite of the fact that the difference in wages between men and women is among the lowest in EU (women's average salary being 93% of the men's – SORS, 2006), there is a perceived difference in job performance evaluation, occupation related benefits and possibilities of upward mobility (Kanjuo Mrčela, 2000). However, increased female economical dependence on men might be expected in older age. As already said before, women are involved in informal household and caring activities (housework, taking care of children, older people and supporting men) to a much greater extent than men. This can cause a decrease in their work-related benefits. It shows in labour market discrimination as well as accumulating at the material level in later life (lower pension benefits, less income from assets, lower involvement in additional social and health security schemes etc.). Another relevant element for those who are married or living in partnership is the so-called spousal impoverishment. In Slovenia, as in other developed countries, women are expected to outlive their partners. There is a risk of an economical impoverishment in case their partners need to be institutionalized or extra care at home needs to be provided. After their partner's death they might be left with fewer economic resources and might become more dependent on the social security system.

2.2 Conceptualization of Older Women in Slovenia – Literature Review

Quantitative data can be valuably supplemented by qualitative interpretations. Decision-making and policy-planning is based not only on statistical data but also on knowledge on the health of older people. To identify and critically evaluate the nature and quality of this knowledge at the macro societal level, a literature review of expert and scientific publications on older women and health was performed. According to Hart, literature review is: "The selection of available documents (both published and unpublished) on the topic, which contain information, ideas, data and evidence written from a particular standpoint to fulfil certain aims or express certain views on the nature of the topic and how it is to be investigated, and the effective evaluation of these documents in relation to the research being proposed." (Hart, 2001: 13)

Relevant publications were searched through COBISS bibliographic database. Cobiss stands for Co-operative Online Bibliographic System & Services - it is a Slovenian interdisciplinary bibliographic database. Data collection was performed according to selected keywords (health, aged, aging, older people etc.) and took place from the end of April to the middle of June 2004. Only publications of expert and scientific nature were considered (monographies, scientific and professional articles, PhD, MSc and specialist theses, research reports and conference papers). The total number of bibliographical units directly relevant to the health of older people and taken for further analysis was 352. They were grouped into thematic categories. On their basis the map of the prevalent conceptualisation of the older people's health was constructed (Pahor, Domajnko, 2005)[2].

Nearly a quarter of the analysed bibliographical units present the medical viewpoint, stressing the physical and potentially pathological aspect of aging. The prevailing image of older people is therefore one of aging bodies, prone to medical risks and disease. It is important to stress and criticize that sometimes they are perceived and described in terms of a potential burden to the society. The prevailing model of older people's health treatment is the bio-medical one, which, among other things, strengthens the medicalisation of aging. Medicalisation is a process that interprets aging as pathological and in turn legitimizes medical intervention. It is usually associated with deviant behaviour and its social control. However, aging as such is not a pathological process. Rather, its medicalisation might be the sign of its perception as a socially disruptive process.

There is little evidence of active cooperation between older people, their families and professionals. Within the analysed literature the lay-experience of aging is largely ignored. By this we mean that the voice and opinion of older people themselves is not heard. Formal professional help is mainly designed in a way that presupposes older people and their families as passive recipients. Various forms of professional help are undoubtedly extremely important and may substantially contribute to the quality of life of older people. Still, help that is offered may not be the most suitable support for all as each older person has his/her own specific needs. This neglect of the voice of older people is also reflected in the lack of literature on stereotypes, prejudices, vulnerability, discrimination, exclusion and older people abuse. One of the conclusions to be drawn is that old age is still very much tabooed, probably due to its close association with dying. On the positive side, there are also some texts on empowerment, values in old age and interpretation of old age as a value in itself.

We also looked at the use of terminology from the gender point of view. Its characteristic is that masculine perspective is generalized to women. Namely, despite the capacity of the Slovenian language to speak of the older people with gender-neutral expressions, most frequent reference to older people is in masculine gender (in plural and singular). Although it is not uncommon in the Slovenian language to use masculine gender with gender-neutral meaning, on the im-

---

2 Literature review and the map are results of the research conducted within the framework of the project "Integrated care of the elderly" - J3-6423 (2004-2007), funded by the Slovenian Research Agency

plicit level masculine gender is thus taken to be representative of both sexes. This means that old age issues are old men's issues. Although selected literature may not talk about exclusively masculine characteristics of aging, they implicitly generalize the masculine perspective on aging across the whole population, as if there was nothing specific or worth mentioning about aging of women alone.

This is backed up by very scarce evidence of publications focusing on the specifics of aging of women. Out of 352 bibliographic units relating to the health of older people only seven were found addressing women-specific aspects of aging. Six of them were medical, focusing on women-specific diseases, only one of them addressed women's quality of life. Although the number of older women is increasing, older women's issues are largely neglected in Slovenian (scientific/expert) literature on the health of older people. The prevailing conceptualization of older women that is conveyed by this literature can be summarized as aging bodies, highly prone to medical risks and illness, passive, socially marginal, meritless and masculinised.

3 The Role of Social Networks in Relation to the Health of Older People

Positive influence of the social support on the basis of the involvement in social networks is a »solid fact« of human health (WHO, 2003). Many research studies found that the inclusion in social networks is a factor affecting general mortality (Berkman et al, 2000). On the basis of these findings they assumed that social isolation, disintegration and disconnection influence mortality and life expectancy by enhancing aging processes. Studies on aging from the social and biomedical point of view concluded that social isolation is a chronic stress condition, to which the body reacts by aging even faster. Isolation is therefore connected with old age morbidity and functional decline. On the other hand, the strengthening of social ties also improves the cognitive functions of older people (Cotman, 1985). Relationships have an impact on the immune response as well. Older studies already documented an immunity decline in people, who were grieving or living with a seriously sick family member. They also proved the influence of less dramatic aspects of relationships, such as disagreement with partner, or feeling of loneliness. Social isolation can influence immune responses, which regulate latent infections. Conflicts and stress can have strong negative influence on health, and on the other side different forms of support enhance health. But there is a need for more research in order to identify interconnections between these phenomena (Kiecolt-Glaser et al, 1984,1987).

When discussing health of older people, it is important to identify different factors that can help in the aging process, when need for help may increase, for example help with house keeping or shopping etc. One of the influential negative factors is lack of social interaction, as many studies have shown (overview in Kiecolt-Glaser et al, 1987). More recent research is oriented towards the question of how social support helps older people to remain healthy. Of course social support is not the only factor of health – equally important is the influence of class, gender, family and environment in the community. Also special historical circumstances should be taken into consideration, such as actual transitional changes in post-socialist countries in Central and Eastern Europe. How do social networks support health in older people (Ashley, Wasserman, 2002)? The basic assumption of these research studies is that social support mitigates stressors like illness. Research (Choi, Wodarski, 1996) showed that the amount of help one gets is more connected with the size of the network than with the need for help of older people, it is therefore all the more likely that an older person's need for support is met the larger his or her help-network is. There are also indicators that help received may have a sustainable effect – a longitudinal study found that people who had received help at point 1 in time, had less health problems at point 2 as well (Choi, Wodarski, 1996). Similar longitudinal consequences of social support were found in other USA studies (Unger et al, 1998): respondents with more social ties experienced fewer declines of functional abilities in the seven-year period of observation. This applied especially to men and to those who were in worse physical condition at the first measurement. There is a gender-related difference in the relation between the size of the network and the person's benefit – for men already a small network is beneficial, while it seems that women need larger networks for the same amount of support (Shye et al, 1995).

4 Social Networks in Slovenia

The aim of the research project Social Integration of Older People During Transition Period[3] was to evaluate the changes in social support providers for residents of Slovenia over a longer period of time, and to establish whether and to what extent the change in the social, political and economic systems played a part in those changes. The purpose of the study was to analyze the existing secondary data on social support provision, collected in 1987 and in 2002, that is, before and after the change in the system at the beginning of the 90s. However, those data were collected for different purposes and using a different methodology, which prevented us from conducting complex statistical analyses. In the

3 Funded by Slovenian Research Agency: contract. no. 631-10/2003/20.

following paragraph, the original 1987 and 2002 studies are briefly described. Two cross-sectional studies in 1987 (The Stratification and Level of Living Survey in Yugoslavia, 1987; see Boh et al. 2000) and 2002 (Social support networks of residents of Slovenia; see Ferligoj et al. 2002) include data on the personal support networks of the residents of Slovenia (Boh et al., 1987a; Ferligoj et al., 2002). These studies differ in many characteristics:

- sample size: 289 in 1987 and 5013 in 2002;
- interview mode: face-to-face interviews (partly self-administered) in 1987 and computer-assisted telephone interviews in 2002;
- age of respondents: in 1987 the lower age limit was 15 and the upper age limit was 75; in 2002 data were collected only on respondents 18 and over, with no upper limit.

Regardless of these differences, both studies contain basic information about various support provisions. Both surveys provide representative samples of the Slovenian adult population after weighting. In both surveys several social support provisions were assessed, namely minor material aid, social support in case of illness, financial support, emotional support in case of trouble with a partner and in case of sadness or depression, and advice support. However, only three social support provisions were comparable across the studies, among which was also support in case of illness[4] (for further detail see Hlebec, Kogovšek, 2005). All calculations in the tables below were done on these two data sets and for this indicator of social support in the case of illness.

We have data for changes of the role of social networks in the provision of support in case of illness for the years 1987 and 2002, which can illuminate the role of different sources of support. However, the small sample for the year 1987 does not allow for the separate analysis of older women.

Before turning our attention to the support that older women get when they are ill, let us look at who are the sources of support in illness and whether they remain the same over time. The most significant change is a general decrease in the role of the partner and closer family as sources of support, with the exception of the oldest group. There are three sources of support whose importance has

4 Social support in the case of an illness: Suppose you had the flu and you had to stay in bed for a few days and needed help around the home, with shopping and such. Whom would you turn to for help? In 1987 survey only role relationships were measured for the first and the second support provider whereas in 2002 names of actual people were recorded and later coded into roles such as mother, daughter, friend, neighbour, etc. Methodological comparisons showed that only the first provider could be compared across studies (for further discussion see Hlebec and Kogovšek 2005b).

increased: friends, wider family and neighbours. We estimate that we are still far from a possible explanation of these phenomena. There are still open questions about what these changes mean and why they occur. Maybe we could find the reason for the smaller role of the close family in its decreasing size in Slovenia. Namely, in the 2002 census the number of families increased by 33.000 in comparison to 1981, but they are smaller: in 2002 only 3.1 members (SORS, 2005). But still, what does the decrease of the role of the partner in providing social support mean? Does it mean that the networks are opening up from families to include the social environment? Are the relations between family members less and less supportive? Or is this a result of a growing number of households with one member only?

Table 1: Basic differences of sources of social support in case of illness

year/sources of social support	1987[5], n= 274	2002[6], n= 4612
partner	52%	41%
parents	23%	14%
siblings	5%	7%
children	14%	18%
other relative	3%	6%
neighbour	2%	5%
friend	2%	9%

Source: Pahor, Hlebec 2006

5 Gender Differences

General trends are similar for men and women. The role of the partner and the closer family decreased, and the role of the wider family, neighbours and friends increased. The last three sources of support, namely wider family, neighbours and friends, are still marginal, but the growth rates are dramatic. For example: friends are five times more important a source for women in 2002 than in 1987. Also, the importance of the partner decreased more for women than for men, and it was replaced by the close family as the principal support provider.

Table 2: The most important sources of social support in relation to gender (1987n = 273 , 2002 n = 4615)

gender	male		female	
sources of social support// year	1987	2002	1987	2002
partner	57 %	49 %	46 %	34 %
close family[7]	38 %	33 %	45 %	42 %
extended family[8]	0 %	4 %	5 %	8 %
neighbour	2 %	5 %	2 %	6 %
friend	2 %	8 %	2 %	10 %

Source: Pahor, Hlebec 2006

6 Differences Regarding Age

But, if we look at the decreased rate of the role of the partner in different age groups, we see that it is smaller in the oldest group (only for 6% comparing with 27% in the 25-34 years group). The over-65 is the only age group with extended family as an important source of support. It seems that as close family is becoming increasingly small, there is a need to look for support elsewhere.

Table 3: The most important sources of social support in relation to age (1987 n = 273 , 2002 n = 4615)

age	18–24		25–34		35–49		50–64		65–75	
year/ source of social support	1987	2002	1987	2002	1987	2002	1987	2002	1987	2002
partner	17 %	13 %	75 %	48 %	75 %	55 %	52 %	46 %	32 %	26 %
close family	75 %	69 %	26 %	33 %	25 %	27 %	38 %	34 %	41 %	44 %
extended	2 %	2 %	0 %	5 %	0 %	5 %	0 %	4 %	16 %	11 %

7 Parents and children.
8 Siblings and other relatives.

family										
neigh-bour	0 %	2 %	0 %	3 %	0 %	4 %	4 %	7 %	8 %	12 %
friend	6 %	14 %	0 %	12 %	0 %	9 %	6 %	8 %	3 %	6 %

Source: Pahor, Hlebec 2006

7 Age and Gender Combined: Social Support of Older Women and Men

Finally, let us have a look at the sources of social support in illness of older women, on the basis of the data from 2002. We can see that the role of the partner decreases with age, while the role of the close and extended family increases, together with the roles of neighbours and friends.

Table 4: The most important sources of social support in relation to age and gender

age	**50–64**			**65–75**		
source of social support/ gender	**male**	**female**	**total**	**male**	**Female**	**total**
partner	58%	35%	46%	37%	21%	27%
family	23%	45%	34%	40%	48%	45%
ded family	3%	6%	4%	9%	12%	11%
neighbour	8%	6%	7%	9%	13%	12%
friend	7%	9%	8%	6%	6%	6%

Taking into consideration only the 65 to 75 age group, we see that for women the close family (meaning children) is the most important. Partners are less than half as frequent. In general, it seems as if older women's sources were more spread out and more often include extended family and neighbours than men's, whose main sources are (in 77% of the cases) partners and children, while in women those are 69%. Does this distribution represent free choice or is the result of need? Perhaps older women need to rely on other people, because either there are no partners (more women than men in that age group) or the partners are not able or not willing to help. It is possible that men and women mean different things when talking about social support, but we were not able to find that out with the quantitative methodology used in the study. Only qualitative approaches could shed light on the subjective understanding of these phenomena.

8 Conclusions

If we understand vulnerability as a state of exposure to life situations or conditions rendering people susceptible to being disadvantaged in a physical, emotional and/or economic way, we can conclude that older women in Slovenia experience double vulnerability: first, they are women in a still patriarchal society (and belong to the generation with even more pronounced male domination); second, they are old in a social order that more and more celebrates youth, power, flexibility and individualism.

Statistic review shows that women in Slovenia live longer than men and make up the majority in the oldest old age group (older than 100 years). Taking into account unpaid housework and caring for others, they work more and have less leisure time than men. The incidence of stress is higher, increasing related risks for disorders and disease. Slovenian society is currently facing growing privatisation within the healthcare system and a decrease of social security benefits. With the ongoing trend of medicalisation of aging this situation is becoming critical for people dependent on the social security system. With the addition of a weak social image of older people, their enduring passive role within society and especially the neglect of gender-related issues our thesis is confirmed. Older women in Slovenia are a progressively vulnerable social group, not all of them to the same extent, but more or less so. There are structural differences in the older women group and these need further systematic exploration.

These are serious inadequacies hampering the quality of life of older women, but perhaps their involvement in social networks, where they are central figures, might have a compensating effect. Although they are more often on the giving than on the receiving end of social support, there is always reciprocity in human relations. So, do they gain when they give? Anyway, we should not accept the actual lack of structural and formal support as inevitable and transfer the locus of the older female health in the private sphere. It is not uncommon to hear the actual leading Slovenian politicians mention family as the main care provider for older people, accompanied by a progressive retreat of the state/public health from caring for them. The quality of life of older women should be achieved by both approaches: on one hand, by supporting their informal social networks and, on the other, by the formation of formal older-women-centred support-schemes, which would take into consideration their expressed needs.

We have revealed some of the core statistical data and given the idea of what the conceptualisation and the quality of life of older women in Slovenia at this historical moment are like. We have taken into account the importance and relatedness between social networks and health-related issues of older women. At the same time we are aware that we have only scratched the surface. When drawing conclusions, special attention needs to be given to the gaps in research on the health of older people (with a focus on older women) in Slovenia. Literature review showed a lack of research on the lay experience of health and aging, on stereotypes, prejudices, discrimination, abuse, lay attitudes towards death and dying, and on old age as a value. Especially the specifics of aging women (women's issues), their experience and perspectives, and to a lesser degree, health related problems of older women are neglected. Further research is needed into the role of social networks in relation to the health of older women. Interconnections between involvement, partnership, isolation, psychological condition, immune response, life expectancy etc. are complex. They also need to be interpreted in the light of the specifics of the transitional socio-economic process in Slovenia. On the one hand, finding these gaps reflects the limitations of this chapter, but on the other hand it contributes to a more complete epistemological characterization of the study phenomenon and it suggests future research.

References

Ashley DF, Wasserman S. Social support and social networks: synthesis and review. In: Levy JA, Pescosolido BA (ed.). Social networks and health. Oxford: Elsevier Science Ltd., 2002: 29–72.

Berkman LF, Glass T, Brissette I, Seeman TE. From social integration to health: Durkheim in the new millenium. Soc Sci Med 2000, 6: 843–57.

Boh, K. in skupina. Stratifikacija in kvaliteta življenja v Jugoslaviji 1987 [kodirna knjiga]. Ljubljana: Univerza v Ljubljani. Institut za sociologijo in filozofijo pri Univerzi v Ljubljani, 1987. Ljubljana: Univerza v Ljubljani. Arhiv družboslovnih podatkov [i-zdelava, distribucija], 2000.

Bosma H, Marmot G, Hemingway H, Nicholson AC, Brunner E, Stansfeld SA. Low job control and risk of coronary heart disease. In: Whitehall II (prospective cohort) study. BMJ 1997;314: 558-65.

Choi NG, Wodarski JS. The relationship between social support and health status of elderly people: Does social support slow down physical and functional deterioriation? Social Work Research 1996, 20: 52–63.

Cotman C. Synaptic plasticity. New York: Guilford Press, 1985.

Černigoj Sadar N. Spolne razlike v formalnem in neformalnem delu. V: Jogan M. (ed.). Tranzi-cija in (ne)enakost med spoloma. Ljubljana: Univerza v Ljubljani, Fakulteta za družbene vede: Slovensko sociološko društvo, 2000 (Družboslovne razprave, 2000; 16: 31-52), available from URL: http://dk.fdv.uni-lj.si/dr/dr34-35cernigoj.PDF, accessed: July 14, 2006.

Černigoj Sadar N. Stress in the work-place [in Slovene]. Teorija in praksa. 2002,39:81-102.

Doyal L. What makes women sick? Rutgers University Press, New Brunswick, New Jersey, 1995.

Ferligoj, A. et al. Omrežja socialnih opor prebivalstva Slovenije. 2002 [kodirna knjiga]. Ljubljana: Fakulteta za družbene vede in Inštitut Republike Slovenije za socialno varstvo.

Grundy E. Ageing and Vulnerable Elderly People: European Perspectives. Ageing & Society, 2006; 26: 105-134.

Hanžek M (ed). Human development report. Slovenia 1998. Ljubljana: Institute of Macroeconomic Analyses and Development & United Nations Development Programme; 1998.

Hanžek M (ed). Human development report. Slovenia 1999. Ljubljana: Institute of Macroeconomic Analyses and Development & United Nations Development Programme; 1999.

Hart C. Doing a Literature Review: Releasing the Social Science Research Imagination. London (etc.): SAGE Publications, 2001.

Hlebec V, Kogovšek T. The stick and the carrot of secondary data in social network analysis [in Slovene]. Družboslovne razprave 2005; 21:189-203.

Hlebec V, Kogovšek T. Hypothetical versus actual support providers in comparative network research. Metodol. zv., 2005; 2(1): 73-93, available from URL: http://mrvar.fdv.uni-lj.si/pub/mz/mz2.1/hlebec.pdf., accessed: July 14, 2006.

Hvalič Touzery S. The oldest old in Slovenia: a demographiccal overview [in Slovene]. Kakovostna starost 2005; 8: 2-20.

Jakoš A. Elderly population in Slovenia – demographic situation and projections [in Slovene]. Zdrav var 1999; 38: 50-53.

Jakoš A. The demographic threshold [in Slovene]. Urbani izziv 2002; 13: 60-66.

Javornik J, Korošec V (eds). Human development report. Slovenia 2003. Ljubljana: Institute of Macroeconomic Analyses and Development & United Nations Development Programme; 2003.

Jogan M. (ed.). Tranzicija in (ne)enakost med spoloma. Ljubljana: Univerza v Ljubljani, Fakulteta za družbene vede : Slovensko sociološko društvo, 2000.

Konjuo Mrčela A. Spolna konstrukcija menedžerskih vlog: stekleni organizacijski stropovi v devedesetih. V: Jogan M. (ed.). Tranzicija in (ne)enakost med spoloma. Ljubljana: Univerza v Ljubljani, Fakulteta za družbene vede : Slovensko sociološko društvo, 2000 (Družboslovnerazprave, 2000; 16: 53-78), available from URL: http://dk.fdv.uni-lj.si/dr/dr34-35mrcela.PDF, accessed: July 14, 2006.

Kiecolt-Glaser J et al. Psychosocial modifiers of immunocompetence in medical students. Psychosom Med 1984, 46: 7–14.

Kiecolt-Glaser J et al. Marital quality, marital disruption and immune function. Psychosom Med 1987, 49: 17–27.

Klemenc D, Pahor M (eds). Nurses in Slovenia [in Slovene]. Ljubljana: DMSZT, 2001.

Matcha DA. The sociology of aging. A social problem perspective. Boston (etc.): Allyin and Bacon, 1997.

Mohorčič-Šolar V, Bergant M, Emeršič B, Ivančič A, Kodelja-Starin J, Kraigher T. Women in education and work [in Slovene]. Ljubljana: ACS, 1995.

Novak M. Hazardiranje s starostjo. Teorija in praksa, 1998; 35: 1042-1056.

Pahor M, Domajnko B. An integrated approach to the health of the elderly people in Slovenia: literature review from 1994 to June 2004 [in Slovene]. Kakovostna starost, 2005; 8: 20-31.

Pahor M, Hlebec V. Social netwoks and health: transition in Slovenia (in Slovene). To appear in: Zdravstveno varstvo/Slovenian journal of public health, 2006
Schroder B E, Marianty R. A Framework for Understanding Old-Age Vulnerabilities. Ageing & Society, 2006; 26: 9-35.
Shye D et al. Gender differences in the relationship between social network support and mortality: a longitudinal study of an elderly cohort. Soc Sci Med 1995, 41: 935–47.
SORS - Statistical Office of the Republic of Slovenia. Družine v Sloveniji (12.5.2005), available from URL: http://www.stat.si/novice_poglej.asp?ID=549, accessed: October 8, 2005.
SORS - Statistical Office of the Republic of Slovenia. Ob dnevu žena (7.3.2006), available from URL: http://www.stat.si/novice_poglej.asp?ID=980, accessed: July 6, 2006.
Šelb-Šemerl J, Rok-Simon M, Kelšin N, Ivas N. Aging of population in Slovenia: demographic changes and some health care consequences [in Slovene]. Zdrav vestn 2004; 73: 526-531.
Švab A. Kako skrbna je država? : konceptualizacija skrbi v družinski politiki v Sloveniji = Does the state really care? : conceptualisation of care in family policy in Slovenia. V: SEVENHUIJSEN, Selma (ur.), ŠVAB, Alenka (ur.). *Labirinti skrbi : pomen perspektive etike skrbi za socialno politiko*, (Zbirka Politike). Ljubljana: Mirovni inštitut, Inštitut za sodobne družbene in politične študije, 2003, str. 51-73.
Toš N., Malnar B. Družbeni vidiki zdravja. Ljubljana: FDV-IDV, 2002.
Unger JB et al. Stress, coping and social support among young homeless youth. Journal of Adolescent Research 1998, 13: 134–57.
Ule M. Spregledana razmerja: o družbenih vidikih sodobne medicine. Maribor: Aristej, 2003.
World Health Organization. Social determinants of health: the solid facts. Available from URL: www.who.dk/healthy cities/Documentation/, accessed: December 1, 2003.
Zaletel-Kragelj L, Pahor M. Risk factors for non-communicable diseases in adults in Slovenia. Frequency of observed phenomena. Stress and related phenomena in women [in Slovene]. Ljubljana: Katedra za javno zdravje Medicinske fakultete Univerze v Ljubljani, 2005.

Quality of Life and Health of Ageing Women in Hungary: Characteristics and Bio–psycho–social Background Factors[1]

Mónika Erika Kovács

1 Introduction: Ageing and Quality of Life

Similarly to the international tendencies, the remarkable and increasing ageing of the population and the phenomenon of the "feminisation of ageing" are characteristic to Hungary, as well. Life expectancy of Hungarian women in 1900 was 38.2 years and that of men was 36.6 years (gender difference: 1.6 years), while these rates in 2000 were 75.6 and 67.1 years (gender difference: 8.5 years) (Table 1). In 1990 the rate of those older than 60 years was 18.9%, in 2001 this rate was 20.4%, while it is expected that by 2050 the rate of those older than 65 years will be more than 25% (Jeszenszky, 2003). The life expectancy is worse, and the gender difference is more remarkable in the East European region than in Western Europe. While in the 1970s the life expectancy of the Hungarian men and women was better than in the neighbouring Austria, today Austrian men live 7.7 years longer and Austrian women 5.2 years longer than their Hungarian counterparts.

Table 1: Mean life expectancy in Hungary between 1900 and 2000 (Source: Jeszenszky, 2003)

Year	Men (years)	Women (years)	Gender differences (years)
1900	36.6	38.2	1.6
1960	65.9	70.1	4.2
1980	65.5	72.2	7.2
2000	67.1	75.6	8.5

Regarding mental health – which is one of the main indicators of quality of life – international and also Hungarian data show that about twice as much women

1 This study is based on the database of the Hungarostudy 2002 health survey that was supported by the NKFP 1/002/2001, and OTKA TS040889 grants.

than men are suffering from depressive and anxiety disorders (Szádóczky, 2000). Additionally, data from three Hungarian national representative health surveys - Hungarostudy 1988, 1995, 2002 (Kopp et al, 2005; Skrabski et al, 2004, 2005; Rózsa et al, 2006) - show that both the prevalence and the gender difference of depressive symptomatology are increasing by age (Figure 1). According to these data, that the female older population is growing and that mood and anxiety disorders affect more women than men, we can imagine what a big challenge our nations need to face to give not only years to our older women but also life quality.

Figure 1: Beck Depression (BDI) means scores by age in 1988, 1995 and 2002, and BDI mean scores by age in women and men in 2002

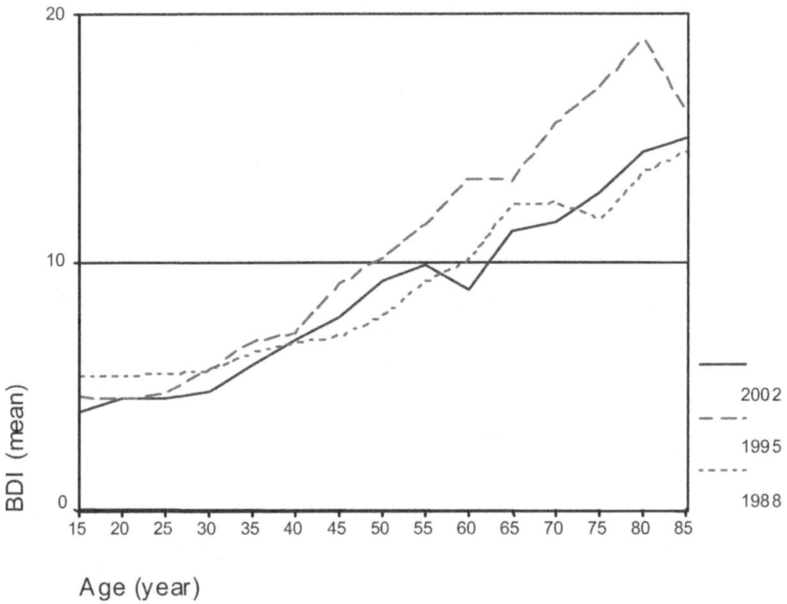

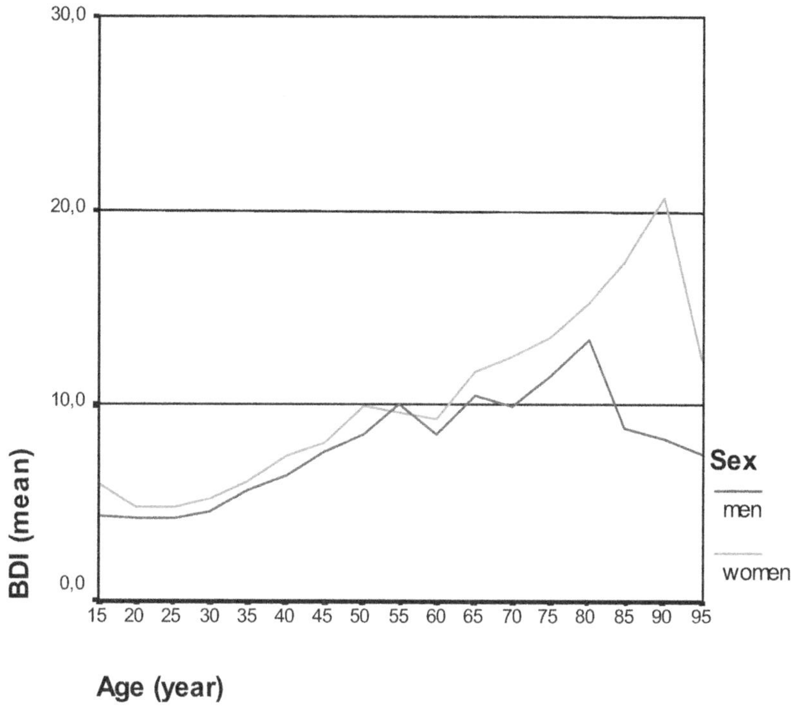

However it is also important to be aware of the following paradox phenomenon of depression and suicide in late life. Generally women marry with older men, and in many cases older women have to take care of their spouse for some time in their later life stages. Additionally, women have better life expectancy, so they have a higher risk to become a widow and live and cope with their own declining physical and mental health alone for years after the death of their spouse. Nevertheless from the aspect of completed suicide – the saddest evidence of unsuccessful ageing – it is the population of older men who is at the highest risk, especially those who are older than 75 years and live alone. On the other hand mental problems of the older men remain hidden more often than those of older women (Laidlaw, 2003).

It is a natural process that older individuals have a decline in physical health, mobility, physical power and ability, and also in their everyday functioning in more or less extent, which may interfere with their participation in the activity of the society. On the other hand the most serious "myth" about ageing is that it is normal to have physical and mental diseases and suffering. Many of the oldest old persons – even with serious diseases – do not feel mentally or physically disabled. The decline that can be seen in some older individuals, is rather due to their isolation or limitation in mobility (Vaillant, Mukamal, 2001; Baltes, Smith, 2002).

It is important to know the dimensions and the positive or negative background factors of quality of life, and as well as of the subjective and objective health in late life, so as to be able to evaluate the extent of *excess disability*. Excess disability is the part of the disability that can be detected in addition to the part that is proportional with the actual physical disease or cognitive impairment, in other words, that part, which cannot be explained by the objective severity of the actual physical or mental disease. Excess disability can be decreased or eliminated, and consequently the quality of life can be improved if we find its psychological and/or social background factors.

Knowledge about the factors of quality of life in the older population is significant also from the aspect of *"active and successful ageing"*. This model - developed by the WHO (2002) - pay our attention to that older people should be regarded as active participants of a society, and should be supported to have the best health and the highest level of functional independence as possible. The society should also provide the old individuals with safe and protected life circumstances, independently from their health and socio-economic state.

Table 2: The most important quality of life dimension reported by the Hungarian ageing population (Source: Tróznai, Kullmann, 2003)

The most important quality of life dimensions:
Health versus illness and pain
Family versus loneliness
Giving and getting help / support
Love and human relations
Talking with others
Peace "inside" and "outside"

When talking about the quality of life of the ageing population, we can differentiate *"welfare"* and *"wellbeing"*. Analyses and also media reports in Hungary generally focus on the "welfare" of the older people (Kovács, Jeszenszky, 2006). However the significance of the dimensions of "wellbeing" in late life was underlined by the results from the Hungarian adaptation of the *WHOQOL-Old* questionnaire, which was developed by the WHO to assess the different facets of quality of life in the ageing population. Old population reported the following quality of life dimensions as the most important ones in their life (Table 2.) (Tróznai, Kullmann, 2003). In our data below – resulted from Hungarian national representative health survey, Hungarostudy 2002 – we will focus on the wellbeing, not on the welfare of the Hungarian population.

2 Data from a Hungarian National Representative Health Survey – Hungarostudy 2002

2.1 Subjects and Methods of the Survey

Data were obtained from a national health survey – Hungarostudy 2002 – representative for the adult (aged 18 years or older) Hungarian population by age, sex and settlement size (Kopp et al, 2005; Skrabski et al, 2004, 2005; Rózsa et al, 2006). The whole sample size was 12,668 persons. Participants were asked in their homes by a set of questionnaires containing 117 group of questions, including validated questionnaires. Data were obtained about health and illnesses, and their bio-psycho-social background factors.

In this chapter, I will analyse the following quality of life measures and background factors (Table 3).

Table 3 Analysed variables

Quality of life measures	**Background factors**
Self-reported physical illnesses	Age, gender
Pain symptoms	Socio-economic state
Depressive symptomatology	Family state
Anxiety symptoms	Coping (emotionally- and problem-based)
Self-assessed general state of health	Dysfunctional attitudes
Illness intrusiveness	Life purposes
Vital exhaustion	Hostility
Working disability	Social support
General quality of life (well-being)	Life events
	Sleep disturbances

2.1.1 Quality of Life Measures

Rate of self-reported physical illnesses: The Hungarostudy 2002 questionnaire contains a detailed, 22-item list of different diseases. Participants were asked whether they had been treated due to any of these diseases. They had the following options to answer: "No", "Yes, previously", "Yes, in the previous 12 months as an out-patient", "Yes, in the previous 12 months as an in-patient/in hospital". After asking all the 22 diseases, they were asked: *"Which disease from this list had the major impact on your everyday life in the previous 12 months?"*. In order to make the statistical analysis and the comparisons easier, we formed disease groups from the 22-item list, and created a 10-item list from the disease that were signed the most frequently by the participants as their major health problem. The list of the most frequent *"main diseases"* are the following:

- Musculosceletal diseases,
- Cardiovascular diseases,
- Allergy and asthma,
- Gastrointestinal diseases,
- Diabetes,
- Eye diseases,
- Depression,
- Cerebrovascular diseases,
- Tumours,
- Renal diseases.

All the other diseases that were signed less frequently were categorised into the "Other diseases" group. When talking about the rate of "main diseases" we do not mean the absolute prevalence of the different diseases, but the proportion of the whole sample that signed e.g. diabetes as the disease that has the major impact on their everyday life, as we explained above.

Pain symptoms were analysed by the following two questions: *"Do you actually have pain symptoms?"*, answer options: "yes"/"no". *"If yes, do they limit your daily activities?"*, answer options: "not", "yes, moderately", "yes, markedly".

Depressive symptoms were assessed with the 9-item *Shortened Beck Depression Inventory* (BDI)[2] (Beck et al, 1961; Beck AT, Beck RW, 1972; Kopp et

2 Question within the Shortened Beck Depression Inventory: I have lost all of my interest in other people/ I can't make decisions at all any more/ I wake up several hours earlier than I used to and cannot get back to sleep/ I am too tired to do anything/ I am so worried about my physical problems that I cannot think about anything else/ I can't do any work at all/ I feel that the future is hopeless and things cannot improve/ I am dissatisfied or bored with everything/ I feel

al, 1995, 2000). The 9 items contain the following characteristics of the depressive symptomatology: social withdrawal, problems with decision making, sleep disturbances, fatigue, extensive worry about body symptoms, working disability, pessimism, inability to feel joy, self-blaming. Sum of the shortened version can be reliably transformed into the full score (Kopp, Skrabski, Szedmák, 2000), which can be categorised in the following manner (Eaves, Rush, 1984): 0-9: not depressed, 10-18: mild, 19-25: moderate, >25: severe depressive symptomatology. Analysis of the psychometric characteristics of the shortened BDI showed, that its cut-point 19 gave the closest rate of depressed individuals to that of found by structured diagnostic interview (DIS), based on clinical depression categories (Rózsa, Szádóczky, Füredi, 2001).

Anxiety symptoms was measured how characteristic the following statement one assessed to herself/himself: *"Recently I feel tense or wound up."* (According to Zigmond, Snaith, 1983). Answer options: "not characteristic", "slightly characteristic", "characteristic", "totally characteristic".

Self-assessed general state of health was measured on a 5-point scale: 1 = poor, very bad, 2 = bad, 3 = fair, acceptable, 4 = good, 5 = very good, excellent. This 5-point self-rating scale was shown to be a simple but reliable and valuable measuring tool of the general health state (Idler, Benyamini, 1997).

Illness Intrusiveness Scale[3] (Devins et al, 1983; Devins et al, 2001; Novák et al, 2005): The 13-item self-administered scale assesses to what extent the symptoms of a chronic disease affect the different fields of everyday life and functioning, such as health, eating, work, relaxation, rest out, financial state, partnership, sexual life, family and other relationships, self-development, religious life, social activity, sleep and daytime freshness, fatigue, daytime sleepiness, sense of well-being, mood. These items create a 3-factor model: 1) relationships and personal development, 2) intimacy, 3) instrumental life domains. Answers are from 1 (not at all) to 7 (considerably) on a visual-analogue scale. Minimum point is 0, maximum is 91.

---

guilty all of the time. *Answer options:* 0. Not characteristic at all, 1. Scarcely characteristic, 2. Characteristic, 3. Fully characteristic

3 *Question within the Illness Intusiveness Rating Scale (IIRS)*: How much does your illness and/or its treatment interfere with your: Health/ Diet (i. e., the things you eat and drink)/ Work/ Active reaction (e. g., sports)/ Passive recreation (e. g., reading, listening to music)/ Financial sitution

Relationship with your spouse (girlfriend or boyfriend if not married)/ Sex life/ Family relaitons/ Other Social Relations/ Self-expression / self-improvement/ Religious expression/ Community and civic involvment. *Answer options:* Not very much 1 2 3 4 5 6 7 Very much/ Not at all = 0

Vital exhaustion was measured with the *Shortened Vital Exhaustion Questionnaire*[4] (Falger, Appels, 1982; Appels, Mulder, 1988; Kopp et al, 1996; Kopp et al, 1998) that was developed to measure the symptoms of vital exhaustion, which is the most important measure of the physiological and psychological state of chronic stress. In Hungarostudy 2002 we used a 5-item shortened version with answer options 0=not, 1=yes. Minimum point is 0, maximum is 5.

Working disability was measured on a 7-point scale: 0 = no working disability,1 = mild working disability, 2 = moderate working disability, 3 = marked working disability, 4 = not able to do paid work (as an employee), 5 = bound to chair or wheelchair, 6 = bound to bed.

General quality of life was measured with the 5-item *WHO Well-Being Index* (Bech et al, 1996). Possible total scores are from 0 to 15. We formed four categories: "totally missing well-being (0)", "decreased well-being (1-5)", "well-being (6-10)", and "total well-being (11-15)".

2.1.2 Background Factors:

Shortened Ways of Coping Questionnaire[5]: The original questionnaire (Folkman és Lazarus, 1980) - that contained 68 items – was developed to analyse what kind of cognitive and behavioural coping strategies individuals use in difficult life situations. The 16 shortened Hungarian version is based on the factoranalysis

---

4 Question within the Shortened Vital Exhaustion Questionnaire:
Do you often feel tired?/ Do you often have trouble falling asleep?/ Do you wake up repeatedly during the night?/ Do you feel weak all over?/ Do you lately feel more listless than before?/ Do little things irritate you more lately than they used to?/ Do you sometimes feel that your body is like a battery that is losing its power?/ Do you feel dejected?/ Do you ever wake up with feeling of exhaustion and fatigue? *Answer options:* 0 no, 1 uncertain, 2 yes.

5 *Question within the Shortened Ways of Coping Questionnaire:* Recall a difficult situation in your life, try to put yourself into your state of mind at that time and indicate on the list of answers given below which occurred to you and to what extent in the weeks following the event.
1. Went over the problem again and again in my mind to try to understand is/ 2. Bargained or compromised to get something positive from the situation/ 3. Made light of the situation; refused to get too serious about it/ 4. I was inspired to do something creative/ 5. I changed or grew as a person in a good way/ 6. I tried to get rid of the problem for a while, I tried to rest, I went on holidays/ 7. I tried to make myself feel better by eating, drinking, smoking/ 8. I tried to make myself feel better by using drugs or medication/ 9. I put everything on one card and began something very risky/ 10. I asked a relative or friend I respected for advice/ 11. I tried to keep my feelings to myself/ 12. I took out my feelings on others/ 13. I came up with a couple of different solutions to the problem/ 14. I prayed/ 15. I tried to see things from the other person's point of view/ 16. I tried to see the humorous side of the situation. *Answer options:* 0. was not characteristic, 1. was scarcely characteristic, 2. was characteristic, 3. was very characteristic.

of Hungarostudy 1988 and 1995 representative health survey results (Kopp et al, 1996). We compared those using problem-based with hose using emotionally-based coping in the majority of their problems.

Shortened Dysfunctional Attitudes Scale[6] (Weisman, 1979; Kopp et al, 1996): This scale was developed by Weisman & Beck (1979), and shortened to 35 items by Burns (1980). In Hungarostudy 2002 we used the 7-item shortened scale of the Hungarian version (Kopp, 1985, 1996). The questionnaire assesses seven attitudes: 1) need for external appreciation, 2) need to be loved, 3) need for achievement, 4) perfectionism, 5) rightful expectations, 6) omnipotency, 7) external control / autonomy. Based on the research of Beck and his colleagues, there is a strong association between depression and anxiety and dysfunctional attitudes. If someone strongly agree with many of these attitudes, that is a risk for depression, since the person has difficulty to fulfil his strict internal expectations. Answer options: 0 = disagree very much, 1 = disagree slightly, 2 = agree slightly, 3 = agree strongly. Minimum point is 0, maximum is 21.

Purposes of Life Scale[7] (Crumbaugh, Maholick, 1964): In Hungarostudy 1988 and 1995 we used a 4-item shortened version of the originally 20-item scale. In Hungarostudy 2002 we asked only those two items, which had higher factor-weight after the factor-analysis of the of the database of Hungarostudy 1995 (Kopp et al, 1996, 1998, 2000).

Hostility-score was measured with the shortened – 5-item version – of the *Cook-Medley Hostility Scale*[8] (Cook, Medley, 1954; Kopp et al, 1996). Answer options: 0 = disagree very much, 1 = disagree slightly, 2 = agree slightly, 3 = agree strongly. Minimum point is 0, maximum is 15.

---

6 Question within the Shortened Dysfunctional Attitudes Scale:
My value as a person depends greatly on what others think of me./ If a person I love does not love me, it means I am unlovable./ If I fail at my work, then I am a failure as a person./ I should be upset if I make a mistake./ If I do nice things for someone, I can anticipate that they will respect me and treat me just as well as I treat them./ I must try to help everyone who needs it./ My happiness is largely dependent on what happens to me. *Answer options:* 0. Disagree very much, 1. Disagree slightly, 2. Agree slightly, 3. Agree strongly.

7 Question within the Shortened Purposes in Life Questionnaire:
I am reliable (Used in Hungarostudy 2002), I have no goals in life, Every single day is new and different, I am generally bored (Used in Hungarostudy 2002).
Answer options: 0. Not characteristic at all, 1. Scarcely characteristic, 2. Characteristic, 3. Fully characteristic. 0 Not characteristic at all - 3 totally characteristic

8 *Question within the Shortened Hostility Scale*: People are honest because they fear from the exposure
My every relative is well meaning with me/ Nobody takes care of the others/ The best is if you distrust anybody/ If I have heard the success of a friend of mine, I feel I am frustrated
Answer options: 0. Not characteristic at all, 1. Scarcely characteristic, 2. Characteristic, 3. Fully characteristic.

Social Support Scale[9] (Caldwell, Pearson, Chin, 1987): We used a 13-item version based on the Hungarian adaptation and the Hungarostudy 1988 health survey (Kopp et al, 1996). It assesses whose help and to what extent someone can count on in a difficult situation. Answer options are 0 = none, 1 = little, 2 = moderate or average, 3 = a great deal.

Live events was asked with the Hungarian adaptation of the *Rahe-Holmes Life Event List* from the *Brief Stress and Coping Inventory*[10] (Holmes, Rahe, 1967; Rahe, 1975; Miller, Rahe, 1997; Rahe, Tolles, 2002), which contains 27 items on the positive and negative changes in someone's work, economic situation, home, family, personal life and social relationships (Skrabski, Kopp, Kawachi, 2004, Szabó, Rózsa, 2006 Participants of our survey answered whether they had the given life event in the previous 5 years, and if yes, to what extent the event affected them emotionally (on a 1-10 scale, 1 = very negative, 5 = indifferent, 10 = very positive impact).

Sleep disturbances was measured with the *Athens Insomnia Scale* (Soldatos, Dikeos, Paparrigopoulos 2001, 2003; Novák et al, 2004), a self-administered psychometric instrument based on ICD-10 and consisting of 8 items. The first 5 (assessing difficulty with sleep induction, awakenings during the night, early morning awakening, total sleep time, and overall quality of sleep) correspond to criterion A for the diagnosis of insomnia according to ICD-10, while the requirements of a minimum frequency (at least three times a week) and duration (1 month) of any complaints correspond to criterion B of the ICD-10. The ICD-10 requirements of marked distress caused by the sleep problem and/or interference

9 *Question within the Social Support Questionnaire*: In a difficult situation, whose help can you count on from: parents/ parents, but already died/ husband / wife/ husband / wife, but already died / spouse

schoolmates, co-workers / neighbours/ friends/ child/ relatives/ helping professionals/ religious group/ civil group, association. *Answer options:* 0 = none, 1 = little, 2 = moderate or average, 3 = a great deal.

10 *Question within the* Shortened Rahe and Holmes Life Event Scale (from the Brief Stress and Coping Inventory): Have the following events happened to you in the previous 5 years? If yes, please assess on a 10 point scale to what extent it affected you emotionally (0 = did not happen, 1 = affected very negatively, 5 = indifferent, 10 = very positively affected).

1. Change in your work conditions/ 2. Loss of your job/ 3. Retirement/ 4. A serious illness or injury

Spouse leaves home/ 5. Divorce/ 6. Death of a spouse/ 7. Death of a close relative (other than spouse)/ 8. Marriage/ 9. Major change in health or behavior of a family member/ 10. Pregnancy, birth of child/ 11. Miscarriage or abortion/ 12. Change in relationship with spouse/ 13. Separation from spouse/ 14. Child leaves home/ 15. Change of work, school/ 16. Change in political beliefs/ 17. Change in religious beliefs/ 18. New, close, personal relationship/ 19. Major decision about your future/ 20. Major personal achievement/ 21. Death of a close friend/ 22. Major loss of income/ 23. Major increase in income/ 24. Loss/damage to personal property/

11 Troubles at work/ 26. Credit difficulties

with ordinary activities of daily living (criterion C) are covered through the strictly subjective nature of the response options for every item of the scale as well as through the content of the last three items pertaining to the next day consequences of insomnia (problems with sense of well-being, functioning, and sleepiness during the day). Each item of the AIS can be rated 0-3, (with 0 corresponding to "no problem at all" and 3 "very serious problem"). Total score ranging from 0-24.

In my analysis I compare the data of the population aged 65 years or older (20.5% of the whole sample, N=2589, 1635 women and 950 men) with the population younger than 65 years (79,5% of the whole sample, N=10050, 5346 women and 4707 men). Besides descriptive statistics I used odds ratio (OR) 95% confidence interval (95%CI), ANOVA and Tukey post-hoc analysis to investigate whether the different quality of life measure scores are significantly different in the different diseases, and linear regression and General Linear Model as multivariate analyses. Associations of the different quality of life measures were analysed by partial correlation, controlled for age, sex, socio-economic and family state. All statistical analyses were done by the SPSS 10.0 version.

2.2 Results – Physical and Mental Health and Illnesses, General Health State, and Their Impact on Everyday Psychosocial Functioning

The rate of self-reported main diseases: Table 4 shows the rate of the main diseases in the older and younger male and female population.

Not surprisingly, the older population reported to have at least one main disease that affects their everyday life more frequently than the younger one (82.2% vs. 51.6%). The two most frequent main diseases are musculosceletal and cardiovascular diseases both in the older and the younger population, in both sexes, but the third one is diabetes in the old, and allergy/asthma in the young. Altogether, more women (84.6%) than men (78.1%) aged 65 years or above reported to have one main disease (OR: 1.5, 95%CI: 1.2-1.9). In 31.4% of women musculosceletal diseases, in 23.8% cardiovascular diseases, and in 5.1% diabetes was the main disease. Cardiovascular diseases (25.2%), musculosceletal diseases (21.9%), and diabetes (4.3%) were reported as the main disease in men.

Table 4: Distribution of the main diseases in the populations above and below the age of 65 years in men and women.

Main disease (%)	**65+ years**			**18-64 years**		
	Men	**Women**	**Total**	**Men**	**Women**	**Total**
1. Musculoscele-letal	21.9	31.4	28.0	13.8	16.4	15.2
2. Cardiovas-cular	25.2	23.8	24.3	9.9	10.7	10.3
3. Diabetes	4.3	5.1	4.8	2.2	1.6	1.9
4. Eye	3.6	4.4	4.1	1.7	1.2	1.4
5. Cerebrovas-cular	3.7	3.5	3.6	1.0	.5	.7
6. Gastrointes-tinal	3.0	2.5	2.7	3.4	3.0	3.2
7. Allergy. asthma	2.1	2.5	2.3	4.2	6.6	5.5
8. Tumor	2.9	1.3	1.9	.9	1.1	1.0
9. Depression	.8	1.3	1.1	.8	2.7	1.8
10. Renal	.9	.8	.8	1.0	.9	.9
All other	9.5	7.9	8.5	8.8	10.1	9.5
None	21.9	15.4	17.8	52.2	45.0	48.4
Total	100.0	100.0	100.0	100.0	100.0	100.0

Pain symptoms: Risk of having pain symptoms are three times higher in the population older than 65 years than in the younger one (71.4% vs. 42.4%, OR: 3.4, 95%CI: 3.1-3.7), this difference is a little bit bigger in women than in men (OR_{women}: 3.5, 95%CI: 3.1-3.9 vs. OR_{men}: 3.1, 95%CI: 2.7-3.6). Actual pain symptoms cause *daily limitations in a high extent* in 35.6% of women, *moderately* in 46.6%, and *does not limit* 17.9% of women. These rates in men are: high limitation: 29.0%, moderate: 50.6%, no limitation: 20.3%. Daily limitations caused by pain symptoms are significantly lower in the population younger than 65 years: in women high limitation: 18.9%, moderate: 51.7%, no limitation: 29.3%, in men high limitation: 18.7%, moderate: 47.3%, no limitation: 34.0%.

Mental health – depression and anxiety symptoms: Beck Depression (BDI) mean scores are increasing by age both in women and men. Although they are higher in women than in men in every age group, this gender difference is increasing above the age of 55 years (Figure 1). BDI mean score is higher than the cut-point 10 both in women and men older than 65, so we can say that the average old population is at least mildly depressed. The risk of having clinically significant depressive symptomatology (BDI≥19, moderate or severe depressive symptoms) is three times higher in the older population than in the younger one (25.3% vs. 10.4%, OR: 2.9, 95%CI: 2.6-3.3). Beck depression severity categories in women and men older than 65 years are shown in Figure 2. These categories in the population younger than 65 are the following:

not depressed:	men: 77.1%,	women: 74.2%,
mild depressive symptomatology:	men: 13.0%,	women: 14.9%,
moderate:	men: 5.0%,	women: 5.0%,
severe:	men: 4.9%,	women: 5.8%.

Only 7.3% (women: 8.5%, men: 4.6%) of those who have clinically significant depressive symptomatology was treated due to depression in the previous 12 months of the survey. The rate of the recognised and treated depressive cases are slightly higher - 10.4% - in the younger population (women: 13.7%, men: 6.2%).

The rate of those who reported that it is characteristic or totally characteristic to them that they have anxiety symptoms (tension or nervousness) is similar in the older than in the younger population (25.7% vs. 25.2%). However these rates are higher both in the older and the younger women than in the men (65+: women 29.1%, men 19.8%, age less than 65: women 27.9%, men: 22.1%).

Self-assessed general state of health: Not only the rate of self-reported diseases was higher in the ageing population, but also they assessed their general state of health as much worse than the younger population. Self-assessment of the general health state is getting worse by age, this worsening is more remarkable from the age of 40, and another less strong worsening comes after the age of 60. This worsening tendency is parallel in women and men until the age of 60, but after this age women assess their general health state as worse than men (Figure 3). 11.9% of individuals older than 65 years assesses their state of health as very bad, 24.2% as bad, 47.3% as fair, 15.1% as good, and 1,4% as very good, excellent. These rates in the population younger than 65 are: very bad 2.8%, bad 8.6%, fair 37.0%, good 42.7%, and excellent 8.9%. Significantly more older person assesses their health state as very bad or bad, than younger ones (36.2% vs. 11.4%, OR: 4.4, 95%CI: 3.9-4.9). This difference is even higher in women

(women: 38.8% vs. 11.4%, OR: 4.9, 95%CI: 4.3-5.6; men: 31.8% vs. 11.2%, OR: 3.7, 95%CI: 3.1-4.3).

Figure 2: Beck Depression Inventory severity categories in the population aged 65 or more years

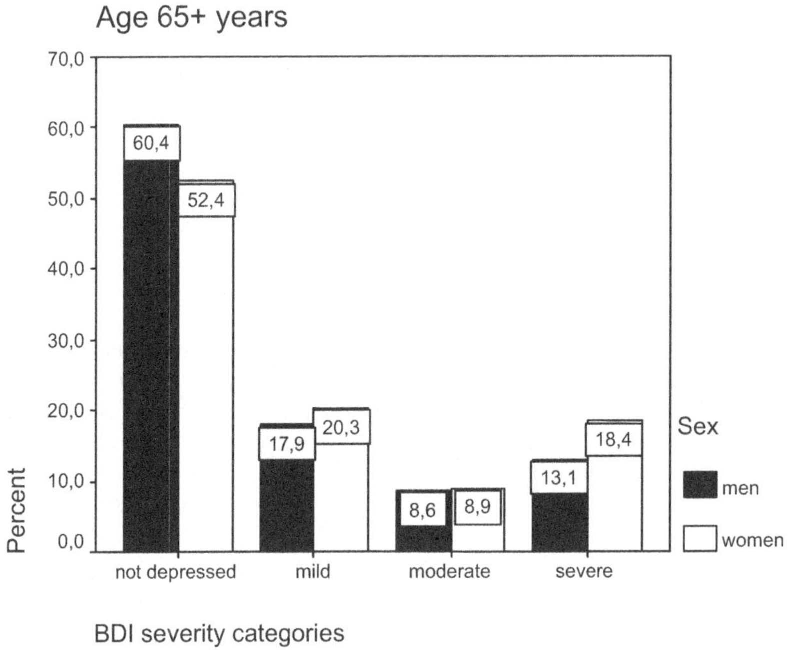

Illness intrusiveness: The extent of the impairment in everyday psychosocial functioning caused by diseases is significantly ($p<0.001$) higher in the older than in the younger population. Illness intrusiveness scores are higher in women than men in every age group. However the three most frequent illnesses that cause the major impact on everyday life are the musculosceletal and cardio–vascular diseases and the diabetes in the older population, and the musculosceletal and cardiovascular diseases and allergy or asthma in the younger one, it is depression and the cerebrovascular diseases that are accompanied by the highest illness intrusiveness scores in both women and men (Figure 4, 5).

Figure 3: Self-assessed general health state mean scores by age (in 5-year age groups) in women and men. (Minimum point – very bad – is 1, maximum point – very good – is 5).

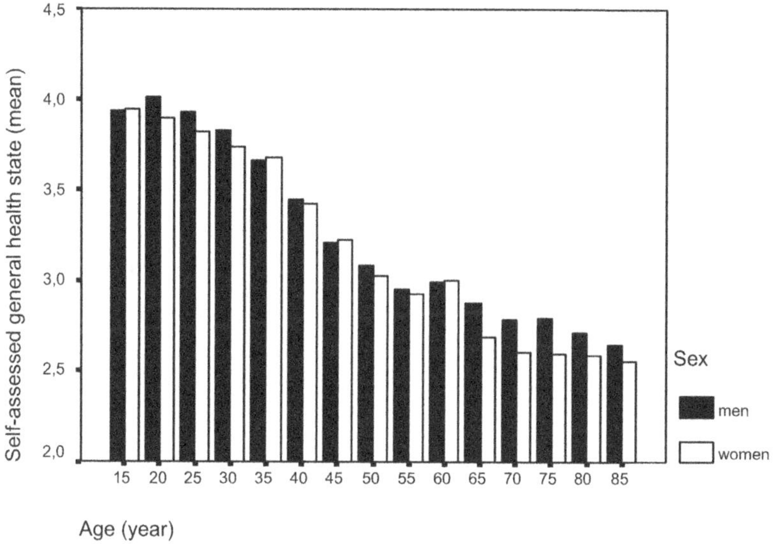

Vital exhaustion: The frequency of complains due to vital exhaustion are also increasing with age both in women and men, and are significantly ($p<0.001$) more frequent in women, both in the younger than in the older population. According to a multivariate analysis (General Linear Model) factors having significant association with vital exhaustion in women are sleep disturbances, anxiety and depressive symptoms, daily limitations caused by pain symptoms, family state (live alone or widow), and lack of social support. These factors are also sleep disturbances, anxiety and depressive symptoms, daily limitations caused by pain symptoms, and working disability in men.

Working disability was measured on a 7-point scale (from 0 = no working disability to 6 = bound to bed). Men have a marked decline in working ability from the age of 40 years until 55, the most remarkably between 50 and 55 years. This decline is slowing down after the age of 55. In women this decline lasts from the age of 40 to 50, it does not change between 50 and 65, but is worsening again after 65 years (more remarkably than in men), and especially in the "old-old" (85+) population. It is an expected result that the population aged older than

65 have higher working disability than the younger one (p<0.001). There is no significant gender difference under the age of 65, but older women report significantly higher working disability than men (p=0.038). Interesting result is that less older women and men – even with severer working disability – report that they are unable to do paid work than younger ones (even with less severe disability). Only one fourth of older women and one third of older men who have severe working disability or are bound to chair or bed assesses that is unable to do paid work, while these rates are more than 50% in younger men and women. These tendencies may refer to the differences of attitudes and needs toward work (and to some useful activity) in the different generations.

Figure 4: Illness intrusiveness mean scores in the 10 „main diseases" in the older population in women and men. (Minimum point is 0, maximum is 91.)

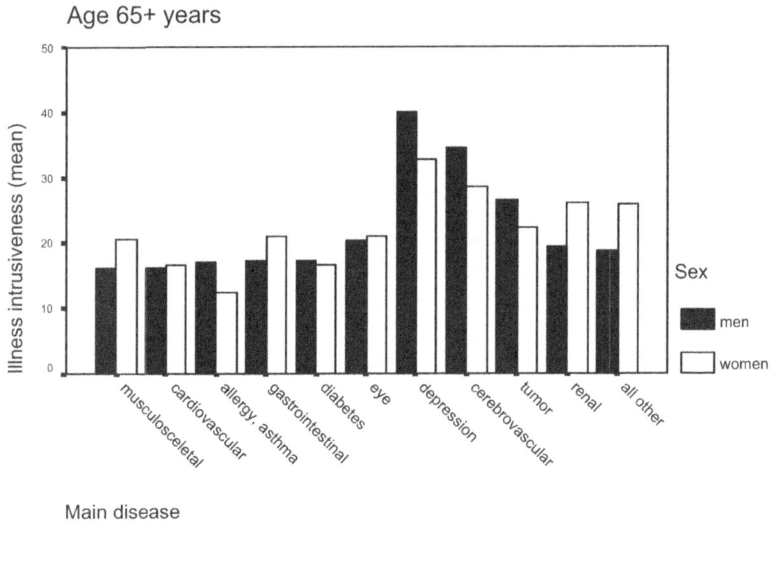

Figure 5: Illness intrusiveness mean scores in the 10 „main diseases" in younger population in women and men

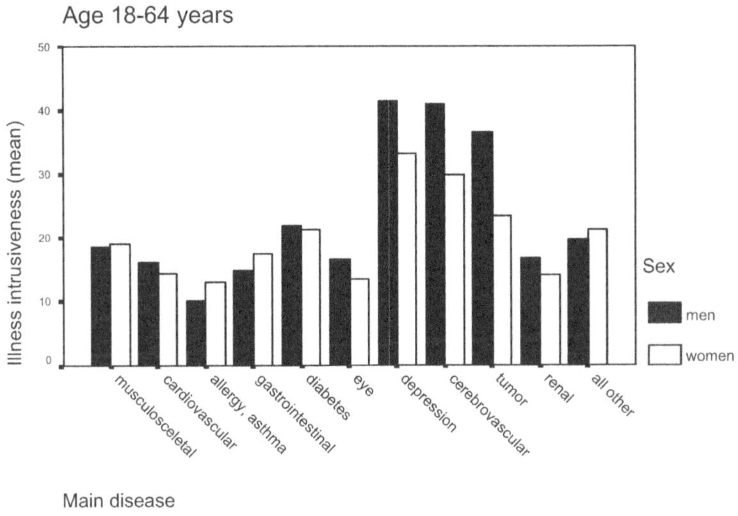

2.3 *General Quality of Life and Its Background Factors*

WHO Well-being Index mean scores are decreasing by age (Figure 6) and are significantly lower in the population older than 65, than in the younger one (means 6.63 vs. 8.04, p<0,001). 8.2% of the ageing population reported totally missing well-being, 32.9% decreased well-being, 42.9% well-being, and 16,1% total well-being. These rates in those younger than 65 are: 3,8% / 20,7% / 52,5% / 22,9%, respectively. Figure 7 shows the gender difference of these rates in the older and younger population. Women reported worse general well-being in all age groups.

Figure 6: WHO Well-being Index mean scores by age (in 5-year age groups) in women and men

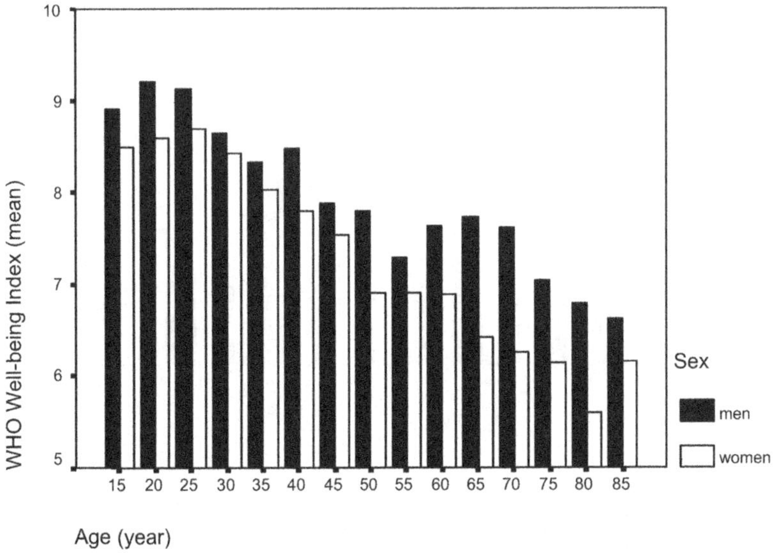

Variables measuring different aspects of quality of life – like the pain symptoms, Beck Depression Inventory, anxiety symptoms, Illness Intrusiveness Scale, self-assessed general health state, vital exhaustion, working disability and the WHO Well-being Index – are strongly associated with each other, as well. Positive factors – like the general well-being and health state – are positively correlated with each other, and negatively with the negative factors – like pain, depressive and anxiety symptoms, illness intrusiveness, vital exhaustion and working disability, while these negative factors are positively correlated with each other (analysed by partial correlation controlled for age, sex, socio-economic and family state).

Figure 7: WHO Well-being Index categories in women and men in the population older and in that of younger than 65 years

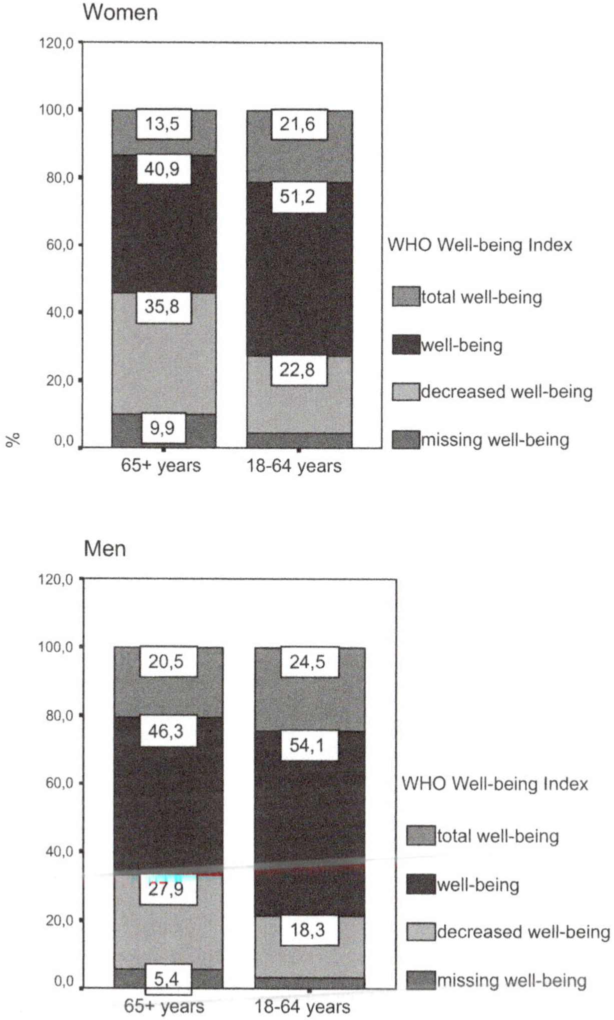

I investigated the associations of the different quality of life measures and their background factors by a multivariate analysis (linear regression). The dependent

variable was the WHO Well-being Index, that measures the general quality of life, and the independent variables were the other quality of life measures - like pain, depressive and anxiety symptoms, illness intrusiveness, self-assessed general health state, vital exhaustion and working disability, and also other background factors – like age, gender, socio-economic state, coping (emotionally- and problem-based), dysfunctional attitudes, life purposes, hostility, social support, life events, sleep disturbances. To analyse the differences along the life span, we made the multivariate analysis separately in the three age groups of young adults (18-44 years), middle aged (45-64), and older (65+) (Table 5).

Table 5: Variables significantly associated with WHO Well-being Index in order of effect size by linear regression in the three age groups.

18-44 years	45-64 years	65+ years
1. Vital exhaustion** (-)	1. Vital exhaustion** (-)	1. Vital exhaustion** (-)
2. Anxiety** (-)	2. Anxiety** (-)	2. Self-assessed health state** (+)
3. Problem-based coping** (+)	3. Self-assessed health state** (+)	3. Working disability** (-)
4. Self-assessed health state** (+)	4. Problem-based coping** (+)	4. Depressive symptoms** (-)
5. Purposes of life** (+)	5. Purposes of life** (+)	5. Problem-based coping** (+)
6. Dysfunctional attitudes** (-)	6. Dysfunctional attitudes** (-)	6. Anxiety** (-)
7. Hostility** (-)	7. Depressive symptoms** (-)	7. Purposes of life** (+)
8. Sleep disturbances* (-)	8. Sleep disturbances** (-)	8. Dysfunctional attitudes** (-)
9. Working disability* (-)	9. Social support** (+)	10. Gender** (wellbeing is worse in women)
	10. Gender* (wellbeing is worse in women)	11. Social support * (+)
	11. Working disability* (-)	12. Limiting pain symptoms* (-)
		13. Negative life events * (-)
The 9 variables altogether explains 32.8% of the variances.	The 11 variables altogether explains 40.0% of the variances.	The 12 variables altogether explains 46.3% of the variances

* p>0.05, ** p>0.001The order of the variables show which variables have the strongest positive (+) or negative (-) association with better self-assessed well-being.

The three variables that have the strongest association with quality of life in the population older than 65 years are: vital exhaustion, self-assessed general health state and working disability. Vital exhaustion is the most important factor in the younger age groups, as well, that is followed by anxiety. As life is going ahead, the impact of factors connected to health and illnesses - like general health state, working disability, pain symptoms that cause daily limitations - is getting stronger, and depression becomes a more significant factor, as well. The role of gender and social support also have an increasing importance by age: women and those without sufficient social support are more likely to report worse general quality of life. The impact of negative life events is among the significant factors associated with the general well-being only in the ageing population.

2.4 *Relations of Mental and Physical Health and Quality of Life*

In general among the main diseases, depression, cerebrovascular diseases and tumours are associated with the worst quality of life measured by the different scales, however there are some gender and age differences as it is shown in Table 6. Additionally to these three diseases, diabetes and renal diseases become a major health problem in the ageing population, as well.

There is a strong association with mental and physical health. Those who reported to have at least one main disease have significantly more depressive symptoms than those without any significant diseases (BDI mean 11.3 vs. 4.3, $p<0.001$). 22.0% of those who signed to have a main disease had clinically significant - moderate or severe - depressive symptomatology (BDI≥19), while only 4.2% of those who did not (OR=6.4, 95%CI: 5.4-7.5). In the whole population the highest rate was found in those with cerebrovascular diseases (women 40%, men 42%), and tumour (women 35%, men 31%). Figure 8. and 9. show the rate of those with BDI≥19 (depressive symptomatology that is likely to reach the clinical level) in the different "main diseases" separately in those above and below 65 years. In the ageing population the highest rate of those with moderate or severe depressive symptomatology was found in women suffering from tumour (65%), cerebrovascular (46%) or renal diseases (45%), and in men with cerebrovascular (45%), other diseases (32%), or cardiovascular diseases (25%).

Table 6: The 5 main diseases that are associated with the worst quality of life measured by the different scales in the three age groups in women and men

	♂ 18-44 years	♂ 45-64 years	♂ 65+ years	♀ 18-44 years	♀ 45-64 years	♀ 65+ years
WHO[12] 1.	cerebrovascular	depression	depression	depression	depression	tumour
2.	tumour	tumour	tumour	cerebrovascular	cerebrovascular	depression
3.	depression	cerebrovascular	cerebrovascular	renal	diabetes	renal
4.	other	other	other	cardiovascular	other	other
5.	musculosceletal	gastrointestinal	allergy/asthma	eye diseases	musculosceletal	cerebrovascular
GHS 1.	cerebrovascular	depression	tumour	tumour	cerebrovascular	tumour
2.	tumour	tumour	depression	musculosceletal	depression	cerebrovascular
3.	depression	cerebrovascular	cerebrovascular	depression	diabetes	renal
4.	cardiovascular	musculosceletal	allergy/asthma	gastrointestinal	tumour	other
5.	musculosceletal	cardiovascular	other	cardiovascular	musculosceletal	depression
BDI 1.	cerebrovascular	depression	depression	depression	depression	tumour
2.	depression	tumour	cerebrovascular	tumour	cerebrovascular	depression
3.	tumour	cerebrovascular	other	renal	tumour	cerebrovascular
4.	renal	other	tumour	cardiovascular	eye diseases	renal
5.	cardiovascular	eye diseases	musculosceletal	other	other	gastrointestinal
WDIS 1.	cerebrovascular	depression	cerebrovascular	tumour	cerebrovascular	cerebrovascular
2.	tumour	cerebrovascular	tumour	depression	tumour	renal
3.	diabetes	tumour	other	musculosceletal	depression	other
4.	depression	other	tumour	other	diabetes	tumour
5.	musculosceletal	musculosceletal	renal	cerebrovascular	musculosceletal	gastrointestinal
IIRS 1.	cerebrovascular	depression	depression cere-	depression	cerebrovascular	depression
2.	tumour	cerebrovascular	brovascular	tumour	depression	cerebrovascular
3.	depression	tumour	tumour	other	tumour	renal
4.	renal	other	eye diseases	musculosceletal	other	other
5.	diabetes	diabetes	renal	gastrointestinal	diabetes	tumour

12 WHO = WHO Well-being Index, GHS = general health state, BDI = Beck Depression Inventory, WDIS = working disability, IIRS = Illness Intrusiveness Rating Scale.
The table shows that when analysing the different quality of life measures in which diseases we found the worst results. E.g. in middle aged men (45-64) depression caused the worst general well-being (WHO), next worst results were found in tumor, cerebrovascular diseases, o-ther diseases, and the fifth worst was gastrointestinal diseases.

Figure 8: The rate of clinically significant depressive symptomatology (BDI≥19) in the different "main diseases" in the older population in women and men measured by the Beck Depression Inventory (BDI).

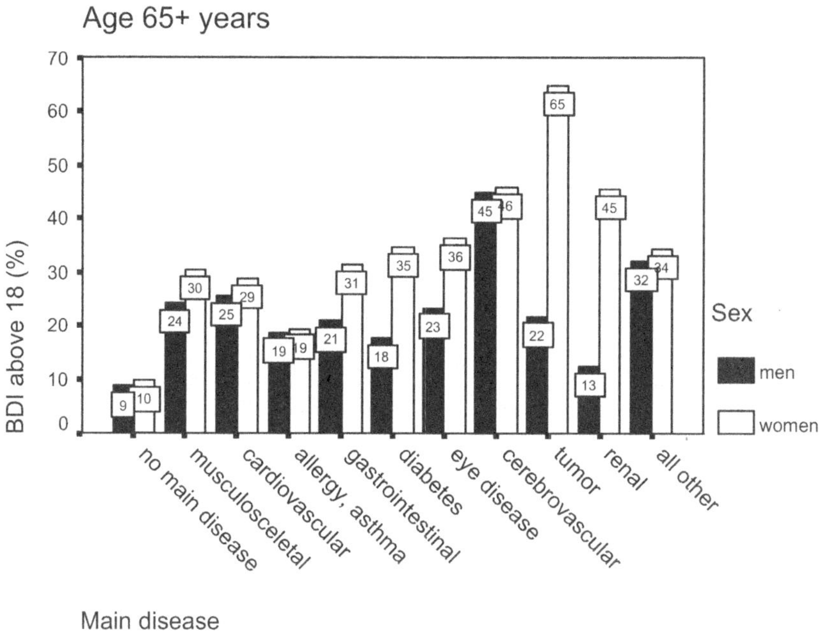

Figure 9: The rate of clinically significant depressive symptomatology (BDI≥19) in the different "main diseases" in the younger population in women and men measured by the Beck Depression Inventory (BDI).

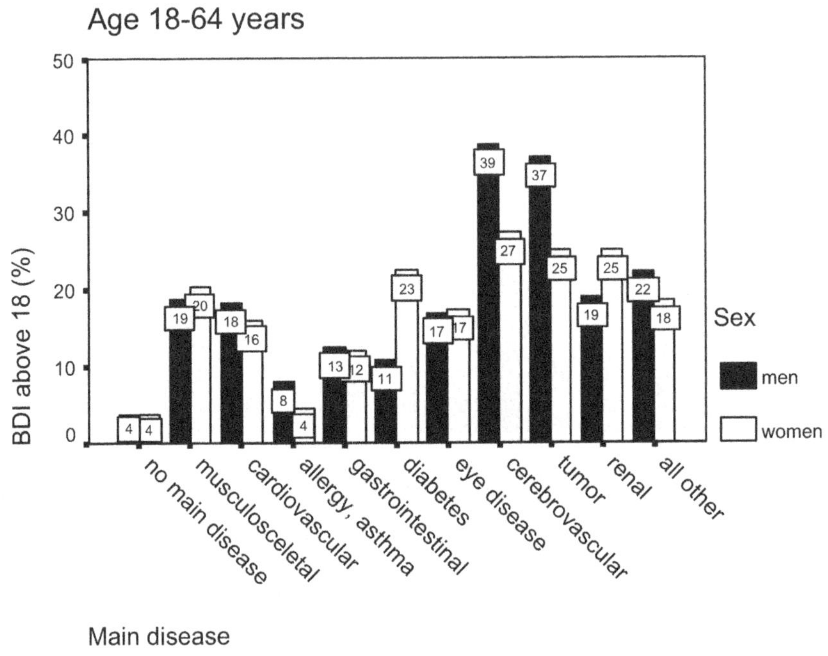

Summary

Older Hungarian population aged more than 65 years reported worse quality of life than the younger population in every analysed well-being factor. It is even more remarkable in the older female population. Up to 40% of the older women and more than 30% of older men assesses their general health as bad or very bad. These rates in the younger population are only slightly above 10%. More than 70% of the population in late life report actual pain symptoms, and these pain symptoms cause marked daily limitations in 36% of women and 29% of men. It is a natural process that the prevalence of significant diseases, and their impact on everyday psychosocial functioning (illness intrusiveness) is increasing by age. However interesting and important result that – although the three main diseases in late life are the musculosceletal, cardiovascular diseases and diabetes in both sexes, it is depression that cause the highest illness intrusiveness, followed by the cerebrovascular diseases.

Beside dementia, depression is the most significant mental illness in late life that causes a high burden on the ageing population. The average population above 65 years suffer from mild depression, and about twice and a half times more older individuals are likely to have clinically significant depressive symptomatology than the younger ones (25.3% vs 10.4%, women: 27.3% vs 10.9%, men: 21.7% vs 10.0%). Older women have more depressive symptomatology, however it is important to emphasise that depression in older men – who have the highest risk for completed suicide - remain unrecognised and untreated more often than in older women. On the other hand depression remains unrecognised and untreated in the older population even more frequently than in the younger one. Depression without treatment cause not only significant subjective suffering and decreased quality of life, but also are in a mutually negative relation with physical health. Those who reported to have at least one main disease have significantly more depressive symptoms than those without any significant diseases. And vice versa, depression negatively affect the severity, course and outcome of physical illnesses (Beckman et al, 1992; Bush et al, 2001; Cavanaugh, Wettstein, 1989; Holzberg et al, 1996, Kovács, Stauder, 2003; Lustman et al, 1997; Lyketsos et al, 1987, Pohjasvaara et al, 2001, Sacks et al, 1990; Wells et al, 1989). The significance of anxiety symptoms are also high in late life. Although the prevalence of anxiety symptoms does not increase by age, the rate of those, who have significant anxiety symptoms that influence their everyday life is very high above the age of 65, as well. About one fourth of the old population has significant anxiety symptoms, more frequently affecting women than men (30% vs. 20%).

According to the WHO Well-being Index scores, about 10% of the older women, and 5% of older men reported totally missing well-being. The three most important factors that are associated with worse well-being in late life are vital exhaustion, worse self-assessed general heath state, and working disability. Important protective factors are problem-based coping, presence of life purposes and social support. Further risk factors are depressive and anxiety symptoms, dysfunctional attitudes, female gender, pain symptoms with daily limitation, and negative life events.

In summary, the impact of the demographic changes that cause the increasing proportion of the ageing populations, as well as the "feminisation of ageing" with all of its psychosocial and economical consequences is a great challenge for the Hungarian population, as well. Investigation of the different domains of quality of life and their bio-psycho-social background factors could help to direct the actions of health care and social affairs professionals, as well as the policy makers.

This study is based on the database of the Hungarostudy 2002 health survey that was supported by the NKFP 1/002/2001, and OTKA TS040889 grants.

References

Baltes PB, Smith J. New frontiers in the future of aging: From successful ageing of the young old to the dilemmas of the fourth age (2002): Paper presented at the Valencia Forum, Researchers, Educators and Providers contribution to the Second World Assembly on Ageing. 2002, Valencia, Spain.

Bech P, Staehr-Johansen K, Gudex C (1996): The WHO (Ten) Well-Being Index: validation in diabetes. Psychotherapy and Psychosomatics 65: 183-190.

Beck AT, Beck RW (1972): Shortened version of BDI. Postgrad Med 52: 81-85.

Beck AT, Ward CH, Mendelsohn M, Mock J, Erbaugh J (1961): An inventory for measuring depression. Arch Gen Psychiatry 4: 53-63.

Beckman JC, D'Amico CJ, Rice JR, Jordan JS, Divine GW, Brook WB (1992): Depression and level of functioning in patients with rheumatoid arthritis. Can J Psychiatry 37: 539-543.

Bush DE, Ziegelstein RC, Tayback M, Richter D, Stevens S, Zahalsky H, et al. (2001): Even minimal symptoms of depression increases mortality risk after acute myocardial infarction. Am J Cardiol 88: 337-341.

Caldwell RA, Pearson JL, Chin RJ (1987): Stress-moderating effects: social apport in the context of gender and locus of control. Personal Soc Psychol Bulletin 13 (1): 5-17.

Cavanaugh S, Wettstein RM (1989): Emotional and cognitive dysfunction associated with medical disorders. J Psychosom Res 33: 505-514.

Cook W, Medley D (1954): Proposed hostility and pharisaic-virtue scales for MMPI. Journal of Applied Psychology 38: 414-418.

Crumbaugh JC, Maholick LT (1964): An experinmental study in existentialism: the psychosomatic approach to Frankl's concept to noogenic neurosis. Journal of Clinical Psychology 20: 200-207.

Devins GM, Binik YM, Hutchinson TA, et al. (1983): The emotional impact of end-stage renal disease: Importance of patients' perceptions of intrusiveness and control. International Journal of Psychiatric Medicine 13: 327–343.

Devins GM, Dion R, Pelletier LG, Shapiro CM, Abbey SE, Raiz L et al. (2001): The structure of lifestyle disruptions in chronic disease: A confirmatory factor analysis of the illness intrusiveness ratings scale. Med Care 39: 1097-1104.

Eaves G, Rush AJ (1984): Cognitive pattern in symptom and remitted unipolar major depression. Abnorm Psychol 93: 31-40.

Falger P, Appels A (1982): Psychological risk factors over the life course of myocardial infarction patients. Advances in Cardiology 29: 132-139.

Folkman S, Lazarus R (1980): An analysis of coping in a middle aged community sample. Journal of Health and Social Behavior 21: 219-239.

Holmes TH, Rahe RH (1967): The social adjustment rating scale. J Psychosom Res 11: 213-218.

Holzberg AD, Robinson ME, Geisser ME, Gremillion HA (1996): The effects of depression and chronic pain on psychosocial and physical functioning. Clin J Pain 12: 118-125.

Idler EL, Benyamini Y (1997): Self-rated health and mortality: A review of twenty-seven community studies. J Health and Social Behavior 38: 21-37.

Jeszenszky Z (2003): Az időskori mentálhigiéné társadalmi jelentősége. In: Kovács M (ed.): Időskori depresszió és szorongás. Budapest: Springer Tudományos Kiadó.

Kopp M, Falger PRJ, Appels A, Szedmák S (1998): Depressive symptomatology and vital exhaustion are differentially related to behavioral risk factors for coronary artery disease. Psychosomatic Medicine 60: 752-758.

Kopp M, Skrabski Á, Szedmák S (1995): Socioeconomic factors, severity of depressive symptomatology, and sickness absence rate in the Hungarian population. J Psychosom Res 39: 1019-1029.

Kopp MS, Skrabski Á (1996): Behavioural Sciences Applied to a Changing Society. Budapest: Bibliotheca Septem Artium Liberalium.

Kopp MS, Skrabski Á, Kawachi I, Adler NE (2005) Low socioeconomic status of the opposite gender is a risk factor for middle aged mortality. J Epidemiology and Community Health 59: 675-678.

Kopp MS, Skrabski Á, Szedmák S (2000): Psychosocial risk factors, inequality and self-rated morbidity in a changing society. Social Sciences and Medicine 51: 1350-1361.

Kovács M, Stauder A. Szedmák S (2002): Severity of allergic complaints: the importance of depressed mood. J Psychosom Res 54: 549-557.

Kovács ME, Jeszenszky Z (2006): Időskor és életminőség. In: Kopp M, Kovács ME (eds.): A magyar népesség életminősége az ezredfordulón. Budapest: Semmelweis Kiadó.

Laidlaw K (2003): A mentális egészség és betegségek hatása a sikeres öregedésre. In: Kovács M (ed.): Időskori depresszió és szorongás. Budapest: Springer Tudományos Kiadó.

Lustman PJ, Griffith LS, Clouse RE (1997): Depression in adults with diabetes. Semin Clin Neuropsychiatry 2: 15-23.

Lyketsos GC, Lyketsos GC, Richardson SC, Beis A (1987): Dysthymic states and depressive syndromes in physical conditions of presumably psychogenic origin. Acta Psychiatr Scand 76: 529-534.

Miller M, Rahe RH (1997): Life changes scaling for the 1990s. J Psychosom Res 43 : 279-292.

Novak M, Mah K, Molnar MZs, Ambrus Cs, Csepanyi G, Kovacs A, Vamos E, Zambo M, Zoller R, Mucsi I, Devins G (2005): Factor structure and reliability of the Hungarian version of the Illness Intrusiveness Rating Scale: invariance across North American and Hungarian dialysis patients. J Psychosom Research 58 (1): 103-110.

Novak M, Mucsi I, Shapiro CM, Rethelyi J, Kopp MS (2004): Increased utilization of health services by insomniacs - an epidemiological perspective. J Psychosom Res 56 (5): 527-536.

Pohjasvaara T, Vataja R, Leppavuori A, Kaste M, Erkinjuntti T (2001): Depression is an independent predictor of poor long-term functional outcome post-stroke. Eur J Neurol 8: 315-319.

Rahe RH (1975): Epidemiological studies of life change and illness. Int J psychiatr Med 6 : 133-146.

Rahe RH, Tolles RL (2002): The Brief Stress and Coping Inventory: A Useful Stress Management Instrument. International Journal of Stress Management 9 (2): 61-70.

Rózsa S, Réthelyi J, Stauder A, Susánszky É, Mészáros E, Skrabski Á, Kopp M (2006): A Hungarostudy 2002 országos reprezentatív tervezése, statisztikai módszerei, a minta leíró jellemzői és az alkalmazott kérdőívek. In: Kopp M, Kovács ME (eds.): A magyar népesség életminősége az ezredfordulón. Budapest: Semmelweis Kiadó.

Rózsa S, Szádóczky E, Füredi J (2001): A Beck depresszió kérdőív rövidített változatának jellemzői hazai mintán (Characteristics of the Shortened Version of the Beck Depression Inventory in a national sample). Psychiatria Hungarica 16:384-402.

Sacks CR, Peterson RA, Kimmel PL (1990): Perception of illness and depression in chronic renal disease. Am J Kidney Dis 15: 31-39.

Skrabski Á, Kopp M, Kawachi I (2004): Social Capital and Collective Efficacy in ungary: Cross-sectional Associations with Middle-Aged Female and Male Mortality Rates, Journal of Epidemiology and Community Health 58: 340-345.

Skrabski Á, Kopp MS, Kawachi I (2004): Social capital and collective efficacy in Hungary: cross sectional associations with middle aged female and male mortality rates. J Epidemiology and Community Health 58: 340-345.

Skrabski Á, Kopp MS, Rózsa S, Réthelyi J, Rahe R (2005): Life meaning: an important correlate of health in the Hungarian population. Int J Behavioral Medicine 12: 78-85.

Soldatos CR, Dikeos DG, Paparrigopoulos TJ (2000): Athens Insomnia Scale: validation of an instrument based on ICD-10 criteria.J Psychosom Res 48 (6): 555-560.

Soldatos CR, Dikeos DG, Paparrigopoulos TJ (2003): The diagnostic validity of the Athens Insomnia Scale. J Psychosom Res 55 (3): 263-267.

Szabó G, Rózsa S (2006): Az életesemények hatása az életminőségre. In: Kopp M, Kovács ME (eds.): A magyar népesség életminősége az ezredfordulón. Budapest: Semmelweis Kiadó.Szádóczky E (2000): Kedélybetegségek és szorongásos zavarok prevalenciája Magyarországon. Budapest: Print-Tech Kiadó.

Tróznai T, Kullmann L (2003): Életkor és életminőség. In: Kovács M (ed.): Időskori depresszió és szorongás. Budapest: Springer Tudományos Kiadó.

Valliant GE, Mukamal K. Successful Aging (2001): Am J Psychiatry 158: 839-847.

Weissman A (1979): The Dysfunctional Attitude Scale: a validation study. Unpublished dissertation. Dissertation Abstracts 40: 1389-1390.

Wells KB, Golding JM, Burnam MA (1989): Affective, substance use, and anxiety disorders in persons with arthritis, diabetes, heart disease, high blood pressure, or chronic lung conditions. Gen Hosp Psychiatry 11: 320-327.

WHO (2002): Active Ageing: A Policy Framework. Geneva: World Health Organisation.

Zigmond AS, Snaith RP (1983): The Hospital Anxiety and Depression Scale. Acta Psychiatr Scand 67: 361-70.

Elder Abuse, Older Women and Considerations of Mental Health

Bridget Penhale

Summary

In recent years there has been an increased emphasis on violence and abuse within society and in particular the abuse and neglect of older people. It therefore seems appropriate to consider the potential role that issues related to violence, gender and mental health might contribute towards providing a greater understanding of the linked phenomena of elder abuse and neglect. This chapter aims to provide a brief overview of current knowledge about elder abuse and neglect and a consideration of factors from the fields of gender (in particular relating to older women) and mental health which might assist in the development of both knowledge and understanding of elder abuse and abusive situations.

1 Introduction

In the last two decades, there has been a gradual increase throughout the world of concern about the abuse and neglect of elderly people. The principal focus of concern has been on abuse of elders by their carers in the domestic setting although more recently there has been a move towards consideration of abuse occurring within institutional settings.

Elder abuse is not a new phenomenon (Stearns 1986), but it is effectively only since 1988 that the problem has really begun to be explored in the United Kingdom (UK). In many respects, it is still quite early in the stages of problem identification and the development of positive action to combat elder abuse and neglect is only just beginning to happen. Whilst a number of Western European countries such as Sweden, the Netherlands and France similarly recognised the existence of abuse at about the same time as the UK, there are others such as Spain, Italy and Belgium where the existence of abuse has only been acknowledged in recent years. Others still (Iceland, Czech Republic, Slovenia) are only now beginning to consider issues relating to elder abuse. There are yet other countries (Denmark and some of the accession countries) that do not really appear to have recognised elder abuse up until this time.

2 What is Known about Elder Abuse?

Elder abuse and neglect is a complex and sensitive area to investigate adequately. This also appeared to be the case with both child abuse and domestic violence against younger women by men known to them. For example, comparative and developmental norms are much more difficult to establish for older people than with children who have been abused (Bennett et al, 1997). Additionally, there have been real difficulties in trying to determine a sound theoretical base to the phenomena. This is in part because of the lack of agreement concerning a standard definition of abuse, but also due to problems in researching the topic (see for example Bennett and Kingston 1993; Ogg and Munn-Giddings 1993). For instance, many of the research studies that have been carried out consist of very small-scale samples and have tended to concentrate on cases already known by professionals. This means that there are a number of difficulties in attempts to establish the exact nature of the field of enquiry.

Although English doctors identified the phenomena in the mid 1970s, it was not until the mid 1980s that the issue was really picked up on in the UK. By contrast, in the USA the issue was identified from the mid 1970s and was researched from that time in attempts to clarify the problem and to provide solutions to it. It is not entirely appropriate to draw generalisations from results of surveys in the USA, due to problems with definitions and with the research data (Cloke, 1983). However, in order to give some idea as to the potential magnitude of the problem, it is worth noting that the majority of research results emanating from the US originally suggested that somewhere between 4-10% of the elderly population were either at risk of, or were experiencing, abuse from their caregivers (Gioglio and Blakemore, 1985; Pillemer and Finkelhor, 1988; US House of Representatives, 1981). Most US researchers nowadays accept that somewhere in the region of 4-5% of the population of older people are potentially affected by abuse or neglect (Lachs and Pillemer, 1995).

3 Definitions

Despite the difficulties already mentioned a number of definitions of elder abuse have emerged. The usual types of abuse included within most definitions were: physical, psychological, financial and neglect. To this list have been added sexual abuse, as distinct from physical abuse, and also, within a number of definitions, social abuse. A typical breakdown of behaviours falling into each category would include:

- Physical abuse: the infliction of physical harm, injury, physical coercion, sexual molestation and physical restraint;
- Psychological abuse: the infliction of mental anguish, verbal and emotional abuse;
- Material abuse: the illegal or improper exploitation and /or use of funds or materials, including property;
- Active neglect: the refusal or failure to undertake a care-giving obligation (including a conscious and intentional attempt to inflict physical or emotional stress on the elder);
- Passive neglect: the refusal or failure to fulfil a care-taking obligation (excluding a conscious and intentional attempt to inflict physical or emotional distress on the elder). (Wolf and Pillemer 1989)

It is also possible to list indicators of abuse, although it is difficult to diagnose mistreatment using these indicators in isolation. To link a bruise to mistreatment for example would require much more evidence than just the injury.

As stated elsewhere, it is possible that different groups may require different definitions to suit their own purposes (Penhale & Kingston, 1995). Researchers, politicians and practitioners may all need their own working definitions of what constitutes abuse (Bennett & Kingston, 1993). Rather than lose time on searching for the ideal definition, covering all situations, it is probably better to accept and work with the different definitions that are currently in use or being developed.

Reports of which type of abuse is most common varies between surveys. Early research from the US suggested that most instances of elder abuse are recurrent and part of a pattern, rather than a single incident (O'Malley et al, 1981). Other researchers in the US found that neglect is the most commonly found type (Valentine & Cash, 1986), whilst yet other research from the US has suggested that psychological abuse (Block & Sinott, 1979) or physical abuse (Lau & Kosberg, 1979) are the most common. These early studies were, however, small-scale samples using different definitions and are thus difficult to generalise from.

4 The Dynamics of Abuse

In trying to determine the dynamics of elder abuse, most of the early research concentrated in attempts to establish a profile of victims of abuse. Initial studies did, unfortunately, settle on the "typical victim" as being a frail, dependent female of 75 + years who is impaired (either physically, mentally or both) and living with an adult child (O' Malley et al 1981; Lau & Kosberg 1979). The levels of dependency of the older person due to the degree of impairments experienced were considered to be a source of extreme stress for the caregiver. Additionally, the degree of frailty of the victim was felt to put them in a position of high vulnerability and risk of abuse occurring. There seemed to be an assumption within such studies that the abuser was not really concerned with the well-being of the victim and that they were motivated by greed.

However, such a view of elderly people as being dependent and vulnerable may add to widely held negative views and attitudes about older people that appear throughout society. And at least one commentator from the US has suggested that one of the reasons that elder abuse gained currency in the US (and the status of a legitimate social problem) may be strongly connected with the fact that it accorded with the predominant focus of research on ageing in the US: a focus on the problems associated with ageing (Baumann, 1989).

From more recent research in the US, it would seem that there are different characteristics of victims, depending on the type of abuse that is present. To expand slightly, after considering the U.S. research over the past two decades, Wolf (1989) suggests that older people who are subject to neglect appear to fit the characteristics of the stereotypical victim (as presented above), and are a source of extreme stress to their caregiver. Those elders who are physically or psychologically abused are less likely to be physically dependent, but may have emotional difficulties. This group of older people usually live with their abuser who is dependent on them, especially financially. Elders who are victims of financial abuse are also less dependent on physical care from relatives, and are more likely to be unmarried and to live alone, although in comparatively isolated situations (Wolf, 1989, cited in Bennett & Kingston, 1993).

Research that followed some of the early US studies has tended to focus on the characteristics of abusers. These studies should be considered to be empirically more informative, because of their case control methodology. The assumptions outlined above about the stress of caring have generally not been upheld. Instead, those people involved in abusive situations as abusers appear to be more likely (when compared with non-abusive carers) to have alcohol or drug related problems and mental health/psychological problems (Pillemer, 1986; Bristowe and Collins, 1989; Wolf, 1986; Homer and Gilleard, 1990; Grafstrom, 1992, Anetzberger, 1994).

These patterns seem to be particularly relevant in those situations that involve physical or psychological abuse. There may also, within such situations, be a history of long-term difficulties in the relationship between the parties (Homer and Gilleard, 1990; Grafstrom, 1992). In the debate concerning dependency, some investigators have indicated that abusers may be very dependent on their victims. The principal areas of dependence that have been identified are finance (Hwalek et al, 1986) and also housing and transportation (Pillemer, 1986). With regard to the characteristics of those who abuse, in general terms research from the US tends to suggest that physical and financial abuse are linked with the dependency of the abuser on the abused, whilst psychological abuse and neglect may perhaps be more associated with care-giver stress.

Although there is still uncertainty regarding the rates of elder abuse either as an overall figure or with regard to the various sub-types, it can be stated with some certainty that abuse within the domestic setting occurs across all ethnic and socio-economic groups and in both urban and rural areas (Steuer & Austin, 1980).

5 Considerations of Gender

Whilst both men and women are abused, the majority of victims of elder abuse are female, even when this is corrected for by the fact that there are more older women in the population. Rates of abuse and neglect do not appear to be higher for elders from ethnic minority populations than for white elders; nor are the rates higher for people over 75 years rather than those between 64-74 years. In addition, particular religious, cultural and economic backgrounds of individual elders do not appear to be of particular significance within the development of abusive situations (Pillemer & Finkelhor, 1988).

Those who abuse may be male or female partners, adult children, or other relatives. They may also be non-relatives, perhaps especially considering abuse within institutional settings. However, it seems that as with other forms of interpersonal violence, specifically situations of child abuse and violence towards younger women, the majority of those who abuse are men. Finkelhor (1983) proposed that when the probability for abuse is corrected for by the amount of time that the abuser spends with the victim, men are much more likely to be involved in abusive acts, particularly physically violent acts.

When considering the gender of those who abuse, many of the early studies and reports indicated that abusers were more likely to be female, usually relatives (Eastman, 1984). This was in part based on the analysis of the causation of abuse as being predominantly related to caregiver stress and the fact that the majority of unpaid caregivers are female relatives, often daughters. However, further analysis of the early data, which differentiated between physical abuse and neglect, discovered a significant sex difference, that men were more likely to be involved in physical violence and women in neglectful acts (Miller & Dodder, 1989; Sengstock, 1991). The former researchers suggested that because categories of neglect (including self neglect) were very high in the studies they reviewed, this to a large extent explained why it had previously looked as if the majority of perpetrators were women.

In a further study, Pillemer & Finkelhor (1988) reported that abusers appeared more likely to be spouses than adult children or non-relatives. In the majority of cases abusers were close family members, usually living with the victim. This study was a well publicised random sample study in the Boston area of the US. In this research, Pillemer & Finkelhor discovered that in their sample, 3.2% of older people could be expected to be either experiencing abuse or be at risk of abuse. Within this study, the highest levels of abuse were found between spouses/partners. When all types of abuse were taken into consideration, the abuser was a spouse in 58% of situations, compared to the abuser being a child (or other individual) in 42% of the cases. When physical abuse alone was considered, 60% of situations were of spouse abuse (Pillemer & Finkelhor, 1988).

It is relevant in this context to note that this study consisted of a telephone survey. Therefore it is perhaps likely that those who might be considered the most vulnerable and at risk, notably those who are very frail, either physically, mentally, or both, did not participate. Of consideration also was the finding that more men than women were reported as victims (1: 1.6 wives to husbands as the ratio of victims). Following adjustment of the figures to account for the actual numbers of men and women in the total population of older people, the risk of abuse for men appeared to be twice that which existed for women. Due to the fact that there were fewer older men in the population, the numbers of men and women seemed to be about the same. When the severity of abuse was considered, however, it was apparent that this was greater for women (Pillemer and Finkelhor, 1988).

There are a number of possible reasons why a higher number of women may come to the attention of professionals and thus become "abuse statistics". Women may be more likely to seek assistance or to report abuse than men. In general terms, the populations surveyed may be made up largely of either women or of very elderly people, most of whom are female (O'Malley et al 1981). It is also possible that because of the severity of their injuries more assistance is necessary for women, which means that they come to the attention of professionals.

This may result in the conclusion that the risk to older women of being abused is higher than the risk to men (Pillemer & Finkelhor 1988).

The proposition is that if most elder abuse is abuse between partners in later life, and the prevailing type of abuse for male abusers is physical violence towards women; this is more likely to result in a need for intervention due to major, or serious injury, especially as the woman's ability to withstand or recover from abuse may well diminish with age. It could therefore appear that there are more older women who are abused than men. Abusive behaviour by women, which is perhaps more likely to be psychological or passively neglectful in nature, may be much less likely to result in any treatment (of injury) for the male victim. It is thus more likely to be almost unnoticed by professionals. Sexual abuse in later life, as for younger women, is highly gendered: those who are victims are female; those who abuse are male. Such aspects as these are likely to benefit from further research.

The effects of gender within abuse are influenced and mediated by a number of factors. These include the type of abuse which occurs; the fact that there are more older women within the population and also in living relationships: more women than men live alone in later life, yet there appears to be a higher risk of abuse occurring when people live together. In addition, as already indicated, elder abuse consists of a number of different types of abuse and in many abusive situations several different types of abuse may co-exist. This does not help in trying to ascertain the role of gender within such situations.

There have been relatively few attempts until now to fully consider the role of gender within elder abuse (Aitken and Griffin, 1996; Leeder, 1994; Mears, 1995; Whittaker, 1995). In one attempt to consider aspects of gender more fully within elder abuse, Whittaker proposes that the consideration of differing types of abuse, for example 'family violence' or 'carer stress' has resulted in a confounding and obscurity of gender (Whittaker, 1995a). As such approaches appear to have neutralised deliberation of the role of gender. For Whittaker, the general concept of 'elder abuse' should be looked at within more precisely defined categories and in her view, far more emphasis should be given to the role of power within relationships:

> "The nature and extent of power held by a woman at any point in time may vary according to her position...In respect of elder abuse this leads to a concern with how power operates in different contexts" (Whittaker, 1995b, p.152)

To pursue such a feminist analysis a little further, stating the position perhaps rather baldly, the starting point is the oppression of women: women being socially, economically and politically controlled by men. Such control is not infrequently seen within the appearance of male violence against women, one aspect of which is abuse between partners within a relationship. As Whalen states:

> "According to the ideological analysis offered by the (contemporary feminist) movement, men batter the women they supposedly love because they benefit from such abuse, individually and collectively. We live in a patriarchal society that has promoted and supported male violence over women: male authority, male power, male control (Whalen, 1996, p.110).

What is now required is a more rigorous examination of the extent of fit of this analysis when considering elder abuse and perhaps more specifically the abuse of older women. Further such analyses will be welcomed in future in attempts to clarify the role of gender within elder abuse.

6 Elder abuse in Institutional Settings

Abuse in care settings and environments is also an important area that is difficult to resolve and could be a topic for further discussion in its own right. Although the main focus of concern has been on abuse of older people by their caregivers and relatives in the domestic setting, in recent years there has been a welcome and much needed move towards consideration of abuse occurring within institutional settings (Glendenning and Kingston, 1999; Stanley et al, 1999). The abuse of older people who live in institutions is seemingly part of the experience of many residents in a number of different settings and such abuse may be both widespread and systematic (Glendenning 1999a). As Glendenning (1999b) observed, there has been a lengthy tradition in the UK of scandals in institutional care relating to older people and, in the United States, detailed research concerning this aspect stretches back to the early 1970s. However, such scandals tend to have been investigated and treated as separate inquiries into standards of care rather than as directly concerned with abuse. Unfortunately, interest tends to be short-lived and rather superficial following such reports, including at a political level.

Abuse in institutions may take place at an individual level, between staff member and resident, resident to resident, or relative to resident, or it may take place at a structural level concerning the fabric of the establishment and how it is run. It appears that often in such circumstances, this is largely for the benefit of the workforce and the organisation rather than for the older people who live in the setting. There are a number of reasons for institutional abuse, but the nature and impact of ageism and ambivalence concerning the care offered to older people in institutions may be important factors. Systems of detection of abuse need to be in place within care settings and there also need to be associated guidance and protocols for professionals to follow when abuse or neglect are identified. This includes some protection for 'whistleblowers', who are members of the staff workforce who report abuse within an institution.

Licensing of homes and regular inspections of care facilities by an independent authority may be valuable in preventing abuse from developing in such environments, together with developing a culture of open-ness in the setting (more links with local communities, open visiting times) and recognised systems for complaints to be made and acted upon. Processes for staff support and development together with the maintenance of morale for the workforce in order to prevent 'staff burn-out' may also assist. If there is very serious abuse or gross neglect of a substantial number of older residents of a care facility, then the closure of that establishment and transfer of residents may be necessary. Generally, action to improve standards in the home ad to prevent abuse and/or neglect from re-occurring may be the preferred approaches taken in order to minimise trauma and distress for the older residents of the home.

7 Causation and Management of Elder Abuse

In terms of possible causative factors it appears unlikely that any one factor causes abuse, but rather that there is a complex interplay between a number of different factors. There are many possible reasons why abuse happens. Such factors as the following may be implicated in the development of abuse:

- a history of long-standing poor relationships within the family
- the dependency of the abuser for finance, accommodation or emotional support on the victim
- the abuser having a history of mental health problems or a substance misuse problem
- a pre-existing pattern of family violence (inter-generational transmission of violence)
- the social isolation of the victim and the abuser

A number of additional risk factors have also been identified. Such aspects as an inability of a carer to care for the older person; other stressors within the family system (for example, unemployment, finance, overcrowding) and inadequate support for the carer may all be implicated.

Although it has been indicated that there does not appear to be any simple or linear causal relationship between caregiver stress and abuse, as clearly not all caregivers perpetrate abuse, it is apparent that some caregivers ultimately find the task of caring for a frail, dependent older person (often a close relative) too stressful and difficult and in some situations, abuse and/or neglect can develop and take place. In addition, it would appear that there are some caregivers who are not suited to provide care, either physically or psychologically, but who are expected to take up the care-giving role for their relative. These individuals may also have their own difficulties relating to relationships, finance or accommodation. If there is not sufficient support for caregivers to provide care, or if their own difficulties are not recognised and assistance offered, as relevant, a difficult and stressful state of affairs may escalate into an abusive situation.

Although awareness and recognition of abuse and neglect have recently been developing across the world, the identification of abuse by professionals has at time proved problematic, however. In many countries, guidance and protocols have been developed in order to assist in this area, with definitions of abuse provided, together with the types of abuse and lists of possible indicators of abuse and neglect (see DOH, 2000 for an example of this type of guidance). Training and education for professionals as also been developing in order to equip professionals to detect abusive situations (at an initial part of the process) and provide knowledge and information concerning when and how to intervene (when situations have been identified or referred). In some countries, screening tools for the detection of abuse are in development (see WHO, 2006 for a report of a project relating to this area).

Interventions within abusive situations have recently begun to be developed in a number of countries. Many such strategies have focused on the provision of practical support and assistance (DOH, 1993) in order to relieve stress from situations. The provision of respite care services, alternative accommodation away from the abusive environment either temporarily or permanently, counselling for individuals or the family as a whole, telephone help-lines or even legal remedies to resolve situations are essential strategies to be developed further. In addition, systems of family therapy and/or relationship therapy to assist in the resolution of fractured relations between family members also need to be devised. A range of interventions with those who abuse, such as treatment for substance abuse, or techniques to enhance anger management are also likely to be necessary (Penhale, 1993).

It is important to try and identify the primary or main cause of the abuse in order to target interventions appropriately. For instance, if the abuse is principally due to the stress of care-giving, then the provision of services within the community may be appropriate in order to support and alleviate the situation. If however, the abuse results from the psychopathology of the abuser, then an approach that provides for treatment of the abuser, together with any necessary protection of the older person is more likely to be indicated.

Good practice within elder abuse should include such elements as a distinction between initial referral (or report) and subsequent investigation; the careful co-ordination of the investigation; separate, sensitive and suitable arrangements for interviews. The use of case conferences in order to determine a protection plan for an individual, where necessary and as an effective means to promote shared decision making is also suggested as indicative of good practice. Clearly a balance between the needs of the older person for support and protection and the possible need for sanction for the abuser is necessary here. The protection plan is likely to include attention to the needs of the elder for safety, support and service provision (or treatment), together with issues relating to the ongoing management of risk. Multi-disciplinary working between the different agencies involved with individuals and with abusers, is an essential part of the process here.

Having briefly outlined the more general aspects of elder abuse it seems appropriate to move to a consideration of elder abuse in relation to issues surrounding mental health of both the individual who experiences the abuse and those who abuse.

8 Elder Abuse and Mental Health

8.1 Dementia and Elder Abuse

The first area to consider within this section, is the situation of older people with cognitive impairments, in particular those with dementia. As seen earlier in this chapter, some of the early research in the area of elder abuse suggested that the dependence of the victim was a risk factor associated with abuse. Therefore it is necessary here to consider whether people with dementia and associated mental health difficulties are more likely to be victims of elder abuse than unimpaired individuals. However, it is perhaps not surprising, given the previous comments made about lack of research generally in elder abuse to find that there is limited research and no definitive answer concerning this question. There may also be an associated question as to whether an abusive situation, particularly one that is of a long-standing nature, may result in a mental health problem for the individual.

Within the literature on elder abuse there are a number of examples that include dementia as a component factor (Homer and Gilleard, 1990; Grafstrom et al, 1992; SSI, 1992). There have also been several studies in recent years which have begun to explore the extent of the relationship between dementia and abuse and it is worth reviewing these, albeit briefly. Two UK based articles have suggested that rates of abuse among older people with mental health problems, in particular those relating to dementia, are higher than in the general population of older people (Wilson, 1994; Cooney and Howard, 1995). The first of these studies looked at levels of elder abuse among older people using a psycho-geriatric service, but living in the community. Although this was a survey of staff of the service and did not just consider dementia, the findings are of some relevance in this context (Wilson, 1994). The second article consists of a review of existing knowledge (at that point) concerning elder abuse and dementia (Cooney and Howard, 1995). Several of the studies reviewed by these researchers will be outlined in the following sections.

The first such study from the USA to be considered is that by Coyne and colleagues who sent out questionnaires to carers who had contacted a free dementia help-line (Coyne, Reichman and Berbig, 1993). Of the third of carers, mostly women, who responded (342), some 33.1% (92 carers) stated that their relative with dementia had physically abused them. The survey also found that 11.9% of respondents (33 carers) indicated that they had physically abused the person they cared for by a number of different acts (biting, kicking and hitting, for example).

In this study, there appeared to be a relationship between those caregivers who had been abusive towards their relatives and those who had themselves been the subject of abuse by their relatives. Just over a quarter of those carers who reported being abused (26%) stated that they had been abusive to their relative. By contrast, only 4.8% (10 carers) who had not been abused reported that they had been abusive towards their relative (Coyne et al, 1993). It is possible that aggressive or violent behaviour by the 'patient' might provoke a similar response by the carer, that in effect the abuse is mutual and dual directional in certain situations.

Certainly, this finding relates to earlier research by Levin and colleagues, in the UK. This research was not specifically looking at elder abuse but rather considered the situation of families caring for 'confused older people' (Levin et al. 1989). One of the key findings, however, was the high risk to carers of both verbal and physical abuse by the person receiving care (the care recipient). A later Australian study by Cahill and Shapiro asked a group of female carers of people with dementia about physical and verbal abuse and sexual violence by the care recipient (Cahill and Shapiro, 1993). Of the 39 respondents, 44% said that pushing and shoving had occurred, whilst 25% stated that hitting and pinching had happened to them. With regard to verbal abuse, 61% stated that shouting had occurred, whilst 48% reported verbal threats and swearing.

Similarly, a later US study by Pillemer and Suitor, concerning caregivers of people with Alzheimer's disease, indicated that those carers who were caring for relatives who were violent on occasion were themselves fearful of becoming violent and had violent feelings. Although this fear of becoming violent was not significantly different between groups of married and non-married caregivers, spouses were much more likely to be violent in response to violence by the care recipient (in this case their partner) and to act on violent feelings than other caregivers (Pillemer and Suitor, 1992).

In this study, violence appeared to be related to disruptive behaviour by the care recipient and also to the caregiver and the care-receiver living together. Caregiver distress generally concerning caring for people with dementia appears to be greatest when the two parties live together; this is perhaps because stressors, tensions and conflicts are more difficult to avoid in such situations (George and Gwyther, 1986; Long, 1981). In addition, in the Pillemer and Suitor study, both higher levels of stress and greater degrees of opportunity from more frequent, perhaps even unavoidable, contact seemed to contribute to the positive relationship between co-residence and caregiver fear of becoming violent (Pillemer and Suitor, 1992).

Suitor and Pillemer conducted a further study considering the effects of network factors on the support of caregivers in 1993; however, this did not consider the possible effects of support networks on violence by caregivers. This aspect was therefore the subject of a subsequent study by Kilburn, which used the same dataset but slightly different analyses (Kilburn, 1996). This latter study confirmed many of the earlier findings, for example that violence and disruptive behaviour by the care recipient was significantly related to the fear of care-givers of hurting the person with dementia; however, being married was not significantly related to violent feelings. Additionally, the study suggested that the characteristics of networks may well be of significance in the development and maintenance of violent feelings of caregivers. The exact nature of these relationships appears somewhat unclear at present: for instance, the relationship of a number of people in close contact with the caregiver did not appear to be significant (i.e. contact with close relatives), whilst contact with a number of others with caregiving experience did appear to give the caregiver significant support. However, this was also often linked with raised stress levels for the caregiver. This survey did not consider attitudes of caregivers or the degrees of support given to the caregiver or even what the experience of the caregiver was. Further examination of the nature of caregivers' support systems might well assist in relation to such aspects.

There have been a number of other studies concerning the possible links between dementia and elder abuse and it is worth mentioning several of these. One study in the Netherlands found high levels of verbal aggression (30.2% of caregivers stated they had been verbally aggressive) whilst 10.7% of respondent caregivers reported that they had been physically aggressive towards the person with dementia whom they cared for (Pot et al, 1996). Both types of aggression appeared to be related to living in the same household as the person they were caring for, caring for a male, and caring for a person with high levels of cognitive impairment and physical dependence (Pot et al, 1996). Australian research by Kurrle and colleagues determined that within their sample, 46% of those abused had significant dementing illness, whilst 65% had major disabilities (Kurrle et al, 1992).

In their U.K study of older people receiving respite care, Homer and Gilleard found no apparent association between a diagnosis of dementia and abuse but did find that violence (or threat of violence) by the person with dementia seemed to lead to a violent response by the caregiver (Homer and Gilleard, 1990). This finding lead the researchers to suggest that it was disturbed and disruptive behaviour by the care recipient which was likely to result in abuse by the caregiver, rather than simply the presence of cognitive impairment such as dementia.

A small-scale study of 38 carers in Northern Ireland seems to echo this finding as those factors of apparent significance within abusive situations were poor pre-morbid relationships; abuse (physical or verbal) or problem behaviours by the person being cared for and poor health of the carer (Compton et al, 1996). Within this study, 34% (13) of the carers admitted to verbal abuse and 10% of carers admitted to physical abuse. A further UK study by Cooney and Mortimer focused on asking carers of people with dementia about the possible occurrence of physical and verbal abuse and neglect of the person they were caring for. This was achieved by way of an anonymous questionnaire which was completed by carers, which were distributed by a voluntary organisation for carers of individuals with dementia (Cooney and Mortimer, 1995).

Although there was a relatively low response rate (33.5%), of those who replied, 55% admitted to being involved in at least one type of abuse, with verbal abuse being the most common. Verbal abuse appeared to be linked with the degree of social isolation of the carer and with an existing poor relationship; it also appeared to be a risk factor for physical abuse. Those carers who scored highly on the General Health Questionnaire (measuring psychological health of carers: i.e. carers in poorer psychological health) and who had been caring for longer periods appeared to be most at risk of abusing the person for whom they were caring. Within this study, other variables such as satisfaction with services provided and amounts of both informal and formal support did not appear to be related to abuse (Cooney and Mortimer, 1995).

There seemed to be some evidence supporting reciprocity of abuse in that carers who admitted to either physical or verbal abuse were also more likely to report concurrent abusive behaviour of a similar type by the care recipient as being problematic. Caution should be exercised in relation to his latter finding, however, as these reports by carers were not substantiated at all in any objective sense. Such 'patient' variables as degrees of physical dependency or behaviour and mood disorder did not appear to be of significance as there was no difference found between individuals who had been abused and those who had not. This suggests some discrepancy between the perceptions of the carers and the actual behaviour of the individual, which the researchers were aware of from the findings (Cooney and Mortimer, 1995).

8.2 Abuse and Mental Health

Much of the research attention in this area appears to have focused on the possible relationships between psychological and emotional ill-health of care givers and elder abuse. Some of the most well known research in this field is that of US researchers Wolf and Pillemer, who discovered from their sample that 38% of the abusers had a history of mental ill health and that 46% of abusers reported a recent decline in their mental health (Wolf and Pillemer, 1989). Psychological and physical abuse appeared to be most related to the deterioration in health of the caregiver. In a further related study, some 41% of abusers had a history of mental health problems (Godkin, Wolf and Pillemer, 1989).

This finding appears consistent on an international basis: from the UK, Clarke and Ogg found in their small sample of 11 cases of abuse that 3 of the abusive care-givers had a problem of mental ill health (Clarke and Ogg, 1994) whilst Cooney and Mortimer found that care-givers who admitted being physically abusive in their sample had significantly higher rates of poor psychological health than non abusive caregivers (Cooney and Mortimer, 1995). Research by Saveman and Norberg in Sweden indicated that some 15% of abusers had mental health problems (Saveman and Norberg, 1993). A study from the Netherlands also suggests that physical aggression by caregivers of care-recipients who had dementia appeared to be associated with a higher degree of psychological disturbance of the caregiver as well as caring for a spouse (Pot et al, 1996).

Canadian research also supports the evidence concerning the mental distress of abusive caregivers. From this study, Podnieks found that within her sample, 56% of spouses who were physically abusive reported psychiatric or emotional problems as compared with 3% of spouses who did not act abusively. Those spouses who were abusive were also much more likely to report serious problems with their physical health: 70% as compared to 33% of non-abusers (Podnieks, 1990). Further Canadian research by Penning indicated that 27% of abusers had 'psychiatric problems' (Penning, 1992).

The study by Homer and Gilleard also reported a notable finding in relation to this aspect. Those caregivers who admitted to physical and verbal abuse were significantly more likely to be depressed than those caregivers who were not involved in abusive situations (Homer and Gilleard, 1990). This finding has been found in several other studies (Paveza et al, 1992; Coyne et al, 1993). As McCreadie astutely recognised:

'Mental and emotional problems may be both a cause and an effect of elder abuse. It would hardly be surprising if people living with abuse, some of which may be long term, displayed psychological effects' (McCreadie, 1996, p.43)

And, in addition to this there is a great deal of information available, collated over the past three decades, concerning the stressful effects of care-giving, especially in relation to caring for people with dementia. A useful review of the psychiatric and physical effects of caregiving in situations of dementia, albeit not specifically concerning elder abuse, was provided by Schulz and colleagues in 1995. However, what is not yet clear is the exact nature of the relationship between care-giving and stress, let alone abuse, stress and caregiving.

When considering the stress of caregiving and the possible relationship of this to the aetiology of abusive situations, there appear to be several relevant factors. Firstly, despite an early and possibly lasting perception of much elder abuse being caused by the stress of caring, it is clear that there are many dependent older people who are cared for and who are not abused, even when the caregiving experience is stressful. It is therefore necessary to develop an explanation that focuses on the differences between abusive and non-abusive situations. Secondly, there has been a tendency to equate stress with high levels of physical dependency. This has failed to satisfactorily examine the potential importance of such factors as psychological and emotional dependency within abusive situations (Nolan, 1993). Thirdly, research conducted by Steinmetz indicates that it is the perception of the situation by the caregiver as stressful which appears to correlate with the existence of abusive situations rather than stress per se (Steinmetz, 1990). Whilst stress may indeed contribute to the development and continuation of abusive situations, it appears insufficient, in isolation from other factors, to provide a satisfactory explanation for elder abuse and neglect.

As seen earlier, a great deal of the early research within the field of elder abuse set out to determine the 'typical characteristics' of victims of abuse, resulting in some unfortunate stereotypes (see Penhale, 1992 in relation to this). Subsequent research has focused on establishing profiles of those individuals who abuse. Although similar suggestions may be made concerning stereotypes, such research has value in that it has produced useful information in relation to the psychopathology of at least a proportion of those individuals who act abusively. Further, the research has indicated that there are likely to be a number of individuals who take on caring roles (no doubt for a variety of reasons, some willing, some unwilling) who are wholly unsuited to such tasks. Such individuals may well be practically, psychologically, emotionally and physically unsuited to caring. For those people with existing or previous mental health or emotional problems, personality or relationship difficulties, the tasks associated with caring may prove too difficult and problematic. If deterioration occurs in their own health or that of the person they care for, an abusive relationship may develop (or possibly continue at a more severe level). Further, if there are reductions in the availability and amount of welfare provision to assist such situations, this will not assist in the resolution of such problems.

Finally, there is an additional group of individuals who have been identified as causing potential concern within the arena of abuse and mental health. These are severely mentally ill adults who are living with and being cared for by their ageing parents. McCreadie described many of these individuals as being the legacy of UK community care policies of two decades and more ago: those individuals who as young adults were discharged from large psychiatric hospitals back into the community on the closure of the institution. Some of those individuals who found themselves unable to live independently in the community returned to live with their parents who provided care for them. As these parents grow older, however, some of those adults with mental health problems may be lead into caring for their parents (McCreadie, 1996). Yet as we have seen, these individuals may not be able to provide care at the level at which it is required and abuse and/or neglect may ensue. An American study of over 200 confirmed cases of abuse involving older parents and their adult children indicated that in some 16% of situations, the adult children had some form of mental illness and a large number of these were also receiving care from their parent (Greenberg et al, 1990). These results substantiate earlier reported work concerning the difficulties for older parents caring for a severely mentally ill individual (Lefley, 1987). And as was apparent earlier, it is likely that difficult, provocative, even aggressive behaviour by the care-recipient may be contributory factors within the development of abusive situations by the caregiver. Similar mechanisms may well be present whether the care-recipient has a severe mental illness, a severe learning disability or is significantly cognitively impaired due to an illness such as dementia.

References

Aitken, L. and Griffin, G. (1996): Gender and Elder Abuse, London, Sage.

Anetzberger, G. J., Korbin, J.E. and Austin, C. (1994): "Alcoholism and Elder Abuse". Journal of Interpersonal Violence, 9 (2): 184-193.

Baumann, E. (1989): "Research rhetoric and the social construction of elder abuse" in Best, J. (ed) Images of Issues: Typifying Contemporary Problems, New York, Aldine de Gruyter

Bennett, G.C. and Kingston, P.A. (1993): Elder Abuse: Theories, Concepts and Interventions, London, Chapman & Hall.

Bennett, G.C., Kingston, P.A. and Penhale, B. (1997): The Dimensions of Elder Abuse: Perspectives for Practitioners. Basingstoke, Macmillan.

Block, M.R. and Sinott, J. D. (1979): The Battered Elder Syndrome: An exploratory study, College Park, University of Maryland Centre on Ageing.

Bristowe, E. and Collins, J. (1989): "Family mediated abuse of non-institutionalised frail elderly men and women in British Columbia". Journal of Elder Abuse and Neglect, 1 (1): 45-64.

Cahill, S. and Shapiro, M. (1993): "'I think he might have hit me once': aggression towards caregivers in dementia", Australian Journal on Ageing, 12, 4, 10-15.

Clarke, M. and Ogg, J. (1994): "Recognition and prevention of elder abuse", Journal of Community Nursing, 8, 2, 4-6.

Cloke, C. (1983): Old Age Abuse in the Domestic Setting- A Review, Portsmouth, Age Concern.

Compton, S.A, Flanigan, P. and Gregg, W. (1996): Elder abuse in people with dementia in Northern Ireland: prevalence and predictors in cases referred to a Psychiatry of Old Age Service. International Journal of Geriatric Psychiatry

Cooney, C. and Howard, R. (1995): "Abuse of patients with dementia by their carers: out of sight but not out of mind" International Journal of Geriatric Psychiatry, 10, 735-741.

Cooney, C. and Mortimer, A. (1995): "Elder Abuse and Dementia" International Journal of Social Psychiatry, 41, 4, 276-283.

Coyne, A, Reichman, W.E. and Berbig, L.J.(1993): "The relationship between dementia and elder abuse" American Journal of Psychiatry, 150, 4, 643-646.

Department of Health (DOH) (1993): No Longer Afraid: the safeguard of older people in domestic settings, London, HMSO.

Eastman, M. (1984): Old Age Abuse, Portsmouth, Age Concern.

Finkelhor, D. (1983): "Common Features of Family Abuse" in: Finkelhor, D.; Gelles, R. J.; Hotaling, G. and Straus. M. (Eds) (1983) The dark side of Families: Current Family Violence Research, Newbury Park, Sage.

George, L. K and Gwyther, L. P. (1986): "Caregiver well-being: A multi-dimensional examination of family caregivers of demented adults", The Gerontologist, 26, 253-259.

Gioglio, G.R. and Blakemore, P. (1985): "Elder abuse in New Jersey: The knowledge and experience of abuse among older New Jerseyians. " Trenton: New Jersey Division of Youth and Family Services, Bureau of Research and New Jersey Department of Community Affairs, New Jersey Division of Aging.

Glendenning, F. and Kingston, P. (eds) (1999): Elder Abuse and Neglect in Residential Settings: Different National Backgrounds and Similar Responses, New York, Haworth Press.

Glendenning, F. (1999a): "The abuse of older people in institutional settings: An overview", in N. Stanley, J. Manthorpe and B. Penhale (eds) Institutional Abuse: Perspectives Across the Life Course, London: Routledge.

Glendenning, F. (1999b): "Elder abuse and neglect in residential settings: The need for inclusiveness in elder abuse", in F. Glenndenning and P. Kingston (eds) Elder Abuse and Neglect in Residential Settings: Different National Backgrounds and Similar Responses, New York, Haworth Press.

Godkin, M.A., Wolf, R. S. and Pillemer, K. A. (1989): "A case comparison analysis of elder abuse and neglect" International Journal of Aging and Human Development 288, 3 207-225.

Grafstrom, M., Norberg, A. and Wimblad, B. (1992): "Abuse is in the eye of the beholder. Reports by family members about abuse of demented persons in home care. A total population-based study". Scandinavian Journal of Social Medicine. 21, 4, 247-255.

Greenberg, J.; McKibben, M. and Raymond, J. (1990): "Dependent adult children and elder abuse" Journal of Elder abuse and Neglect, 2, 1/2, 73-86.

Homer, A. and Gilleard, C. (1990): "Abuse of Elderly People by their Carers," British Medical Journal, 301: 1359-1362.

Hwalek, M., Sengstock, M. and Lawrence, R. (1986): "Assessing the probability of abuse of the elderly" Journal of Applied Gerontology, 5, 153-173.

Kilburn, J.C. (1996): "Network effects in Caregiver to Care Recipient Violence: A study of caregivers to those diagnosed with Alzheimer's disease", Journal of Elder Abuse and Neglect, 8,1, 69-81.

Kurrle, S. E.; Sadler, P.M. and Cameron, I.D. (1992): "Patterns of Elder Abuse", Medical Journal of Australia, 157, 673-676.

Lachs, M. and Pillemer, K. (1995): "Abuse and Neglect of Elderly Persons", New England Medical Journal, 332, 7, 437-443.

Lau, E. E. and Kosberg, J. I. (1979): "Abuse of the elderly by informal care providers" Aging, 299, 10-15.

Leeder, E. (1994): Treating Abuse in Families: A Feminist and Community Approach, New York, Springer Publications.

Lefley, H.P. (1987): "Aging parents as caregivers of mentally ill adult children: an emerging social problem" Hospital Community Psychiatry, 38, 10, 1063-70

Levin, E; Sinclair, I and Gorbach, P (1989) Families, services and confusion in old age, Aldershot, Avebury.

Long, C. (1981): "Geriatric Abuse" Issues in Mental Health Nursing, 3: 123-135.

McCreadie, C. (1996): Elder Abuse, London, Age Concern Institute of Gerontology.

McCreadie, C. (1996): Personal communication to B. Penhale.

Mears, J. (1996): Triple Jeopardy: Gender and the Abuse of Older People, University of Western Sydney, Macarthur; Discussion Paper.

Miller, R. B. and Dodder, R. A. (1989): "The Abused: Abuser Dyad; Elder Abuse in the State of Florida" in Filinson, R. and Ingman, S. R. (Eds) (1989) Elder Abuse: Practice and Policy, New York, Human Sciences Press.

Nolan, M. (1993): "Carer-dependent relationships and the prevention of Elder abuse" in Decalmer P. and Glendenning, F. (Eds) (1993) The Mistreatment of Older People, London, Sage.
O'Malley, H.; Segars, H. Perez, R. (1981): "Elder Abuse in Massachusetts: A Survey of Professionals and Paraprofessionals" Boston, Ma, Legal Research and Services for the Elderly.
Ogg, J. and Munn-Giddings, C. (1993): "Researching elder abuse", Ageing and Society 13 (3): 389-414.
Paveza, G.J.; Cohen, D.; Eisdorfer, C.; Freels, S.; Semla, T.; Ashford, J. W.; Gorelick, P.; Hirshman, R.; Luchins, D. and Levy, P. (1992): "Severe family violence and Alzheimer's Disease: prevalence and risk factors" Gerontologist, 32, 4, 493-497.
Penhale, B. (1992): "Elder Abuse: an overview", Elders, 1, 3, 36-48
Penhale, B. (1993): "The Abuse of Elderly People: Considerations for Practice" British Journal of Social Work, 23, 2, 95-112.
Penhale, B. and Kingston, P. (1995): "Social perspectives on Elder Abuse", in Kingston, P. And Penhale, B. (eds): Family Violence and the Caring Professions, Basingstoke, Macmillan.
Penning, M.J (1992): Elder Abuse resource centre: Research component-final report, Winnipeg, University of Manitoba Centre on Aging.
Pillemer, K. A. (1986): "Risk factors in elder abuse: Results from a case-control study" in Pillemer, K. A. and Wolf, R. S. (Eds) (1986) Elder Abuse: conflict in the Family, Dover, Ma, Auburn House.
Pillemer, K. A. and Finkelhor, D. (1988): "The prevalence of elder abuse: A random sample survey" Gerontologist, 28, 51-57.
Pillemer, K. A. and Suitor, J.J. (1992): "Violence and violent feelings: What causes them among family caregivers?" Journal of Gerontology, 47, 4, 165-172.
Podnieks, E. (1990): National Survey on abuse of the elderly in Canada: The Ryerson Study Toronto, Ryerson Polytechnical Institute.
Pot, A. M.; van Dyck, R.; Jonker, C. and Deeg, D. J. H. (1996): "Verbal and Physical Aggression against Demented Elderly by Informal Caregivers in the Netherlands" Journal of Social Psychiatry and Social Epidemiology (forthcoming)
Saveman, B.I and Norberg, A. (1993): "Cases of elder abuse, intervention and hopes for the future, as reported by home service personnel" Scandinavian Journal of Caring Science, 7, 21-28.
Schulz, R.; O'Brien, A. T; Bookwala, J. and Fleissner, K. (1995): "Psychiatric and Physical Morbidity Effects of Dementia Caregiving: Prevalence, Correlates and Causes" Gerontologist, 35, 6, 771-791.
Sengstock, M. C (1991): "Sex and gender implications in elder abuse" Journal of Women and Aging, 3, (2), 25-43
Social Services Inspectorate (SSI) (1992): Confronting Elder Abuse , London, HMSO.
Steinmetz, S. K. (1990) "Elder Abuse: Myth and Reality" in Brubaker, T. H. (Ed.): Family Relationships in Later Life, (2nd ed.) Newbury Park, California: Sage.
Stanley, N., Manthorpe, J and Penhale, B. (eds) (1999): Institutional Abuse: perspectives across the Lifecourse, London: Routledge.

Stearns, P. (1986): "Old Age Family Conflict: The Perspective of the Past". In Pillemer, K. A. and Wolf, R.S. (eds): Elder Abuse: Conflict in the Family. Dover Massachusetts, Auburn House.

Steuer, J. and Austin, E. (1980): "Family Abuse of the Elderly" Journal of the American Geriatrics Society, 28, 372-376.

Suitor, J.J. and Pillemer, K.A. (1993): "Support and interpersonal stress in the social networks of married daughters caring for parents with dementia", Journal of Gerontology, 48, 1, S1-S8.

United States House of Representatives, Select Committee on Aging (1981): Elder Abuse: The Hidden Problem. Washington, DC: US Government Printing Office.

Valentine, D. and Cash, T. (1986): "A definitional discussion of elder mistreatment" Journal of Gerontological Social Work, 9, 17-28.

WHO (2006): A Global Response to Elder Abuse and Neglect: Building PHC Capacity to Deal with the Problem Worldwide, Geneva: WHO.

Whalen, M. (1996): Counseling to End Violence Against Women: A Subversive Model, Thousand Oaks, Sage.

Whittaker, T. (1995a): "Violence, Gender and elder abuse: towards a feminist analysis and practice", Journal of Gender Studies, 4, (1), 35-45.

Whittaker, T. (1995b): "Gender and elder abuse" in Arber, S. and Ginn, J. (1995) (Eds): Connecting gender and ageing: sociological approaches to gender relations in later life, Buckingham, Open University Press.

Wilson, G. (1994): "Abuse of elderly men and women among clients of a community psychogeriatric service" British Journal of Social Work, 24, 4, 681-700.

Wolf, R. S. (1986) "Major findings from three model projects on elder abuse" in Pillemer, K. A. and Wolf, R.S. (Eds) (1986): Elder abuse: conflict in the family, Dover, Ma, Auburn House.

Wolf, R. S.; Godkin, M. and Pillemer, K. A. (1984): Elder Abuse and Neglect: Final report from three model projects, Worcester, Ma, University Centre on Aging: University of Massachusetts Medical Centre.

Wolf, R. S. (1989): "Testimony before the Subcommittee of Human Services: Select Committee on Aging; U.S. House of Representatives Hearings on Elder Abuse" in Bennett, G. & Kingston, P. (1993): Elder Abuse: Concepts, theories and interventions, London, Chapman & Hall.

Wolf, R.S. and Pillemer, K.A. (1989): Helping Elderly Victims: The reality of elder abuse. New York, Columbia University Press.

III. Challenges of Care – Gender and Health Perspectives

Ageing and Demographic Change: European Research Resources

Vera Lasch & Katja Reimann

1 Introduction

The European Union faces the challenges of demographic change such as growing need for and changing conditions in care for the elderly, and the impact of the changing conditions in care on life quality in old age. In 2002 the WHO reinforced the importance of the topic and defined determinants and challenges of the ageing society, outlined in the WHO's strategy paper "Active Ageing. A Policy Framework“ (2002), a vision of ageing as "the process of optimizing opportunities for health, partizipation and security in order to enhance quality of life as people age" (WHO 2002: 12).

Most of the important research knowledge is a result of the 5th EU research framework programme. In the sub-programme „The Ageing Population and Disabilities“ (Programme Acronym: LIFE QUALITY) cross-country research co-operations have been realized, investigating the needs and resources of the elderly and their impact on quality of life and health in old age. Thus the potential and developments in care are highlighted to face the challenges of ageing societies in Europe, and to assure life quality in old age as well as sustainable concepts of care structures. Important steps to crossnational and comparative European research have been made. The EU resources for research in that field have not proceeded in the 6th RF, and may not be so intensive in the current 7th. However, for further European and national research debates on different results, the theoretical models and methodological approaches introduced by these projects are substantial. For national research development, the integration of databases and results from both national and crossnational research resources in the field of quantitative as well as qualitative methodologies are necessary to improve (national) research strategies, enhance its efficiency and to widen research approaches to more internationality. Therefore a short overview of the different projects focused on the 5th framework program will be presented on the next pages. The presentation focuses all research projects with aspects on ageing, demographic change, quality of life for elderly and formal or informal care funded by the European Union in international cooperation. Research results here are important for further research development. As our investigation shows the funded topics focus on care, care structures, on future challenges for social security frameworks and life quality in old age – in the field of gender analysis more descriptive concepts occur. Care is a traditional workspace for women; quality of work in care, qualifications in care and career opportunities in professions relating to care, their remuneration and acknowlegdement in formal and in informal settings will remain important topics in the discussion of new concepts. The question of how ageing and care may be included as a societal and private challenge in future requires the review of the already-existing results from a wide range of European states, offering a first glimpse on the differences as well as the common ground.

2 Data on Ageing, and Demographic Change

The following projects combine a variety of aspects of ageing: they encompass the currents demographic and societal changes, and their implications on the systems of social security (i.e. pension funds), on public health policy and familial networks, and create a database for future research. Contributing countries for the research project "Ageing, Health and Retirement in Europe (AGIR)" were: Luxembourg, the Netherlands, France, Germany, Spain, Finland. The aim was to verify whether people do not only live longer but also in better health and to analyse how the economic impact of population ageing could vary health developments and retirement behaviour.

"The principal objectives of the study were to:

- document developments in the health of the elderly, ideally since 1950, based on a systematic collection of existing national data on the health and morbidity of different cohorts of the population;
- analyse retirement decisions and the demand for health care as a function of age, health and the utility of work and leisure;
- combine these results, and on that basis elaborate scenarios for the future evolution of expenditure on health care and pensions; and
- analyse the potential macroeconomic consequences of different measures aiming at improving the sustainability of European pension systems." (Mortensen 2005: III)

The AGIR project identified important developments for public health policy such as an increase in the number of visits to health-care providers accompanied by a decline in the duration of hospital stays; a decline in the capacity for informal and family care in response to changing family structures and increasing labour force participation by women; and the unavoidable increase of the number of elderly persons and associated with this an increase in the need for long-term care for the oldest old (see Mortensen 2005: 31). It is therefore a vital political requirement for the future to create care schemes, concepts for the care of the oldest old, maintaining their quality of life, and the shaping of care settings (allowing for as much self-determination of those concerned as possible) and support systems for carers (relatives, volunteers and professionals).

The demographic research project „Future Elderly Living Conditions in Europe: Who Will Care" (FELICE) has ascertained and analysed data to forecast future care needs 2000 – 2030 of the population 75+, classified according to family status, future personal and family relationships and socio-economic situations in the nine countries involved (Belgium, Czech Republic, Finland, France, Germany, Italy, the Netherlands, Portugal and United Kingdom). One of their results is:

> For assessing care needs in decades to come, the incorporation of marital status in projections which show a relatively much smaller increase in those without a spouse, as compared to those with a spouse, may suggest some shift in the proportion of care-giving towards that given by spouses in the informal sector. (Murphy, Kalogirou 2006: 5)

According to these results, private care relationships will remain a relevant factor in the future, necessitating promotional measures for the maintenance of familial care relationships. Together with knowledge of ongoing changes concerning familial structures (increase of the number of women seeking professional careers, labour-market participation by older workers, increase of oldest old), the type and quality of public care-infrastructures enabling a positive ageing process and allowing for a high degree of self-determination and integration in spite of health restrictions, will be of the utmost importance.

In the EU research project SHARE "Survey of Health, Ageing and Retirement in Europe" a wide range of comparable micro data on health, socio-economic status and social and family networks of individuals over the age of 50 was collected to display these three equally important dimensions of daily life and their linkages. As a cross-national data base it represents diverse regions in Europe, from Scandinavia (Denmark and Sweden) through Central Europe (Austria, France, Switzerland, Belgium, and the Netherlands) to the Mediterranean (Spain, Italy, and Greece). The results from SHARE are mostly descriptive, but are meant to be analysed further by researchers (see Börsch-Supan 2005). SHARE has been designed after the model of the U.S. Health and Retirement Study of Aging (HRS) and the English Longitudinal Study of Ageing (ELSA). It may well be advisable to set up cross-connections to national data resources (such as German and Dutch SOEP) and to use them jointly.

3 Quality of Life

The EU and the WHO aim to develop more knowledge about the aspects, and the requirements of life quality in old age.

The project „Extending quality of life in old age – the state of the art (EQUAL)" concerns the social and economic determinants of life quality in old age in six European countries. It consists of a review of literature documenting the current state of the art in relation to the definition of the concept of quality of life (see Brown et al. 2004: 5). The EQUAL project, aimed at reviewing the factors which extend or limit quality of life among older people in Germany, Italy, the Netherlands, Sweden and the UK (see Brown et al. 2004: 6), has come to the following conclusions:

> "[…], the components […] were remarkably consistent: These were family and other relationships/contact with others, emotional well-being, religion/spirituality, independence/mobility/autonomy, social/leisure activities, finances/standard of living, own health, health of others.
>
> There was some evidence to suggest that context had an effect on the level of importance given to the nominated components. The frequency of mentioning health as the most important thing in the respondents lives, for example, was found to increase for those not in good health." (Brown et al. 2004: 87).

These results demonstrate the complex interplay of conditions resulting in what is popularly termed 'quality of life': individual, cultural and infra-structural resources are all contributing factors, while at the same time they indicate the relevance of the health system particularly for advanced age.

The WHO promoted the development of standartised, comparable and intercultural instruments for conducting quantitative surveys of factors determining life-quality, translated into several languages, within the project Quality of Life (WHO-QOL). One of these tools still to be developed focuses on the quality of life in old age (WHO-QOL-Old). The project tests the dimensional structure of the quality of life concept of health professionals and lay persons. Quality of life was associate with social, physical as well as environment-related aspects (Winkler et al. 2003).

One of the most exiting objectives of present-day research is to render the existing tools for investigation applicable in a multitude of countries, in order to create comparable data, to open 'quality of life' to co-operative research and based on this, to discuss strategies for change and improvement. The book at hand presents a wide range of aspects connected to ageing, gender, social and cultural differences, offering an opportunity to raise new questions and to deepen already existing knowledge.

4 Research on Formal and Informal Care for the Elderly

The emphasis of EU-research lies in the area of care. Aimed at improving the quality of life and at meeting the challenges presented by demographic changes both within the context of formal and of informal care, a host of projects has been realised.

The EU-project CARMA "Care for the aged at risk of marginalization" (1/2003–12/2005) aims to analyse current social care services for the aged and the social situation of care-dependent older people in five different countries, each with distinctive approach to elderly care (Austria, Belgium (Flanders), Germany, Italy and Northern Ireland). It included longitudinal studies on coping skills of the aged, a comparative study of care arrangements, and a comprehensive literature review. Thus the concept of social exclusion is used to analyse care arrangement patterns, the access to care resources and the social situation of care dependent older people:

> "On the basis of an investigation, [...] two issues have been chosen for a detailed analysis. The comparison of the combination of care resources as well as the related care- and economic burdens reveals accessible care resources and their consequences for care receivers and informal carers. The analysis of social contacts to relatives, friends and neighbours and the psychological situation is undertaken to illuminate levels of social integration." (Theobald 2005: 23)

Within all countries impacts of social class on care provisions were visible. Theobald gives a detailed insight in this volume and points out the importance of keeping processes of social exclusion in mind in order to prevent marginalisation of the elderly in European societies.

The research project PROCARE "Providing integrated health and social care for older persons; issues, problems and solutions" identified structural, organisational, economic and social-cultural factors and actors involved in the integration of health and social care for the elderly and constituting a system of integrated services in nine European countries (Austria, Denmark, Finland, France, Germany, Greece, Italy, the Netherlands, United Kingdom). The aim is to define a new concept of integrated health and social care for older persons in need of care. This is done by comparing and evaluating different modes of care delivery. The research report identifies missing implementation programmes to realise the politically underlined necessity for integrated services in most countries (see Leichsenring 2003).

In the same period, political and thematical networks have been initiated in the field of care for the elderly. One of them is CARMEN – "Care and Management of Services for Older People: a European Network". Members of the CARMEN network are 40 European organisations working in the field of managing services for older people in 11 European countries. CARMEN established a network of organisations involved in managing services for older people with participants in Greece, Sweden, Finland, United Kingdom, Italy, the Netherlands, Belgium, Denmark, Ireland, Spain, and Germany. In this context, research and innovative activities/examples of good practice have been identified in the field of integrated care for older people. Furthermore the CARMEN projecthas carried out a 3-year cross-national comparison of methods of integrated care in 5 different countries,

> "which included methods of assessment and service delivery, new methods of planning care provisions, monitoring, and management of care performance and methods of network co-ordination. In its work the CARMEN project closely examined the fragmentation, common to all the countries involved, which exist between care segments, i.e. acute care, long-term care, social care, housing and welfare." (See CARMEN)

To increase life quality of the elderly in the European countries, the project CareKeys (http://www.carekeys.net) emphasises the quality of care in a three-year-project within the „Quality of Life"-programme under the European Commission, with partners from Finland, the United Kingdom, Sweden, Spain, Germany and Estonia.

The aim of CareKeys is to develop an effective tool for performance management and evaluation of the quality and efficiency of long-term social and health care for older persons. The tool combines three key principles:

- Target efficiency – does the care provided meet clients' needs?
- Quality of life – are people satisfied with the care they receive and does it improve quality of life? And
- Quality of care – are high standards of care and service delivery achieved? (see http://www.carekeys.net).

On the other hand, many of the EU-research projects focused on informal and family carers as an important resource in the care for the elderly, but one which has long been neglected in studies. For example, the project OASIS "Old Age and Autonomy: The Role of Service Systems and Intergenerational Solidarity" investigated the roles of family carers and service systems in care for the elderly and their impact on the quality of life of older persons in five different countries (Norway, England, Germany, Spain, Israel) by analysing survey and qualitative data from questioning family carers.

> „The aim has been (1) to explore the variation in intergenerational solidarity and ambivalences across countries, (2) to study the interacting roles of family care and service systems and (3) to analyse the impact of families and services on quality of life in old age". (OASIS Findings 2003)

The project findings show that the family solidarity and filial norms to support older parents are still strong in the enlisted countries (stronger in Spain and Israel compared to Norway, England and Germany). But ambivalences between older parents and children were found in negotiating autonomy and dependence.

> "The findings indicate that the balance between services and family care is different in the five countries. In Germany and Spain, and less so in England, when the 75+ elderly are 'at risk of dependency' and in the need of support, they actually receive this support from their informal networks – mostly the family.
>
> In Norway and Israel where there is a wide range of services available [...], the family provides less instrumental and personal care. But the total help levels (family and services) are higher. Hence, family dominated models of services, such as Germany and Spain, are vulnerable, and in contrast to what both older and younger generations themselves prefer. [...] Service development however, should follow the path relevant to each country, because the family continuous to play an important role – even in Norway with its wide network of services." (Lowenstein et al. 2003: 310f)

The data shows a complementarity effect, rather than a substitution effect between services and families and that "the welfare state services do not erode family solidarity. But they may change the way that solidarity is expressed within the family." (Lowenstein 2003: 311). Therefore more significance should be given to providing a wider range of care services in order to give older people more choices, and to maintain their independency and autonomy. At the same time building, protecting and maintaining individual resources requires support, concurring with a redefinition of the role of the family, allowing for a mix of family care and formal services, but with the state in a more central role than at present. These findings point out the importance of an integrated view on carers, family members, social networks and other formal and informal care networks and gives insights into the needs of comparable support strategies oriented towards everyday life and the maintenace of habitual environments. An exchange on communal, everyday-life-oriented concepts on a European level is highly advisable. The knowledge about the complementarity of care service structures and family care needs to be grounded on information about needs, wishes and quality of life of the elderly in the different care cultures, underlining the overall results in different countries. Additionally, the future role of family and family support in the care process of coming generations needs to be discussed in these different European cultures.

Pursueing a similar question, the research project "Services for Supporting Family Carers of Elderly People in Europe: Characteristics, Coverage and Usage" (EuroFamCare) investigated the situations and conditions of family carers and other care providers, services and measures to support family carers in six countries (Germany, Greece, Great Britain, Italy, Poland and Sweden). The aim was to examine services to help and support family carers in Europe in the light of features, awareness and utilisation. In many EU-countries, family carers are largely unseen and are not publicly acknowledged. They need political recognition, accompanied by financial and practical support. To support older people living at home in maintaining a social life, mobility, health care, personal needs, financial management and in general organisation and care management, services should support family carers by providing information services, financial and service support and flexible day care or support of self-help groups. Other important issues discussed were the working conditions of formal and informal care work, particularly in caring for the elderly, and the need of public appreciation for this work.

The project SOCCARE "Informal and Formal Social Care Arrangements for Young Children and Older People in a Comparative European Perspective" examined the impact of changes in demography, economy and the labor market within the European societies, on the informal care for children and older persons in five countries (Finland, France, Italy, Portugal, and the UK). The project focused on four family types that are strongly effected by the current demographic, socio-economic and structural changes. They are single-parent households, dual-career families, immigrant families, and "double front carer" families.

> "Recommendations were given for policies on formal care, policies on informal care, labour market policies and other social policies (including housing policies, immigration policies, social security policies and social work). [...] According to the final and most general recommendation of the SOCCARE Project, it is highly necessary that policies do away with strict dichotomies. Citizens of Europe are not either workers or carers. They are both at the same time. As well, children, disabled people and older people are not in need of either informal or formal care. Both are essential and practically always, there is a need to integrate both at the level of everyday family life. To face the challenges of the future, an integrated policy perspective on work and care is required in Europe." (SOCCARE 2003: 2)

In this area a new European network „Eurocarers: European Organisation on Informal Care" was initiated to promote awareness of carer issues and to influence policies in the fields of employment, health care, social exclusion and poverty. The aims of Eurocarers are:

- "exchanging ideas and information about new developments, policies and practice
- promoting awareness of carer issues, particularly in EU countries where the profile of carers in research and policy is low
- influencing policy at both national and EU levels, including the translation of EU policies into national and regional actions
- developing and influencing the research agendas of both the EU (eg the forthcoming 7th Framework Programme) and national governments
- providing new opportunities for disseminating research and for developing new cross-national research on family care-giving, in order to improve the evidence base for policy and practice" (see EUROCARERS homepage)

First results of this projects may be viewed on their homepage (http://www.uke.uni-hamburg.de/extern/eurofamcare-de). There have also been several initiatives for supporting family carers on a European level. (Kohler, Döhner 2006).

5 Older Women

The majority of these European research projects focus on conditions of care and well-being, linkages between health and socio-economic circumstances, or family carers, but they do not sufficiently highlight the different implications of gender on old age health and care issues. In particular, care is a highly gendered issue due to women's longevity: The majority of the elderly to be cared for are women. The same is true of carers, irrespective of whether they are family or formal carers..

The European cross-national research project MERI – "Mapping existing research and identifying knowledge gaps concerning the situation of older women in Europe" gathered information on the life situation of older women in twelve European countries (Austria, Belgium, Finland, France, Germany, Greece, Italy, the Netherlands, Portugal, Spain, Sweden and the United Kingdom). They outlined available investigations, data, and studies, and knowledge gaps in this field (see Stiehr 2004, for results from the Swedish report see Lindencrona, Westerholm in this volume).

6 Outlook

The projects and networks included offer an encompassing base of knowledge for further research in the area of care (both formal and informal), care for the elderly, data on ageing, health and retirement, as well as for the development of concepts of quality of life. Most projects mention gender as a purely descriptive aspect; while MERI does explicitly broach the issue of gender, it also does so in a more or less descriptive way.

The compilation of existing research results and the accompanying materials and insights into country-specific structural differences offer an excellent basis for the identification, investigation and cross-disciplinary discussion of related topics. Above all other advantages, it may serve to facilitate further European comparative research and cross-border cooperation. What is still missing, though, in addition to an in-depth theoretical and methodical sighting and evaluation of the results at hand, is an effort to include the project results into some of the ongoing discourses on separate fields within gerontology, and to develop them further. By supporting this research focus in the 5th Research Framework Programme, the EU has placed particular emphasis on the demands raised by care, care structures and their (financial) implications. In order to develop appropriate strategies for the future, it is still necessary to compile knowledge on the complex interplay between ageing, gender and health, in addition to research into care structures and cultures. Several important fields have yet to be researched; particular attention should be given to a joint treatment of age(ing) and gender. This is apparent if we look at a topic such as the maintenance and the support of familial care. There are several factors at play, which cannot be separated from each other: family, its networks, the involvement of both men and women in care-giving, the ease of compatibility of gainful employment and care-giving, flexible combinations of formal and informal care elements, the maintence of the care-receivers' independency, their social inclusion and quality of life. Each one of these factors contributes to the success of care relationships within families. Furthermore, each one of these questions includes gender constellations strongly influencing resources and potentials. The following fields of research seem to warrant further investigation:

- Migration, ageing and gender: A condensed elaboration of the information and results provided by the various projects, focusing on questions relating to the influence of cultural differences on societally relevant problems in old age. Research on culturally induced needs and requirements faced by formal and informal care, and on experience with the implementation of this knowledge into effective integration strategies in various fields related to ageing (residence and living conditions, work, mobility, political participation). There is a specific lack of research results pertaining to gender differences, gender-specific resource-allotment and problems.

- Work, ageing and gender: The OECD as well as the WHO have defined requirements for improving the integration of older citizens into the labour market. It is therefore relevant to widen research into feasible concepts for the transition from gainful employment to retirement, workload and ageing workforce, inclusion of expertise and life-time experience of older employees, qualifying measures etc. (also see EU-project: ActivAge: http://www.iccr-international.org). This project focuses on the integration of results in gerontological research and processing the differences found on a regional and gender level, and their implications on health and care.
- Volunteer work, ageing and gender: The country-specific experiences relating to questions on the integration of volunteer work into formal and informal care structures, recognition of volunteer work, possibilities of improving cooperation and honoring merits, strategies for the combination of different types of services and qualifying measures for volunteers etc need to be investigated. It may also be necessary to inquire into the existence of gender-specific approaches to support, and whether these are at all needed.
- Education and ageing: The demands on and structure of educational institutions for the ageing; the provision of educational material for a cross-generational cooperation, for ageing workforces, for communal and for private care settings, for the qualification of volunteers, provision of low-threshold modular education and leisure opportunities, etc.. What is needed here is an exchange of experience among the various realms of research and practice: education, gerontology, operational professional training, care, volunteerism, and technological research. Still missing is a differentiated analysis of gender-specific differences and needs.
- Social integration of the aged: Positive strategies for the integration and the development of meaningful areas of activity for the fourth stage of life, strengthening of self-help and self-determination, creation of infrastructures and spheres of life preventing the exclusion of the aged. Here too, a cross-border exchange of experience is still missing, together with gender-specific analyses of potentials and resources, and particularly support systems for the oldest old.
- Cross-generational exchange and cohesion: knowledge on new strategies, such as the relevance of networks including grandchildren, parents and grandparents; possibilities of applying mentoring-approaches to creating cross-generational cohesion; creation of communal and cross-disciplinary projects.

- Integration of new technologies into social spheres of life, and the avoidance of replacing social contacts by technologies in the process of ageing. Missing here are cross-disciplinary and knowledge-integrative approaches and methods. Also lacking are approaches taking into account the highly differentiated needs and modes of access to technology and to technology-backed processes, varying in accordance with gender, ethnicity and educational differences.

In the introduction, we have already argued that research strategies should take into account the heterogenous life-worlds of the ageing, gender-specific differences and life-course variations. We would like to instill yet another strategy into the ongoing discourse: what we would like to emphasise is a focus on innovative practice, devoid of the connotations of obsolescence or dequalification, but rather with an aim for raised quality of life during the last stages of life. In the Fedarl Republic of Germany, a number of initiatives have sprung up, in part supported by the Federal Ministries, committed to re-determining/re-defining the notions on ageing. Some of the areas these initiatives have touched upon are residential and living arrangements for the elderly, i.e. cross-generational residential projects, mentoring projects in a host of industrial and professional branches. There are also numerous "Time Exchanges", or bartering systems, particularly suited to include the daily needs of the elderly, as well as other projects tailored to the needs of migrants. A great variety of ideas and initiatives which have come up during the last years, even though they may not offer whole-sale solutions to the problems faced by the ageing, may still offer interesting opportunities and new approaches. It seems practicable to pick up on these new concepts, to investigate them and to evaluate them as possible enrichments. This could be an interesting venue for international cooperation.

It may be possible to institutionalise regular European research symposia on a European level in the next years, which could be given to the continuous development of theoretical concepts, methodological tools and filling reserach gaps, facilitating, promoting and structuring cross-border exchange (also on strategies). It would well fit the importance of the topic of ageing to strengthen the competence of research institutions within the separate member-states by creating European institutions (which of course need to include gender related questions in their agenda).

References

Börsch–Supan, Axel, Brugiavini, Agar, Jürges, Hendrik, Mackenbach, Johan, Siegriest, Johannes, Weber, Guglielmo 2005: Health, Ageing and Retirement in Europe. First Results from the Survey of Health, Ageing and Retirement in Europe, Mannheim Research Institute for the Economics of Aging, available http://www.share-project.org/index.php?page=Documentation&menue=4&sub=, access date

Brown, Jackie; Bowling, Ann; Flynn, Terry 2004: Models of Quality of Life: A Taxonomy, Overview and Systematic Review of the Literature. Available under http://www.ageing-research.group.shef.ac.uk/pdf/qol_review_complete.pdf, access date 2006/05/30.

CARMEN – "Care and Management of Services for Older People: a European Network", available under http://www.ehma.org/projects/default.asp?NCID=111, access date 2006/05/16.

EUROCARERS – European Organisation on Informal Care: Homepage: http://www. york.ac.uk/inst/spru/eurocarers.htm. last updated 27 March, 2006, access date 12.06.2006.

Jackie Brown, Ann Bowling, Terry Flynn (2004): Models of Quality of Life: A Taxonomy, Overview and Systematic Review of the Literature, available under http:// www.ageingresearch.group.shef.ac.uk/pdf/qol_review_no_tables.pdf

Kohler, Susaanne; Döhner, Hanneli 2006: European Initiatives for Family Carers. EUROFAMCARE Group, available under http://www.uke.uni-hamburg.de/extern /eurofamcare/documents/european_initiatives.pdf, access date 11.07.06.

Kröger, T. 2003: Families, Work and Social Care in Europe. A qualitative study of care arrangements in Finland, France, Italy, Portugal and the UK. SOCCARE Project Report 6, verfügbar unter http://www.uta.fi/laitokset/sospol/soccare/report6.pdf, Zugriff 12.06.2006.

Leichsenring, Kai 2003: Providing integrated health and social care for older persons – A European overview. European Centre for Social Welfare Policy and Research. Available under http://www.euro.centre.org/procare/procare_european_overview. pdf, access date 2006/03/01.

Mortensen, JØrgen 2005: Ageing, Health And Retirement In Europe. The AGIR Project. Final Report On Scientific Achievements http://www.enepri.org/ Publications/ RR11.pdf

Murphy, M.; Kalogirou, S. 2006: A summary of key results of population projections of those aged 75 and over by material status, age, sex for the nine FELICIE countries over the next three decades. Available under http://www.felicie.org, access date 2006/05/14.

OASIS Findings 2003: Verfügbar unter http://oasis.haifa.ac.il/downloads/findings.pdf, access date 12/06/2006.

Stiehr, Karin 2004: MERI – "Mapping existing research and identifying knowledge gaps concerning the situation of older women in Europe" Final European Synthesis Report, available under http://www.own-europe.org/meri/pdf/synthesis.pdf, access date 2006/06/12 .

Theobald, Hildegard (2005): Elderly care and social exclusion: Concepts and empirical findings in five European countries. Paper presented at the 7th European Sociological Assoziation Conference, Research Network on Ageing in Europe, Torun Poland, 9–12 September 2005. Available under http://www.ageing–in–europe.de/torun-papers/ESA_RN_Ageing_Torun2005_Theobald.pdf, access date 2006-06-27.

World Health Organization WHO 2002: Active Ageing. A Policy Framework.. Noncommunicable Disease and Mental Health Cluster, Noncommunicable Disease Prevention and Health Promotion Department, Aging and Life Course.

Care Resources and Social Exclusion: A European Comparison

Hildegard Theobald

Introduction

Social Exclusion and the Accessibility of Care Resources in European Countries[1]

Since the 1990s the concept of social exclusion has gained significance in the scientific and political debate in Europe as a tool to analyse exclusionary processes in society. Research guided by the concept began within the area of unemployment and was only recently transferred to the areas of old age, care dependency and elderly care. The issues of social exclusion in old age, care dependency and the accessibility of formal and informal care resources in European countries with different elderly care approaches are at the focus of this contribution.

I commence with a discussion of the basic assumptions of the concept of social exclusion, as well as its transfer to the area of old age, care dependency and care. As prerequisite, the dimensions of the ageing process are worked out, which allows us to analyse causal factors and processes of social exclusion in old age and care dependency.) Social exclusionary processes become manifest in everyday situations, where actors encounter problems. With the help of accessible, adequate resources people at risk of social exclusion can develop action strategies and prevent or counteract social exclusionary processes. In case of care dependency in old age, access to adequate care resources enable the elderly or their family members to promote social integration and to counteract social exclusion. Care for the elderly is often provided by different actors, i.e. professional carers, privately hired helpers, volunteers, family members, friends and neighbours. The issue of accessibility of care resources requires the analysis of the contribution of different care resources and their combination.

On the basis of an investigation into care arrangements in five European countries, the accessibility of care resources, their combination and the conse-

---

1 The article is based on an investigation carried out within the framework of the EU-project "Care For The Aged At Risk Of Marginalization (CARMA)" (QLK6-CT-2002-02341). Funding from the European Commission within the 5th Framework programme is gratefully acknowledged but the views remain those of the author alone.

quences for the care situation for different groups among the elderly are analysed in a greater detail. The countries selected – Austria, Belgium, Italy, United Kingdom (Northern Ireland) and Germany – represent countries with different approaches with regard to elderly care. The influence of the country-specific approaches is shown in the care arrangement patterns of the country samples, which differ for certain groups among the elderly, and the consequences for the elderly and for the informal carers.

Conceptual Framework: Social Exclusion and the Combination of Care Resources

Social Exclusion in Old Age

Despite various attempts to clarify the concept, "social exclusion" is still criticized as incoherent and elusive, which diminishes its analytical capacity (see e.g. Room 2000). Nevertheless, some basic assumptions of the concept are outlined in the following as a prerequisite for the discussion of the issues of social exclusion in old age related to care dependency and elderly care (see e.g. Silver 1994; Jordan 1996; Littlewood/ Herkommer 1999).

A pivotal characteristic of the concept is its assumption of multidimensionality. Kronauer (1997), for example, lists different dimensions, in which processes of social exclusion may occur:

- economic exclusion, e.g. lack of an adequate standard of living
- institutional exclusion, e.g. lack of access to public institutions
- cultural exclusion, e.g. due to expectations towards certain groups in a society
- social exclusion, e.g. lack of social relationships
- spatial exclusion, e.g. local segregation of living areas

The multiplicity of the concept pertains to its cumulative nature. Social exclusion is viewed as a continuum of combined and accumulated disadvantages, which gradually emerge in a process of reduced social participation. The term 'marginalization' was coined to define this gradual process of becoming detached from the organization and the communities a society is composed of, as well as from the rights and obligations that it embodies. Marginalization focuses on relational issues, such as inadequate social participation, lack of social integration and lack of power. Thus, it is closely connected to a denied access to the principal social areas and, on the basis of this, to processes of multidimensional and cumulative disadvantage. The described patterns of multidimensional disadvantages enable the identification of vulnerable groups within a society (Room 1995).

The assumption of the multiple and cumulative nature of the concept raises the question as to how these dimensions reinforce each other. Whelan and Whelan (1995) describe this as the "need for conceptual clarity". From their perspective, simply identifying dimensions of social exclusion does not allow conclusions to be drawn on their significance and their interplay. "If the identification of distinct dimensions of exclusion is to be fruitful we must direct our attention to the somewhat different factors that are involved in producing different types of deprivation and consider the variable consequences of specific types of exclusion" (Whelan/Whelan 1995: 37). In their view, distinguishing between determinants and outcomes seems to be fundamental in order "to understand the dynamics of social change and processes by which certain social groups are excluded" (Whelan/Whelan 1995:37). As a consequence, the systematic analysis enables the identification of the (cumulative) factors that trigger an entry to and an exit from situations of social exclusion.

Blackman et al. (2001) transferred the concept of social exclusion to the issue of old age. The starting-point of their analysis is the definition of an ageing process as the interaction of genetic, environmental, cultural and social factors reflecting the multidimensional and cumulative character of the concept. Hence, in their definition of social exclusion processes in old age, they combine a broad range of dimensions, which, in consequence, is a complex, still elusive concept of social exclusion. This complex nature of their definition enables us to re-evaluate the interplay of the different dimensions related to care provision on the basis of further empirical findings and conceptual approaches.

The findings of the European project "OASIS" confirm the broad approach for an analysis of the ageing process. The researchers emphasize economic situation, educational background and health status as decisive for the degree of autonomy in old age (Tesch-Römer et al. 2003). The Berlin Aging Study has proved that the health status is decisive for the performance of daily functions (Baltes/ Mayer 1999). The maintenance of these functions forms a precondition for the involvement in social or leisure activities, whereas the participation in such activities is further determined by the status and income mediated by personality and cognitive competences. Both the performance of daily functions and the participation in leisure and social activities are identified as two basic elements of a "successful ageing process" (Baltes/ Mayer 1999).

Strong networks of families, friends and neighbours are regarded as vital to older people and have been revealed to be a significant source of social integration, especially for elderly people living in areas characterized by social deprivation (Scharf et al. 2001). Both social relations and social activities also correlate positively with the health-related quality of life (George 2001). Furthermore, ideological aspects reflecting cultural expectations in relation to elderly people within a society contribute to processes of social exclusion (Blackman et al. 2001). Ageism, i.e. a set of beliefs based on the variations between people according to their age, generates stereotypes regarding competence and the need for protection, which can be used to systematically deny resources and opportunities that others enjoy (Bytheway 1995).

All of the disadvantages within the different dimensions outlined above contribute to a gradual process of social exclusion in old age. Blackman et al. (2001) define social exclusion of the aged as a lack of participation in social life, as well as a lack of autonomy in daily life due to the changes related to the ageing process. Life situations, which may counteract processes of social exclusion, depend on the provision of the elderly with basic needs, such as nutrition, housing, social support, etc., and are all strongly connected to social class or gender (Baltes/Mayer 1999; Kruse 2002). Consequently, changes inherent to the ageing process not only affect the elderly to varying degrees and in different ways, but according to the degree of vulnerability of the elderly themselves and the coping resources and styles available to them.

According to Blackman et al. (2001) social exclusion occurs when an old person cannot control the resources needed to meet the demands of an everyday life of autonomy that most take for granted.

> "Social exclusion exists because access to a resource – including both material and social resources – is prevented by economic, political, and social barriers. These barriers are constructed by a mechanism of exclusion controlled by people with more power than those who are excluded. Exclusion for some is created by the actions, words and beliefs of others ..." (Blackman et al. 2001:162).

Situations, Agency and Power

A more detailed analysis of the development of processes of social exclusion requires an investigation into the situations in which they occur. The situational dynamics of processes of social exclusion is at the focus of an analysis by Wessels and Mediema (2002). In their approach, they turn their attention to situations in which the dynamics of exclusion materialize and the actors involved encounter problems, analyze their situation and develop action strategies. Agency, ability and the competence of the actors, as well as the domain of exclusion and the available resource structures provide the framework of action. Wessels and Mediema emphasize a positive self-concept based on notions of belonging, trust and access to relevant resource structures as a prerequisite for the development of successful action strategies. If one of these notions is lacking, effective action-strategies are impeded and processes of social exclusion may ensue. The authors conclude

> "that the consideration of social exclusion needs to address the nature and processes of belonging, trust and accessibility of the resource structures (Wessels/Mediema 2002:62)".

In their work they analyze the notions of belonging, trust and accessibility of resources on three levels, on a micro-level, i.e. individual biography, on a meso-level, i.e. in close environments such as neighbourhoods, networks etc, and on the macro-, the societal, level. The positive function of belonging refers to integration and participation on all three levels; by contrast the absence of belonging refers to societal fragmentation, social disorganization and feelings of loneliness. Reliance on government combined with the expectation of fair treatment characterize the positive functions of trust, while a lack of trust, or mistrust, appears towards authorities or institutions as well as towards others in the social environment. Finally, the positive functions of accessibility of resources lie in the opportunities to mobilize power and resources for social empowerment as well as resources for personal development and social participation. A lack of access is characterized by an increase in dichotomies between different groups in society, a low-quality infrastructure and obstacles for personal development in individual life courses.

Objective control, which is defined as having the power to control significant resources, constitutes only one prerequisite in the exercise of control. The actual exercise of control is additionally influenced by an individual's beliefs in his or her capacity to control environmental factors (Tesch-Römer et al. 2003). The exercise of power and control, or the lack of these resources are treated as key issues in Gibson's (1998) analysis of the situation of care-dependent elderly. Lack of power and control are defined as negative dimensions of dependency or, in her terms, "negative dependency", which may occur in the life situation of care-dependent elderly people. As a result of her analysis, Gibson (1998) claims the enhancement of access to power or control as the central challenge towards the avoidance of negative dependency. She develops three criteria to define the extent of negative dependency in a given situation:

- the extent to which the dependent individual needs the required services,
- the availability of alternative resources and,
- the level of discretion of the resource holder in providing the required assistance.

Access to resources, the power of decision-making and a broad definition of the ageing process, including genetic, economic, social and cultural dimensions, proved to be significant variables that must be taken into account in any analysis of the interaction between processes of social exclusion, care-dependency in old age and care. The findings place demands on the quality of existing care services and their accessibility. Formal care services provide only a part of the necessary care. The bulk of care for the elderly is provided by informal carers within the family framework. Care provision is typically requisite on a whole pattern where different types of care or help resources are combined.

The Combination of Different Care Resources

For an analysis of the relationship of formal care services and informal care, different models have been conceptualized and empirically investigated. The substitution model proceeds on the assumption that needs and corresponding caring tasks have a final character. Both paid and unpaid carers can carry out the necessary caring tasks and are thus seen as functionally equivalent and substitutable (Lingsom 1997). From the perspective of the model, the changing family structures require the development of paid social services, which in turn reinforce the decline of the level of family responsibility, and as a consequence, the decline of informal family care. In contrast, the complementary model views needs as socially defined and not as final, and emphasizes processes of negotiation between paid and informal care workers where needs and caring tasks have to be discussed and agreed upon. The complementary model hypothesis assumes that professional services strengthen informal care because they lower the burden on the informal carer, so that both informal carers as well as care receivers are more willing to give and to accept informal care. Empirical findings clearly demonstrate that the substitution of informal care work by formal care services is not a very common phenomenon and that no substantial reduction of levels of family help even in more service-oriented countries can be found (Denton 1997; Daatland/ Herlofson 2003).

The link between formal and informal care is revealed as a multifaceted interplay, which is dependent on the family situation, the level and type of help required as well as on the approach and organisation of formal care services in a country (Chappell/Blandford 1991; Daatland/Herlofson 2003; Denton 1997). Various conceptual approaches and research findings show that different variables – the individual experiences within the family context, the social position of the elderly and the potential family carer, and the country-specific elderly care approaches influence the negotiation of the care arrangement in an individual situation of care dependency.

In their research on family responsibility, Finch and Mason (1991) emphasize that publicly expressed norms on responsibilities and duties attached to the family do not seem to be acknowledged automatically. Family responsibilities do not operate by way of substantive, fixed rules showing what must be done, but are used within a negotiation process as procedural guidelines, which indicates how to work out the appropriate level of help and assistance to relatives in defined situations of need. Present actions are only understandable on the basis of existing commitments to giving support to each other, developed in the course of the individual biography. Thus, family responsibilities are not automatically connected to the family status but are created in a biography embedded in the individual family context. Due to the special status assigned to the parent-child relationship, people usually do agree that children have a responsibility to do something to support their older parents, but views vary on what they should do. In their empirical research, no systematic variations on the level of the guidelines according to socio-economic class, gender and ethnicity were found. To reveal the importance and influence of social position, they suggest that a new definition of social structure is necessary. Finch and Mason (1993) define the term "effective structural position" in order to examine not only formal definitions, but also to investigate how the position will constrain human agency.

Finch and Mason (1991;1993) examined familial responsibility in a wide range of areas. Care for the elderly is a sphere where responsibilities are often not only assigned to the family but also to the society as a whole. The availability of services embedded in a specific elderly care approach provides the framework for the negotiation of an individual care arrangement. Within the negotiation processes, welfare states with their capacity to define the needs, responsibilities, and standards play an active role in delivering a framework for discussion.

Accessibility of resources is seen as a major dimension with regard to processes of social exclusion (Wessels/Mediema 2002). Within the area of care for the elderly, the issue of accessibility of resources refers to both formal care services and informal family care as well as to their combination. In the following this major issue is addressed on the basis of empirical findings. The accessibility of care resources will be shown by an analysis of the combination of various care resources for different groups among the elderly and in different care situations. In addition, an investigation into the situation of the informal carers and the financial burdens due to the purchase of different types of paid services reveals the consequences of different care arrangements for users and informal carers.

Empirical Research: Care Resources in Five European Countries

The following research is based on the assumption that the patterns of care arrangements differ between European countries. Findings from a questionnaire survey and an in-depth interview study on care arrangement patterns and the situation of the informal carers in five European countries are used as an empirical basis to discuss the issues. The investigation was carried out in Austria, Belgium, Germany, Italy and Northern Ireland (as a part of the United Kingdom), i.e., five countries with distinctive approaches to elderly care.

Austria, Belgium and Germany represent the continental European approach, within which care benefits have been introduced since the 1990s, together with efforts to develop the concomitant care services. In all three countries the care benefits aim at facilitating the purchase of paid services and at supporting family care. Significant differences exist between these countries with regard to the level of available professional care services, with Belgium at the top and Austria and Germany at lower levels (Pacolet et al 2000; Bettio/Plantenga 2004). The services are also financed in different ways. In Germany, comparatively high care insurance benefits (up to 1918 € per month in home-based care) paid to the care receivers form the only financial basis for the services, which are delivered to the care receivers at cost-effective, non-subsidized prices. Elderly people on low incomes can receive additional means-tested care benefits from the state.

In Austria and Belgium, in addition to the care benefits paid to the care receivers, the delivery of services is directly subsidized. On the basis of the subsidization the user prices are reduced dependent on the individual income of the users.

Despite this subsidization, in Austria the care benefits are comparatively high (up to 1531.50 € per month). Care benefits in Belgium are comparatively low (125 € per month) but care services may be subsidized by up to 80% (Cuyvers/Pintelon 2003; Egger de Campo/Just 2003, Theobald 2004).

The Italian approach towards care for the elderly is characterized by a strict family orientation; the family is seen as the main provider of long-term care services, while professional care services are widely underdeveloped (Pacolet et al 2000; Bettio/Plantenga 2000). Professional care services in Italy are delivered according to the principles of income and very often even according to the family-situation, i.e. they are oriented towards the lower socio-economic classes in society and the elderly without adequate family support. In contrast, provision of long-term care in cases of care dependency is seen as a societal task in Northern Ireland, where care services are universally provided free of charge or at low costs to the receivers, on the basis of need (McCormick/Harpur 2003). Thus, elderly care policies in Northern-Ireland differ significantly from the policy approaches in other regions of the United Kingdom, especially in England, where after commonly occurring means-testing the services are mainly delivered to the members of the lower socio-economic classes.

At least 90 care-dependent elderly people living in urban areas in each country, or their informal carers if the care receivers themselves were unable to participate, were interviewed for the questionnaire survey.[2] In a next step 40 participants of the questionnaire survey study in each country were selected for in-depth interviews. The samples are not representative according to the selection criteria - care dependency and urban living. Due to the access to the respondents mainly via different types of services in Germany, Italy and Austria the users of professional services are over-represented in these samples. Especially in Italy, where professional care services are selectively provided according to the criteria "income" and "family-situation", the sample represents a certain, often disadvantaged group among the care dependent elderly. The findings of the investigation cannot, therefore, provide exact numbers about the situation of care dependent elderly in urban areas of the countries in question. They can, however, be used for a detailed, qualitative analysis of the combination of different types of care resources and their relationship to different social groups and care situations.

Combination of Care Resources: A European Comparative Perspective

With the exception of the Italian sample, family and professional services are the main care providers in all samples (see footnote).[3] In the Austrian sample, a high

---

2 With 115 respondents the Belgian sample is the only exception.

3 Proportion among the elderly, who receive care from the following care resources:
Austria: Professional care services: 70.8%; Relatives within the same flat/house: 60.7%; Relatives within easy reach: 58.4%; Privately hired helpers: 44.9%; Neighbours: 24.7%; Friends: 15.7%; Volunteers: 3.4%
Belgium: Professional care services: 78.3; Relatives within the same flat/house: 44.3%; Relatives within easy reach: 82.6%; Privately hired helpers: 17.4%; Neighbours: 44.3%; Friends: 46.1%; Volunteers: 7.8%
Germany: Professional care services: 78.9%; Relatives within the same flat/house: 38.9%; Relatives within easy reach: 57.8%; Privately hired helpers: 55.6%; Neighbours: 33.3%; Friends: 20.0%; Volunteers: 8.9%
Italy: Professional care services: 44.9%; Relatives within the same flat/house: 17.8%; Relatives within easy reach: 23.3%; Privately hired helpers: 8.9% Neighbours: 68.9%; Friends: 10.0%; Volunteers: 0%

level of professional care services is combined with a high level of care by relatives or partners sharing living accommodation or by relatives living within easy reach. In the Belgian, German and Northern Irish samples a high level of service use is combined with a high level of support from relatives within easy reach but with a lower level of assistance – compared to Austria – of relatives or partners sharing living accommodation. In contrast to the other countries, in the Austrian sample professional care services are provided less frequently. One reason for the pattern characteristic in the Austrian sample may be the high proportion of the elderly who live with relatives, especially with their children. Here, the service provision supports this type of living-situation.

In addition, in the Austrian and German samples about half of the elderly privately hire helpers, while the support of wider networks, i.e. help from friends or neighbours is quantitatively low.[4] In Belgium, by contrast, privately hired helpers are much less common, with nearly 50% of the elderly receiving support from friends and neighbours. The Northern Irish sample takes a position in the middle, with about 30% receiving help from privately hired helpers, friends and neighbours.

In the Italian sample a low level of family support from relatives sharing accommodation or relatives living nearby is combined with a low level and less frequent assistance by professional care services and even less assistance by privately hired helpers. With 68% among the respondents, neighbours are most often reported as care providers. These neighbours assist the elderly on a weekly basis; i.e. 95% of the respondents supported by their neighbours report assistance once or several times a week. Despite this support, only in the Italian sample do the elderly complain about unmet needs in a wide range of daily caring activities. Also the low number of help resources indicates a lack of assistance. According to the samples in our study, in Italy the elderly can draw on an average of 1.8 help resources, compared to 2.8 in Austria and Northern Ireland, 2.9 in Germany and 3.2 in Belgium. The differences cannot be explained by the level of care dependency of the elderly.

On the basis of the variables "living-situation, level of care dependency, socio-economic class and gender" the patterns of care arrangement and the allocations of different care resources can be revealed in greater detail. In all country

---

Northern-Ireland: Professional care services: 83.0%; Relatives within the same flat/house: 31.8%; Relatives within easy reach: 60.2%; Privately hired helpers: 30.7%; Neighbours: 28.4%; Friends: 37.5%; Volunteers: 3.4%

4 Within the questionnaire survey a distinction was made between professional care services and privately hired helpers. Professional care services are defined as services delivered by public or private service providers. Privately hired helpers are directly hired by the care dependent elderly or the informal carers. The latter also includes also assistance and help offered on the black market.

samples, care arrangement patterns are most influenced by different living situations, i.e. living alone or sharing accommodation, but decisive country differences can be observed when it comes to the kind of help afforded.[5] In all countries included in our study the elderly who live alone receive significantly more assistance from professional care services or privately hired helpers with housekeeping chores, with housecleaning and laundry as the only two tasks where a significant proportion of assistance is carried out by privately hired helpers.[6] The country differences concern basic nursing care. In the German sample, all activities within this area are far more frequently provided to the elderly living alone. In the Belgian and Northern Irish samples the differences in the area of basic nursing care concern only some activities and are less pronounced, while in the Austrian and Italian samples the provision of professional care services or assistance by privately hired helpers concerns housekeeping chores only.[7] With the exception of Northern Ireland and Germany, additional care resources are used more often, mainly the help of relatives within easy reach, but also neighbourhood support and the assistance of privately hired helpers in the Austrian sample.

In all samples, higher levels of care dependency are related to different patterns of care arrangements.[8] One difference concerns the help provided by family

---

5 Elderly living on their own receive almost/ significant more care from (Chi-Square): **Austria:** Relatives within easy reach: .059; Neighbours: .009; Privately hired helpers: .083; Prof carers/paid helpers related to the following activities: Cold meals: .000; Cooking: .000; Food shopping: 000; Laundry: 011; House cleaning .003, Repair work: .002;

Belgium: Relatives within easy reach: .010; Prof carers/paid helpers related to the following activities: Personal hygiene: .065; Dressing/Undressing: .032; Going to bed: .094; Check/control: .006; Eating: .013; Cold meals: .086; Cooking: .002; Laundry: .061; Housecleaning: .000; Repair work: .024

Germany: Professional care service in general: .001; Prof carers/paid helpers related to the following activities: Personal hygiene: .000; Shower/Bath: .004; Pedicure: .003; Toileting: .035; Dressing/Undressing: .000; Going to bed: .033; Check/control: .016; Eating: .000; Cold meals: .000; Cooking: .000; Food shopping: .000; Laundry: .000; Housecleaning: .004; Repair work: .081; Errands: .000;

Italy: Relatives within easy reach: .075; Neighbours: .015; Professional care services in general: .000; Prof carers/paid helpers related to the following activities: Cold meals: .000; Cooking: .000; Food shopping: .000; Laundry: .000; Housecleaning: .000; Social activities: .011

Northern-Ireland: Prof carers/paid helpers related to the following activities: Pedicure: .000; Dressing/Undressing: .075; Eating: .046; Cold meals: .002; Cooking: .000; Food shopping: .005; Laundry: .001; Housecleaning: .001

6 In the Northern Irish and Belgian samples it applies to housecleaning only. In addition, in the Belgian sample even housekeeping is mainly carried out by professional services.

7 In the Belgian, German and Northern Irish samples basic nursing tasks are conducted by professional services.

8 Elderly with an increasing level of care dependency receive almost significantly more care from (Mann-Whitney U):

members. In the German, Austrian and Northern Irish samples, elderly people with a higher level of care dependency receive more help from relatives with whom they share accommodation, i.e., they are more likely to be living with a partner or relatives. Only in the German sample does one find a significant increase in the level of assistance from relatives living nearby. The second difference is related to the use of professional care services. A significant increase in the take-up rates of professional care services exists in the samples of Italy, Belgium and Austria, and there are indications in Northern Ireland of an increase in the frequency of the delivered services.[9] In the German sample, more care-dependent elderly use the assistance of privately hired helpers significantly more often but not professional care services. A third difference exists with regard to assistance provided by wider networks – friends and neighbours – in the German and Italian samples.

As a third variable the position in the socio-economic class structure (indicators: income, education, occupational status) is analyzed.[10] With the exception

---

Austria: Relatives within the same flat: .000; Professional care services in general: .029; Volunteers: .051; Prof carers/paid helpers related to the following activities: Food shopping: .084; Transport: .070

Belgium: Professional care services in general: .000; Prof carers/paid helpers related to the following activities: Shower/bath: .020; Laundry: .051; Transport: .006.

Germany: Relatives within the same flat: .002; Relatives within easy reach: .020; Friends: .071; Privately hired helpers: .025; Prof carers/paid helpers related to the following activities: Pedicure: .013; Dressing/Undressing: .090; Cooking: .092; Housecleaning: .055; Errands: .044

Italy: Neighbours: .094; Friends: .042; Professional carers in general: .000; Prof carers/paid helpers related to the following activities: Cold meals: .000; Cooking: .000; Food shopping: .007; Laundry: .018; Housecleaning: .000

Northern-Ireland: Relatives within the same flat: .000; Prof carers/paid helpers related to the following activities: Pedicure: .029; Toileting: .074; Cold meals: .018; Cooking: .014; Food shopping: .002; Laundry: .004; Housecleaning: .009; Repair work: .001

9 The frequency of professional care services is related to the availability of a main informal carer in the Northern Irish sample (Chi-Square .005). Further, the availability of a main informal carer is closely related to the living situation (80% of the main informal carer are sharing accommodations), which in turn is related to the increase of the level of care-dependency.

10 **Austria:** Elderly with a higher socio-economic status receive almost significantly more care from (Chi-Square):

Prof carers/privately hired helpers related to the following activities: Transport

Elderly with a lower socio-economic status receive almost/significant more care from (Chi-Square):

Professional carers in general: Income: .093; Education: .010

Prof carers/privately helpers related to the following activities: Cold meals: .062 (Education); Laundry .013 (Education).

Belgium: Elderly with a higher socio-economic status receive almost significantly more care from (Chi-Square):

of the Northern Irish and Austrian samples, there is a tendency in all samples for those of the lower socio-economic classes to more frequently draw on support from relatives or partners.[11] Only in the Austrian sample do care receivers in this situation tend to use professional care services more often. Interestingly, there is an almost significant inverse correlation concerning the use of the assistance of privately hired helpers, i.e. the elderly receiving fewer professional services are more often supported by privately hired helpers.[12]

In the Belgian, Northern Irish and the German samples the elderly who are higher up on the socio-economic scale receive more professional care services. In the German, and even highly significant in the Northern-Irish samples, it is related to the use of professional care services in general. In the Belgian sample it applies to different activities within the area of housekeeping and basic nursing care.[13] In addition, in the German and Northern Irish samples those higher up on the scale are more frequently supported by privately hired helpers. Even a significant positive correlation between both types of help resources can be stated in these two countries. In the Italian sample, no significant correlation can be found with regard to professional care services, privately hired helpers and support by friends and neighbours, and social class.

With the exception of the Austrian sample, a gender influence in the care patterns can be found in all country samples. In general, there is a trend for men to receive more informal family help in general or with regard to different activities, and women receiving more professional care services. In the Northern Irish sample, the differences are not very pronounced, as they apply to merely one daily help activity for men – going to bed - and one for women – assistance with

---

Prof carers/private helpers related to the following activities: Going to bed:. .082; Eating: .006; Cold meals: .030;Cooking: .009;Laundry:.000; Housecleaning: .065; Repair work: .000; Social activities: .026 (All education)

Germany: Elderly with a higher socio-economic status receive almost significantly more care from (Chi-Square):

Professional carers in general :.062 (Occupational status); Privately hired helpers: .003 (Income); Prof carers/paid helpers related to the following activities: Pedicure:.046 (Income); .070 (Occupational status); Dressing/Undressing; .012 (Occupational status); Housecleaning: .047 (Income) .033 (Occupational status); Social activities: .054 (Occupational status)

Northern Ireland: Elderly with a higher socio-economic status receive almost significant more care from (Chi-Square):

Professional carers in general: .000 (Income); Privately hired helpers: .072 (Education); Prof carers/paid helpers related to the following activities: Shower/bath: .007; Dressing/Undressing: .035; Going to bed: .029; (All income); Laundry: .071; Housecleaning: .070 (All Education)

11 Chi-Square: Belgium: Relatives within the same flat: .076 (Income); .044 (Education); Germany: Relatives within easy reach. .033 (Occupational status); Italy: Relatives within the same flat: .067 (Income)

12 Chi-Square: .064

13 In the Belgian sample private hired helpers are only active in the area of housecleaning.

pedicure.[14] More pronounced are the differences in the Italian and German samples. Care-dependent women of the Italian sample receive highly significant more often professional care services, while care-dependent men more often draw on informal help.[15] In the German sample, care-dependent women receive more professional services in a wide range of daily activities, while care-dependent men are more often supported by relatives within the same flat and by privately hired helpers.[16] Italy and Germany are the two countries with the highest level of elderly women living on their own, and the greatest difference between men and women with regard to the living-situation "living-alone".[17] In addition, the criterion "living alone" determines – compared to the other country samples – the care pattern to a large extent (see above). In the Belgian sample, a different trend can be found, i.e. female respondents are more often supported by relatives within easy reach.[18] A reason for this pattern may be the high proportion of women living on their own and the active involvement of the relatives within easy reach in daily care provision within this sample. A last interesting point is the provision with professional care services concerning social activities. Only in the Northern Irish and in the Belgian samples can a gender difference in favour for men be noticed. [19]

Informal Carers, Care Burdens and Economic Costs

In a next step the characteristics of informal care giving, the situation of the main informal carers, their care burdens and the financial burden arising from delivered paid services are discussed in order to reveal the wider consequences of the care arrangement patterns for the elderly themselves and their main informal carers.

The availability of a main informal carer is taken as a starting point for the analysis of their situation. In the Austrian, Belgian and Northern Irish samples,

14 Northern-Ireland: Chi-Square Eating men: .013; Pedicure women: .033

15 Chi-Square: Italy: Women Professional care services .002; Men informal help with regard to Eating: .028; Food shopping .035; Laundry. .003

16 Germany: Chi-Square: Women. Dressing/Undressing .053; Going to bed . 004; Cold Meals .007; Cooking .001; Food shopping .001; Laundry .026; Men: Relatives within the same flat .000; Privately hired helpers .049

17 Proportion of the respondents of the samples who are "living alone": Germany: Men: 31.0%, Women 72.1%; Italy Men 48.6%; Women 80.0%

18 Belgium: Chi-Square: Relatives within easy reach .091

19 Chi-Square Belgium: .010; Northern-Ireland. .013

between 66% and 77% of the elderly are supported by a main informal carer.[20] The corresponding figure in the German sample is 54% and in the Italian sample just 22%. The proportion in the Italian sample may be an underestimation.[21]

Table 1: Availability of a main informal carer

	No		Yes	
	Count	**%**	**Count**	**%**
Austria	21	23.3	69	76.7
Belgium	30	26.1	85	73.9
Germany	41	45.6	49	54.4
N-Ireland	31	34.4	59	65.6
Italy	70	77.8	20	22.2

Only 31.9% of the elderly report their partner or relative whom they live with under one roof as an informal carer, while the proportion is 92.6% in the Austrian, 91.9% in the German, and 79.3% in the Northern Irish sample. In the Belgian sample, there is also a low proportion 38.7% of elderly who regard the partner or relative with whom they live as their main informal carer. This is, however, compensated for here by a high level of main informal carers who live nearby–in contrast to the Italian sample. Nevertheless, even if the figure is underestimated in the latter due to the low proportion of the elderly who share accommodation with someone, it does not change the picture as a whole. With the exception of the Belgian sample, the elderly living on their own in all countries can rely significantly less on a main informal carer.[22]

Differences between the country samples can be found with regard to the familial relationship and gender of the main informal carers. Within the Austrian, Belgian and Northern Irish samples the children are reported to be the main group among the informal carers. Different patterns of care provision and living situations of the elderly form the background of this finding. While within the Austrian sample the elderly more often live together with their children respectively one child, in the Belgian sample the children living within easy reach take over this responsibility, even if their elderly relative lives together with a partner. In the Northern Irish sample it can be explained by the high proportion among the elderly – 67.8% - living on their own. Even if the daughters represent the

20 A main informal carer is defined as: "A person who organises and/or carries out the caring activities"

21 The interviewer in Italy reports that care receivers often consider the care of their partners as natural and as a part of their role within marriage.

22 Chi-Square: Austria: .00; Germany; .00; Northern Ireland: .00 and Italy: .013

majority of care providers, sons are frequently involved. The proportion of the sons among the main informal carers ranges from 13.0% in the Austrian sample to 18.8% in the Belgian, and 23.3% in the Northern Irish samples.

Table 2: Who is the main informal carer?

	Austria	Belgium	Germany	N-Ireland	Italy
Daughter(in-laws)	34 49.3%	51 60.0%	20 40.8%	12 40.0%	1 5.3%
Partner female	10 14,5%	9 10.6%	20 40.8%	5 16.7%	9 47.4%
Son (in-laws)	9 13.0%	16 18.8%	2 4.1%	7 23.3%	1 5.3%
Partner male	8 11.6%	5 5.9%	6 12.2%	1 3.3%	0
Other relatives	6 8.7%	3 3.5%	1 2.0%	4 13.3%	5 26.3%
Friends/neighbours	2 2.9%	1 1.2%	0	1 3.3%	3 15.7%
Total	69 100%	85 100%	49 100%	30 100%	19 100%

Note: Italian sample: Two of the friends/neighbours are paid by the elderly, Northern Irish sample: While 59 % of the elderly report having an informal carer, only 30 give information about who the carer is.

Within the German and Italian samples, the partners are most often the main informal carers with 53.0% in the German, and 47.4% in the Italian. While within the Italian sample, no male partner is reported as a main informal carer, within the German sample the proportion of 12.2% male partners among the main informal carers is comparatively high. A further quantitatively important group among the main informal carers within the German sample are the daughters and within the Italian sample "other relatives", i.e. nieces or nephews as well as neighbours and friends.

The reasons for the involvement of the informal carers differ between the countries. In the in-depth interviews the respondents of the Austrian, Belgian and German samples partly describe their caring activities as self-evident, meaningful or as based on a positive close relationship. But around half of the interview partners within the Austrian, around one third within the German and even two respondents of the Belgian samples complain about the lack of alternatives, i.e.. no adequate professional care services being available. The respondents within the German and Austrian samples express their desire to avoid admission to a nursing home. Within the Italian sample, informal care giving is based on the norms of familial responsibility even for members of the wider family, e.g. by nieces, nephews and mutual solidarity in the neighbourhood. Due to the idea of societal responsibility the informal carers within the Northern Irish sample describe their engagement as voluntary, i.e. they offer the help they are prepared to provide. Typically, the tasks within care provision are negotiated in a round table conversation between the professional carers and the family members.

Table 3: Main informal carer is exhausted in %

	Yes	**Somewhat**	**No, don't think so**	**Don't know**
Austria	36.2	37.7	23.19	2.9
Belgium	8.2	15.3	65.9	10,6
Germany	46.9	16.3	34.7	2.0
N-Ireland	11.8	27.9	42.6	17.6
Italy	0	12.5	43.8	43.8

In the German sample about half of the main informal carers are reportedly exhausted. In the Austrian sample it is about one third, with lower exhaustion rates in the Northern Irish and Belgian samples. Of the Italian respondents, almost half point out that they "don't know" which indicates that the dimension "exhaustion" is not noticed by a considerable proportion of the care receivers.[23]

23 The question is answered by informal carers and care-dependent elderly respectively. The care receivers may underestimate the level of exhaustion, but it does not change the picture in gene-

For the Northern Irish respondents the availability of a main informal carer is significantly related to an increase of the frequency of professional care services.[24] Within the German sample, the elderly with a main informal carer use professional services significantly less often; in the Italian sample the same trend is discernible, but the correlation is not significant.[25] The low level of support by professional care services in the German sample and in contrast the intense support in the Northern Irish sample may explain the different levels of reported exhaustion. Professional care services within the Northern Irish sample are initiated by professionals within hospitals or by the General practitioners, who refer the elderly or the family members to the care manager or social service office. The German interview partners emphasize the important role of the professionals for the initiation and arrangement of professional care provision. The hospital discharge proved to be decisive for the access to professional care services, and the care needs of the elderly are brought forward as reason for service use. Despite the high level of exhaustion among the main informal carers, no interview partner reports the desire to unburden the informal carer as a reason for the involvement of professional care services. Within the Italian sample professional services are used either when the family is not longer able to carry out the caring activities or when no family carer or informal network for care provision is available. The care needs of the elderly are pointed out as the basis for the arrangement of professional care services by the interview partners of the Belgian sample. The low level exhaustion of the main informal carers indicates that the support of professional services and further informal carers is sufficient.

Characteristic for the care provision within the Austrian sample is the high proportion of the elderly living together with their children and the use of professional care services on a low frequency. Furthermore, professional care services are used more often in case of a more severe care dependency. However, the increase of support may be not sufficient. Within the Austrian sample, feelings of exhaustion are more often reported in cases of a more heavily care-dependent elderly. At the same time, far fewer reports of exhaustion are made where privately hired helpers support the elderly, respectively the informal carer.[26] Only the interview partners of the Austrian sample justify the arrangement of professional care services by both the care needs of the elderly and the desire to unburden the informal carers or to enable labour market participation, with both reasons being provided to the same extent. Professional care services are mainly

ral. With the exception of the Italian sample between 15-23% of the care receivers do not know whether the main informal carer is exhausted.

24 Chi-Square. Northern Ireland: .005

25 Chi-Square: Germany: .000; Italy: .159

26 Chi-Square: Austria: .067

initiated and arranged by the family members or social networks, which may underline the interest of the informal carers to be unburdened. However, the high level of exhaustion may indicate insufficient relief of the care burden of the main informal carers.

Table 4: Costs for services paid by the care receivers[27]

	Yes, (almost) all		Yes, some		No	
	Count	**%**	**Count**	**%**	**Count**	**%**
Austria	14	15.9	32	36.4	42	47.7
Belgium	73	66.4	20	18.2	17	15.5
Germany	5	5.7	44	50.0	39	44.3
N-Ireland	4	4.5	15	17.0	69	78.4
Italy	11	13.4	45	54.9	26	31.7

Table 5: Costs for care services are a burden

	Yes, a severe one burden		Yes, a minor one Burden		No	
	Count	**%**	**Count**	**%**	**Count**	**%**
Austria	18	35,3	28	54.9	5	9.8
Belgium	20	21.1	33	34.7	42	44.2
Germany	26	53.1	15	30.6	8	16.3
N-Ireland	0		2	10.5	17	89.5
Italy	24	43,6	31	56.4	0	

With regard to the costs of care services to the elderly themselves, the respondents in the Northern Irish sample experience the most favourable situation. Only 21.6% of the respondents pay at least some of the paid services and 10% of these assess their costs as a burden. In the Austrian, German and Italian samples, about half of the elderly have to pay for some of the services. In these country samples more than 90% of them assess the private payments as a burden. Half of the respondents in the German and Italian samples even describe them as a severe burden. In the Belgian sample the largest proportion of the elderly have to

27 The costs include payments for all types of services respectively privately hired helpers.

pay for the services and very often for almost all care services. However, only 55.8% of these respondents consider this to be a burden and only 21.1% as a severe burden.

Whether the respondents experience a financial burden or not is related to an increasing level of care dependency and their income situation. In the Belgian sample a higher level of care dependency is strongly related to the experience of a financial burden.[28] This may explain the ambivalent relationship between privately paid services and financial burdens. Elderly people who have to pay all services themselves more rarely complain of a financial burden than the elderly paying only some of the services. It can be assumed that the first group only needs assistance in some areas due to a lower level of care dependency. In the Belgian system, care services are highly subsidized and often not too expensive, i.e. if one only needs a small number of the services, it will be affordable. However, if one is more heavily care-dependent one receives only a very small flat-rate care benefit, which takes no account of the level of care dependency. Also in the German sample the reported financial burden increases significantly with the level of care dependency and the same trend can be seen in the Italian sample, which reveals insufficient covering of costs in case of a more severe care dependency.[29] The income situation is related to the financial burden in the German sample and is visible as a trend in the Austrian sample, which indicates difficulties with the purchase of care services, especially for the elderly on lower incomes.[30] In the Belgian sample, the relationship between socio-economic class and an experienced economic burden is more contradictory. Elderly people with a higher occupational status report significantly more often that they experience the costs as a burden, however, this also applies – almost significant – to the elderly with a lower income.[31]

Conclusion: Accessibility of Care Resources – The Interplay of Elderly Care Approach, the Social- and the Care Situation

Only recently the concept of social exclusion has been transferred to the area of care for the aged. The conception of an ageing process as an interplay of different dimensions – genetic, social, environmental, economic and cultural - forms the starting-point, which have to filled with empirical results for a more in-depth analysis. Dynamics of social exclusion materialize within situations where actors

28 Mann-Whitney U: Belgium: .004
29 Mann-Whitney U: Germany: .035; Italy: .078
30 Chi-Square: Germany: .081; Austria: .164
31 Chi-Square: Belgium: Occupational status: .031 and Income .075

encounter problems and develop action strategies (Wessels/Mediema 2002). The accessibility of resources is viewed as one precondition for the establishment of successful action strategies. In case of care dependency in old age adequate care resources aim at supporting the elderly in maintaining activities of daily living and promote social integration. Care for the elderly is provided by different actors, i.e. professional carers, privately hired helpers, volunteers, family members and wider networks of friends and neighbours. Thus, the analysis of accessibility of care resources includes the access to care provided by different actors, their combination and interplay.

On the basis of an investigation into care arrangements in five European countries – Austria, Belgium, Germany, Italy, United Kingdom (Northern-Ireland) care arrangement patterns, their development and their consequences with regard to the situation of the informal carers and economic burdens due to the purchase of paid services have been analysed. The samples are not representative, but provide a basis for a qualitative analysis of care arrangement patterns and their relationship to elderly care approaches in the participating countries.

The findings reveal different patterns of combination of formal, paid care and informal care by the family or wider social network in the participating countries. The patterns differ within a country according to the living – and family situation, socio-economic class, gender and level of care dependency. The country-specific elderly care approach with its characteristic sharing of responsibility between the family and the society and the related regulations interact with the different care- and social situations of the elderly and their family and wider social network. Within the framework various combinations of formal and informal care develop.

Austria, Belgium and Germany represent countries with approaches, where both society and family are assigned major responsibilities. Despite the common basic assumption, the elderly care approaches differ, as do the observed combinations of different types of care. In Germany, the strict orientation of professional care services towards the elderly living on their own leave in particular the main informal carers with a high care burden. Within the Austrian sample, professional care services are oriented towards both the elderly living alone and those sharing accommodation, but the low frequency of professional care services also results in a high care burden for the informal carers, which can be relieved more effectively by privately hired helpers. Only in these two countries, dissatisfaction of the main informal carers, particularly daughters, with the arrangements can be found. Within the Belgian sample, the care burdens of the main informal carers are low due to the mutual support of family members, in particular the active involvement of the children living within easy reach and the simultaneous use of professional care services.

The elderly care approaches in Northern Ireland and Italy form a contrast. While in the Italian approach the family is seen as the main provider, in Northern Ireland society is assigned the major responsibility. The findings of the Italian sample show the difficulties of care provision in a family-oriented approach, when the close family is not available to take over the care provision, particularly for those of the elderly with limited private means. Despite the support provided by the members of the wider family, e.g. nieces and nephews, and neighbours, only for the Italian respondents a lack of assistance with regard to daily activities can be observed. In contrast in Northern Ireland, the involvement of the informal carers is seen as voluntary and the sharing of tasks between the family and professional carers is a matter of negotiation. Only a small proportion among the main informal carers report being exhausted, which indicates an adequate support in daily care provision.

The findings prove the importance of sharing daily care provision between informal carers as well as between informal carers and professional care workers, to reduce feelings of exhaustion of the main informal carers. The country-specific involvement of male offspring, with the higher proportion in the Northern Irish or Belgian samples, reveals that sons are more actively included in care arrangements, when care burdens are lowered due to professional care services or due to the support provided by further informal carers. Furthermore, in country samples where the main informal carers feel highly burdened – Germany and Austria – the dissatisfaction with the situation increases.

Costs related to the purchase of paid services may either impede the use of care services, or, if the use of paid services is seen as unavoidable, may lead to an economic burden. The most favourable situation for the elderly may be observed in the Northern Irish sample, where elderly care is provided publicly, free of charge or at low costs. Only a small proportion among the elderly has to pay something for the use of paid services and if so, it is not viewed as an economic burden. Austria, Germany and Belgium (Flanders), the countries that have introduced care benefits to support the elderly, differ with regard to the regulations in detail. The differences explain the research findings of the country samples. Within the Belgian sample, most of the elderly have to pay for a proportion of the paid services, but the costs are typically not viewed as a severe burden. Highly subsidized prices of the professional services enable even elderly with a lower level of care-dependency to use these services. In contrast, in case of a more severe care dependency, costs may add up and are not adequately covered by the very low and flat rate care insurance benefits. In Austria care benefits are higher than in Belgium (Flanders), and adapted to the level of care dependency and in addition, professional care services are subsidized. Here, around 60% of the respondents report to pay something for the services. In general the payments are viewed as a burden, but often as a minor burden only. In contrast to the Belgian sample, no increase of economic burdens due to the level of care dependency can be observed. Two explanations can be pointed out for the finding. In Austria (Province of Styria) the frequency of service delivery is limited by regulations and there are indications that the assistance of professional care services does not adequately cover the increasing care needs. Furthermore, care allowances are adapted to the level of care dependency.

Although care insurance benefits are comparatively high in Germany, due to the unsubsidized, cost-effective prices the benefits are meant to cover basic needs only. That around 40% of the elderly do not pay anything is due either to the limitation of the use of paid services to the amount of care insurance benefits or that in addition means-tested welfare state benefits are granted. If the elderly cover some costs on their own, it is experienced as an economic burden and often even as a severe burden. Despite the increase of care insurance benefits according to the level of care-dependency, the more severe care-dependent elderly within the German sample more often assess these costs as an economic burden. About 70% of the elderly in the Italian sample have to pay something for paid services and all respondents describe it as an economic burden, with about 40% describing it as a severe burden. In Italy, costs are adapted to the economic situation of the users but for the respondents – very often with limited private means in general – the adaptations are not sufficient. Even here the increase of the level of care dependency strengthens the economic burden.

Within all country-samples an impact of social class on care provision is visible, however, the type of influence and the situations of the further social groups differ. Within the Northern Irish, German and Belgian samples, the members of the higher socio-economic classes are served more often by professional carers and within the German and the Northern Irish samples in addition by privately hired helpers. The range of caring activities also differs between the countries. For the German and Northern Irish respondents, it applies to the professional care services in general; for the Belgian it holds true for the area of housekeeping services only. Furthermore, the situation of the care dependent elderly in general can be distinguished. Despite the privileged situation of the higher socio-economic classes within the Northern Irish sample the elderly in general receive sufficient, affordable professional care services. This is indicated by the low level of exhaustion of main informal carers or the almost not-existent economic burden accompanying the purchase of services. Also within the Belgian sample, the low proportion among the main informal carers reporting exhaustion indicates that the level of assistance by professional care services and the mutual family help is sufficient. The costs for paid services are not adequately covered wherever an influence of the income situation but also of the occupational position– elderly with lower income and in contrast with a higher occupational status more frequently complain of a burden - can be observed. Within the German sample, a lack of support for the main informal carers in general and the high economic burden in case of professional service use exist simultaneously with an advantaged care situation for the members of the higher socio-economic classes.

Within the Austrian sample, the members of the lower socio-economic classes receive more professional care services, while simultaneously the members of the higher socio-economic classes are oriented towards privately hired carers. One reason may be the regulations limiting the frequency of service provision. The insufficient frequency of care provision may induce members of the higher socio-economic classes to look for private solutions. Within the Italian sample, no impact of socio-economic class can be observed. But according to the rules of service provision, professional care services are mainly delivered to the elderly with limited private means.

Gender patterns in care provision, i.e. the major responsibility of female main informal carers but also the inroad of men, has already been discussed (see above). From the perspective of the elderly care users the situation is not so straightforward. Whether a gender impact can be observed depends on the proportion of women living on their own in a sample and the orientation of the professional care services towards elderly living on their own. A considerable gender influence can only be stated for the German and Italian samples.

References

Baltes, P. B./Mayer, K. U. (eds.). (Hardback 1999, Paperback 2001). The Berlin Aging Study: Aging from 70 to 100. New York: Cambridge University Press

Bettio, F./ Plantenga, J. (2004). Comparing Care Regimes in Europe. Feminist Economics,10 (1), March 2004, 85-113

Blackman, T./Brodhurst, S./Convery, J. (eds.) (2001). Social Care and Social Exclusion. Houndsmills, Basingstoke: Palgrave

Bytheway, B. (1995). Ageism. Buckingham: Open University Press

Chappell, N.L./Blandford, A. (1991) Informal and Formal Care: Exploring the complementarity. Ageing and Society, 11, 299-315.

Cuyvers, G/ Pintelon, A. (2003). Documentation of Services for Reintegration of the Aged in Belgium. Report Workpackage two. EU-Project CARMA. www.cooss.marche.it/Carma

Daatland, S.O. /Herlofson, K. (2003) Families and welfare states: Substitution or complementarity. Final Report (unpublished). EU-Project OASIS (pp. 285-308).

Denton, M. (1997) The Linkages between Informal and Formal Care of the Elderly. Canadian Journal on Aging, 16, 1, 30-50.

Egger deCampo, M./Just; B. (2003). Documentation of Services for The Aged at Risk of Marginalization in Austria. Report Workpackage two. EU-Project CARMA. www.cooss.marche.it/Carma

Finch, J./ Mason, J. (1991) Negotiating family responsibilities. London/New York: Tavistock/Routledge.

Finch, J. / Mason, J. (1993) Obligations of kinship in contemporary Britain. Is there normative agreement? British Journal of Sociology, 42, 3, 345-67.

George. L. (2001). The social psychology of health. In: Binstock, R.H./George, I.K. (eds.). Handbook of aging and the social sciences. (5ed.).San Diego: Academic Press, 217-237

Gibson, D. (1998). Aged Care. Old Policies, New Problems. Cambridge: University Press

Jordan, B. (1996). A Theory of Poverty & Social Exclusion. Cambridge: Polity Press

Kronauer, M. (1997). „Soziale Ausgrenzung" und „Underclass" Über neue Formen gesellschaftlicher Spaltung. Leviathan, 25, 28-49

Kruse, A. (2002). Gesund Altern. Stand der Prävention und Entwicklung ergänzender Präventionsstrategien. Expertise im Auftrag des Bundesministeriums für Gesundheit.

Lingsom, S. (1997) The substitution issue. Care policies and their consequences for family care. Report 6-1997. Oslo: NOVA.

Littlewood, P./Herkommer, S. (1999). Identifying Social Exclusion. Some problems of meaning. In: Littlewood, P./ Glorieux, I./Herkommer, S./Jönsson, I. (eds.). Social Exclusion in Europe: Problems and paradigms. Aldershot: Ashgate, 1-21

McCormick, W./Harpur, J. (2003). Documentation of Services for The Aged at Risk of Marginalization in N.-Ireland. Report Workpackage two. EU-Project CARMA. www.cooss.marche.it/Carma

Pacolet, J./ Bouton, R./Lanoye, H./Versieck, K. (2000). Social Protection for Dependency in Old Age. A study of fifteen EU Member States and Norway. Aldershot: Ashgate

Room, G. (1995). Poverty in Europe: competing paradigms of analysis, Policy & Politics, 23 (2), 103-113

Room, G. (2000). Social Exclusion, solidarity and the challenge of globalisation, International Journal of Social Welfare, 9, (2), 103-119

Scharf, T./Philippson, C./Kingston, P./ Smith, A.E. (2001). Social Exclusion and Older People: exploring the connections, Education and Ageing, 16, (3), 303-320

Silver, H. (1994). Social Exclusion and social solidarity: Three paradigms, International Labour Review, 133 (5-6), 531-578

Tesch-Römer, C./ Motel-Klingebiel, A./ Von Kondratowitz, H.J. (2003). Quality of Life. Project OASIS: Final Report, 259-284

Theobald, H. (2004) Care services for the elderly in Germany. Infrastructure, access and utilisation from the perspective of different user groups. (SP I 2004-302). Discussion-paper. Working Group on Public Health Policy. Social Science Research Center (WZB). Berlin

Wessel, B. /Mediema, S. (2002). Towards understanding situations of social exclusion In: Steinert, H./ Pilgrim A (eds.). Welfare Policy From Below: Struggles Against Social Exclusion in Europe. Aldeshot: Ashgate, 61-74

Whelan, B./Whelan, C.T. (1995). In what sense is poverty multidimensional? In. Room, G. (ed.) Beyond the threshold. The Measurement and Analysis of Social Exclusion. Bristol: Policy Press, 29-48

Future Elderly Living Conditions In Europe: Demographic Insights

Gabriele Doblhammer & Uta Ziegler

During the last three decades, low birth rates and increasing life expectancy have led to the ageing of the European population, which is expected to accelerate during the coming decades. The proportion of the population 60+ and 80+ in the 15 member states of the European Union will increase from 22.4 percent and 4.3 percent, respectively, in 2004 to about 32.4 percent and 7.5 percent in 2030. Trends are similar in Germany: between 2001 and 2035 the share of the population aged 60+ will increase from 24.1 percent to 34.4 percent and the share of over 80-year-olds will increase from 3.9 percent to 7.3 percent (Eurostat 2005, Statistisches Bundesamt 2003). In 1950, this share of people aged 60+ and 80+, respectively, was still as low as 14.0 percent and 1.0 percent in West Germany and 16.0 percent and 1.0 percent in East Germany.

The projections by Eurostat and the Statistical Office of Germany are based on the assumption that fertility will remain below the replacement level, and on moderate improvements in future life expectancy. The assumptions about life expectancy have recently been challenged as being too conservative for Germany (Bomsdorf 2004, Schnabel, Kistowski and Vaupel 2005) as well as for the world in general (Oeppen and Vaupel 2002). The latter show that the life expectancy of the respective country leading world wide in a particular year has been increasing linearly by 3 months per year since 1840, and no levelling off of the situation is detectable. Thus, life expectancy in Europe in 2030 could be higher than currently assumed, resulting in an even higher proportion of elderly people.

These tremendous changes in the population structure will have far-reaching consequences for society as a whole. It has repeatedly been pointed out that the increasing share of an elderly population may result in a raised demand for care, particularly if the health status of the elderly remains unchanged as compared to today. On the other hand, the supply of private care may diminish in the coming decades due to changes in the family structure, brought about by the second demographic transition.

Whether and to what extent demand and supply of care will change in the near future is at the heart of the project FELICIE – Future Elderly LIving Conditions In Europe - funded by the European Commission, under the 5th Framework.

The core objectives of the project are (1) a 2000-2030 forecast of care need among the population aged 75+ by family status; (2) a forecast of their future kinship structures; and (3) of their socio-economic status in Belgium, the Czech Republic, Finland, France, Germany, Italy, the Netherlands, Portugal and the United Kingdom.

Whether a person is in need of care primarily depends on his or her status of health; whether care is provided in institutions or at home is in turn determined by family status, living arrangement and socio-economic background. The choice of a specific living arrangement is a step-wise decision within which the marital/conjugal status, the existence of family support, the health conditions and socio-economic conditions are the most important determinants. Old people can live on their own as long as they are in good shape or if they reside with someone who is willing and able to provide care.

Projections of care need, thus, primarily depend on assumptions about future trends in health status, while projections of care supply need to draw into consideration the support structure future elderly may expect from their partner and from their children. This chapter addresses both the questions of care demand and of care supply. First we present the current situation in the nine FELICIE countries regarding prevalences of disability, marital status, living arrangements, and childlessness. In the second part we shall provide a short overview of the main projection results of future care need and discuss future trends in marital status and childlessness. Particular emphasis will be placed on the German situation.

Marital Status-specific Prevalences of Severe Disability in the FELICIE Countries

A long and extensive literature has shown correlations between marital status and indicators of health, with married individuals enjoying the best health, followed by the never-married and finally, the formerly married. This association is hypothesised to reflect both positive health selection (unhealthy people are less likely to marry, to stay married or to remarry) and the protective effects of companionship: care when ill, sexual intimacy, material advantages (especially for women), domestic services and control of unhealthy behaviours (especially for men) (Hahn 1993; Glaser, Murphy and Grundy 1997). It has been suggested that this correlation may diminish, or even be reversed, in older women. Goldman, Korenmen and Weinstein (1995) found that never-married older women enjoyed better states of health than their married counterparts, a result the authors attributed to more extensive social ties built up as an alternative to marriage. However, this analysis was based on a private household sample (the US Longitudinal Study of Ageing). Analyses of British data including the institutionalised population have shown a continuing, although weaker, advantage for the married, even in the oldest age groups (Glaser, Murphy and Grundy 1997).

Within the FELICIE project, health profiles of nine European countries have been compared. Special emphasis is placed on marital status-specific differences in health in each of the countries. International comparisons, however, are clearly hampered by differing definitions of health. A recent Eurostat publication (2003) gives an overview of the health questions asked in European health surveys and assesses their comparability. According to the report, questions about self-perceived health belong to those indicators with relatively high levels of comparability, which are commonly asked in national health interviews. Therefore, we decided to base our study on an indicator of subjective health that is closely linked to disability: the ability to independently perform activities of daily life.

Even if similar questions are asked in national surveys there are some variations among the countries, not only in wording, but also most importantly in the response categories. Within the FELICIE project we, therefore, opted for using an international survey – the European Community Household Panel (ECHP) as the starting point of our comparative analysis. The ECHP contains the question "Are you hampered in daily activities by any physical or mental health problem, illness or disability?" with the answer categories `severely´, `to some extent´, and ‚no'. Although the ECHP to a certain degree solves the problem of comparability by asking a uniform question in all countries, there are additional challenges. Firstly, the same health questions may be answered differently in different countries, depending on the exact wording and cultural differences in the perception of health. Secondly, the ECHP is restricted to private households only. It therefore excludes the large proportion of elderly living in institutions. Furthermore, living in institutions is related to health and marital status. On the basis of the ECHP alone, one, therefore, would underestimate the prevalence of disability. This underestimation would be more serious for the unmarried than for the married: since the unmarried usually do not have a partner who takes care of them in case of sickness, they experience a higher likelihood of living in an institution. Thirdly, sample sizes in the ECHP are generally small, particularly at older ages. It is therefore impossible to derive age-specific prevalences of health for the unmarried population, particularly when looking for distinctions between the single, widowed and the divorced.

Within the FELICIE project we therefore resolved upon the following procedure consisting of three steps: on the basis of the ECHP we first analyse the question about limitations in daily activities "Are you hampered in daily activities by any physical or mental health problem, illness or disability" (severely, to some extent, no) and assume that participants selecting the first answer are in need of care. The decision to restrict those who are in need of care to the category "severely" was taken after extensive cross-country comparisons. These comparisons show that defining care need in terms of the two categories "severely" and "to some extent" would result in large differences between countries that may mainly reflect differences in the cultural perception of moderate disability. Between-country-differences are much smaller and more reasonable when only severe disability is used.

Since the sample sizes in the ECHP are generally small, particularly at older ages, we could not discern any reliable age-specific prevalences of disability for the unmarried population. We therefore restricted our analysis to the married population only and calculated age-specific profiles of disability for the married. Using the proportion of married people living in institutions provided by national statistics, we then adjusted the age-profile in order to reflect the prevalences in the total married population rather than in the married population living in private households. In a third step we used national health surveys to estimate odds ratios of disability for the widowed, single and divorced as compared to the married and applied these odds ratios to the age-specific prevalences of the married. We used logistic regression to calculate the age-specific and marital status-specific prevalences of disability.

The international comparison of the prevalence of disability among the married in the eight FELICIE countries Belgium, France, Finland, Germany, Italy, Netherlands, Portugal, United Kingdom (in the ECHP no data are available for the Czech Republic) divides the countries into two broad groups: The first group is outstanding insofar as these countries exhibit particularly low prevalences of disability for both sexes, and consists of Italy, Belgium and the Netherlands (dashed lines in Figures 1a and 1b). The remaining countries form a more or less consistent group with prevalences at age 85+ for males ranging from 38 percent in Germany to 46 percent in France, and for females from 44 percent in Portugal to 53 percent in France and UK, respectively. Finnish males stand out because of their extremely high prevalence of severe disability from age 70 onwards, which reaches a level of 60 percent at age 85+.

Figures 1a and 1b: Prevalence of severe disability among married people in eight FELICIE countries: logarithmic scale

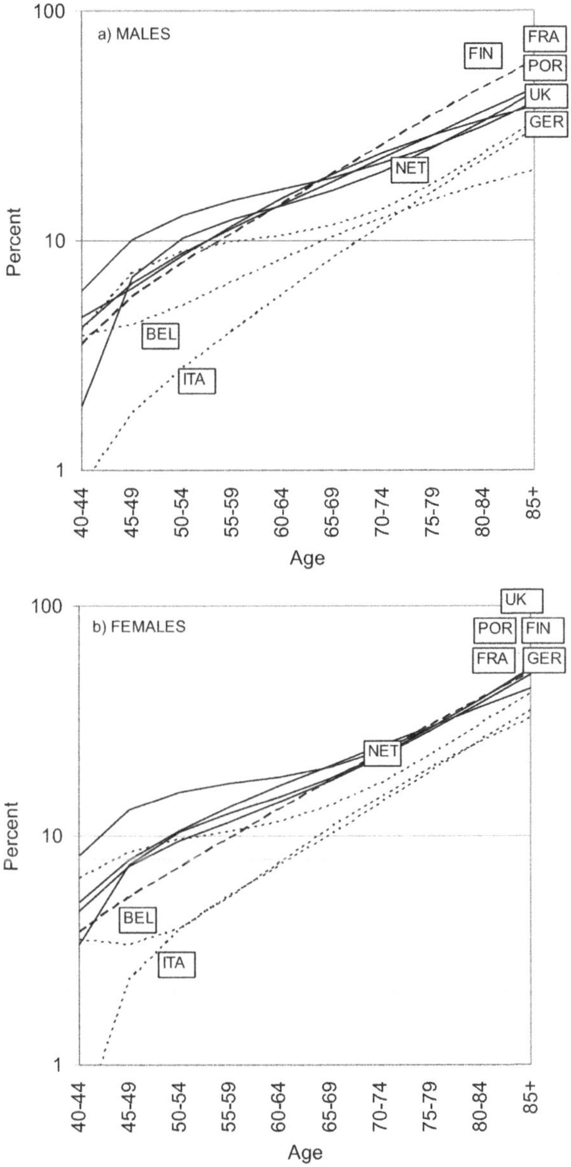

A comparison of the level of disability with remaining life expectancy among the married elderly (figure not shown) reveals no correlation when corrected for sex. It is, thus, not possible to infer whether increased life expectancy is a result of years spent in disability or in good health. On the contrary, it seems that these two factors are independent of each other.

The question as to why arises. Although we can only speculate, one possible explanation is the influence of social factors on the process from functioning loss to disability. There is a long way from the healthy state to disease and impairment which may lead to functioning loss that may finally result in disability. Whether functioning loss, which mainly captures physical decline, leads to disability depends largely on the social environment. The question asked in the ECHP contains both aspects. Differences in the prevalence of severe disability may therefore not only capture differences in physical health but also in the social environment. Which are these social factors? On the one hand there may be differences in the medical systems, on the other hand there may be differences in family structures, economic status and cultural norms. An Italian, who is taken care of by his or her family, which may provide financial resources and accepts functional loss as an obligation to personally take care of its elderly relatives, may feel less hampered and disabled than a Fin who lives alone in an institution with little financial resources remaining at his disposal.

Turning to marital status-specific odds ratios of severe disability, we generally find that the married experience the best health status (Table 1). As mentioned before, this is consistent with a large body of literature. As expected, considerable differences exist between marital status- specific odds ratios on the basis of the ECHP and national sources. This partly stems from different definitions of disability, but also from the inclusion of the institutional population in some of the national surveys. In France a particularly strict definition of disability is used in the national survey, resulting not only in extremely low levels of disability but also in marital status- specific odds ratios that are lowest for the widowed and divorced. With the exception of France, the widowed generally seem to fare best behind the married while the never-married are the most disadvantaged in terms of disability. Differentials are similar among females and males. Comparing the odds ratios derived from national sources with those based on the ECHP (not shown) we find that the ECHP generally underestimates the differentials (with the exception of France). This may be explained by the exclusion of the institutionalised population from the ECHP. Since institutionalisation depends both on health status and marital status, selection effects into institutions are stronger among the unmarried than the married.

Table 1: Marital-status-specific odds ratios in disability in comparison to the married, ages 45+ based on national sources

	Males						Females					
	Never married		Wid-owed		Divorced		Never married		Wid-owed		Divorced	
Bel-gium	1.71	**	1.04		1.47	**	1.32	**	1.02		1.47	**
Finland												
France	2.38	**	0.66	*	0.56	*	1.70	**	1.17	*	1.03	
Ger-many	1.21	**	0.99		1.44	**	1.34	**	1.37	**	1.73	**
Italy	2.42	**	1.53	**	1.53		3.33	**	1.40	*	1.05	
Nether-lands	1.43		0.84		1.39		1.35		1.00		1.69	**
Portu-gal	3.67	**	1.17	**	1.52	**	2.61	**	1.26	**	1.43	**
UK	1.32	*	1.03		1.36	**	1.13		1.27	**	1.48	**

**: significant at the 1% level, *: significant at the 5% level

No correlation exists between country patterns in marital status-specific odds ratios in disability and differences in remaining life expectancy at age 45 by marital status (Figure 2). For example, the country with the largest odds ratios in disability is Italy, while differences in life expectancy are largest in Germany. This again points to the explanation that country-specific social factors influence the relationship between functioning loss and disability.

Trends in Healthy Life Expectancy in Germany Between 1992 and 2001

Three scenarios have been proposed concerning the future developments of mortality and health. The first scenario assumes that the increase in life expectancy is caused by a reduction of the fatality rate of chronic diseases rather than by a decline of the incidence of the disease (Gruenberg 1977; Olshansky et al. 1991). This scenario is generally called the "expansion of morbidity" theory. The increase in life expectancy goes hand in hand with a growing number of years spent in poor health.

In contrast, Fries (1989) proposed the "compression of morbidity" scenario, which assumes that the onset of morbidity will be postponed while the average lifespan will not exceed 85 years. This implies that morbidity will be compressed into an ever-shorter period at the end of life.

The third theory was proposed by Manton (1982) and combines both the compression and expansion scenario. The "dynamic equilibrium" scenario implies that the increase in life expectancy will be associated with a redistribution of disease and disability from severe to moderate states. Life expectancy with severe disability will therefore decrease while life expectancy with moderate disability will increase.

Figure 2: Scatterplot marital status-specific odds ratios in disability and differences in remaining life expectancy as compared to the married; ages 45+ FELICIE countries

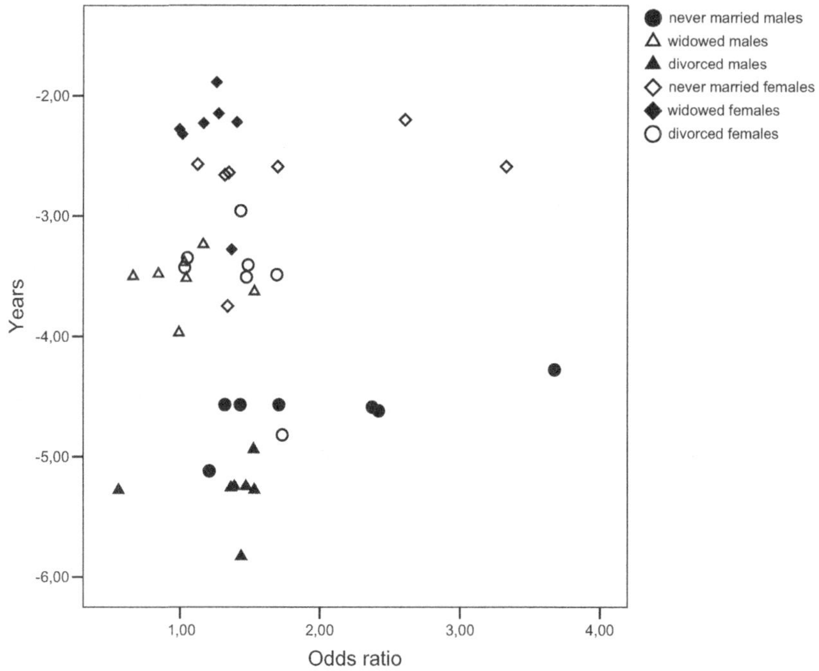

Health trends have been widely analysed on the basis of health expectancies, which combine information about mortality and health trends at the population level (Crimmins, Saito and Ingegneri 1989, 1997, Bebbington 1991, van Ginneken et al. 1991, van de Water, Boshuizen and Perenboom 1996, Valkonen, Sihvonen and Lahelma 1997, Robine, Mathers and Brouard 1996, Doblhammer and Kytir 2001, Robine, Romieu and Cambois 1997, Robine et al. 2003). The results of these studies, however, tend to depend on the indicator of health that is used in the study and on the time period of the study. For example, Crimmins, Saito and Ingegneri (1989) use disability as an indicator of health in the US in the 1970s and conclude that increases in life expectancy lead to an expansion of morbidity. For the 1980s Crimmins, Saito and Ingegneri (1997), however, come to the opposite conclusion and support the scenario of a compression of morbidity, particularly at older ages. Grundy, Ahlburg and Ali (1999) report that the prevalence of disability was much higher in the 1996/97 UK disability survey than in the earlier 1985 survey, and that these results are therefore not in concordance with those from the United States. Contradictory results exist for Finland (Robine et al. 2003), with an increase in the proportion of people reporting long-standing illnesses over the time period 1964 to 1996, a decrease in the proportion of people with ADL disabilities (1986 to 1994) and a decrease of the proportion of people reporting poor or rather poor health (1979-1998). Studies based on self-reported health tend to find a compression of morbidity, particularly among middle-aged men (van de Water, Boshuizen and Perenboom 1996) but also among the elderly in general (Doblhammer and Kytir 2001).

Despite all these discrepancies in the results, Robine et al. (2003) in their overview of health trends in low-mortality countries over a 25-year period from 1970 to 1995, support the dynamic equilibrium scenario. The authors conclude that "disability-free life expectancy has evolved very differently depending on the severity level of disability: a decrease for the most severe levels of disability (institutionalisation and/or bed confinement), and an increase for the less severe levels of disability (no Activity of Daily Living (ADL) Dependency)". The general conclusion from the overview of past studies is that "at worst the increase in life expectancy is accompanied by a pandemic of light and moderate but not of severe disability". Countries, however, appear to differ largely in their trends of disability, particularly for less severe levels of disability. The more severe the levels, the more similar are the changes over time, indicating a possible compression of morbidity? (Robine et al. 2003).

The time period covered in the ECHP ranges from 1995 to 1999 and is too short for analysing time trends. Since for Germany the ECHP is based on the German Socio-economic Panel (GSOEP), we use the cross-sections of the GSOEP for the years 1992 and 2001 in order to examine trends in the prevalence of disability in East and West Germany. The Sullivan Method (Sullivan 1971) is applied to the German life tables for the years 1992 and 1999, taken from the Human Mortality Database (Table 2).

In terms of care need, health trends at ages 75+ are of particular interest. Over the period of time mentioned, life expectancy in both parts of Germany rose considerably, particularly among East German females aged 75+ (1.4 years). In this age group the health ratio of moderate and severe disability combined (= number of years with moderate and severe disability divided by the total number of years) remained largely stable among females (East Germany 1992: 86 percent; 2001:84.7 percent; West Germany 1992: 81.8 percent; 2001:80.5 percent), whereas it improved among East German males (1992:89.1 percent; 2001:76.3 percent) and deteriorated among West German males (1992: 73.5 percent; 2001:81.3 percent). In other words, among German females we neither find a compression nor an expansion of disability, but rather a parallel shift of mortality and disability to higher ages. This is different for males: in East Germany there is a compression of disability (increasing life expectancy goes hand in hand with better health), in West Germany an expansion of disability.

Behind these general trends there are opposite trends in moderate and severe disability. With the exception of West German males there is a tendency from severe towards moderate disability. While among females the health ratio of severe and moderate disability combined remained stable over time, the health ratio of severe disability clearly declined. This parallel shift in disability and mortality to higher ages, combined with the trend from severe to moderate disability is consistent with the "Dynamic equilibrium hypothesis" formulated by Manton.

Among East German males, both severe and moderate disability declined. West German males stand out not only because of the deterioration of their health over time but also because of their exceptionally low proportion of years lived with disability. Whether the latter result reflects reality or is due to a data artefact in the GSOEP has still to be investigated.

Table 2: Trends in healthy life expectancy in East Germany between 1992 and 2001, GSOEP

	Males				Females			
	Disability in %		Partial life expectancy		Disability in %		Partial life expectancy	
Disability	1992	2001	1992	2001	1992	2001	1992	2001
EAST GERMANY								
Age 40-59								
No	61.0	59.6	11.67	11.28	51.5	54.3	10.01	10.62
Moderate	30.8	31.0	5.63	6.04	38.8	34.8	7.63	6.90
Severe	8.1	9.4	1.47	1.76	9.7	10.9	1.84	2.09
health ratio moderate & severe			*37.8*	*40.9*			*48.6*	*45.9*
health ratio severe			*7.8*	*9.2*			*9.4*	*10.6*
Age 60-74								
No	32.0	40.8	3.71	4.90	33.0	35.0	4.51	4.79
Moderate	47.2	42.9	5.79	5.68	47.1	48.5	6.39	6.72
Severe	20.7	16.4	2.66	2.18	19.9	16.5	2.58	2.39
health ratio moderate & severe			*69.5*	*61.6**			*66.6*	*65.5*
health ratio severe			*21.9*	*17.1*			*19.1*	*17.2*
Age 75+								
No	9.7	19.7	0.86	2.13	13.8	16.6	1.38	1.72
Moderate	46.5	51.8	3.84	4.17	43.9	50.8	4.28	5.79
Severe	41.0	28.5	3.17	2.71	40.3	32.5	4.20	3.73
health ratio moderate & severe			*89.1*	*76.3**			*86.0*	*84.7*
health ratio severe			*40.3*	*30.1*			*42.6*	*33.2*

WEST GERMANY								
Age 40-59								
No	60.3	64.6	11.57	12.48	53.3	63.1	10.42	12.64
Moderate	29.3	25.3**	5.65	4.83**	35.3	28.1	6.88	5.23***
Severe	10.4	10.1	1.95	1.95	11.4	8.8**	2.26	1.72**
health ratio moderate & severe			*39.7*	*35.2***			*46.7*	*35.5****
health ratio severe			*10.2*	*10.1*			*11.6*	*8.8***
Age 60-74								
No	31.4	40.6**	3.90	5.25	29.2	42.0	3.96	5.89
Moderate	42.0	43.3	5.31	5.67	46.3	42.9	6.40	5.81*
Severe	26.6	16.2**	3.45	2.07***	24.6	15.1**	3.47	2.29***
health ratio moderate & severe			*69.2*	*59.6****			*71.4*	*57.9****
health ratio severe			*27.2*	*15.9****			*25.1*	*16.3****
Age 75+								
No	26.2	19.7	2.31	1.77	18.5	18.5	2.00	2.28
Moderate	44.0	45.9	3.88	4.32	36.0	44.7	3.80	4.55
Severe	29.4	34.1	2.54	3.38	44.1	36.8	5.22	4.84
health ratio moderate & severe			*73.5*	*81.3*			*81.8*	*80.5*
health ratio severe			*29.1*	*35.7*			*47.3*	*41.5*

***: significant at the 1% level; **:significant at the 5% level; *: significant at the 10% level

Marital Status, Living Arrangements and Childlessness in the FELICIE Countries

Living conditions other than health are important determinants of the supply of care, too. They are primarily influenced by age, sex, marital status, the existence of children and the socio-economic status. Old people can live independently as long as they are healthy. If they are in need of care the existence of a partner, children or other relatives and socio-economic status determine whether the elderly can rely on private care arrangements at home, or whether institutional help is needed. Care is most often provided by spouses, while for those who live alone and do have children this task is most likely shifted to their children. (e.g. BMFSFJ 2002; Barkholdt and Lasch 2004; Diewald 1993; Wagner and Wolf 2001; Tinker et al. 2000). Many elderly people in need of care prefer staying at home to life in an institution, and in large segments of society taking care of the elderly is still accepted as a family commitment (Gierveld, de Valk and Blommesteijn 2000; Halsig 1995; Daatland and Herlofson 2004). For example, in Germany in 2003, 69 percent of the people in need of care are taken care of by their family, and 31 percent rely on institutional care (Statistisches Bundesamt 2005).

The degree of institutionalisation has a clear North – South gradient resulting from different cultural backgrounds with stronger family links in Southern Europe and stronger political actions in Northern Europe (for the different systems see e.g. Acker, 2004). While in Northern Europe people without a partner and children more often move into residential homes, a different solution such as living with other relatives is to a much higher proportion found in Southern Europe (Tomassini et al. 2004; Iacovou 2000; Gierveld, de Valk and Blommesteijn 2001). It is interesting to note that the resort to family care is particularly high in those countries where fertility rates are low and that institutionalisation rates are high in countries with comparatively high fertility rates. In 2000, Italy and the Czech Republic showed the lowest institutionalisation rates of the countries included in FELICIE (in Italy 1.8 percent males and 4.5 percent females and in the Czech Republic 2.7 percent males and 5.1 percent females), and experience lowest low fertility with a period TFR of 1.26 and 1.17, respectively, while Finland and the Netherlands belong to the countries with the highest proportion of people living in institutions (in Finland 5.6 percent males and 10.7 percent females and in the Netherlands 7.3 percent males and 15.1 percent females) and show period fertility around 1.7 (Council of Europe 2002). This implies that in the future the question of care supply and the shift from family to institutional care will be more severe in the southern and eastern than in the northern countries.

The FELICIE project uses three different indicators to characterise the living conditions of the elderly and the possible source of care: marital status, living arrangement, and childlessness. A partner will most likely take over care while those who live alone may have to move into an institution in case they do require care. Marital status is highly correlated with living arrangement as the married most likely will be living together with a partner. Divorced or widowed people may possibly rely on children, which is not the case for those never married.

In the last decades considerable changes have occurred in the marital status distribution of the elderly in the FELICIE countries. The mortality decline during the last decades has led to a decreased risk of being widowed. This, in reverse, is reflected by higher proportions of married people. Despite a strong increase in the proportions of divorced people the proportions for people aged 75+ in 2000 are still small, not exceeding 5 percent except for Finnish females with 6.8 percent. (Felicie team 2005).

Also in Germany, older cohorts experience an increasing proportion of people who are married at advanced ages, and a decreasing proportion of elderly widows and widowers between 1991 and 2000. Males have always shown higher marriage rates, as they tend to remarry more often than their female counterparts. When comparing numbers from 1991 to numbers gleaned in 2000, it becomes apparent that particularly elderly women experienced a strong increase in the proportion married at old and oldest ages. The reasons are the delayed risk of widowhood and a higher overall chance of marriage. Over time the proportion of women who could not find a partner due to the war-diminished male cohorts has decreased, as more and more cohorts unaffected by war-induced devastation are coming of age. For males we find a considerable increase in the proportion of the never married, while for females this proportion decreases from a very high level caused by the small number of males available for marriage after the war.

Living arrangements are highly correlated with marital status. Widowed, divorced and never married people generally live without a partner. Cohabitation and remarriage are still not as widespread among the older cohorts as among the younger ones. For the years 1999/2000, there are some general similarities between FELICIE countries concerning the living arrangements of men and women above the age of 75 (Delbès, Gaymu and Springer 2005; Gaymu et al. 2005). In most countries about half of the women aged 75+ live alone; exceptions are Portugal with only 31 percent and Germany with almost 60 percent. Consequently, the proportion of women who live together with a partner is low, ranging between 16 percent in the Czech Republic and 26 percent in Belgium. In all countries more women than men live together with people other than their partners. However, here we find big differences between the Northern European and the Southern and Eastern European countries, which also holds true for those living in collective households. As little as 7 percent of women from the Netherlands live together with others compared to 37 percent of Portuguese women. Only 4 percent of Italian women but 15 percent of women in the Netherlands are living in an institution.

For men, the predominant living arrangement is living together with a partner. The proportions range from 60 percent in the United Kingdom to 69 percent in Germany. Therefore they are less prevalent in the other living forms. Only 14 percent of Portuguese men live alone and 28 percent of men in the United Kingdom. Living together with others is least common for Dutch men (3.7 percent) closely followed by German men (4.6 percent) and most common for Portuguese men (20 percent). The institutionalisation rate is lowest in Italy with 2 percent and highest in the Netherlands with 7 percent (Gaymu et al. 2005).

Figure 3: Proportion of living arrangements in the FELICIE countries at ages 75+.

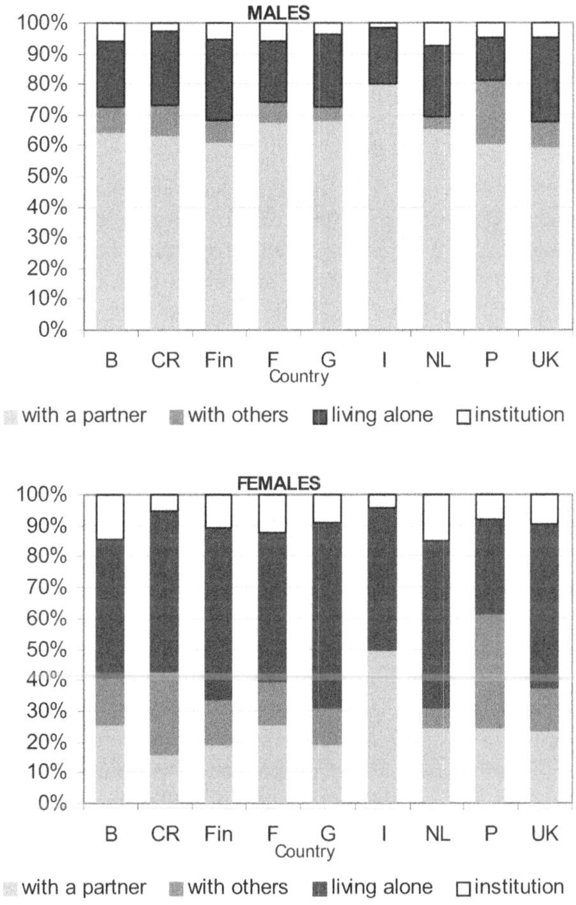

(For Italy the category 'with partner' includes also 'with others')
Source: Gaymu et al. 2005

For Germany the 1999 Microcensus is used to explore living arrangements. Compared with the other FELICIE countries, Germany has the highest proportion of women who live alone (60 percent) and the highest proportion of men who live together with a partner (69 percent). This outstanding position is caused on the one hand by the higher life expectancy of women and on the other hand by the high losses of men during the First and the Second World War (Tomassini et al. 2004). Among the cohorts affected by the war, many women could not find a partner to marry whereas for men, even if they became widowers, the chances to remarry where high. Living together with others is less common in Germany (4.6 percent for men and 12.1 percent for women) while 3.8 percent of the German men and 9.3 percent of the German women live in institutions. This proportion is midway between the other FELICIE countries; Italy, Portugal and the Czech Republic have lower institutionalisation rates, whereas the other countries show higher ones.

Since the number of people who live alone has been increasing in developed countries during the last decades (Grundy 2000), information about the number of children who could take over care becomes even more important. It is widely known that the cohort fertility decreases for cohorts born after the 1930s. The cohort fertility rate (CFR) in the FELICIE countries ranges between 2.94 for Portuguese women born in 1930 and thus entering the age of 75 in 2005, to 2.14 for women born in the Czech Republic in 1930 (then Czechoslovakia). For later birth cohorts it dropped below replacement level. For the French birth cohort 1966 the CFR is still relatively high with 2.0, and women in Italy born in the same year have the lowest CFR with 1.46 children (data from Council of Europe 2004). However, this decline in fertility mostly comes from a decrease in third and higher birth orders. For cohorts born after 1930 children became less important as guarantors of social security, but their emotional value increased. Priority was therefore given to quality versus quantity (van de Kaa 1987, Lesthaeghe 1995). For cohorts born between 1900 and 1940 there is a steady decline in the proportion of childless women (Figure 4). For West Germany we see the highest proportion of childless women born between 1900 and 1924 while among East German women born between 1910 and 1934 the situation is more positive. Generally, only cohorts born after 1940 experience an increase in childlessness (Rowland 1998). This means that the proportion of people aged 80 and above with at least one child will not decrease, but will rather increase in most countries, for at least two decades to come.(Murphy and Grundy 2003 for the United Kingdom).

Figure 4: Proportion of childless women born between 1900 and 1954, in FELICIE countries.

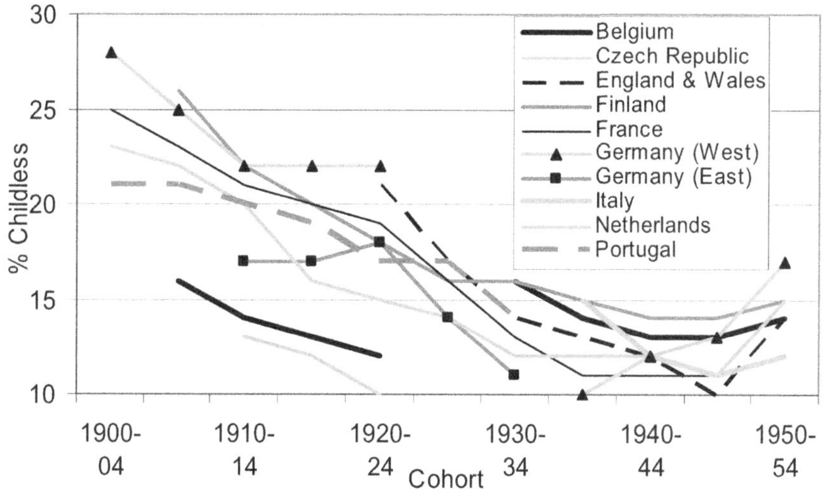

Data collected by Rowland, 1998

Care Need Projections by Marital Status for the Years 2000 to 2030

Care need projections in FELICIE participants consist of two components: first the population aged 45+ in 2000 is projected until 2030, taking marital status into account (Murphy and Kalogirou 2004). As future trends in fertility have not yet been anticipated, it makes sense to start at age 45. Since the aim of the project is to forecast care need of the 75+ year olds, a time span of 30 years is needed to allow the 45 year olds in 2000 to reach age 75. The population forecasts by marital status are calculated using the LIPRO model (van Imhoff and Keilmann 1991). For each country the base population in the year 2000 and the marital status-specific stocks and flows are collected by the national statistical offices in order to calculate the transition rates between marital statuses. Two scenarios of possible future developments concerning marital status in the population are projected: the constant rate scenario which leaves all transition rates between and from marital states at the 2000 year level; and the consistent variable scenario which assumes a continuation of current trends. The assumptions about life expectancy in 2030 follow those of the national statistical offices while pectancy in 2030 follow those of the national statistical offices while migration is assumed to be zero. The consistent variable scenario is the basis of the care need projections.

The second component of the care need projections are the prevalences of disability described above. Two scenarios of future trends in disability have been developed: the Constant Disability Share (CDS) Scenario assumes that the gain in life expectancy results in a proportional growth of years spent disabled. The Healthy Life Gain (HLG) Scenario assumes that all added years in life expectancy are healthy years. The years spent in disability will therefore stay constant (Ekamper, van Wissen, Beets 2005).

The international projections do not concentrate on differences in the prevalence rate of severe disability among the countries as such, but rather on differences in the indexed trends in the period 2000-30. Figure 5 shows these trends for males and females above age 75 in the two scenarios. Only three countries are displayed: Germany in comparison with the country with the least and the largest increase in care need. For each country the CDS and the HLG scenario is displayed.

Figure 5: Index of future care need (base year 2000=100) among people aged 75+ in selected FELICIE countries

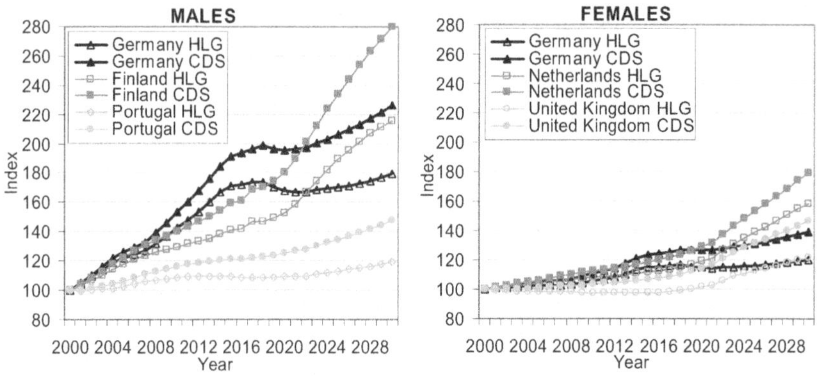

Source: Ekamper, van Wissen, Beets, 2005

In both scenarios, for both males and females, and for all countries a marked increase in the number of severely disabled persons until 2030 is projected. The increase in the number of disabled persons is much larger for men than for women. In the CDS scenario, for example, the 2030 index for males is mostly to be found between 150 and 250, indicating that in all countries the number of men in need of care will at least double if prevalences in disability remain constant. For females in most countries the index is between 120 and 175. It is interesting to note that not only is the growth in care need larger for males than for females (although one has to consider that males start from a lower level than females), there is also a much larger variation in growth indices among the countries for males. In Germany the increase is moderate compared with the other FELICIE countries, for females even low. For the latter the rise will be about 20 to 40 percent, depending on the CDS and HLG scenario and for males between 180 and 220 percent, respectively. In most countries a marked increase in the rate of change in the number of disabled is observed around 2020 when the cohorts born after World War II enter age 75. However, for German men we see that the increase occurs earlier than for males in other countries and than for females. One reason might still be the impact of the Second World War. Cohorts born before the year 1933 that enter our study population of people aged 75 and above in 1998 still belong to the generation that suffered high losses during the War. Thus the general increase of males and disabled males after that year is especially high.

Sensitivity analyses reveal that the national marital status differences in the prevalence of severe disability are of little importance for the future trends of care need: care need projections based on the total population and projections differentiated by marital status come to broadly similar results. The future development in the number of people in need of care is primarily driven by the assumptions about future trends in health. The advantage of marital status specific projections, thus, lies in the insight they provide about the future supply side of care. Whether the future elderly in need of care will be married or divorced has important implications on future trends in formal and informal care.

Figure 6 shows the forecast on future people in need of care by marital status for Germany. The population pyramid for the year 2000 reveals a huge imbalance between males and females and a dominance of widowed females. Until the year 2030 the number of disabled people will rise from 2.4 to 4.0 Million in the CDS scenario and to 3.3 Million in the HLG scenario (Ekamper, van Wissen, Beets 2005). The sex ratio, however, will become more balanced and a much larger proportion of those in need of care will be married, both among males and females. There is also an increase of divorced people; however, this increase is still small.

Figure 6: Population in need of care aged 75+ by marital status in Germany in the year 2000 and 2030: CDS and HLG scenario

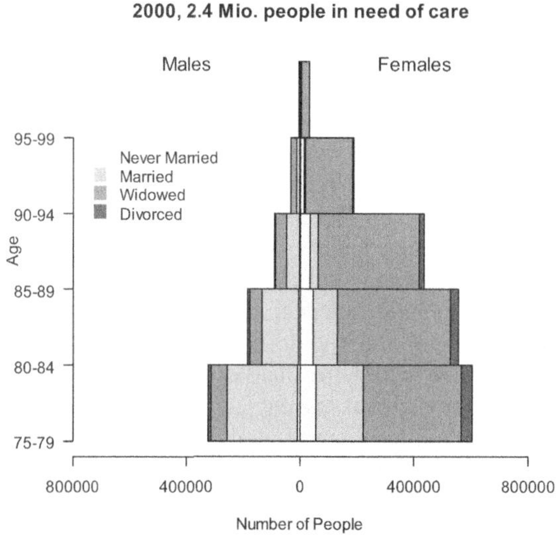

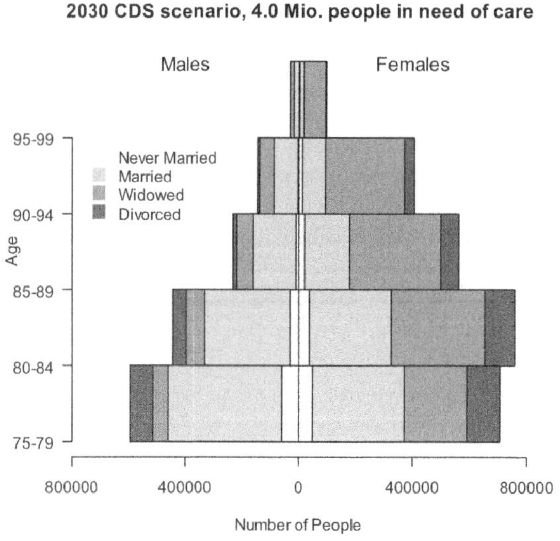

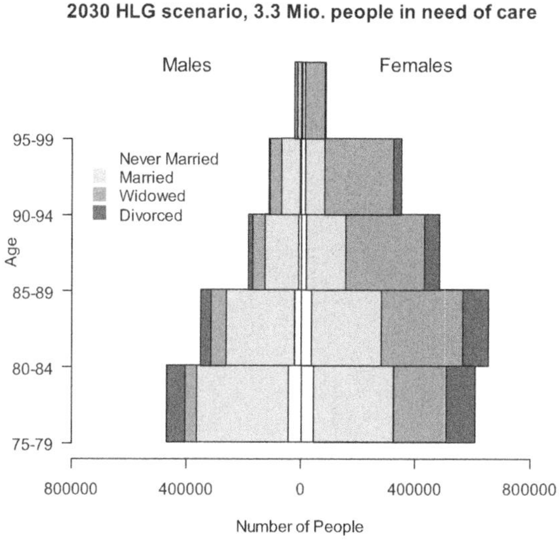

Source: Ekamper, van Wissen, Beets, 2005

Conclusion

The projections of care need in the nine FELICIE countries show that even under the optimistic scenario, within which the years gained in life expectancy will be years without disability, the number of people in need of care will rise by at least 0.50 Million males and 0.37 Million for females in Germany. Constant prevalences in disability imply at least a doubling for males and at least an increase of 50 percent for females. In the next two decades people in need of care, however, to a higher degree will be living together with a partner, and will have at least one child. The marital status projections in the FELICIE project (Figure 7), as well as earlier studies have shown that the number of living partners of elderly people in most European countries is most likely to increase until 2030 (Murphy and Grundy 2003; Tomassini et al. 2004; Dinkel 1997). Reasons for this are first of all a decreasing discrepancy between the number of male and female elderly, as the age gap for male and female life expectancy is shrinking. In addition, the high losses of men during the Second World War, which still impact sex ratios at advanced ages today, will lose their importance for the living arrangements of the future elderly. This effect of higher marriage proportions especially among females will be lowered by an increasing divorce rate among younger cohorts.

Figure 7: Marital status distribution among German males and females 2000 and 2030

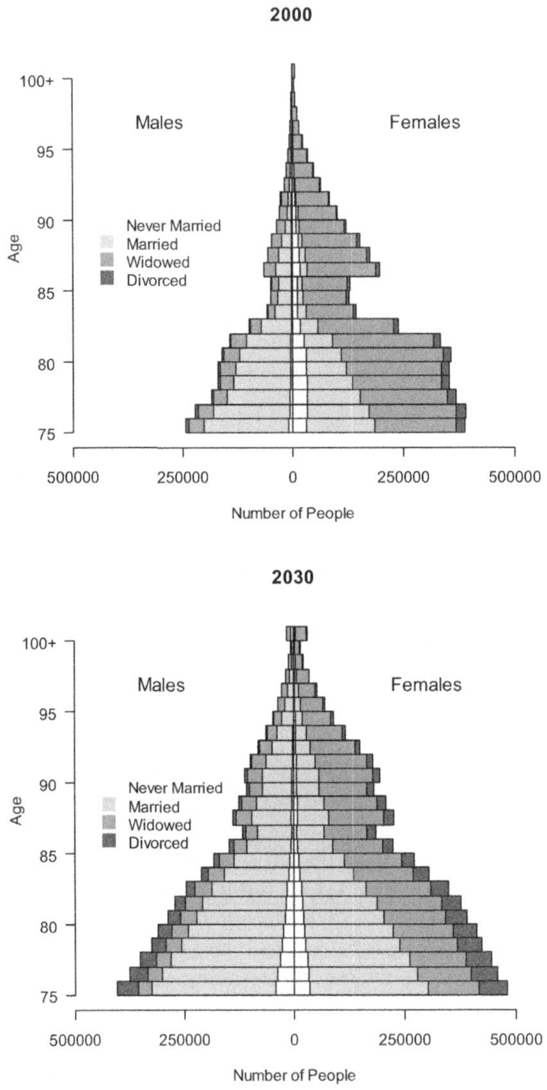

Source: Murphy and Kalogirou, 2005

The second demographic transition led to breaks with the traditional family norms and made other lifestyles possible. The future elderly cohorts reaching ages 75 and above are not yet so much affected, however, by this development and the proportion of divorced will increase from 2.6 to 8.7 percent among males and from 4.6 to 11.3 percent among females (Murphy and Kalogirou 2005).

People who do not receive support from their partner might still be helped by their children – if they have any. The FELICIE projections of childlessness among the future elderly reveal that the increase in childlessness after age 75 will be modest (Grundy et al. 2004; Ekamper, van Wissen, Beets 2005). For a number of countries there is even a decrease in childlessness in the coming decades and only after 2020 the proportion slowly rises again. However, levels of childlessness among countries differ greatly, with northern countries leading far ahead of southern and eastern countries.

The decreasing average number of children does not necessarily have a negative influence on the care provision, as closeness between family-members may turn out to be more important than sheer numbers of children (Diewald 1993; Tomassini et al. 2004). However, the number of elderly people who move into an institution is likely to rise, as social norms and a higher demand for independence and autonomy may motivate elderly people in some countries to choose this lifestyle. Again a North – South gradient can be found, with people in Southern European countries more often living with their families, while in the Scandinavian countries and the Netherlands they increasingly choose to live in institutions (Gierveld, de Valk and Blommesteijn 2001).

From a demographic point of view, after 2030 the situation concerning the demand and supply of care will change. By then the baby boom cohorts will reach ages in which the likelihood of disability and the need for care increases. Among these cohorts childlessness is high, the average number of children low and divorcees will be plenty. Unless new forms of partnerships such as consensual unions will be more readily accepted as a chosen lifestyle for old age, family-supplied care resources will shrink dramatically. The Southern European countries will face a particular challenge, since their fertility rates are the lowest in Europe, their life expectancies among the highest and the reliance on the family as a provider of care is almost universal.

References

Acker, Dominique (2004): Die Rolle der sozialen Sicherheit bei der häuslichen Pflege. Fachausschuss für Gesundheitsleistungen und Krankenversicherung; Fachausschuss für Hilfsvereine auf Gegenseitigkeit, Frankreich.

Barkholdt, Corinna and Lasch, Vera (2004): Vereinbarkeit von Pflege und Erwerbstätigkeit. Expertise für die Sachverständigenkommission für den 5. Altenbericht der Bundesregierung, Dortmund und Kassel

Bebbington, A.C. (1991): The expectation of life without disability in England and Wales: 1976-88. *Population Trends* 66, 26-29.

Bomsdorf, Eckart (2004); Life Expectancy in Germany until 2050, Experimental Gerontology 39(2004)159-163

Bundesministerium für Familie, Senioren, Frauen und Jugend (2002): Vierter Bericht zur Lage der älteren Generation in der Bundesrepublik Deutschland. Risiken, Lebensqualität und Versorgung Hochaltriger – unter besonderer Berücksichtigung Dementieller Erkrankungen. Berlin

Crimmins, E.M., Saito, Y. and Ingegneri, D. (1989): Changes in life expectancy and disability-free life expectancy in the United States. *Population and Development Review* 15/2, 235-67.

Crimmins, E.M., Saito, Y. and Ingegneri, D. (1997): Trends in disability-free life expectancy in the United States, 1970-90. *Population and Development Review* 23/3, 555-572.

Council of Europe (2004): Recent demographic developments in Europe. Council of Europe Publishing F-67075 Strasbourg Cedex ISBN 92-871

Daatland, S. O. and Herlofson, K. (2004): Family Responsibility Norms in European Countries: Contrasts and Similarities; OASIS

Delbès, C. and Gaymu, J. and Springer, S. (2005): The living arrangements of the older population from the past until the present day. INED, Paris; FELICIE contract no. QLK6-CT-2002-02310

Diewald, Martin (1993): Hilfebeziehungen und soziale Differenzierung im Alter. Kölner Zeitschrift für Soziologie und Sozialpsychologie 45(1993)4: 731-754.

Dinkel, Reiner H., Hartmann Kerstin, Lebok, Uwe (1997): Langfristige Veränderungen in der Verfügbarkeit häuslicher Unterstützungspotentiale aufgrund familiärer Strukturverschiebungen – Eine Modellrechnung. in: Gesundheitswesen 59, Sonderheft 1 S. 49-54.

Doblhammer G., Kytir J. (2001) Compression or expansion of morbidity? Trends in Healthy-Life Expectancy of the Elderly Austrian population between 1978 and 1998, *Social Science and Medicine* 52, 385-391

Ekamper, P. and van Wissen, Leo and Beets, Gijs (2005): Population scenarios of health, family and socio-economic status by age, sex and marital status, for the nine FELICIE countries over the period 2000-2030. NIDI, The Hague; FELICIE contract no. QLK6-CT-2002-02310

Eurostat (2005): europa.eu.int/comm/eurostat/

Eurostat (2003): Health Statistics. Key data on health 2002. European Commission. Theme 3 Population and social conditions: 1-475.

FELICIE team (2005): The marital status of the older population. From the past until the present day, INED, France, FELICIE contract no. QLK6-CT2002-02310

Fries, J. F. (1989): The compression of morbidity: Near or far? *Milbank Memorial Foundation Quarterly/Health and Society* 67/2, 208-232.

Gaymu, J. and Delbès, C. and Springer, S. and Binet, A. and Desesquelles, A. (2005): Synthesis report: Determinants of the living arrangements of older people in Europe INED, Paris; FELICIE contract no. QLK6-CT-2002-02310

Gierveld J., de Valk H., Blommesteijn M. (2001): Living Arrangements of Older Persons and Family Support in More Developed Countries. in: United Nations Technical meeting on Population Ageing and Living Arrangements of Older Persons: critical issues and Policy Responses, New York, Population Division, United Nations: 45 p.

Glaser, K., Murphy, M. and Grundy, E. (1997) 'Limiting long term illness and household structure among people aged 45 and over, Great Britain 1991'. *Ageing and Society*, 17, 3-20.

Goldman, N., Korenman, S. and Weinstein, R. (1995): 'Marital status and health among the elderly'. *Social Science and Medicine*, 40(12), 1717-1730

Gruenberg, E.M. (1977): The failure of success. *Milbank Memorial Foundation Quarterly | Health and Society*, 55,3-24.

Grundy, Emily and Kalogirou Stamatis and Tomassini, Cecilia (2004): The future of family networks and the support of older people in Europe: Synthesised report; LSHTM, London, FELICIE contract no. QLK6-CT-2002-02310

Grundy, Emily (2000): Living arrangements and the health of older persons in developed countries. Technical meeting on population ageing and living arrangements of older persons: critical issues and policy responses, New York.

Grundy, E., Ahlburg, D., Ali, M., et al. (1999): Disability in Great Britain. London: HSMO, Department of Social Security (Research Report 94).

Hahn, B. A. (1993): 'Marital status and women's health: the effect of economic and marital acquisitions'. *Journal of Marriage and the Family*, 55, 495-504.

Halsig, N. (1995): Hauptpflegepersonen in der Familie: Eine Analyse ihrer situativen Bedingungen, Belastungen und Hilfsmöglichkeiten. Zeitschrift für Gerontopsychologie und –psychiatrie 8(1995)4: 247-262

Iacovou, Maria (2000): Explaining the living arrangements of older European women. ISER working paper 2000-08, Institute for Social and Economic Research.

Lesthaeghe, R. (1995): The Second Demographic Transition: An Interpretation. in: Mason, K. O. and Jensen, A.-M. (eds.), Gender and Family Change in Industrialized Countries., Oxford

Manton, K.G. (1982): Changing concepts of morbidity and mortality in the elderly population. *Milbank Memorial Foundation Quarterly/Health and Society* 60, 183-244.

Murphy, Mike and Kalogirou, Stamatis (2004): Population projections by sex and marital status and single year of age. LSE, London; FELICIE contract no. QLK6-CT 2002-02310

Murphy, Michael J.; Grundy, Emily (2003): Mothers With Living Children And Children With Living Mothers: The Role Of Fertility And Mortality In The Period 1911-2050. Population Trends no. 112 (2003): 36-44.

Oeppen, Jim and Vaupel, James W. (2002): Broken Limits to Human Life Expectancy Science, 296(2002): 1029-1031.

Olshansky, S.J., Rudberg, M.A., Carnes, B.A., Cassel, B.A. and Brady, J.A. (1991): Trading off longer life for worsening health: The expansion of morbidity hypothesis. *Journal of Aging and Health* 3/2, 194-216.

Robine, J.M., Jagger, C., Mathers, C.D., Crimmins, E.M., Suzman, R.M. (2003): *Determining Health Expectancies*, West Sussex, Wiley.

Robine, J.M., Mathers, C. and Brouard, N. (1996) Trends and differentials in disability-free life expectancy: Concepts, methods, and findings. In *Health and mortality among elderly population*, eds. G. Caselli and A.D. Lopez, pp. 182-201. Clarendon Press, Oxford.

Robine, J.M., Romieu, I, Cambois E. (1997): Health expectancies and current research. *Reviews in Clinical Gerontology* 7:73-81.

Rowland, Donald T. (1998): Cross-National Trends in Childlessness. Working Papers in Demography No. 73, The Australian National University

Schnabel, Sabine; von Kistowski, Kristin; Vaupel, James W. (2005): Immer neue Rekorde und kein Ende in Sicht. Der Blick in die Zukunft lässt Deutschland grauer aussehen als viele erwarten. Demografische Forschung aus erster Hand 2(2005)2: 3.

Statistisches Bundesamt (2005): 2. Bericht: Pflege im Rahmen der Pflegeversicherung. Ländervergleich: Pflegebedürftige. Statistisches Bundesamt, Wiesbaden.

Statistisches Bundesamt (2003): Bevölkerung Deutschlands bis 2050, 10. koordinierte Bevölkerungsvorausberechnung. Statistisches Bundesamt, Wiesbaden

Sullivan, D. F. (1971): A Single Index of Mortality and Morbidity, in: HSMHA Health Reports, Vol. 86, April 1971, pp. 347-354

Tinker, Anthea; Askham, Janet; Hancock, Ruth; Mueller, Ganka; Stuchbury, Rachel (2000): Eighty-Five Not Out. A Study of People Aged 85 and Over at Home. Age Concern Institute of Gerontology King's College, London.

Tomassini, Cecilia; Glaser, Karen; Wolf, Douglas A.; Broese van Groenou, Marjolein I.; Grundy, Emily (2004): Living arrangements among older people: an overview of trends in Europe and the USA. Population Trends 115(2004): 24-34.

Valkonen, T., Sihvonen, A.P. and Lahelma, E. (1997): Health expectancy by level of education in Finland. *Social Science and Medicine*. 44/6, 801-808.

van de Kaa, Dirk J. (1987): Europe's Second Demographic Transition. Population Bulletin 42(1987)1: 1-58.

van de Water, H.P.A., Boshuizen, H.C. and Perenboom, R.J.M. (1996): Health expectancy in the Netherlands 1983-1990. *European Journal of public health* 6, 21-28.

van Ginneken, J.K.S., Dissevelt, A.G., van de Water, H.P.A. and van Sonsbeek, J.L.A. (1991): Results of two methods to determine health expectancy in the Netherlands in 1981-1985. *Social Science and Medicine* 32/10, 1129-1136.

van Imhoff, E. and Keilman, N. W. (1991): LIPRO 2.0: an application of a dynamic demographic projection model to household structure in the Netherlands. NIDI/CBGS Publications No. 23, Amsterdam/Lisse: Swets & Zeitlinger. 245 p.

Wagner, Michael and Wolf, Christof (2001): Altern, Familie und soziales Netzwerk Zeitschrift für Erziehungswissenschaft 4(2001): 529-554.

Care for Old People Between Gender Relations, Gender Roles, and Gender Constructs

Gabriele Kreutzner

1 Point of Departure

As a stage of life, old age, and particularly very old age, comes with its specific chances, yet also implies its own risks. Based on the manifold facets of aging – physical, health-related and medical, psychological and mental, economic, social, cultural - the gerontologist Andreas Kruse considers (very) old age as a period of life characterized by increasing vulnerabilities. This article focuses on one of these vulnerabilities, namely the probability increasing with (very) old age to find oneself in a situation where one is forced to rely on others (much more than one used to) in order to manage daily life. Examples of such an essential reliance start out with seeming trifles such as having to ask for assistance when being confined to a walker and wishing to use an escalator or public transportation. On the next level, they move on to the requirement of support in household performances and proceed to varying degrees of reliance on psychological and physical care and nursing. A special care requirement is owed to the factor that old and particularly very old age implies an increased risk to fall ill with dementia. Statistically speaking, that probability increases significantly by the age of 80 and older. In Germany, about one million people aged 65 and older suffer from dementia; about two thirds of them are more than 80 years old (Bickel 2004).

Dementia, and particularly its most well-known form, Alzheimer's disease, is a disease pattern that effects each person in a different way (as the Alzheimer's Society has put it: "If you know one person with Alzheimer's, you know one person with Alzheimer's "). This also means that the degree and kind of support needed by a person with dementia will significantly vary from case to case. Nevertheless, dementia confronts our highly advanced industrial societies (as well as all other societies, if at a somewhat later point in time) with a tremendous challenge. As for Germany, credible estimations point to an increase to 1,4 million people with dementia over 65 by the year 2020 and to more than 2 million in 2050 in case there is no significant break-through in terms of prevention and therapy (4. Altenbericht, bmfsfj 2002).

Thus, the vulnerabilities of old and very old age require that we cope with an increasing demand for old-age related, and particularly dementia-adequate medical attendance and care services which implies a demand for increased and improved provision of care. In Germany, we have seen an increase of corresponding efforts, for example through the comprehensive model programme "Altenhilfestrukturen der Zukunft" (future care structures for old age) organized and funded by the federal ministry for senior citizens (bmfsfj) and carried out between 2001 and 2005. Yet, with all due appreciation of such efforts and the kinds of advancement achieved so far, the issue of aging as a reasonably expectable period of life, and particularly the issue of dementia, implies a dimension of social and cultural challenges that necessitates more thorough reflections and, ultimately, methods of resolution. As I see it, the present situation implies both the request and the chance to rethink the way in which bourgeois capitalist society conceives of, organizes, structures and values care for the other person, and particularly care for old and very old people in the light of expectable social and demographic changes. As I am going to argue, we will only be able to provide a kind of care to our societies' old and needy members that complies with democratic values and principles if we succeed to profoundly change dominant thinking and acting with regard to care. Central to that requirement for change is the social category of gender.

2 Gender and the Societal Organization of Care

It has become standard practice to rely on the English term "gender" in Germany. This is owed to the fact that "gender" (unlike the German term "Geschlecht") unequivocally refers to something which is socially produced. Therefore, gender does not suggest the kind of natural or biological givenness (and the idea of something beyond scrutiny) which tends to determine concepts of "Geschlecht" ("sex") in common thought. In our context here, gender refers to both a structural category of social inequality and a construct determined in historical, social and cultural ways. Moreover, gender must be conceived both as structure and process: gender is continuously produced and reproduced in the context of social power structures (and, thus, in principle can be subjected to change) while simultaneously forming an integral part of that very structure. While this conception may sound rather abstract, it will hopefully become more concrete in my analysis of the interrelationship between gender and care that is of interest here.

2.1 The Historical Conjunction between Gender and Care - Reflection on the Level of Gender Constructs

Western modern thought has produced a dovetail connection between gender and care. Until today, our dominant concepts of care are inextricably related to the fact that this kind of reasoning conceives of autonomy and dependence as mutually exclusive categories and places them into as structural opposition. Feminist criticism has traced this conceptionalization back to the very beginning of modernity and to early bourgeois thinking (e.g. Benhabib 1995). Shortly put, early bourgeois thinkers such as Thomas Hobbes conceived man (the male subject) in terms of a substantially singular creature. This kind of autonomous male subject finds its supplementation in an inversely constructed female counterpart:

> It is decisive that in that world [i.e. that of early political and moral thought, gkr] there is no space for the early modern female ego. 'Women' simply is that what man is not, i.e. *not* autonomous, not independent and, for the same reason, not aggressive, but caring; not battlesome, but unselfish, not 'public', but 'private'. The woman's world is composed by a series of negations; she is respectively, what he just is not. Thus, her identity is defined as an absence in the sense of what she lacks: autonomy, independence, a phallus. The narcissistic male ego considers her as his equal, yet turned into the opposite. (Benhabib 1995: 173f.; *my re-translation gkr*)

In this way, dependence and care have been tied to the concept of the female and of femininity and assigned to an area conceived as non-societal (the household, the private area). Thus, early modern thought implemented a conceptualization with profound consequences since that perception was integrated into symbolic production where it took on a kind of style-sheet function.

2.2 Care on the Level of the Historically and Socially Concrete

In order to understand the actual organization of care in a given (modern) society, one has to move from the conceptual level and that of symbolic production to that of concrete historical and social circumstance. From a comprehensive and comparative perspective, one of the decisive moments can be seen in the historical development of a given national state and, related to this development, to the formation of a given country's respective welfare system. For Germany, that historical process has been described by the scientific mainstream as a contradictory reaction to the so-called "social question" in the 19th century. As feminist science has demonstrated, the implementation of the welfare system also meant the institutionalization of a modern gender arrangement designed to safeguard social reproduction. "That kind of gender system sought to permanently establish the gendered division of labour in its authoritative validity across classes and social milieus – with the male bread winner on the one hand, and female responsibility for house work, raising children, and caring for the sick and/or old members of the family" (Dackweiler 2004:451). Thus, the "social division of welfare" (Titmus 1963) tied to the (traditional) welfare state has been characterized as a gender-specific arrangement between state, market, and (women working in) the family (Dackweiler 2004: 451).

As a basic social agreement or model, this kind of arrangement differs somewhat from country to country. Social analysis has tried to condense those differences and to make them analytically productive by introducing the model of varying welfare regimes. It must be left to future research to analyze historical differences in terms of a given country's basic social model. What is clear is that national welfare systems evolved in interaction with the kinds of social forces and sectors prevailing their respective context. On the one hand, the results of that process have been codified into constitutions, laws, and regulations. On the other hand, however, they are being subjected to a process of permanent change. Presently, the most recent stage of that process is being fought out and negotiated under the signifier of "the transformation of the welfare state".

What characterizes the present situation in Germany is that the public debate about care for those in need and for old people is carried out in almost exclusively national terms. Moreover, it is a debate which, in its dominating form, is increasingly invaded by arguments of "inherent necessities". This corresponds to the observation that in societal arrangements based on a highly diversified division of labour, care – and particularly care for old people and for vulnerable groups – is inscribed into a hierarchical relationship to other social areas and sectors. In their continuous struggle for allocating and hedging resources (particularly in terms of resources administered and distributed by the state) such areas and sectors seek to secure their supremacy.

> In general terms: a society where agencies of power and their agents primarily insist on their economic and political dominance will be characterized by quite different rules and norms than those essential to a civil society primarily dedicated to social cohesion and the population's vital concerns. Our modern Western societies have seen the historical development of a form of relationality which contradicts the logic of social areas' reciprocal dependency: interdependence is not the decisive criterion for exerting influence on social development. Rather, power is savoured by those sectors representing dominant political-economic interests and (dominant) strategies of socio-cultural hegemony. The economy, state institutions, the military complex and the cultural establishment are given precedence over education, private life worlds, the health system (Becker-Schmidt 2004: 68).

When discussing care for old people, one has to account for the conditional framework that characterizes a given national situation including the specific resources (both in quantitative and qualitative terms) that are available in that context. However, what is decisive is the overall orientation that characterizes a given society. Such an orientation is based on a normative decision and negotiated within concrete relations of power and domination. In the context of the European integration process and, more specifically, that of shaping the European Union, such a decision goes well beyond the level of the singular nation state. Thus, the issue of care for old people and for particularly vulnerable social groups deeply touches the issue of the European Community as a Civil Society. And vice versa: In its approach to health and care, the European Union will reveal its composition and quality as a Civil Society.

2.3 The Concept of Care in the International Feminist Debate

In recent years, it was particularly feminist scholars who took care as their point of theoretical and analytical departure. In doing so, they have criticized and rejected the equation of a reliance on care provided by others with "dependency" as constructed by dominant thought and discourse: "The unilateral linkage between care and dependency is quite misleading, since all human beings – and particularly when living in societies marked by a highly diversified division of labour – are structurally dependent on one another ('interdependent'), if at different times and in quite different ways"(Brückner 2000). Therefore, inevitable (in contrast to unnecessary) dependence must be rehabilitated as a human condition and the concept of autonomy as independence must be exposed as fictitious (Fraser/Gordon 1994; cited in Brückner 2000).

Today, it seems more important than ever to uncover and reject the dominant concept of autonomy because of its fictitious nature. In order to conceive of human beings as essentially social subjects the concept of autonomy remains indispensable. However, autonomy and reliance must be understood as always being mediated with each other. In this sense, care also means *a practice of enabling* (in the sense of supporting or sustaining) *autonomy, and of participation and personhood*[1]. In that respect, feminist thinkers are no longer out on a limb.

1 In the context of dementia care, a non-essentialist, procedural and dialogical understanding of the constitution of the self and, thus, of the person, is of central importance. Whereas I rely on feminist conceptualizations here (e.g. as the one suggested by Benhabib), the expert debate on dementia care and on people with dementia was strongly influenced by the concept of personhood and the person-centered approach to dementia care initiated by the work of the British social psychologist Tom Kitwood. A useful (and bilingual, German and English) insight to the

Meanwhile, a veto has also been expressed by those engaged in the improvement of care for some of the most vulnerable among the old people, i.e. people with dementia.[2]

As has been already suggested, the feminist discussion on care which has been carried out in and across various countries (in Europe and beyond) is also directly tied to the debate about the transformation of the welfare state and the concern to the development of civil society. In that context, care has been defined as the over-all ensemble of caring practices along with the forms of their social organisation (cf. Brückner 2000:45): "In its extensive sense, care not only means the consolidation of formal and informal caring and nursing activities in the course of the life cycle (childhood – age; health – sickness), but also all those pedagogical and social-work related practices provided to people in special situations and life circumstance (from supporting single parents to support services such as shelters for battered women). Like the definition of all these areas themselves, extent and character of care are subjected to societal changes and to political decisions about public and private responsibilities and, thus, about the scale and relevance of education and training as well as about paid and unpaid work" (Fraser 1994, quoted in Brückner 2000).

Against this background, I will now turn to the German context and to a consideration of the dominant gender regime in terms of its status and relevance for accomplishing good care for old people, and particular for people with dementia.

2.4 Under the Spell of the Prevailing Gender Regime: Care for Old People in Germany

In order to adequately grasp the interrelation between care and the category of gender in its concrete societal context, I advance from the conception of "Geschlechterverhältnis" (gender relationship) as it has been theorized in the context of women studies/gender studies in Germany. That conception comprises a specific mode of institutionalized and socially structured relatedness of men and women which characterizes a given society:

---

international debate in dementia care (with particular emphasis on the issue of quality of life) is provided by Christian Müller-Hergl (2005).

2 I am referring here to the national initiative „Gemeinsam für ein besseres Leben mit Demenz" ("Together for a better living with dementia") originated by the Robert Bosch Foundation. The final report produced by the working group "Gemeinsam betreuen" ("caring together") criticizes the dominant model of autonomy and argues in favour of a revision.

> 'Geschlechterverhältnis' (trans.: the gender relationship) means the ensemble of arrangements which relate men and women to one another through forms of division of labour, relations of social dependency, and processes of exchange. Within this allness, men and women are allocated with social status and prestige through a matching of sociocultural valuation. The mode of that relationality, which has to be characterized as a non-egalitarian one in the light of positions of social inequality between the genus groups existing on central levels of social participation (distribution of paid and unpaid, highly or lowly remunerated work, social security, prestige, power), structures private life worlds, the job market, differing public spheres and political arenas (Becker-Schmidt 2004:66).

I shall now try to draw on this conceptualization for an examination of domestic care. As numerous studies have shown, a kind of care which takes place in the care receiver's domestic context is the kind of solution of a social task highly preferred by both informal care givers and care receivers. A representative study carried out in 2002 revealed that "71% of those who are in need of care and even 87% of their relatives [...] hold a negative attitude against the possibility of a transfer to an institutional environment and [...] express that they wish a life in the privacy of their own home" (bmfsfj 2003). What's even more: A majority of the overall population expresses a preference for domestic care provided in familial terms. A survey carried out by the market research institute Emnid in the summer of 2005 asked people whether they were willing to care for their parents in case this was needed. As it turned out, 48% of the inquired expressed their willingness to take their parents into their own home "at any rate" in case care should become necessary. Another 21% stated their willingness to undertake such a move "if my partnership or family will not suffer from such a step". Finally, another 4% said they would take up and care for their parents in case of need "since I won't be able to afford the costs of a nursing home". Both studies demonstrate the strong preference for a care that is provided in a familiar and familial domestic setting and the readiness to take on responsibility accordingly.

2.5 *Care as a Generative Task: Chances and Risks*

Those who take on the responsibility of care for a person close to them are challenged by a task which implies a strong emotional involvement. Also, to accomplish familial care is not rewarded by established gratifications such as a good income or social status. Moreover, taking care of old people means to be confronted with (frequently terminal) disease, with age- and ailment-related cognitive, mental and physical changes, with the eventuality of dying – and, therefore, also with one's own aging and the finiteness of one's own life. Within the familial context, care givers are intensely confronted with anxiety, shame, and emotional entanglements (Gröning et al. 2004). On top of this, care, and particularly dementia care, expects care givers to be able to bear with things that are grave and encumbering and cannot be changed by their doings. It is one of the most difficult demands of formal and informal care to resist the reflex of "wishing to get rid" of such seemingly intolerable instances and one which accounts for the high degree of sophistication needed when caring for people with dementia. In dominant Western thought, such a kind of "having to endure" is conceived as an egregious impertinence and as a mortification, even an insult (in psycho-analytical terms) which undermines the very idea of human competency and capability on which this thinking is built.

And yet, in spite of its demands and impertinences, the task of care also implies the chance to manage and accomplish – life as inter-action, empathy and mutual affection, meaningful action directed to the other person, a care of the self which, following Foucault, also implies the commitment to care for the other person (1986). It depends on both the general social framework and on a multitude of factors related to concrete circumstance and particular conditions whether care can successfully be carried out as a type of positively interdependent action. Katharina Gröning and her colleagues have provided important insights into the complexities of familial care relationships (Gröning et al. 2004). Based on qualitative interviews with female care givers, their seminal study combines empirical with more theoretically oriented work. By critically scrutinizing assessments about the future of aging and care which tend to rely on social theories of detraditionalisation and individualisation, Gröning et al. stress the relevance of care and responsibility for one's own life in a generational context and the persistent willingness to give care found by empirical research as an extremely valuable moral (and, one would like to add, social) resource (2004: 153). While Gröning et al. acknowledge the kinds of strain frequently attached to care (and to dementia care in particular), the authors also highlight that familial care must also be understood in terms of an - at least potentially – extremely positive process for the involved. Based on the work of Erik Erikson, Gröning et al. conceive of familial, and particularly filial care as a developmental task providing the chance of growth and change – yet also the risk of failure and stagnation or even regression.

2.6 The Situation of Domestic Care in Germany – Some Facts and Numbers

What exactly are we talking about when considering domestic care in Germany? What does the actual situation look like? How exactly, and in the context of which kind of societal and legal framework, is this preferred mode of care-giving presently carried out? Does empirical evidence suggest that we can conceive of the actual performance of domestic care as a good practice which accounts for the needs of all of the involved? What about the issue of gender justice in terms of assuming responsibility for care? Is there, in the light of ongoing social and demographic changes, good reason to suggest that the present practices provide us with a sustainable solution? I shall try to at least sketch out an answer on the remaining pages of this article.

Presently, the group of those receiving domestic care[3] comprises 4,4 million people (as of 2002; infratest data, cited in DJI 2005: 336). Two thirds of these people are women over seventy (ibid.). Beyond these general numbers, it is necessary to differentiate between the 1.4 million people receiving benefits from the *Pflegeversicherung* (social long-term care insurance) and the remaining three million who rely on support for running their household and for managing the demands of daily life (bmfsfj 2005). Among those provided with domestic care (covered by the *Pflegeversicherung*), 92% are cared for by family members and, to some extent, by neighbours or friends (7%). A similar situation is found for those in need of support for running their daily life: it is primarily the closest family members who assume responsibility (mostly without payment) for supporting that group and who actually take over the necessary kind of support[4] (infratest 2003; cited in DIW 2004).[5] The picture is completed by another 640 000 people who live in a nursing home due to their dependence on caring and nursing support.

Thus, the data show that the major part of support and care for needy old people is provided by the families. However, familial care does not necessarily take place in one household shared by care givers and care receivers. 31% of those receiving benefits provided by the *Pflegeversicherung* and 41% of those who need "other" support benefits (relating to recipients' need for support for managing their daily life/household) live on their own (infratest 2002 in DJI 2005: 336). This accords to the insight that major parts of what must be con-

3 So far, my reflections have been based on a broad concept of care. At this point, the concept necessarily becomes much narrower in that it relates to the legal definitions of who is entitled to receive support or care. Thus, the numbers do not indicate the actual demand for support and care (which can be assumed to be considerably higher). For example, a person with dementia may not be entitled to receive benefits since the legal definition of care (which is much closer to the British "nursing") excludes major parts of those dimensions of care that do not relate to immediate physical demands. Thus, it may well be the case that taking care of someone who has dementia asks for permanent attendance while that person may not be entitled to certain benefits provided by the German long-term care insurance.

4 About half of these people have to rely on support on a daily basis.

5 Of those receiving forms of support related to managing daily life, about 85% rely on informal, i.e. non-marketed support.

ceived as family life occurs in geographically different places. The fact that as a way of life, family frequently takes on the form of the "multi-local, multiple-generational family" (Bertram 2000) is a very recent insight of social science which must be kept in mind when looking at the present empirical situation with regard to care. What is equally important in our context, however, is the fact that geographical distance between children (mostly daughters) and parents tends to decrease with increasing age on the parents' part (Lauterbach 1998, cited in Gröning et al. 2004: 29).

In order to adequately account for the "social division of welfare" that characterizes the German situation in relation to care for old people, it must be pointed out that domestic care provided in and by the family has been strongly encouraged by a change of general regulation through the introduction of the *Pflegeversicherung* (social long-term care insurance) since 1995. The motivation for this reform can be seen to lie in the ongoing social and demographic change and the expectable modifications with regard to demand for support and care for old people which had been pointed out by various expert commissions and reports. The new law *(Pflegeversicherungsgesetz)* meant a major step forward in that care is now being publicly acknowledged as an important social achievement. In case the legally defined terms apply (need of care must be medically confirmed; care receivers are graded according to three different levels of care), care receivers are provided with a monetary allowance. Also, the so-called primary care giver is entitled to claims for a retirement pension. Last but not least, a package of additional supportive benefits is provided.[6]

This kind of official acknowledgement of privately provided care work for the generations of the old and very old and particularly the award of a long-term care allowance seem to have led to a positive reception of the overall solution package provided by the *Pflegeversicherungsgesetz.* Assessed in a comparative perspective, the advancement implied in this new legal framework must be acknowledged. However, with regard to abolishing social inequality between men and women, the new legal arrangement has also been met with criticism. If po-

6 The book by Katharina Gröning et al. dedicates its final chapter to a detailed analysis of the law on social long-term care insurance. With regard to the reinforcement of domestic/familial care brought about by the new law, Gröning et al. point to three major aspects: 1. the provision of a long-term care allowance; 2. the (partial, gkr) coverage of claims to a retirement pension on the part of the primary care-giver; 3. a system of selective measures of support, i.e. special educational supply (courses on care knowledge, e.g. on dementia care); quality assurance of care by a regular obligatory consultancy for primary care-givers provided by out-patient nursing services and, finally, the possibility to hire a holiday replacement for four weeks per year paid for by the Pflegeversicherung. Gröning et al. also discuss in detail the somewhat problematic construction of care givers and care receivers implied in the new law (Pflegeversicherungsgesetz). For details see Gröning et al. 2004: 141-53.

litical discourse on domestic care persistently foregrounds the role of the family as the agency of accomplishment, it is also evident that the new legislation had been created with a particular eye on women as informal care-givers. A fundamental intention behind the legal changes, improved conditions and the valorising of informal domestic care was to motivate women in particular to hold on to their performance as care givers (Behning 1997: 210).

2.7 The Gendered Division of Domestic Care

In trying to come to terms with the actual situation found in domestic care, I start by looking at the division of care work between men and women in domestic settings. In terms of empirical evidence, I rely on the cited representative survey on people in need of support and care in private households carried out by the research institute infratest in 2002 (Schneekloth und Leven 2003; DJI 2005; bmfsfj 2005).[7] Advancing from this empirical data base, it is hardly surprising to find that women bear the overwhelming part of the weight of domestic/familial care by a share of 73% (infratest 2002 in DJI 2005: 263). By comparison, men not only take over considerably less care work, they also spend less time in providing care.[8] Thus, it is evident that "the nation's largest care service" (i.e. familial care, Gröning et al. 2004) is still predominantly made up of women.

Yet, another source which was equally based on the 2002 infratest data published in 2005 also confirms a significant increase in the number of (primary) male care givers of 10%, since 1990, rising from 17% to meanwhile 27% (bmfsfj 2005: 4). More particularly, the number of care-giving sons has doubled from 5% (1990) to 10% (as of 2002). This means that the 10% increase in men providing informal care in the home is equally split-up between sons and husbands. All in all, that number bears testimony to a notable change with regard to the conventional assignment of care work to women – one which is also confirmed by observations in ordinary daily life.

The present situation can be described in a more detailed way by a comparison between male and female care givers.[9] The majority of female carers is pro-

7 A provisional report on the major results was published by Schneekloth and Leven in 2003. Since the study was commissioned by the Federal Ministry for the Family, Senior Citizens, Women and Youth, the Infratest data have also been assessed in the Gender Report edited by DJI in 2005. It is important to note that the study was based on the concept/construct of a primary care giver.

8 A socio-economic panel (SOEP) worked out by DIW/Infratest found that male care givers spend a total of 2,5 hours per average week day for care work while the temporal amount for women is 3,0 hours.

9 Based on SOEP panel data, DIW 2004.

vided by the group of 45-60 year olds whereas the major group of male care givers consists in men over sixty (DIW 2004). In familial terms, this means that apart from the female partner, the core group of informal female care givers is made up by daughters (infratest 2002: 26%) and, to some extent, also by daughters-in-law (6%) whereas for men, it is predominantly husbands who take on key responsibility for care work.

When comparing the gender-differentiated primary groups of informal care givers, we find that they clearly differ in that a major part of the women does care work while still at an employable age. Upon closer look, however, one finds that about 40-50% of the primary care givers are not gainfully employed while giving care. It should be added, however, that a 1998 study suggested the share of care givers with an occupational status to be 30%. This suggests a quite significant change over a relatively short period of time (DJI 2005: 337). All in all, women as care-givers tend to cut down or even give up their occupational work in order to provide familial care. Of all care givers engaged in occupational work when taking over informal care (59%), 27% eventually abandoned gainful employment. Another 24% cut down on their professional work and 49% did not make any changes with regard to their professional lives (Schnee-kloth/Müller 2000: 60 in DJI 2005: 337).[10] It should also be added that the chance for women to cut back on or even give up professional work decreases with the time spent in full employment before taking on responsibility in familial care. This also corresponds to the finding that women in Eastern Germany tend to interrupt their occupational employment much less frequently when carrying out familial care (DJI 2005: 337f).

2.8 *The* Geschlechterverhältnis *and Social Policy (the Level of Gender System)*

Why is it still predominantly women assuming responsibility for care? And why is it that among those at an employable age, it is exclusively women who cut back on (or even give up) their occupational work? With regard to the situation in Germany, a major reason can be seen in the complicity between the conditions implied in the legal framework and the kinds of dominant care arrangements to be found in families and familial situations. As feminist scholars have argued, institutions produce social injustice in that "the occupational sphere, the family, the dual educational system and social policy form a bonded system characteri-

10 „Thus, what emerges from empirical observation are differing strategies of coping with the conflicting obligations of gainful employment on the one hand and familial care on the other. The decision to interrupt or to even give up gainful employment is actually restricted to married women (Schneider/Drobnic/Blossfeld 2001 in DJI 2005: 337f.)

zed by reciprocal support" (Krüger 2001, cited in Becker-Schmidt 2004: 107). The example of domestic/familial care for old people illustrates how institutional regimes (in this case: social policy) uses gender arrangements (here: the gendered division of labour in the private sphere / the assignment of care work to women) as a principle/means of societal linking. The ultimate result of this is an updating of existing inequalities and their continuation in a "reformed mode".

This is not the place for a detailed discussion of the *Pflegeversicherungsgesetz* in terms of its construction of care givers and its gendered implications (for more detailed accounts, see particularly Gröning et al. 2004: 193-153). What is of primary interest in our context here is the interplay between the legal conditions of domestic care and the warrantee (or lack thereof) of social equality between men and women. With regard to this, it can be put on record that domestic care has not been granted the status of an equivalent to occupational employment by the legislator. In the framework of recently reformed legal conditions, familial care givers remain excluded from social security regarding health, unemployability, casualty, care and unemployment. The new legislation does not recognize informal care work (and that of familial care givers) in the form of a social insurance that is coequal to the kind of social insurance provided by occupational work. Under the new legal conditions, social policy remains centred on marriage and occupational employment (Behning 1997: 110).

2.9 Occupational Employment and Familial Care

When looking at the situation of employed care givers, the following emerges in principle regardless of gender, yet empirically applies almost exclusively to women: if you are occupationally employed and decide in favour of interrupting or even of giving up your professional work because of familial care responsibilities, you have to live with a whole package of considerable disadvantages (if not discriminations). In that respect, the 2005 gender data report states:

> So far, women who take care of family members have to put up with many disadvantages resulting from drop out of professional life because of caring tasks. Apart from losses in income, such disadvantages comprise considerable problems which will have to be met when trying to return to professional life, processes of dequalification due to the interruption of their professional career with long-term consequences for the level of income as well as consequences for their own old age benefits (DJI 2005: 339).

Cutting back on or even giving up one's professional work does not only lead to disadvantages with regard to the social and material safeguarding of one's existence. Such a step also implies increased risks and/or an exposure to loss in terms of one's position or status in professional life. Therefore, it must be conceived as an important intervention that the expert commission responsible for the latest (fifth) age report (*Altenbericht*") ordered a survey on the "compatibility of domestic care and occupational work" (Barkholdt & Lasch 2004). Through that survey, the official reporting on age and aging issues has explicitly addressed gender-related concerns for the very first time. In terms of the approach chosen by the authors, Barkholdt and Lasch argue against the waste of economic power held by women which is caused by the latter's abandonment or significant reduction of occupational work when confronted with familial care requirements. That way, the employment market is deprived of valuable qualified resources – a kind of inefficiency which can no longer be afforded in the future. Assessing solutions established in other European countries, the authors point to alternative schemes for coming to terms with the life-work balance where care is an issue. They argue for more flexible temporal patterns for professional work in Germany by which women's drop out from professional life caused by familial care requirements might be avoided.

It certainly is impressive, particularly from a strategic point of view, to base one's argument in favour of improving the situation of care-giving women on the logic of dominant economic thought. However, the major problem of this kind of reasoning (one that the study's authors are aware of) is that it inevitably implies an act of "doing gender" by substantiating the conventional association between women and care. This is particularly problematic since recently the debate about the "compatibility problem" (i.e. of having to reconcile the requirements of a working life and those of raising a family) has been taken up by the new government. Against the background of persistently low birthrates and a long-standing disregard of the issue of a better life-work balance for men and women on the political side and that of employers, there is now a broad consensus (across the political camps) that the need to reconcile the requirements of professional and family life affects both men and women alike. The urgent task of the present is to extend this discussion to the issue of care for the old and very old and to address it in terms of a concern of equal importance to men and women. Against this background, it is vital to systematically and persistently reject all attempts to naturalize the (symbolic/cultural) conjunction of care and women and all attempts to hold on to that gendered conjunction.

What makes it all the more important to raise the issue of the life-work balance in terms of care requirements for both men and women today is that domestic care's traditional key carrier, i.e. women exclusively dedicated to working the home, is on the decline. In that respect, gender-sensitive scholarship will also have to consider whether and how women's increased participation in occupational life and the job market will actually lead to more gender justice conceived in terms of a more symmetrical division/distribution of care work between men and women. In Germany, regular occupational work is increasingly turning into a "scarce resource" the possession of which marks a central social distinction. Therefore, it must be suspected that the overall situation will lead to a top-down reallocation of domestically provided care work within the female gender group (and that this has already occurred, at least partially) – with well educated women in economically secure and privileged positions on "top" and women in economically and status-wise insecure positions, without a prospect to eventually enjoy regular employment on the first job market (i.e. for the most part migrant, and particularly newly migrating women) fixed to the "bottom".

What does this mean? For one thing, it means that in the area of domestic care, we must turn our concern to a development which in recent years has been addressed and discussed by feminist scholars in relation to family and upbringing work. In Germany, this issue was discussed under the label of "the new class of domestic servants" emerging as a consequence of both globalisation and the European integration process. In relation to the question of care for old people, this discussion takes on a new dimension. A complex field of investigation, endowed with highly explosive components, is waiting for theoretical examination and empirical exploration.

2.10 Domestic Care – the Meaning of Gender Roles

One of the crucial reasons for the prevailing practice to firstly turn to women when care is an issue lies in the significance of what has been termed "gender roles". But what exactly are gender roles? What the numerous conceptualizations have in common is that they seek to grasp a special kind of being interrelated, i.e. an interface between self perception and the way this self is perceived by others as well as an act of adjustment in relation to a (in principle reciprocal) social expectation. It is quite helpful for my reflections here that a more detailed investigation of the existing theories has recently been undertaken by the well-known feminist scholar Regina Becker-Schmidt. Based on her work, we can approach the role concept by starting out with a formal description:

> Social integration assumes that social expectations in terms of coping with a situation, of executing a task, of representing a status group or a position will be met. Therefore, every member of society must learn in the process of socialization and enculturation to move in his or her social environment in such a way that s/he does not permanently offend or has to accept failure or is left misunderstood. (Becker-Schmidt 2005: 90).

With regard to existing gender roles, a major point of criticism is that they all adhere to the notion that gender roles are based on (or relate to) a particular attribute conceived to be a somehow "natural" trait of each member of the respective social group (qua sex or gender) – think, for example, of the role of mother or of the idea of gender-specific working capacities. Because of their reliance on such naturalizations, the existing theories and approaches turn into an integral part of producing/constructing gender and, thus, disqualify as analytic tools.

How, then, can one cope with this problematic concept which, at least at the time being, is nevertheless an indispensable one? First, it is legitimate to assume that conventionalized expectations which differentiate between men and women exist "out there" in our societies (and, upon closer look, will turn out to differ somewhat from society to society). Thus, gender roles are part of the production of men and women as differing social groups and, hence, an integral part of the *Geschlechterverhältnis*. There is a structural and structuring relevance attached to the social expectations implied in gender roles. However, this functional characterization of gender roles (with regard to the social structure) must be supplemented with their principally dynamic composition. Gender roles are constantly (re-)constituted within the framework of communicative, interactive and cooperative processes (Becker-Schmidt 2005:). This basically implies the possibility of (re-)negotiations and modifications.[11]

With regard to assuming responsibility for domestic care, empirical research points out two seemingly contradictory tendencies which I would like to highlight in more detail. First, it is stressed that women frequently consider it as a matter of course to assume responsibility for care (Gröning et al. 2004: 51). On the other hand, however, empirical evidence underscores that there is a considerable degree of social pressure put on women with regard to responsibility for familial care. As numerous studies show, "particularly daughters and, to some extent also daughters-in-law, take on care under familial pressure" (Wahl/Wetzler 1998: 191). In order to reflect on these findings in some more detail, I shall draw on a representative survey investigating the situation in domestic care which is presently carried out at the Free University of Berlin. The project LEANDER is a longitudinal survey funded by the bmfsfj which analyzes strain[12]

11 This also accounts for the relevance of the representation of gender roles in the media.

12 While the authors of the LEANDER project introduce their own concept of strain, I am drawing on the work of K.Gröning et al. which conceives of strain as a multi-dimensional and, following Gunzelmann (1991) transactional construct implying both objective and subjective factors. Regarding the concept's transactional nature, the following situative parameters have to be taken into account: (1) features of the diseased person; (2) features of the primary care giver; (3) features of the specific care demand; (4) features of the care situation with regard to its integration into the familial and immediate social context along with its structural and material characteristics. See Gröning et al. 2004: 33-34.

experienced by familial care givers of people with dementia. First results have been published in a final report on the first project phase (Zank & Schacke 2005). Before discussing these results, it should be pointed out that due to the nature of the disease and its numerous implications, dementia care implies more strain than do other types of care characterized by a more somatic orientation.

According to the final report on the first project phase, women subjectively feel more strained by personal restrictions, lack of social recognition and familial role conflicts than men. With regard to this finding, the authors concede that the two latter aspects possibly reflect objective societal conditions (Zank & Schacke 2005: 66). As the authors emphasize, men experience much more social recognition and acknowledgement for their caring activities than women, whereas women "generally are still held much more responsible for family work" so that they also will tend to suffer more from conflicts between requirements of care and family requirements" (Zank & Schacke 2005: 66). Other than that, the study finds caring spouses to generally take over more caring tasks and to suffer more from feelings of sadness and bereavement due to dementia-related changes in their partner's personality than do children. By comparison children, i.e. particularly daughters, more strongly bemoan the lack of experienced social recognition (Zank & Schacke, op. cit.)

For those engaged in gender-sensitive research, these results will come as no surprise. The intense distress that lies behind them is revealed by so far unpublished project findings. According to these findings, two thirds of the inquired care givers show clinically relevant depression values; for care-giving spouses the share seems to even point in the direction of 50%. Further cause for serious concern is provided by the fact that 68% of the inquired state that they had acted in an aggressive manner towards the person with dementia at least once within the two weeks preceding the interview (data according to Zank in Nationaler Ethikrat 2005). In that context, Susanne Zank points to US-American findings (Schulz et al. 1995) according to which highly stressed caregivers show clearly increased mortality rates (plus 60% within two years after giving care).

The LEANDER study provides us with empirical evidence for an existing paradox: care implies the chance for positive interchange and particularly to assuming generative responsibility as a challenge for personal growth (Gröning et al. 2004). And indeed, familial care givers do conceive of their task in terms of such a chance (Zank & Schacke 2005). At the same time, however, Zank and Schacke argue that care – particularly for informal care givers exclusively dedicated to this task (i.e. for major parts of the female care givers and for the husbands) – sometimes turns into a quite "risky endeavour". This may in part be owed to the particular conditions of dementia care, but also suggests that with regard to women (particularly daughters; see Grond 2002) conventional role expectations leave hardly any space for psychological and emotional regeneration on the part of the care giver: "As far as we know, women scarcely have the chance to work through the feelings in their care for relatives. There is no space for this in the familial context; yet frequently no such space exists in their contact with an ambulant service as well. What comes closest to support for working through their care experiences are self-help groups. Yet even here we find a theoretical as well as diagnostic deficit" (Gröning et al. 2004: 62).

In their analysis of the complex mechanisms which provably lead to high degrees of strain in care and their consequences such as depression or burnout, Katharina Gröning et al. have introduced the concept of "totalization". The latter comprises a whole ensemble of factors such as (1) the expectation towards female care givers to act and operate as a self- and ego-less "ideal mother" untroubled by needs and demands of her own in the vein of Nancy Chodorow's model (or, following Gröning et al., in that of a "super woman"); (2) a decline in contacts outside of the private home due to the task of caring which tends to be both self-induced and externally induced. Contacts outside the family acknowledge the self in its diverse and varied, also non-familial relations and contexts of action and, thus, are essential to its re-constitution. Thus, they open up the chance to a realization of the self beyond the family. Additionally, one has to account for (3) a complex, and usually emotionally close relationship to the person in need of care and, particularly when dementia is an issue, the "impertinence" of having to deal with and accept personality changes in the beloved person due to the illness. What comes in as an aggravating and, ultimately, decisive factor is that under present conditions, familial care frequently is carried out through a disruption (by "doing the splits", K. Gröning et al.) between individual needs and wishes and familial requirements and expectations:

> If that disruption is distributed in a gender-specific way, a gender hierarchy is reproduced in familial care. Thus, the adoption of care, conceived as a familial task of growth, is deprived of its moral ground by that gender hierarchy. (Gröning et al. 2004: 61).

As the results of the LEANDER-project and the seminal work of Gröning et al. suggest, familial care has actually entered a transitory phase with regard to gendered role expectations. One way to read this transition is this: One the one hand, it is blatant how the willingness to care – as a highly valuable social resource – is (and still can be) taken for granted on many levels, particularly when provided by women. On the other hand, however, there is much evidence that female care givers have started to question the way in which their willingness to make their contribution leads to being imposed complete cognizance for the task of care.

Moreover, women are increasingly wondering (if in very diverse ways) about the way in which they are being left alone with coming to terms with the multitude of caring requirements including the extremely sophisticated demand of psychological and emotional coping. With special regard to dementia care, but also other forms of age-related chronic ailments, the discharge of a given family's remaining (adult) members via gender role assignment is a serious hazard for care givers' health and well-being and, thus, must be rejected as intolerable.

Research on domestic/familial care confirms the impressive accomplishment provided particularly by women in the personal sphere for (old) persons in need of support and care. However, surveys such as LEANDER also indicate that in spite of all valuation of that accomplishment, the predominating practice of discharging the familial and larger social system at the cost of one individual is an unsound solution. Moreover, it is a practice which falls behind the state of the art of social coping achieved in societies based on highly advanced division of labour. With regard to domestic care, conventionalized role expectations (still) contribute to maintaining that unsound practice.It is virtually calamitous that the legal conditions established by the long-term care insurance (falling into the domain of the gender system) in its present form "tends to reinforce familial regressions in the form of a congealment (coagulation) in roles, of re-enactment of old patterns and of a social isolation in the role of care-giving since domestic care is not defined in terms of a collective project, but as a task involving at most two persons" (Gröning et al. 2004: 153).

2.11 The Social Division of Care

In order to adequately perceive of familial care within the framework of the overall care structure in Germany, a few – and necessarily quite sketchy – explanatory remarks must be added here. Today, care policies are guided by a clear priority for outpatient care and for informal (care in the private home) over formal care settings (care in the nursing home). This is a comparatively recent trend. Previously, the care-related traditional division of responsibility and tasks between the state, the market and the family was determined by the divide between family (i.e. in terms of care practices: predominantly women) on the one hand, and (largely state-supported) market-mediated institutional solutions in the form of care provided in nursing homes (and/or homes for the elderly) on the other. Because of the historical decision in favour of that particular, and gendered division of care responsibility, and its succeeding implementations, the overall structure of care for old people is presently characterized by a decidedly a-symmetrical shape. For one, this means that the existing supply in domestic care services and also in affordable professional support for informal care givers (particularly in the form of therapeutic counselling and coaching) is quite disproportional to the care capacity provided in the domestic context by informal care givers. This situation is aggravated by the fact that the kind of are provided by home care services is determined by legal regulations strictly oriented at a highly restricted, somatically-centred concept of care. This means that so far, other essential imperatives of care, let alone the necessity to care for the care givers, are excluded by that concept.[13] A second and contributing consequence of the gendered division of care is that the overwhelming share of state funding has gone into institutionally organized care carried out in formal settings.

Meanwhile, this shortcoming has been recognized on the political side. Lately, the Ministry of Health has repeatedly expressed its decided intention to deal with this situation by supporting the upgrading of outpatient care. However, a major difficulty of the present situation is that such corrective policy and action will have to be accomplished in the context of shrinking financial resources. Particularly with regard to the major deficits of adequate (professional) support for care givers in their extremely difficult personal and emotional situations, it will take lots of patience and even more vigour to fight out solutions for meeting these needs. Yet, in order to exempt domestic care from the status of an unsound solution or practice, we have to move far beyond what has been achieved so far in terms of self-help activities and low-threshold services and supply achieved mostly through the tireless work of self-help organizations.

3 Conclusion and Outlook: Towards a Future that Cares!

Working in the business world, I have frequently come across the saying: "If the system works, why change it?" As I have tried to show, the existing system of domestic/familial care does work – yet it works in ways which arguably are costly (particularly in terms of health-related consequences for care givers), cause much avoidable suffering, fall short of existing societal skills and strategies of coping and, finally, do not correspond to democratic principles and standards. Moreover, in its present form, domestic care does not only present an unsound practice; it also must be considered as an unsustainable approach. Based on this insight, I would conclude that the historical division of care between the state, the market and the family has become dysfunctional and calls for a substantial transformation. While on the personal level, and that of gender arrange-

13 One exception which I have already pointed out is the possibility to hire a holiday replacement for four weeks per year paid for by the long-term care insurance.

ments in the family, the first step must be to take on and work out care as a joint project, sustainable solutions will have to substantially reach beyond the family. A similar argument has been brought forward by some of those professionally engaged in improving the conditions for people with dementia. In the context of the initiative "Together for a better life with dementia", it has been suggested that a new social model is needed, one that is based on civil society and, more particularly, on – old and new – networks of support.[14] The Work Group "Caring Together" also points to necessary changes in public consciousness, and calls on citizens' willingness to take over responsibility for care for old people, and particularly for people with dementia.

This must not be read as an argument in favour of a solution that calls for voluntary (and for the most part unpaid) work exclusively. Rather, this is to suggest that new, and networked (and quite heterogeneous) solutions will have to be shaped. In this respect, the Work Group has introduced the concept of dementia care as co-production. As they argue, adequate solutions will have to be found and worked out on the local level, in concrete communities, and on the basis of the specific strengths and weaknesses found in that particular context. It is within the immediate social context that responsibilities will have to be renegotiated, and actors (including business and market forces) as well as particularly helpful forms of contribution will have to be identified. In order for this to happen, it is crucial that the state will accept the challenge and adapt a new, and considerably altered role. Instead of the present directive of "advancing and stipulating" the role and function of the state will have to change into that of enabling and empowering sustainable solutions and good practices.

While it is way beyond this article to deal with the implications of this suggestion in any concrete terms, I would like to close by returning to a social framework that reaches well beyond the nation state. Clearly, the issue of a new social model raises the question about the future of the European Community as a shared basis for the development of Civil Society. Such a shared basis, and appropriate stimulation of action and research, could facilitate the advancement of a new culture of care and the building of new networks of support. Furthermore, such a new model would call for a renegotiation of roles and tasks of – old and new – actors involved in its implementation. The challenges of such an attempt are manifold – but so are its chances. As I see it, the crucial point would be to conceive of care in terms of a basic social principle and a highly valuable social resource. Using it responsibly and in ways that cultivate and sustain it is the key to advancing the great chances implied in the long-living society.

14 This is by no means a merely abstract claim: According to evidence-based estimations, today dementia care is already provided to about 15% by volunteers working mostly in nursing homes (Work Group "Caring Together" 2005).

References

Becker-Schmidt, Regina (2004). Doppelte Vergesellschaftung von Frauen: Divergenzen und Brückenschläge zwischen Privat- und Erwerbsleben. In: Ruth Becker und Beate Kortendieck (Hrsg.) Handbuch Frauen- und Geschlechterforschung. Theorie, Methoden, Empirie. Wiesbaden: VS Verlag für Sozialwissenschaften, 62-71.

Becker-Schmidt, Regina (2005). Von soziologischen Geschlechtsrollentheorien zur gesellschaftstheoretischen Erforschung des Geschlechterverhältnisses. In: Ulrike Vogel (Hrsg.) Was ist weiblich – was ist männlich? Aktuelles zur Geschlechterforschung in den Sozialwissenschaften. Bielefeld: Kleine, 89-112.

Becker, Regina (1997). Häusliche Pflege von Angehörigen. Beratungskonzeptionen für Frauen. Frankfurt am Main.

Behning, Ute (1997). Richtungswechsel in der Sozialversicherungspolitik? Zur Anerkennung von nicht-professionellen häuslichen Pflegeleistungen durch das Pflege-Versicherungsgesetz. In: Ute Behning (Hg.). Das Private ist ökonomisch. Widersprüche der Ökonomisierung privater Familien- und Haushaltsdienstleistungen. Berlin, 103-117.

Bertram, H. (2000) Die verborgenen familiären Beziehungen in Deutschland. Die multilokale Mehrgenerationenfamilie. In: Kohli, M. / Szydlik, M. (Hrsg.) Generationen in Familie und Gesellschaft. Opladen.

Benhabib, S. (1995) Selbst im Kontext. Kommunikative Ethik im Spannungsfeld von Feminismus, Kommunitarismus und Postmoderne. Frankfurt / Main.

Bickel, Horst (2004). Epidemiologische Aspekte: Gegenwärtiger Stand und künftige Entwicklungen von Demenzerkrankungen. In: Forum TTN – Technik, Theologie, Naturwissenschaften. München, 23-35.

bmfsfj (2001). Alter und Gesellschaft. Dritter Bericht zur Lage der älteren Generation in der Bundesrepublik Deutschland. Stellungnahme der Bundesregierung. Bericht der Sachverständigenkommission. Dokumentation. Berlin: Deutscher Bundestag. 14. Wahlperiode/Drucksache 14/5130. available under www.bmfsfj.de/Kategorien/ Publikationen/Publikationen,did=3174.html.

bmfsfj (2002). Alter und Gesellschaft. Vierter Bericht zur Lage der älteren Generation in der Bundesrepublik Deutschland: Risiken, Lebensqualität und Versorgung Hochaltriger – unter besonderer Berücksichtigung demenzieller Erkrankungen. Dokumentation. Berlin: Deutscher Bundestag. Als download verfügbar unter http://www.bmfsfj.de/Kategorien/Publikationen/Publikationen,did=5362.html.

bmfsfj (2003). "Hilfe- und Pflegebedürftige in Deutschland". Pressemitteilung vom 7. November.

bmfsfj (Hg.) (2005). Möglichkeiten und Grenzen selbständiger Lebensführung in Privathaushalten. Ergebnisse der Studie MUG III. Forschungsprojekt im Auftrag des Bundesministeriums für Familie, Senioren, Frauen und Jugend. Durchgeführt durch TNS Infratest Sozialforschung (Ulrich Schneekloth).

Borchers, Hans; Kreutzner, Gabriele, Seiter, Ellen, and Warth, Eva-Maria (1989) ‚Don't treat us like we're so stupid and naive' – Towards an ethnography of soap opera viewers. In: Ellen Seiter, Hans Borchers, Gabriele Kreutzner and Eva-Maria Warth: Remote Control. Television, Audiences, and Cultural Power. London etc.: Routledge, 223-2447.

Brückner, Margrit (2000): Care-Work jenseits von Caritas? Frauenprojekte im Kontext feministischer Sozialstaatsanalysen. In: Fürsorge – Anerkennung – Arbeit. Feministische Studien 18 (extra), 43-53.

Eckart, Christel; Senghaas-Knobloch, Eva (2000): Fürsorge – Anerkennung – Arbeit. Einleitung. . In: Fürsorge – Anerkennung – Arbeit. Feministische Studien 18 (extra), 3-8.

Emnid-Institut (2005). Würden Sie Ihre pflegebedürftigen Eltern bei sich zu Hause aufnehmen? Chrismon Umfrage des Monats September 2005. In: Chrismon, Beilage der Wochenzeitung DIE Zeit 09/2005.

Fraser, Nancy (1994): Widerspenstige Praktiken: Macht, Diskurs, Geschlecht. Frankfurt/Main.

Fraser, Nancy; Gordon, Linda (1994): ‚Dependency' demystified: Inscriptions of power in a keyword of the Welfare State. In: Social Politics. Vol. 1, 1, 4-31.

Gerhard, Ute (1997). Soziale Bürgerrechte – ein Konzept für Frauen? In: Ute Behning (Hg.). Das Private ist ökonomisch. Widersprüche der Ökonomisierung privater Familien- und Haushaltsdienstleistungen. Berlin, 23-39.

Gröning. Katharina; Kunstmann, Anne-Christin; Rensing, Elisabeth (2004). In guten wie in schlechten Tagen. Konfliktfelder in der häuslichen Pflege. Frankfurt am Main: Mabuse.

Grond, E. (2000). Wenn Kinder wieder zu Eltern werden. In: Tackenberg, P. / Abt-Zegelin, Angelika (Hrsg.), Demenz und Pflege. Eine interdisziplinäre Betrachtung. Frankfurt.

Knijn, Trudie; Kremer, Monique (1997): Gender and the Caring Dimensions of Welfare States: Towards Inclusive Citizenship. In: Social Politics, vol. 4, 3, 328-361.

Müller-Hergl, Christian (2005). From a Subjective Point of View / Aus der Sicht des Subjektiven. In: Demenz Support Stuttgart (Hg.) Focus on Quality of Life / Quality of Care. Im Brennpunkt: Lebensqualität / Pflegequalität. North Sea Dementia Research Group. 5th Annual Meeting, Stuttgart, April 22-24, 2005. Stuttgart: Demenz Support Stuttgart, 104-130.

Nationaler Ethikrat (2005). Niederschrift über die Jahrestagung „Altersdemenz und Morbus Alzheimer. (Wortprotokoll) Berlin: 27. Oktober 2005. (Teil 1: Vormittag; Teil 2: Nachmittag). www.ethikrat.org/veranstaltungen/pdf/Wortprotokoll_Jahrestagung_2005-10-27_Vormittag.pdf, http://www.ethikrat.org/veranstaltungen/ pdf/Wortprotokoll_ Jahrestagung_2005-10-27_Nachmittag.pdf.

Seubert, H. (1993). Zu Lasten der Frauen. Benachteiligung von Frauen durch die Pflege alter Eltern. Pfaffenweiler.

Schneekloth, Ulrich; Leven, Ingo (2003). Hilfe- und Pflegebedürftige in Privathaushalten in Deutschland 2002. Schnellbericht. Erste Ergebnisse der Repäsentativerhebung im Rahmen des Forschungsprojekts „Möglichkeiten und Grenzen einer selbständigen Lebensführung hilfe- und pflegebedürftiger Menschen in privaten Hushalten (MuG 3). Infratest Sozialforschung. Im Auftrag des Bundesministeriums für Familie, Senioren, Frauen und Jugend. München.

Schneider, Norbert (2005). Wer pflegt morgen? Wandel der Familie und die Auswirkungen auf die häusliche Pflege. Statement anlässlich des ersten rheinland-pfälzischen Pflegekongresses „Menschen Pflegen – Innovative Modelle in Rheinland-Pfalz. www.menschen-pflegen.de/files/bc075f6cf28749e01cc2c8c0338bba2e/461/ norbert_schneider.pdf.

Schupp, Jürgen; Künemund, Harald (2004). Private Versorgung und Betreuung von Pflegebedürftigen in Deutschland. Wochenbericht des DIW Berlin 20/04. Berlin: DIW 2004. www.diw.de/deutsch/produkte/publikationen/wochenberichte/docs/04-20-1.html.

United Nations, Department of Economic and Social Affairs, Population Division [UNPD] (2005), Population Challenges and Development Goals. New York.

Werkstatt „Gemeinsam Betreuen“ (cited as: Working Group „Caring Together“) (2005). Gemeinsam Betreuen. Abschlussbericht der gleichnamigen Werkstatt im Rahmen der Initiative „Gemeinsam für ein besseres Leben mit Demenz“ der Robert Bosch Stiftung. Unpublished manuscript. To be published under the title „Gemeinsam Betreuen“ by Hans Huber, Bern, later in 2006.

Zank, Susanne; Schacke, Claudia (2005). Projekt LEANDER (Längsschnittstudien zur Belastung pflegender Angehöriger von demenziell Erkrankten) – Abschlussbericht Phase 1. Entwicklung eines standardisierten Messinstruments zur Erstellung von Belastungsprofilen und zur Evaluation von Entlastungsangeboten für pflegende Angehörige demenzkranker Patienten. BMFSFuJ-Nr. 68432. http://ipg. psychologie.fu-berlin.de/projekte/Abschlu%DFbericht_LEANDER_Phase1.pdf.

Notes on Contributors

Ludwig Amrhein, Dipl.-Soz., Dipl.-Psych. Geront., is research fellow and lecturer in Social Gerontology at the University of Kassel. He finishes a Ph.D. thesis about social and individual lifestyle models of ageing. His research interests are the biographies and lifestyles of ageing persons, the social structures of the care for the elderly and the societal discourse of ageing. Contact: University of Kassel, Department Social Services, Arbold-Bode-Str. 10, 34109 Kassel, Germany. Email: lamrhein@uni-kassel.de

Gertrud M. Backes, Prof. Dr. phil., is professor for Ageing and Society at the University of Vechta and Speaker oft the Section "Ageing and Society" of the German Sociological Association. Her research interests are ageing and gender, ageing, social change and social structur, "Lebenslagen", care and gender, gender, body and ageing, life course and gender. Contact: University of Vechta, Driverstr. 23, 49377 Vechta, Germany. +49 4441 15-358 Email: backes@uni-kassel.de; gertrud.backes@uni-vechta.de

Csilla Csoboth, M.D., Ph.D., is an assistant professor at the Semmelweis University Institute of Behavioral Sciences in Budapest and is the program director of the Better Health for Women program. Contact: Semmelweis University Institute of Behavioral Sciences, Nagyvárad tér 4, 1089 Budapest, Hungary.
E-mail: csobcsil@net.sote.hu

Gabriele Doblhammer-Reiter, is professor for empirical research and demography at the University of Rostock and co-director of the Rostock centre, a joint research centre of the Max Planck Institute for Demography and the University of Rostock. Her research interests are on the aging process, biological and social determinants of longevity, validation of the oldest old, health and care projections in Germany. Contact: Universität Rostock, Wirtschafts- und Sozialwissenschaftliche Fakultät, Lehrstuhl für empirische Sozialforschung und Demographie, Ulmenstraße 69, 18057 Rostock, Germany. Phone: +49-381-498-4393.
Email: doblhammer@demogr.mpg.de

Barbara Domajnko, Ph.D., Assistant of Sociology. Research interests: aging, interprofessional collaboration in health care, qualitative research. Contact: University of Ljubljana, College of Health Studies, Poljanska 26a, 1000 Ljubljana, Slovenia. Email: barbara.domajnko@vsz.uni-lj.si

Valentina Hlebec, is assistant professor of statistics at the University of Ljubljana, Slovenia. Her research interests are social network analysis, questionnaire design, the sociology of adolescents and social gerontology. Contact: University of Ljubljana, Faculty of Social Sciences, Kardeljeva pl. 5, 1000 Ljubljana, Slovenia. Phone: +396-1-5805-284. Email: valentina.hlebec@fdv.uni-lj.si

Friederike Kendel, Dipl.-Psych., is a research associate and lecturer at the Institute for Medical Psychology at Charité-Universitätsmedizin Berlin. Research focus on gender differences in cardiovascular health, member of the Center for Gender Medicine at Charité. Contact: Charité-Universitätsmedizin, ZHGB, Institute for Medical Psychology, Luisenstraße 57, 10117 Berlin.
Email: friederike.kendel@charite.de

Mónika Erika Kovács, MD, Ph.D., Assistant professor, psychiatrist, coordinator of the Central Eastern European Behavioural Medicine Network (www.ceebm-net.hu). Institution: Semmelweis University Institute of Behavioral Sciences, Nagyvárad tér 4, 1089 Budapest, Hungary. Contact: E-mail: kovmon@net.sote.hu.

Gabriele Kreutzner, Dr. phil.: M.A. American, German and English Studies; media and cultural studies expert. For the past years, her work has come to focus on the developing field of age, health and gender. She has been working for an NGO dedicated to improving dementia care in Germany and is now in the process of building up her own information agency "age – health – gender". Gabriele is member of the executive committee of the German NGO Aktion Demenz – gemeinsam für ein besseres Leben mit Demenz ("Dementia Campaign – together for a better life with dementia"). Email: gkreutzner@yahoo.de

Vera Lasch, Dr. rer. pol. is research fellow at University of Kassel, Unit Gender Research. Research topics are "Women, Work and Health", "Ageing, Health and Gender", "Higher Education, Gender and the Bologna Process in Germany".

Contact: University of Kassel, IAG FG, Mönchebergstr. 21A, 34109 Kassel, Germany. Phone: ++49-(0)551 541664. Email: lasch@uni-kassel.de

Birgitta Lindencrona, Fil.lic./Ph.D. in Literature, deputy assistant under-secretary, now retired. Birgitta began dealing with matters related to gender equality and the growing field of gender research at the Swedish Ministry and Education and Science in the 1980s. She has also acted as a coordinator of these matters and a senior adviser at the Swedish Research Council, between 2001-2003 also as the secretary of the Swedish Gender Research Committee. Contact: Swedish Association of Senior Citizens, Box 22 574, SE-104 22 Stockholm. E-mail: birgitta.lindencrona@telia.com

Majda Pahor, Ph.D., Assistant Professor of Sociology of Health. Research interests: health professions, interprofessional collaboration, aging. Contact: University of Ljubljana, College of Health Studies, Poljanska 26a, 1000 Ljubljana, Slovenia. Email: majda.pahor@vsz.uni-lj.si

Bridget Penhale, is Senior Lecturer in Gerontology at the University of Sheffield. Bridget has a background in Psychology and Social work and worked for many years as social worker and latterly manager in several locations across the UK. She has held academic posts since 1996 and is recognised internationally for her work on elder abuse. Research topics include elder abuse, adult protection, domestic violence, mental health and older people, bereavement and loss in later life. Contact: Community, Ageing & Rehabilitation Department Department, Universtiy of Sheffield, 301 Glossop Road, Sheffield, S10 2HL, UK. Phone : +44 114 222 8316. Email: B.Penhale@sheffield.ac.uk

Pasqualina Perrig-Chiello, is professor at the University of Bern, Switzerland. Her teaching and major research interests focus on life-span developmental psychology, especially health and well-being, personality, gender roles, and familial intergenerational relations. Teaching appointments at the Universities of Saarbrücken and Frankfurt/Germany and Basel/Switzerland. She is member of the Swiss National Research Council and chairs the Directory Board of the National Research Program 52 "Intergenerational Relations". Contact: Institut für Psychologie, Universität Bern, Muesmattstrasse 45, CH-3012 Bern, Switzerland. Phone: ++41 (0)61 331 75 19. Email: pasqualina.perrigchiello@psy.unibe.ch

Katja Reimann, is Ph.D. student and research fellow in Social Gerontology, at the Department of Social Services, University of Kassel, Germany. She is actually working on her Ph.D. project, exploring lay body and health concepts in older gay and straight men. She is member of the Gender Research Group at the University of Kassel and of the Interdisciplinary Research Training Group "Public Spheres and Gender Relations. Dimensions of Experience" of the Universities Kassel and Frankfurt/Main (Germany). Contact: IAG Frauen- und Geschlechterforschung, Universität Kassel, Mönchebergstr. 21a, 34109 Kassel, Germany. Email: k.reimann@uni-kassel.de

Monika Sieverding, Prof. Dr. phil., is Professor of Differential Psychology and Gender Studies at the University of Heidelberg, Psychological Institute. Her research deals with health psychology (Research project on "Psychological Determinants of Cancer Screening") and especially "Gender Roles and Health". Contact: Psychologisches Institut, Ruprecht-Karls-Universitaet Heidelberg, Hauptstr. 47-51, 69117 Heidelberg, Germany: Phone: ++49-(0)6221 547372. Email: monika.sieverding@psychologie.uni-heidelberg.de

Hildegard Theobald, Dr. phil. is research fellow at the Social Science Research Centre Berlin (WZB), Research Group "Public Health Policy". Her current research interests include international comparative welfare state research on social care, service work as well as on social exclusion and social and gender inequality (Research project on "Care for the Aged at Risk of Marginalization (CARMA), funded by the European Union). Contact: Social Science Research Center Berlin, Research Group "Public Health Policy", Reichpietschufer 50, 10785 Berlin, Germany: Phone: ++49 (0)30 25491 548. Email: theobald@wz-berlin.de

Beata Tobiasz-Adamczyk Prof. Ph.D. is Professor of Medical Sociology and Head of the Chair of Epidemiology and Preventive Medicine and also Department of Medical Sociology at the Jagiellonian University Medical College in Krakow, Poland. Her main topics of interest relate to the quality of life in older people (the role of subjective health, social network, social support), quality of life in cancer patients, illness behaviours and gender-related differences in health as well as to the social and cultural determinants of professional roles in medicine. She is also involved in extensive didactic activity, teaching students of medicine, dentistry, public health and nursing on relevant topics. Contact: Chair of Epidemiology and Preventive Medicine, Jagiellonian University Medical College, Kopernika 7a st., 31-034 Krakow, Poland, Phone: +48 12 423 10 03. Email: mytobias@cyf-kr.edu.pl

Barbro Westerholm, Prof. M.D.. Vice President, AGE (Older People's Platform), Brussels, Belgium and former President of the Swedish Association of Senior Citizens. Barbro's main research is within the field of drug epidemiology. She has among other things chaired the Swedish Gender Research Committee during the years 1991 - 2000 .Contact: Swedish Association of Senior Citizens, Box 22 574, S 104 22 Stockholm. e-mail: barbro.westerholm@spfpension.se.

Uta Ziegler, is a Ph.D. student and research fellow at the chair for empirical research and demography at the University of Rostock. Her research interests are on the living conditions of the elderly population, especially the determinants of care and dementia and their future impact. Contact: Universität Rostock, Wirtschafts- und Sozialwissenschaftliche Fakultät, Lehrstuhl für empirische Sozialforschung und Demographie, Ulmenstraße 69, 18057 Rostock, Germany. Phone: +49-381-498-4396. Email: ziegler@demogr.mpg.de

Made in the USA
Las Vegas, NV
11 November 2024

11544692R00184